T0643904

Preventing Partner
Violence

Preventing Partner
Violence

RESEARCH AND EVIDENCE-BASED
INTERVENTION STRATEGIES

Edited by DANIEL J. WHITAKER and JOHN R. LUTZKER

American Psychological Association • Washington, DC

Published by
American Psychological Association
750 First Street, NE
Washington, DC 20002
www.apa.org

To order
APA Order Department
P.O. Box 92984
Washington, DC 20090-2984
Tel: (800) 374-2721; Direct: (202) 336-5510
Fax: (202) 336-5502; TDD/TTY: (202) 336-6123
Online: www.apa.org/books/
E-mail: order@apa.org

In the U.K., Europe, Africa, and the Middle East, copies may be ordered from
American Psychological Association
3 Henrietta Street
Covent Garden, London
WC2E 8LU England

Typeset in Goudy by Stephen McDougal, Mechanicsville, MD

Printer: Maple-Vail Book Manufacturing Group, York, PA
Cover Designer: Naylor Design, Washington, DC
Technical/Production Editor: Devon Bourexis

The opinions and statements published are the responsibility of the authors, and such opinions and statements do not necessarily represent the policies of the American Psychological Association.

Library of Congress Cataloging-in-Publication Data

Preventing partner violence : research and evidence-based intervention strategies / edited by Daniel J. Whitaker, John R. Lutzker. — 1st ed.
    p. cm.
  Includes bibliographical references and index.
  ISBN-13: 978-1-4338-0434-2
  ISBN-10: 1-4338-0434-4
  1. Marital violence—Prevention. 2. Family violence—Prevention. 3. Child abuse—Prevention. 4. Dating violence—Prevention. 5. Psychological abuse—Prevention. I. Whitaker, Daniel J. II. Lutzker, John R., 1947–
  HV6626.P733 2009
  362.82'927—dc22
                                                   2008036634

British Library Cataloguing-in-Publication Data
A CIP record is available from the British Library.

Printed in the United States of America
First Edition

CONTENTS

CONTRIBUTORS

Marguerite L. Baty, PhD(c), MSN, MPH, RN, Johns Hopkins University School of Nursing, Baltimore, MD

Tina Bloom, PhD, MPH, RN, Oregon Health Sciences University, Portland

Raul Caetano, MD, PhD, University of Texas School of Public Health, Dallas

Jacquelyn C. Campbell, PhD, RN, FAAN, Johns Hopkins University School of Nursing, Baltimore, MD

Deborah M. Capaldi, PhD, Oregon Social Learning Center, Eugene

Vangie A. Foshee, PhD, University of North Carolina at Chapel Hill

Nancy Glass, PhD, MPH, RN, Johns Hopkins University School of Nursing, Baltimore, MD

Grant T. Harris, PhD, Mental Health Centre Penetanguishene, Penetanguishene, Ontario, Canada

N. Zoe Hilton, PhD, Mental Health Centre Penetanguishene, Penetanguishene, Ontario, Canada

Hyoun K. Kim, PhD, Oregon Social Learning Center, Eugene

Kathryn Laughon, PhD, RN, University of Virginia School of Nursing, Charlottesville

Sherry Lipsky, PhD, MPH, University of Washington at Harborview Medical Center, Seattle

John R. Lutzker, PhD, Georgia State University, Atlanta

Catherine L. McMonigle, MS, Virginia Tech, Blacksburg

Heathe Luz McNaughton Reyes, MPH, University of North Carolina at Chapel Hill

Phyllis Holditch Niolon, PhD, Centers for Disease Control and Prevention, Atlanta, GA

K. Daniel O'Leary, PhD, Stony Brook University, Stony Brook, NY

Katherine C. Pears, PhD, Oregon Social Learning Center, Eugene

Chiquita Rollins, MS, PhD, Multnomah County Health Department, Portland, OR

Sandra M. Stith, PhD, Kansas State University, Manhattan

Murray A. Straus, PhD, University of New Hampshire, Durham

Daniel J. Whitaker, PhD, Georgia State University, Atlanta

Erica M. Woodin, PhD, University of Victoria, Victoria, British Columbia, Canada

Anne Woods, PhD, MPH, CNM, Messiah College, Grantham, PA

Preventing Partner
Violence

1

INTRODUCTION

DANIEL J. WHITAKER AND JOHN R. LUTZKER

The popular media is rife with news on violence between intimate partners. A cursory Internet search of news articles on domestic violence reveals many tragic reports, such as the following: "Police and witness accounts show that 24-year-old Jessica Acree was struck down by her boyfriend with her infant child still in her arms outside of her Crescent Drive home" (Sumner, 2007, ¶ 2), and

> when police broke down the door, they found Nichole Snipe, 26, in her house with two gunshot wounds to the head. They also found a man who apparently saved a third round for himself. "Some sort of domestic dispute took place, but we're unsure of what the nature of that dispute was," Thornton said. (WSFA 12 News, 2007, ¶ 4)

These stories are chilling and are experienced by adults and children every day. Further, as will be seen in this volume, there are lifetime serious mental and physical health sequelae and other societal ills that are related to intimate partner violence (IPV). This volume presents research and theory and discusses services aimed at preventing IPV.

The study of aggression and violence among intimate partners has a relatively brief history that has been marked by rapid change. Practice and research on IPV began as part of the women's movement, which sought to promote gender equity, and part of that goal involved stopping violence against women, much of which was perpetrated by intimate partners. The initial perspective of both practitioners and researchers was largely that of the feminist sociocultural theory, which attributed IPV primarily to broad social factors, such as the patriarchal structure of society, and interpreted men's violence toward women as a means to sustain this structure by controlling their partners.

Today, the conceptualization of the nature, causes, and consequences of IPV has expanded and broadened considerably. For instance, although IPV was initially conceptualized as a problem of men's oppression of women, it is now also recognized as a broad public health problem (Campbell, 2002; Hammond, Whitaker, Lutzker, Mercy, & Chin, 2006; Plichta, 2004), a criminal justice problem (Buzawa & Buzawa, 2003), and an economic problem for individual victims and society (National Center for Injury Prevention and Control, 2003). One of the contributing factors to this broadening is the multidisciplinary makeup of the IPV community. Theories, research, and program experiences regarding IPV can be found in journals of various disciplines, including psychology, sociology, criminal justice, public health, medicine, nursing, policy, and economics. The broad IPV community is also influenced by both the research and the practice communities. Each of these different viewpoints has a unique perspective, and this multiperspective approach provides ample opportunities for understanding determinants, along with multiple points of intervention for stopping IPV. Perspectives have clashed, but sometimes those clashes have driven new understandings of IPV. For instance, Johnson's (1995) conceptualization of types of violence arose in part to resolve differing perspectives and interpretations of the data between those taking a feminist perspective on IPV and those taking a family conflict perspective.

Although early views were focused primarily on how broad societal-level factors (e.g., patriarchy) influenced men's violence toward women, more recent views of IPV now discuss factors that cut across levels of the social ecology and thus recognize that partner violence can be influenced by individual, dyadic, community, and societal factors. Multifactor explanations for IPV, such as Riggs and O'Leary's (1989) model of courtship violence, and ecological models (Dutton, 1995; Heise, 1998) are the norm. Such models include discussion about a variety of factors that were once considered off-limits as explanatory factors and remain controversial, such as the role of alcohol use in IPV perpetration (Leonard, 2005) and dyadic influences of IPV perpetration (Capaldi & Kim, 2007). These models also seek explanations of partner violence that can account for the behavior of both sexes rather than focusing exclusively on men's violence toward women.

The field's conceptualization of IPV has also evolved over time. Early work on IPV focused primarily on very serious IPV perpetrated by men against their female partners (Walker, 1984) because those were the cases that were most apparent. IPV was (and still is by some) believed to be a chronic problem that mostly escalated over time and was thought to be motivated by the men's desire to control their partners. However, it has become clear over the years that (a) this early conceptualization describes one but not all forms of partner violence (Holtzworth-Munroe & Stuart, 1994; Johnson, 1995), (b) control is one motive for partner violence but there are other important motives and precursors (Kernsmith, 2005; Stuart et al., 2006), and (c) IPV—at least physical IPV—is perpetrated by both men and women (Archer, 2000; Straus & Gelles, 1995) and in same-sex relationships (McClennen, 2005). Low-level violence is fairly common among relationship partners, especially young adults (Straus & Gelles, 1995; Whitaker, Haileyesus, Swahn, & Saltzman, 2007); often does not escalate but desists (Caetano, Field, Ramisetty-Mikler, & McGrath, 2005; K. D. O'Leary et al., 1989); and is motivated by a range of factors, including escalating conflict, preceding psychological aggression, and anger expression (Cascardi & Vivian, 1995; Johnson, 1995; S. G. O'Leary & Smith Slep, 2006).

Related to this is a relatively new focus on understanding the development of IPV perpetration by itself and in the context of other risk factors. Partner violence, especially among teens and young adults, is increasingly being viewed in a developmental context as a behavior that unfolds over time with individual, dyadic, and broader contextual influences (e.g., see chaps. 5 and 7, this volume). Partner violence is also being studied in the context of emergence of other risk behaviors, such as peer violence and substance use (Connolly, Pepler, Craig, & Taradash, 2000; Gorman-Smith, Tolan, Sheidow, & Henry, 2001). A small body of longitudinal studies has begun to show the importance of risk factors related to individual, family, and peer characteristics as IPV perpetration behavior emerges. For instance, longitudinal studies have shown that early conduct problems and parental discipline styles predict the perpetration of physical IPV in adolescence (see chap. 7, this volume, for an in-depth review). More work is needed to better understand how a full range of risk and protective factors lead to IPV, including broader social-level influences; how more serious IPV develops (i.e., what many have referred to as "battering"); and how findings from a developmental perspective can be turned into prevention programs.

Finally, there has been much development in prevention and intervention strategies in the past 30 years. Initially, prevention and intervention services regarding partner violence were mainly tertiary prevention efforts that focused on victims' safety and recovery from abuse. Intervention programs included shelters, advocacy-based intervention, and legal remedies such as protective orders. Programs for men who abused their partners were developed as part of a criminal justice response to IPV. All of these initial intervention programs and strategies emphasized victim safety, empowering victims, and promoting perpetrator responsibility and attitude change.

Although these ideas are still important and influential today, prevention and intervention efforts have expanded in two major ways. First, there has been increasing attention paid to primary prevention, because it has been recognized that IPV can be prevented before it occurs rather than only reduced after it occurs (Foshee et al., 2004). Two prevention programs have shown a positive preventive impact on partner violence with adolescents (Foshee et al., 2004; Wolfe et al., 2003). It is important to note that these efforts have focused on both boys and girls, as it is seen as critical to intervene early, when physical aggression in relationships is practiced equally by both (Archer, 2000). Second, the universe of potential prevention and intervention points seems to be expanding. In line with a broad social–ecological model, early prevention strategies have focused on various individual factors, such as interpersonal skills, beliefs and norms, and anger responses (Foshee, 1998; Wolfe et al., 2003); family factors (see chap. 7, this volume); and school environments (Foshee, 1998). Intervention efforts have been expanded to examine (a) how treating substance abuse might reduce the occurrence of partner violence (Fals-Stewart, Kashdan, O'Farrell, & Birchler, 2002; O'Farrell, Murphy, Stephan, Fals-Stewart, & Murphy, 2004), (b) whether dyads can successfully be treated together when it is safe to do so (Bograd & Mederos, 1999; K. D. O'Leary, 2002; Stith, Rosen, & McCollum, 2003), and (c) when traditional individual therapies might be used with perpetrators of partner violence (Eckhardt, Murphy, Black, & Suhr, 2006; Sonkin & Dutton, 2003). Although there is clearly much work to do in the development and testing of prevention and intervention strategies, there seems to be some consensus regarding the newer conceptualizations of IPV that are multifaceted, indicating that one size of intervention does not fit all.

The results of many of the evolutions previously described are evident in this volume, which is structured into three parts, as follows.

PART I: FOUNDATIONS

Part I of this volume deals with basic questions regarding IPV. How common is it? Who perpetrates it? What can explain it? What puts a person at risk of experiencing IPV? What are the health effects of IPV? As noted, there has been tremendous growth of knowledge in these areas, and the chapters in Part I heavily reference the body of empirical evidence. Yet, as will become apparent to the reader, there is still a great deal of work to be done.

In chapter 2, Lipsky and Caetano offer a comprehensive discussion of definitions, surveillance issues, and prevalence rates across national studies. Several related issues raised by these authors are worthy of commentary and provide significant substance for further inquiry. It is clear from Lipsky and Caetano's discussion that surveillance of IPV has, in many ways, been patched together from a series of related but not well-coordinated data collection efforts. The authors provide a clear description of the strengths and gaps of various data collection methods (e.g., surveys vs. criminal justice data vs. health-related data). It is clear that greater coordination among the agencies that collect such information is needed, along with a better understanding of the relationship between various data sources. Lipsky and Caetano also discuss types of IPV (i.e., stalking and physical, sexual, and emotional abuse) in the context of surveillance systems and prevalence estimates. This further complicates the overall surveillance issue in that it is critical to understand which types of surveillance systems capture which types of IPV.

Woodin and O'Leary, in chapter 3, provide an overview of theoretical approaches to IPV perpetration, covering considerable ground, from sociocultural theories to intrapersonal theories. They demonstrate the progress made from 3 decades ago, when most work was focused on a single explanation, to the present time by examining social–ecological (Dutton, 1995; Heise, 1998; Riggs & O'Leary, 1989) and developmental (Capaldi, Shortt, & Kim, 2005) theories. Woodin and O'Leary also demonstrate the considerable need for empirical validation of the various theoretical models. There is a strong need to understand how risk factors at various social–ecological levels interact to affect behavior and how their influence may vary across developmental periods.

In chapter 4, Stith and McMonigle discuss risk factors for IPV and distinguish between risk factors for IPV victimization versus intimate partner homicide (IPH). They raise the issue of whether correlates of the most serious IPV, such as homicide, differ from correlates of less serious IPV—a question that has received little attention in the empirical literature to date. There is an increasing agreement that IPV comes in more than one form (Johnson, 1995) and that, for example, low-level, conflict-based IPV may be different from IPV characterized by extreme control and dominance. There is relatively little empirical work, however, and little known about how different forms of violence may develop. Stith and McMonigle also demonstrate the multifactorial nature of IPV by discussing a breadth of risk factors associated with IPV and IPH. They raise an important question that other chapters also touch on—whether risk of any IPV is similar to risk of the most serious forms of IPV.

Capaldi, Kim, and Pears, in chapter 5, focus on the overlap between IPV and child maltreatment and discuss IPV perpetration from a developmental perspective. They tackle the questions of whether risk of perpetrating IPV and child maltreatment is more unique than similar, ultimately arguing that conduct disorder and antisocial behavior are variables common to the two forms of violence. Their dynamic developmental systems approach suggests that the behaviors of IPV and child maltreatment be viewed from an ecological and a developmental perspective in which various levels of risk factors influence behavior, and that those influences may change over time. This is an important perspective for potential primary prevention efforts. As discussed by Foshee and McNaughton Reyes (chap. 7), more information is needed regarding when to intervene and what factors to target with prevention strategies. Capaldi, Kim, and Pears remind the reader that those targets may change over developmental stages.

In chapter 6, the final chapter in Part I, Campbell, Baty, Laughon, and Woods discuss the health effects of IPV, describing them and some of the mechanisms by which IPV victimization leads to poor health. Several points from chapter 6 are important. One is that the health effects from IPV are numerous and severe; IPV victims are at much greater risk of a number of short- and long-term physical and psychological problems. A second point is that therapists need to know more about the mechanisms by which IPV leads to poorer health. Much of the research cited in chapter 6 is correlational, and longitudinal work is needed to more fully understand the physical and psychological mechanisms by which IPV leads to poorer health. Third, on a more positive note, poor health from IPV is not inevitable. This is not to say that some IPV is not harmful, but there is variation in the extent to which IPV leads to poor health outcomes, and understanding that variation can inform the development of intervention strategies for victims to better facilitate the avoidance of negative health outcomes. Finally, Campbell et al. review studies on how IPV victimization affects women. Male victims of IPV have been less well studied, and it is not clear whether men experience the same long-term effects compared with women.

PART II: PREVENTION AND INTERVENTION

Part II of this volume deals with prevention and intervention issues. Five chapters focus on approaches to preventing or reducing IPV, and several themes emerge. One theme is the diversity of intervention strategies that have been and will be needed to effectively address IPV and its negative consequences. There have been and will need to be many sectors involved in a full and effective response to IPV prevention, including community-based agencies (see chaps. 8, 9, and 10), legal and criminal justice agencies (see chaps. 8, 10, and 11), schools (see chaps. 7 and 11), and families (see chaps. 7 and 11). Researchers and practitioners in each of these areas must contribute to the combined effort to address IPV. Each may have a different role, but all are needed to prevent IPV and its negative consequences.

A second related theme apparent across the chapters in Part II is that there is still a great deal of work to be done to understand which strategies are effective. Three of the five chapters present fairly detailed data on intervention effectiveness, and the picture to date is not particularly positive. A few programs have been shown to prevent teen dating violence (chap.7), but among adults and identified perpetrators and victims, there is insufficient evidence for effective psychosocial programs (chap. 8) and relatively little evidence that legal and criminal justice programs are especially effective (chap. 10). Thus, the chapters collectively demonstrate a strong need for further intervention development with rigorous testing of those interventions. Straus (chap. 11) offers many innovative suggestions for new IPV prevention efforts based on his conceptualization of partner violence.

A final theme of Part II is that there is a strong need for interventions that focus on both perpetrators and victims, as well as the need to think more broadly about the roles of perpetrator and victim than has traditionally occurred. Traditionally, the field of IPV has associated perpetration with men and victimization with women. However, after the first family violence survey, by Straus and Gelles in 1975, which found that both men and women reported perpetrating substantial levels of physical IPV, the picture became more complicated. Since that time there has been intense debate about *sex symmetry* in the perpetration of physical IPV and the extent to which prevention and intervention efforts should involve women. Both Foshee and McNaughton Reyes (chap. 7) and Straus (chap. 11) suggest that universal primary prevention programs should focus on boys and girls because perpetration rates for physical violence are about equal among teens. However, they also note (along with Stith and McMonigle in chap. 4) that most of the few longitudinal studies examining precursors of dating violence have focused on boys only. Hilton and Harris (chap. 10) note that the criminal justice system has generally ignored female perpetrators in response to females' portrayal as "weak" victims. Whitaker and Niolon (chap. 8) discuss secondary prevention efforts that might target female perpetrators, noting that there is a dearth of information on female perpetrators and that most intervention programs were developed with men as the target.

In chapter 7, Foshee and McNaughton Reyes discuss primary prevention, addressing the issues of when to begin, whom to target, and how to do it. Although stated plainly, such issues are not simple. With regard to when to begin, the authors make clear that primary prevention must begin in early adolescence or sooner. With regard to whom to target, the authors note the lack of data to suggest that targeting interventions by sex, race, or income is warranted. They point to other factors that could serve as triggers for selected or indicated interventions, such as the use of psychological aggression and having been a victim of child maltreatment. With regard to how to do it, the authors summarize the relatively small body of longitudinal studies and ultimately focus on three points for intervention: the family context, the peer context, and the prevention of behavioral precursors to dating violence. Finally, Foshee and McNaughton Reyes discuss dating violence prevention in the broader context of general prevention research, noting that the prevention research community is beginning to look at more comprehensive general prevention programs that address multiple problems rather than individual programs for each different problem behavior, an important consideration.

Whitaker and Niolon, in chapter 8, discuss intervention approaches for known perpetrators (i.e., secondary prevention programs), including batterer intervention programs (BIPs). The thrust of their chapter is to review what is known about current BIPs and to review the literature on what other forms of treatment might prevent the recurrence of IPV, including therapeutic approaches, dyadic approaches, and substance abuse treatment. The authors discuss several issues that may affect the development and testing of secondary prevention strategies, including typologies, female perpetrators, motivation for treatment, and cultural issues. Two important points that emerge from chapter 8 for the successful treatment of violent partners are that multiple intervention strategies will likely be needed and that much more rigorous intervention development and testing is required.

In chapter 9, Glass, Rollins, and Bloom focus on expanding the treatment responses to victims by adopting a human rights approach to IPV, proposing that a reconceptualization of IPV as a human rights issue suggests different approaches to victim services than the current state of the field. After describing the various forms of victim services (e.g., shelters, advocacy, legal assistance), Glass et al. provide a human rights framework and discuss how it would be applied to IPV services in the United States. For example, they argue that framing IPV victimization as an issue of human rights puts responsibilities squarely on the shoulders of government and institutions, who would be responsible for ensuring those rights by enacting appropriate legislation, policy, and practice. Likewise, they suggest that adopting a human rights framework for IPV victimization would cause various outcomes that could (and should) be measured as indicators of success, measures that reach beyond the more simple indicators of reabuse as suggested by other authors (e.g., see chap. 8). Like other chapter authors (i.e., see chaps. 8, 10, and 11), Glass et al. clearly assert that addressing IPV will require coordination and collaboration of multiple sectors, including government, organizations, and educational institutions.

Hilton and Harris, in chapter 10, describe efforts and findings regarding criminal justice approaches to address IPV, including legislative efforts, policing strategies, prosecutorial strategies, and coordinated criminal justice and community responses. As with other interventions, the authors note that many criminal justice interventions for IPV have not been rigorously evaluated (nor were they designed to be rigorously evaluated). The authors then discuss six principles from the broader criminal justice literature regarding criminal justice intervention strategies. These principles are critical in guiding one's thinking about the criminal justice response to IPV. Several are consistent with the writing from other authors. For example, the principle that intervention targets are not always obvious is consistent with the recommendation by several chapter authors (see chaps. 7, 8, and 11) that there is a need to look broadly rather than narrowly for solutions to partner violence. The principle that risk factors are highly general is also consistent with the notions posed by other chapter authors (see chaps. 5 and 7) who speculate whether more general positive youth development programs can be used to prevent dating violence.

In chapter 11, the final chapter in Part II, Straus focuses specifically on the notion of sex symmetry (i.e., the notion that men and women perpetrate physical violence equally) in partner violence and the implications for primary and secondary prevention strategies. The debate about sex symmetry in physical IPV has been ongoing and heated. Straus argues that the acceptance of the notion of sex symmetry in physical IPV implicates a host of prevention principles that have not been widely implemented or tested. For instance, prevention strategies would include targeting messages about physical violence to both boys and girls, recognizing gender in the development of prevention messages, and focusing on the development of healthy relationships as means to prevent partner violence. For treatment with known perpetrators of IPV, recommendations include assessing all violent relationships for dangerousness and symmetry and focusing on the treatment needs of the perpetrators rather than using more simple educational approaches.

PART III: CONCLUSION

The study, prevention, and treatment of IPV perpetration and victimization has evolved considerably over the past 30 years. The concluding chapter, chapter 12, summarizes the main themes of this volume and discusses future directions in preventing and treating IPV. It will be clear from the chapters herein that there is much, much more work to do. It is critical that researchers, practitioners, and policymakers be open to new and multiple solutions to fully address the problem of partner violence, as several of the authors in this volume make clear. It is our hope that this volume will inform and provoke readers to understand and ultimately stop the tragedy of IPV.

REFERENCES

Archer, J. (2000). Sex differences in aggression between heterosexual partners: A meta-analytic review. *Psychological Bulletin, 126*, 651–680.

Bograd, M., & Mederos, F. (1999). Battering and couples therapy: Universal screening and selection of treatment modality. *Journal of Marital & Family Therapy, 25*, 291–312.

Buzawa, E., & Buzawa, C. G. (2003). *Domestic violence: The criminal justice response* (3rd ed.). Thousand Oaks, CA: Sage.

Caetano, R., Field, C. A., Ramisetty-Mikler, S., & McGrath, C. (2005). The 5-year course of intimate partner violence among White, Black, and Hispanic couples in the United States. *Journal of Interpersonal Violence, 20*, 1039–1057.

Campbell, J. C. (2002, April 13). Health consequences of intimate partner violence. *The Lancet, 359,* 1331–1336.

Capaldi, D. M., & Kim, H. K. (2007). Typological approaches to violence in couples: A critique and alternative conceptual approach. *Clinical Psychology Review, 27,* 253–265.

Capaldi, D. M., Shortt, J. W., & Kim, H. K. (2005). A life span developmental systems perspective on aggression toward a partner. In W. M. Pinsof & J. L. Lebow (Eds.), *Family psychology: The art of the science* (pp. 141–167). New York: Oxford University Press.

Cascardi, M., & Vivian, D. (1995). Context for specific episodes of marital violence: Gender and severity of violence differences. *Journal of Family Violence, 10,* 265–293.

Connolly, J., Pepler, D., Craig, W., & Taradash, A. (2000). Dating experiences of bullies in early adolescence. *Child Maltreatment, 5,* 299–310.

Dutton, D. G. (1995). *The domestic assault of women: Psychological and criminal justice perspectives.* Vancouver, British Columbia, Canada: University of British Columbia Press.

Eckhardt, C. I., Murphy, C., Black, D., & Suhr, L. (2006). Intervention programs for perpetrators of intimate partner violence: Conclusions from a clinical research perspective. *Public Health Reports, 121,* 369–381.

Fals-Stewart, W., Kashdan, T. B., O'Farrell, T. J., & Birchler, G. R. (2002). Behavioral couples therapy for drug-abusing patients: Effects on partner violence. *Journal of Substance Abuse Treatment, 22,* 87–96.

Foshee, V. A. (1998). Involving schools and communities in preventing adolescent dating abuse. In X. B. Arriaga & S. Oskamp (Eds.), *Addressing community problems: Psychological research and interventions* (pp. 104–129). Thousand Oaks, CA: Sage.

Foshee, V. A., Bauman, K. E., Ennett, S. T., Linder, G., Benefield, T., & Suchindran, C. (2004). Assessing the long-term effects of the Safe Dates program and a booster in preventing and reducing adolescent dating violence victimization and perpetration. *American Journal of Public Health, 94,* 619–624.

Gorman-Smith, D., Tolan, P. H., Sheidow, A. J., & Henry, D. B. (2001). Partner violence and street violence among urban adolescents: Do the same family factors relate? *Journal of Research on Adolescence, 11,* 273–295.

Hammond, W. R., Whitaker, D. J., Lutzker, J. R., Mercy, J., & Chin, P. M. (2006). Setting a violence prevention agenda at the Centers for Disease Control and Prevention. *Aggression and Violent Behavior, 11,* 112–119.

Heise, L. L. (1998). Violence against women: An integrated, ecological framework. *Violence Against Women, 4,* 262.

Holtzworth-Munroe, A., & Stuart, G. L. (1994). Typologies of male batterers: Three subtypes and the differences among them. *Psychological Bulletin, 116,* 476–497.

Johnson, M. P. (1995). Patriarchal terrorism and common couple violence: Two forms of violence against women. *Journal of Marriage and the Family, 57,* 283–294.

Kernsmith, P. (2005). Exerting power or striking back: A gendered comparison of motivations for domestic violence perpetration. *Violence and Victims, 20,* 173–185.

Leonard, K. E. (2005). Alcohol and intimate partner violence: When can we say that heavy drinking is a contributing cause of violence? *Addiction, 100,* 422–425.

McClennen, J. C. (2005). Domestic violence between same-gender partners: Recent findings and future research. *Journal of Interpersonal Violence, 20,* 149.

National Center for Injury Prevention and Control. (2003). *Cost of intimate partner violence against women in the United States.* Atlanta, GA: Centers for Disease Control and Prevention.

O'Farrell, T. J., Murphy, C. M., Stephan, S. H., Fals-Stewart, W., & Murphy, M. (2004). Partner violence before and after couples-based alcoholism treatment for male alcoholic patients: The role of treatment involvement and abstinence. *Journal of Consulting and Clinical Psychology, 72,* 202–217.

O'Leary, K. D. (2002). Conjoint therapy for partners who engage in physically aggressive behavior: Rationale and research. *Journal of Aggression, Maltreatment, and Trauma, 5,* 145–164.

O'Leary, K. D., Barling, J., Arias, I., Rosenbaum, A., Malone, J., & Tyree, A. (1989). Prevalence and stability of physical aggression between spouses: A longitudinal analysis. *Journal of Consulting and Clinical Psychology, 57,* 263–268.

O'Leary, S. G., & Smith Slep, A. M. (2006). Precipitants of partner aggression. *Journal of Family Psychology, 20,* 344–347.

Plichta, S. B. (2004). Intimate partner violence and physical health consequences: Policy and practice implications. *Journal of Interpersonal Violence, 19,* 1296–1323.

Riggs, D. S., & O'Leary, K. D. (1989). A theoretical model of courtship aggression. In M. A. Pirog-Good & J. E. Stets (Eds.), *Violence in dating relationships: Emerging social issues* (pp. 53–71). New York: Praeger Publishers.

Sonkin, D. J., & Dutton, D. (2003). Treating assaultive men from an attachment perspective. In D. Dutton & D. J. Sonkin (Eds.), *Intimate violence: Contemporary treatment advances* (pp. 105–133). New York: Haworth Press.

Stith, S. M., Rosen, K. H., & McCollum, E. E. (2003). Effectiveness of couples treatment for spouse abuse. *Journal of Marital & Family Therapy, 29,* 407–426.

Straus, M. A., & Gelles, R. J. (1995). How violent are American families? Estimates from the National Family Violence Resurvey and other studies. In M. A. Straus & R. J. Gelles (Eds.), *Physical violence in American families: Risk factors and adaptations to violence in 8,145 families* (pp. 95–112). New Brunswick, NJ: Transaction.

Stuart, G. L., Moore, T. M., Gordon, K. C., Hellmuth, J. C., Ramsey, S. E., & Kahler, C. W. (2006). Reasons for intimate partner violence perpetration among arrested women. *Violence Against Women, 12,* 609–621.

Sumner, J. D. (2007, August 24). *Kids may have seen mother die*. Retrieved November 5, 2008, from http://www.albanyherald.com/archives/News/2007/front082407a.html

Walker, L. (1984). *The battered woman syndrome*. New York: Springer Publishing Company.

Whitaker, D. J., Haileyesus, T., Swahn, M., & Saltzman, L. S. (2007). Differences in frequency of violence and reported injury between relationships with reciprocal and nonreciprocal intimate partner violence. *American Journal of Public Health*, 97, 941.

Wolfe, D. A., Wekerle, C., Scott, K., Straatman, A.-L., Grasley, C., & Reitzel-Jaffe, D. (2003). Dating violence prevention with at-risk youth: A controlled outcome evaluation. *Journal of Consulting and Clinical Psychology*, 71, 279–291.

WSFA 12 News. (2007, September 5). *Attempted murder–suicide sparked by domestic dispute*. Retrieved August 31, 2007, from http://www.wsfa.com/Global/story.asp?S=6981631&nav=0RdE

I

FOUNDATIONS

2

DEFINITIONS, SURVEILLANCE SYSTEMS, AND THE PREVALENCE AND INCIDENCE OF INTIMATE PARTNER VIOLENCE IN THE UNITED STATES

SHERRY LIPSKY AND RAUL CAETANO

Epidemiological studies are necessary to establish the basic frequency indicators of intimate partner violence (IPV) in the population, such as prevalence and incidence, as well as to identify risk factors. This in turn forms the base for the identification of high-risk groups and the development and implementation of prevention and intervention in the community. These studies are most fruitful when they share common methodological characteristics, including definitions of constructs being studied, standard methodology of measurement for these constructs, and standardized data collection. When repeated at regular intervals, population-based studies can become the backbone of surveillance systems. *Surveillance* is typically defined in public health as the ongoing and systematic collection, analysis, and interpretation of outcome-specific data essential to the planning, implementation, and evaluation of public health practice (Thacker, 1996).

Important components of IPV surveillance systems include population-based studies, such as the Behavioral Risk Factor Surveillance Survey (BRFSS) and the proposed National Intimate Partner and Sexual Violence Survey (NISVS) developed by the Centers for Disease Control and Prevention (CDC). Health care data collected systematically by states, including trauma registries and injury surveillance systems, and criminal justice data, such as the Supplementary Homicide Reports (SHR) and the National Incident-Based Reporting System (NIBRS), are additional sources of national surveillance data on IPV.

The overall objectives of this chapter are to describe definitions of terms necessary for the surveillance and study of IPV, describe the structure of current IPV surveillance systems and potential improvements to those systems, and review the prevalence and incidence of IPV in the U.S. population. The discussion here of prevalence and incidence focuses on national-level data and, to the extent possible, on differences across ethnic groups.

TERMS AND DEFINITIONS

Researchers have used terms related to IPV in a number of different ways and have used different terms to describe the same acts. These inconsistencies have contributed to a wide range of estimates of the incidence, prevalence, and predictors of IPV. It is essential that researchers clarify the specific measurements used in any given surveillance system or survey to accurately report findings, draw appropriate conclusions, and formulate relevant recommendations. In assessing measures and survey instruments, it is also important to determine whether severity and different forms of IPV (e.g., psychological abuse, physical violence, sexual violence) are included, because each of these measures adds important information necessary to fully understand the nature of IPV (Gordon, 2000; R. S. Thompson et al., 2006) and potential sequelae (Bonomi et al., 2006; Coker et al., 2002). In the sections that follow, we review terms and definitions proposed by the CDC for surveillance systems as well as those used by general population surveys.

Surveillance Terms Proposed by the Centers for Disease Control and Prevention

In an attempt to improve the quality of the available data about violence against women, the CDC's National Center for Injury Prevention and Control initiated a process in 1994 to begin addressing some of the conceptual and logistical issues of IPV surveillance. To narrow the scope of the task and increase its effectiveness, the CDC decided to concentrate on developing data elements for IPV surveillance (Saltzman, Fanslow, McMahon, & Shelley, 1999). Although originally intended to describe IPV against women, the proposed terms may apply to either men or women in same-sex or hetero-

TABLE 2.1
Terms and Definitions Proposed for the Surveillance
of Intimate Partner Violence

Term	Definition
Victim	Person targeted for violence or abuse.
Perpetrator	Person who inflicts or causes the violence or abuse.
Intimate partners	Current or former spouses, partners, dates, boyfriends, or girlfriends.
Physical violence	Intentional use of physical force with potential for causing harm or death.
Sexual violence	Use of physical force to compel a person to engage in a sexual act against his or her will or a sex act with someone unable to consent (attempted or completed).
Abusive sexual contact	Intentional touching directly or through clothing of genitalia, anus, groin, breast, inner thigh, or buttocks of a person against his or her will or of a person who is unable to consent.
Threat of physical or sexual violence	Communicating the intent to cause physical or sexual violence or abusive sexual contact.
Psychological–emotional abuse	Trauma to victim caused by acts, threats of acts, or coercive tactics on a repeated basis or with prior threat of or actual physical or sexual violence.

Note. Data from Saltzman, Fanslow, McMahon, and Shelley (1999).

sexual relationships. This is an important consideration given that general population surveys have revealed both male-to-female (MF) and female-to-male (FM) partner violence among heterosexuals (e.g., see Caetano, Cunradi, Clark, & Schafer, 2000; Straus & Gelles, 1990) as well as IPV among individuals in same-sex relationships (Tjaden, Thoennes, & Allison, 1999).

The first set of proposed definitions relates to the involved parties and relationships between them and includes victim, perpetrator, and intimate partners (see Table 2.1). Intimate partners may or may not be cohabiting, and the intimate relationship need not involve current sexual activities. For instance, if the victim and the perpetrator have a child in common but no current relationship, then by definition they fit in the category of former marital or nonmarital partners.

Violence and terms associated with violence are also defined. Violence is divided into four categories: physical violence, sexual violence, threat of physical or sexual violence, and psychological–emotional abuse (see Table 2.1). Physical violence may include acts such as pushing, biting, choking, slapping, punching, burning, use of a weapon, and use of restraints or one's body against another person. Physical violence also includes coercing other people to commit any of these acts. Sexual violence can be divided into three categories: (a) the use of physical force to compel a person to engage in a sexual act against his or her will, (b) an attempted or completed sex act involving a person unable to consent, and (c) abusive sexual contact. Threat of physical or sexual violence involves communicating through the use of words, gestures or weapons the intent to cause death, disability, injury or physical harm or the intent to compel a person to engage in sex acts or abusive sexual contact when the person is either unwilling or unable to consent. Psychological or emotional abuse may involve humiliating the victim, controlling or isolating the victim, coercing the victim to engage in illegal activities, using the victim's children to control the victim's behavior, and destroying property. Some behaviors may not be perceived as psychologically or emotionally abusive by all victims. Furthermore, other behaviors may be considered emotionally abusive if they are perceived as such by the victim.

In addition, episodes and patterns of violence were defined by Saltzman et al. (1999). A *violent episode* is defined as a single act or series of acts of violence that are perceived to be connected to each other and that may persist over a period of minutes, hours, or days and may involve single or multiple types of violence. *Most recent violent episode* refers to the violent episode perpetrated most recently by any violent partner. *Pattern of violence* is the way that violence is distributed over time in terms of frequency, severity, or type of violent episode.

Measurement of each of these elements can be complex. Two commonly used measurements are lifetime IPV or past-year IPV (i.e., in the previous 12 months). These measures can be further categorized as any lifetime IPV (dichotomized as ever vs. never experienced IPV), number of episodes by any partner ever, number of episodes in the past 12 months by any intimate partner, or number of episodes in the past 12 months by perpetrator of most recent episode (Saltzman et al., 1999). These measures can also include separate counts for the different types of violence. It is unlikely that any one surveillance method would incorporate all of these measures. Each surveillance system or survey has a specific purpose, making it difficult to recommend one set of measures across systems. If the purpose is to estimate the total burden of partner violence in a population, lifetime measures would be most appropriate. Estimating the current prevalence by type and severity (e.g., severe physical IPV by any intimate partner in the previous 12 months), however, would provide IPV programs more up-to-date data for planning purposes and would allow one to track trends over time. Specific populations or outcomes must also be taken into account. For instance, the time frame for IPV during pregnancy should be specific to the referent pregnancy period if maternal and infant outcomes are to be measured. At the very least, however, one should strive to standardize within surveillance systems.

A subsequent workshop recommended that stalking be included as a form of violence and abuse against women (CDC, 2000). These measures may be applicable to men experiencing stalking, although the majority (80%) of stalking victims are women (Basile, Swahn, Chen, & Saltzman, 2006). An explicit definition of stalking was not included in the work group summary, although it was reported that the work group did not resolve the issue of whether stalking requires the presence of a clear threat to do physical harm. Consensus in this work group was also not reached regarding whether stalking should be included in the narrower category of violence against women (considered psychological–emotional abuse) or treated as a discrete category.

Negative physical health, social, and psychological effects of stalking have been well documented (Basile, Arias, Desai, & Thompson, 2004; Davis, Coker, & Sanderson, 2002; Turmanis & Brown, 2006), and stalking may have predictors and sequelae distinct from other forms of IPV (Logan, Shannon, Cole, & Walker, 2006; Mechanic, Uhlmansiek, Weaver, & Resick, 2000; Mechanic, Weaver, & Resick, 2000). Furthermore, stalking in intimate relationships has been associated with previous psychological abuse without physical violence (Logan, Leukefeld, & Walker, 2000; Mechanic, Uhlmansiek, et al., 2000; Mechanic, Weaver, & Resnick, 2000) and without current physical abuse or victim injury (Tjaden & Thoennes, 2000d). For these reasons, we suggest that a definition of stalking (a) need not require a clear and present threat to do physical harm and (b) should be included as one distinct aspect of IPV.

Survey Terms and Measurement

One of the more widely known and used set of scales in the measurement of IPV in surveys is the Conflict Tactics Scales (CTS; Straus, 1979). Two versions are most often used: the CTS Form N (CTS1) and the Revised CTS or CTS2 (Straus, Hamby, Boney-McCoy, & Sugarman, 1996). As the name implies, the CTS was intended to measure the choice of tactics individuals use in dealing with conflict within families and is introduced in the interview as such.

The CTS1 includes three scales: Reasoning, Verbal Aggression, and Violence. The CTS2 includes Negotiation, Psychological Aggression, Physical Assault, Injury, and Sexual Coercion. The most commonly used CTS1/CTS2 scales are the Verbal/Psychological Aggression and Violence/Physical Assault scales. For the purposes of this chapter, we do not include a discussion of the Reasoning/Negotiation scale. Within each scale are subscales with specific behaviors or acts listed for each. The respondent indicates how many times he or she did each of these acts and how many times his or her partner did them in the past year.

Straus (1979) defined *verbal/psychological aggression* as "the use of verbal and nonverbal acts which symbolically hurt the other" (p. 77). *Violence/physical assault* is defined as the use of physical force against another person as a means of resolving conflict. Straus et al. (1996) defined *sexual coercion* as "behavior that is intended to compel the partner to engage in unwanted sexual activity." The Injury scale measures "partner-inflicted physical injury resulting in bone or tissue damage, a need for medical attention, or pain continuing for a day or more" (p. 290).

All of the CTS2 scales have good internal consistency, with coefficients as high as or higher than those for the CTS1 (Straus, 1979; Straus et al., 1996). Construct validity, although found to be adequate, is more complex, and the evidence in support of those findings is limited.

A number of criticisms of the CTS have been articulated by other researchers (DeKeseredy, 2000; Gordon, 2000), many of which have been addressed by Straus (1990). These include the rank ordering and counting of behaviors, which may be misleading; the inability to address issues of power and control; the lack of context of the event; and the situating of IPV only in the context of settling family conflicts. Although the CTS has advantages as well as limitations, using these scales in combination with other measures is critical to one's understanding of IPV in its entirety (Campbell, 2000; Gordon, 2000).

Several other population-based surveys have used the CTS1/CTS2 or adaptations of these measures, including the National Longitudinal Couples Survey (NLCS; Caetano et al., 2000) and the National Violence Against Women Survey (NVAWS; Tjaden & Thoennes, 2000b). The NVAWS defined *IPV* as rape, physical assault, and stalking perpetrated by a current or former date, boyfriend, girlfriend, spouse, or cohabiting partner (National Center for Injury Prevention and Control, 2003). Same-sex and opposite-sex cohabitants are included in the definition. The assessment of physical assault was adapted from the CTS. *Completed and attempted rape* (with and without penetration, respectively) were defined as the use of force, without the victim's consent, or threat of force to penetrate the victim's vagina, anus, or mouth by penis, tongue, fingers, or object. Follow-up questions were used to ascertain the relationship of the perpetrator. The rape questions were adapted from those used in the National Women's Study (National Victim Center & Crime Victims Research and Treatment Center, 1992). *Stalking* was defined as repeated visual or physical proximity, nonconsensual communication, and/or written, verbal, or implied threats directed at a specific individual that would arouse fear in a reasonable person. Stalking also included vandalizing the victim's property or destroying something they loved.

Other general population surveys, including the National Survey of Families and Households (NSFH), the National Survey on Drug Use and Health (NSDUH; formerly called the National Household Survey on Drug Abuse), and the National Crime Victimization Survey (NCVS), have defined and measured IPV in a variety of different ways. The NSDUH, for example, asked married or cohabiting respondents one question on IPV victimization (i.e., "How many times during the past 12 months did your spouse or partner hit or threaten to hit you?") and one question on perpetration (i.e., "How many times during the past 12 months did you hit or threaten to hit your spouse or partner?").

The NSFH, however, asked married or cohabiting respondents and their spouses about how they handled disagreements and if arguments sometimes become physical. They were further queried as to how many of these arguments resulted in the respondent being hit or shoved or had things thrown at him or her, and how many resulted in the respondent hitting, shoving, or throwing things at his or her partner. Finally, the respondent was asked whether he or she (or his or her partner) had been cut, bruised, or seriously injured in an argument. All of the physical violence and injury questions were referenced for the past year. These questions were also asked of respondents who had experienced marital disruption (e.g., "In the last year before your separation . . ."). Only the questions on physical arguments and injury were used to measure physical IPV in research papers emanating from this study (Rodriguez, Lasch, Chandra, & Lee, 2001; Sorenson, Upchurch, & Shen, 1996; Zlotnick, 1998; Zlotnick, Johnson, & Kohn, 2006).

The NCVS did not originally ask specific questions about incidents that were perpetrated by relatives or offenders known to them, although the survey did ask about victim–perpetrator relationship. With the redesign of the survey in 1992, however, new questions were added to increase the reporting of IPV. *Intimate relationships* are defined as spouses, ex-spouses, and current or former boyfriends and girlfriends, including same-sex relationships. Physical violence is assessed by asking whether anyone attacked or threatened the respondent in any of a number of listed ways (including sexual assault and threats). Additional questions ask about forced or coerced unwanted sexual activity (including rape or other type of sexual attack).

Considerations for Survey Measurement

Surveys typically have specific and often unique objectives that distinguish them from each other, making it difficult to propose a single set of measures. However, lack of comparability in the methodology for assessing IPV creates considerable difficulties for comparing results across surveys. In the case of surveillance, which has as one of its main purposes to monitor the level of IPV, differences across survey methodology make it almost impossible to decide, say, if an increase in prevalence is a true increase or just an effect of survey methods.

Another important consideration is the context in which the survey is conducted and in which the questions are framed. For example, the NCVS collects data in the context of crimes an individual has experienced, whereas surveys using the CTS frame questions in the context of partner conflict situations or personal safety (Straus, 1993, 1999; Tjaden & Thoennes, 2000a). This may affect an individual's response to questions and, consequently, prevalence estimates. Furthermore, general population surveys tend to measure less severe violence compared with agency data. There is an ongoing debate in the literature and among researchers regarding this issue, particularly because typologies of violence and the related issue of gender symmetry may be measured differently depending on data sources. We cannot give these issues adequate voice here because of space limitations, but the controversy has been addressed most recently in the Gender Symmetry workshop sponsored by the CDC and the National Institute of Justice (see Rosen, 2006, and related workshop papers).

It is essential in all studies, whenever possible, to specify the relationship and gender of victim and perpetrator, time frames, and context. In addition, collecting data from both partners in cohabiting relationships will expand the ability to estimate the prevalence of IPV (Schafer, Caetano, & Cunradi, 2004). Using the guidelines, terms, and definitions proposed by the CDC (Saltzman et al., 1999) will increase the comparability among surveys and improve one's ability to compare findings across populations and across time. It is important to note, however, that although the development of these definitions is a valuable step toward standardization, other measurement issues, such as those discussed here, must be addressed.

Another endeavor to improve the scientific quality of survey research is the compilation of IPV measures recently published by the CDC: *Measuring Intimate Partner Violence Victimization and Perpetration: A Compendium of Assessment Tools* (M. P. Thompson, Basile, Hertz, & Sitterle, 2006) includes measures for IPV victimization and perpetration in four areas—physical, sexual, psychological, and stalking. Psychometric data and target groups are provided for each measure. More research will be necessary to determine whether these scales are reliable and valid, especially among ethnic and sexual minority populations.

CURRENT SURVEILLANCE EFFORTS

The ability to gauge the magnitude of IPV in relation to other public health problems, identify those groups at highest risk who might benefit from focused intervention or increased services, and monitor changes in the incidence and prevalence of IPV over time would enable public health, healthcare, and other service providers as well as policymakers to better respond to the problem of IPV (Saltzman et al., 1999). Currently, there are a number of different data sources and systems from which to estimate prevalence and incidence, but these resources have been developed for a variety of different purposes (CDC, 2000). In the sections that follow, we review those sources that currently collect data on IPV and potential sources that could incorporate IPV-specific data in the future.

National Survey Surveillance

The CDC conducts two ongoing surveys that include questions on IPV. First, the BRFSS, an annual telephone survey, tracks health risk behaviors in the United States. Two optional modules covering IPV and sexual violence are available to states conducting the survey, but not all states have implemented them. Second, the Pregnancy Risk Assessment Monitoring System (PRAMS) is an ongoing state- and population-based surveillance system designed to monitor selected self-reported maternal behaviors and experiences that occur before, during, and after pregnancy among women who deliver a live-born infant. This survey also provides information on physical abuse by a spouse or partner.

In addition, the CDC has conducted a pilot study of the NISVS to gather information about IPV, including physical and emotional abuse, sexual violence, and stalking victimization and perpetration. The survey will inform the development of an ongoing national IPV, sexual violence, and stalking surveillance system.

The NCVS, sponsored by the Bureau of Justice Statistics, is the primary source of information on criminal victimization in the United States. Each year, incident data are obtained from a nationally representative sample of persons age 12 years or older. Although the survey does not specifically address IPV victimization, the victim–perpetrator relationship is assessed. Questions on rape, sexual assault, physical assault, and threats of violence, in addition to other types of crimes, are specifically asked of all respondents.

Health Data Sources

The National Electronic Injury Surveillance System (NEISS), which includes a national sample of hospitals, conducted the Survey of Injured Victims of Violence (SIVV; Rand, 1997) in 1994 as a supplement to NEISS. SIVV gathered data from hospital emergency departments, including intentional injuries brought to the attention of hospital personnel, and identified victim–offender relationship, including intimate partner. The CDC, in collaboration with the Consumer Product Safety Commission, expanded the NEISS in 2000 to include all types and external causes of nonfatal injuries, including intentional injuries such as assaults, treated in U.S. hospital emergency departments. This ongoing surveillance system is called the NEISS All Injury Program (NEISS-AIP) and includes data on victim–offender relationship and the context of the assault (e.g., altercation, robbery, sexual assault). The CDC uses NEISS-AIP to generate national estimates of nonfatal injuries, including those related to IPV.

There are important limitations to NEISS-AIP data. The majority of emergency and primary health care providers do not ask their patients about IPV, and victims seeking medical care for IPV-related injuries may not disclose the true cause of their injuries (Glass, Dearwater, & Campbell, 2001; Kothari & Rhodes, 2006; Kramer, Lorenzon, & Mueller, 2004). Even if they do, the information may not be recorded in the medical record (Kothari & Rhodes, 2006) or it may be incomplete (Biroscak, Smith, Roznowski, Tucker,

& Carlson, 2006). It is also important to note that the NEISS data will provide information on only those IPV incidents that result in injury and for which victims seek medical attention.

Criminal Justice Data

The two main national sources of criminal justice data for the surveillance of IPV are the NIBRS and the SHR, components of the Uniform Crime Reports (UCR) compiled by the Federal Bureau of Investigation (FBI). Data are reported annually. Although the UCR does not provide the detail necessary to identify violent crimes by intimate partners, the NIBRS and the SHR do provide detail on the victim–perpetrator relationship in violent crimes recorded by police agencies. The NIBRS obtains information on 57 types of crimes. Intimate relationships include spouse, ex-spouse, common-law spouse, boyfriend, girlfriend, and same-sex relationships. The SHR gathers data from local police departments on each homicide. This dataset provides 28 categories for the victim–offender relationship; intimate relationship definitions are comparable to the NIBRS. Thus, the SHR is a source for intimate partner homicide (IPH) data.

These data can provide information on nonfatal and fatal IPV, but the data are limited by the accuracy and reliability of police reports (Gelles, 2000). These data also likely underestimate the counts because not all states report—in fact, only a small percentage of the U.S. population resides in jurisdictions certified to report in the NIBRS. In 2004, 5,271 law enforcement agencies contributed NIBRS data to the UCR program (FBI, 2006). The data from those agencies represent 20% of the U.S. population and 16% of crime statistics collected by the UCR program. A large portion of reports also contain missing or misclassified data on victim–offender relationships. In addition, only about 25% to 50% of IPV is reported to the police (McFarlane, Soeken, Reel, Parker, & Silva, 1997; Tjaden & Thoennes, 2000a; U.S. Department of Justice, 1995).

The limitations of the SHR in terms of IPH also have been well documented (Biroscak, Smith, & Post, 2006; Langford, Isaac, & Kabat, 1998; Maxfield, 1989; Pampel & Williams, 2000). Notable issues include underreporting due to missing data within reported cases, exclusion of ex-boyfriends and ex-girlfriends as relationship types, and the inability to identify IPH deaths.

The full extent of nonfatal and fatal IPV, then, is not known. To better document the scope of the problem of IPV and identify trends in incidence and prevalence, researchers must improve the quality and consistency of data collection at national, state, and local levels. It will also be necessary to use multiple sources for the detection of nonfatal as well as fatal IPV.

One effort to better estimate fatal IPV is the development of the National Violent Death Reporting System (NVDRS; CDC, 2006b). The CDC funded 17 states to assist in developing a system that would (a) link records from violent deaths that occurred in the same incident; (b) provide timely information through faster data retrieval; (c) describe the circumstances that may have contributed to the violent death; and (d) better characterize perpetrators, including their relationship to the victim(s). The NVDRS will help to provide a more comprehensive picture of violent incidents and aid in the design and implementation of potentially successful prevention plans. The CDC will eventually incorporate NVDRS into the Public Health Information Network to integrate it with other public health surveillance systems.

Future Work

Several potential sources for national data on violence and abuse against women have been identified that do not currently collect specific data or include direct questions regarding IPV (CDC, 2006b). For example, the National Ambulatory and Hospital Medical Care Surveys, National Hospital Discharge Survey, National Health Interview Survey, National Survey of Family Growth, Youth Risk Behavior Surveillance System, and the Monitoring the Future surveys are possible sources to tap for future incorporation into a broad national surveillance system. Furthermore, modules or IPV-specific questions could be added to those surveys that do not routinely and systematically collect these data, such as the BRFSS.

Future additions to the surveillance system could increase surveillance accuracy and assist in the identification of trends, particularly in subpopulations with increased prevalence. Together with more specific research efforts and evaluation of the prevalence of known predictors of IPV, surveillance data could be used to develop and implement targeted prevention and interventions in these subgroups.

Limitations of Surveillance Systems

Each type of surveillance system has a number of limitations. Many of these issues have been reviewed at length in the background papers commissioned for the Building Data Systems workshop (Campbell, 2000; Orchowsky & Weiss, 2000; Waller & Martin, 2000). These issues include nondisclosure or self-report bias in health care settings and surveys, the framing of questionnaires or interviews, psychometric properties of survey instruments, coding in health care systems, and separate, disparate, and incomplete criminal justice and health-related databases, to name but a few. These limitations must be taken into account when using individual as well as linked data sources and in planning for more a comprehensive and cohesive surveillance system.

To address some of these problems, the CDC has established cooperative agreements with several states to conduct state-based IPV surveillance

(CDC, 2006a). These activities are designed to help states identify existing data sources, recognize opportunities to link data sources, and develop and implement more comprehensive systems for surveillance of fatal and nonfatal IPV. The states are also to support, to the extent possible, the integration of IPV surveillance systems into existing injury surveillance systems. Most of the funded states have conducted local or statewide surveys on IPV, used data linkage to improve IPV surveillance, and examined mortality data and/ or developed surveillance systems to estimate the number and characteristics of IPH victims.

PREVALENCE AND INCIDENCE

Prevalence refers to the proportion of cases of a disease or condition present in a population at a specific point in time or period of time. *Incidence* is the rate at which new cases of a disease or condition occur in a population within a defined time period, usually 1 year. As Campbell (2000) pointed out, however, it is important to consider how incidence is used in the course of IPV surveillance. Incidence may not be appropriate for ongoing acts such as IPV because it would be difficult to determine whether an individual is a "new case" even in a systematic surveillance system, given the multiple ways in which a victim or perpetrator may enter the system (e.g., criminal justice, victim services, emergency departments). Researchers must be specific, then, in how the term *incidence* is used to accurately reflect the data. Although most of the data presented herein refer to the prevalence and incidence of nonfatal IPV, a brief review of IPH incident data is also included.

General Population Estimates

Several national surveys in the United States have estimated the prevalence of IPV among men and women, including the National Family Violence Survey (NFVS; Straus & Gelles, 1990), conducted by Straus and Gelles in 1975 and repeated in 1985; the NSFH, conducted in 1987 with a follow-up in 1992 (Sorenson et al., 1996; Zlotnick, 1998; Zlotnick et al., 2006); the National Longitudinal Couples Survey (NLCS; Caetano et al., 2000), conducted in 1995 with a follow-up in 2000; the NVAWS (Tjaden & Thoennes, 2000b), conducted in 1995; and the annual NCVS (Rennison & Planty, 2003). A few of these surveys have also estimated the incidence of IPV by either identifying new cases in follow-up surveys (e.g., NLCP) or counting the number of incidents per person per year (e.g., NVAWS, NCVS).

Prevalence

The 1975 and 1985 NFVS are two of the earliest and most detailed national surveys on IPV. The 1975 survey was conducted with face-to-face

TABLE 2.2
Prevalence of Past-Year Intimate Partner Violence (IPV)

Survey	Any IPV (%)	Minor IPV (%)	Severe IPV (%)	Any MFPV (%)	Any FMPV (%)	Severe MFPV (%)	Severe FMPV (%)
NFVS (1985)[a]	16.0	—	6.3	11.6	12.5	4.8	3.4
NLCS (1995)[b]	21.5	12.8[c]	8.6	13.6	18.2	3.6	7.5
NSFH (1987)[d]	4.9–6.2	—	—	2.5	3.3	—	—
NVAWS (1995)[e]	0.9–1.5	—	—	—	—	—	—

Note. MFPV = male-to-female partner violence; FMPV = female-to-male partner violence. [a]NFVS = National Family Violence Survey; refers to physical IPV (Straus & Gelles, 1990). [b]NLCS = National Longitudinal Couples Survey; refers to physical or sexual (forced sex) IPV (Caetano, Cunradi, Clark, & Schafer, 2000, and original analysis conducted for this chapter). [c]Minor violence only. [d]NSFH = National Survey of Families and Households; refers to physical IPV; "Any IPV" refers to male and female respondents, respectively, reporting any physical arguments (Sorenson, Upchurch, & Shen, 1996). [e]NVAWS = National Violence Against Women Survey; refers to rape or physical assault by any intimate partner; "Any IPV" refers to reporting by male and female respondents, respectively; gender of perpetrator not identified (Tjaden & Thoennes, 2000).

interviews in English or Spanish with a nationally representative sample of heterosexual married or cohabiting individuals. The survey was repeated in 1985 via telephone and only in English. As shown in Table 2.2, approximately 16% or one out of six married or cohabiting heterosexual couples in the United States experienced physical IPV in 1985 (Straus & Gelles, 1990). Among these couples, 39% experienced severe physical IPV. MF and FM physical violence estimates were comparable overall, and women initiated the violence about as often as men did. Men, however, were somewhat more likely to perpetrate severe violence. The prevalence rates by gender of respondent differ, though. Men were significantly more likely than women to report MF minor violence only (9.2% vs. 6.9%), and women were more likely to report MF severe violence (4.9% vs. 1.3%). In contrast, men and women reported FM violence at comparable rates, both minor-only (7.5% and 7.7%, respectively) and severe (4.7% and 4.4%, respectively) violence.

The NLCS, a component of the Ninth National Alcohol Survey of 1995, was a nationally representative household survey of married and cohabiting couples in the 48 contiguous United States. Although conducted 10 years later, the estimates from the 1995 NLCS are similar to those of the NSFH (see Table 2.2). More than one in five couples experienced physical (including sexual) IPV (Schafer, Caetano, & Clark, 1998). The majority of violent acts reported were relatively minor in severity. Overall, women were more likely than men to report IPV regardless of whether they were the victim or perpetrator. Among MF violent acts, women were significantly more likely to report minor violence as well as a few of the more severe acts (e.g., beat up, choked), but reporting differences by gender were significant among only the minor FM violent acts. Sexual violence (forced sex) victimization and perpetration were more likely to be reported by women than men, but these differences were not statistically significant because, in part, of the small number of couples reporting sexual violence.

The estimates from the NFVS and NLCS are higher than those of the 1987 NSFH (Sorenson et al., 1996), a nationally representative household survey (see Table 2.2). Similar proportions of men and women reported perpetration and victimization in the NSFH, which is consistent with the findings of the NFVS. These estimates differ, however, from the NLCS, in which women were more likely to report IPV victimization as well as perpetration, regardless of which partner perpetrated the violence.

In contrast, the 1995 NVAWS (Tjaden & Thoennes, 2000b) found lower rates of past year IPV victimization compared with the other national surveys (see Table 2.2). The NVAWS was a nationally representative telephone survey of adult men and women, regardless of marital or cohabiting status. Among all respondents, a statistically significant higher annual prevalence of physical IPV victimization was found among women compared with men. To assess whether the lower rates of the NVAWS were due to marital or cohabiting status, Tjaden and Thoennes (2000c) reanalyzed the survey data, restricting the analysis to physical assaults perpetrated by marital or cohabiting partners. The authors found similarly low rates of IPV victimization among both women (1.1%) and men (0.6%).

The NVAWS is also one of few national population-based surveys to estimate IPV among same-sex couples (Tjaden et al., 1999). Using lifetime prevalence, the survey found that individuals who had ever lived with a same-sex intimate partner (i.e., *same-sex cohabitants*) reported significantly more IPV than did individuals reporting a history of cohabitation with only opposite-sex partners (i.e., *opposite-sex cohabitants*). When comparing prevalence rates by perpetrator gender, however, female same-sex cohabitants were more likely to report past victimization by a male partner (30.4%) than by a female partner (11.4%). In comparison, 20.3% of female opposite-sex cohabitants reported being victimized by a male partner. Male same-sex cohabitants were more likely to report having been victimized by a male partner than a female partner (15.4% and 10.8%, respectively). A smaller proportion (7.7%) of male opposite-sex cohabitants reported victimization by a female partner. These findings suggest that perpetrators are more likely to be male, whether against same-sex or opposite-sex partners.

Incidence

In the NVAWS, the number of physical IPV victimizations per victim per year in the full sample was comparable between women and men (3.4 and 3.5, respectively), but the annual rate of victimization per 1,000 persons was 44.2 among women and 31.5 among men because of the higher proportion of women reporting IPV. The majority of assaults were relatively minor in severity. IPV stalking was reported by 0.5% of women and 0.2% of men with an average of one victimization per victim per year, although stalking by definition involves repeated acts. In all, 1.8% of women and 1.1% of men reported any victimization, including rape and stalking (the number of men reporting rape was too small to calculate separate estimates of rape).

The overall IPV victimization rates in the NCVS also have been higher among women than men (Rennison, 2003). In 2001, the rates were 5 and 0.9 per 1,000 persons, respectively. These incidents included rape or sexual assault, robbery, aggravated assault, and simple assault. The rate per 1,000 persons for simple assault, which accounts for the majority of crimes, was 3.6 for women and 0.5 for men in 2001.

These rates are much lower than those found in the NVAWS, even after the redesign of the NCVS. Nevertheless, a reanalysis of the NCVS and NVAW, which calculated rape and physical assault estimates using the same counting rules and age populations for both surveys, revealed higher levels of rape but comparable levels of physical assault against adult women (Bachman, 2000).

Ethnic-Specific Estimates

In addition to overall estimates of IPV, population-based surveys have generated ethnic-specific prevalence and incidence rates. Disparities have been revealed in some, but not all, studies. In sections that follow, we review these findings among the three major racial and ethnic groups in the United States: non-Hispanic Whites, non-Hispanic Blacks, and Hispanics.

Prevalence

Overall, the literature suggests that IPV occurs more frequently among Blacks and, to a lesser extent among Hispanics, compared with Whites in general population surveys. The NFVS of 1975 (Cazenave & Straus, 1990) found the prevalence of minor violence (i.e., slapping) and severe violence perpetrated by Black men and women greater than that of White men and women (see Table 2.3). In stratified analyses, however, these differences did not persist when controlling for class and social network embeddedness. Likewise, the prevalence of any or severe MF and FM partner violence among Hispanics was greater than that of non-Hispanic Whites in the 1985 resurvey (Straus & Smith, 1990). Again, ethnicity was no longer significant after taking into account other factors, including urbanicity, family income, and age of respondent. That said, Sorenson et al. (1996) found race/ethnicity to be a significant factor in an analysis of married respondents in the 1987 NSFH. After controlling for sociodemographic factors, Sorenson et al. discovered that Black respondents were 1.6 times (95% confidence interval [CI] = 1.1–2.3) more likely than Whites to report physical IPV, whereas Hispanics were less likely than Whites (adjusted odds ratio [AOR] = 0.5, CI = 0.3–0.9) to report IPV.

TABLE 2.3
Prevalence of Past-Year Intimate Partner Violence (IPV) by Race/Ethnicity

Survey	Black MFPV (%)	Black FMPV (%)	Hispanic MFPV (%)	Hispanic FMPV (%)	White MFPV (%)	White FMPV (%)
NFVS[a]						
Any[b]	N/A	N/A	17.3	16.8	10.8	11.5
Minor[c]	12.0	6.0	N/A	N/A	5.0	3.0
Severe[d]	11.0	8.0	7.3	7.8	3.0	4.0
NLCS[e]						
Any	22.9	30.4	17.0	21.2	11.5	15.5
Minor	14.0	12.0	10.8	10.8	9.5	10.6
Severe	9.4	19.0	6.3	10.5	1.9	4.8

Note. MFPV = male-to-female partner violence; FMPV = female-to-male partner violence; N/A = not available.
[a]NFVS = National Family Violence Survey; refers to physical IPV (Cazenave & Straus, 1990; Straus & Smith, 1990). [b]1985 data. [c]1975 data; "Minor" refers to slapping. [d]1975 data for Blacks; 1985 data for Hispanics; 1975 and 1985 data comparable for Whites. [e]NLCS = National Longitudinal Couples Survey 1995 data; refers to physical or sexual (forced sex) IPV (Caetano, Cunradi, Clark, & Schafer, 2000, and original analysis conducted for this chapter).

Baseline data for the NLCS conducted in 1995 (Caetano et al., 2000) indicated that the prevalence of MF and FM partner violence was greater among Blacks and Hispanics compared with Whites (see Table 2.3). After multivariate analysis, however, the only significant effect of race/ethnicity was a higher prevalence of FM violence among Blacks. Table 2.3 also illustrates similar patterns for MF and FM minor violence among the three groups, but substantially higher rates of severe MF and FM violence among Black and Hispanic couples compared with White couples.

The NVAWS also examined the relationship of IPV and race/ethnicity among married or cohabiting respondents (Tjaden & Thoennes, 2000a). Only lifetime prevalence rates were reported; 26% of Black women and 21% of White women reported physical IPV; intimate partner rape estimates were comparable between the two groups (7%). However, Hispanic women (of any race) and non-Hispanic women had similar prevalence rates of physical assault (21% and 22%, respectively) and partner rape (8% and 6%, respectively). In multivariate analysis, Black women were more likely than White women to report IPV victimization by their current partner, after controlling for sociodemographic factors, childhood violence, and partner characteristics (e.g., jealous, controlling, verbally abusive). Among men, there were no significant differences for IPV victimization overall between Blacks and Whites (12% and 8%) or Hispanics and non-Hispanics (7% and 8%). Race/ethnicity also was not associated with IPV victimization among men in multivariate analysis, but the risk of IPV increased for those respondents whose race/ethnicity differed from their partner.

Incidence

Two national surveys have examined the incidence and recurrence of IPV among ethnic groups over time. Jasinski (2004) used data from the first (1987) and second (1992) waves of the NSFH to examine changing patterns of physical violence against women among married and cohabiting couples still together at the second wave. The incidence (proportion of couples newly violent) of MF violence was significantly higher among Hispanics compared with Blacks and Whites (9.7%, 5.8%, and 3.8%, respectively). Rates of recurrence (couples persistently violent) were comparable between groups (3.9%, 4.1%, and 2.8%, respectively). In multivariate analyses, however, no significant ethnic differences were found for either incidence or recurrence.

In contrast, the 2000 NLCS resurvey of intact couples (Caetano, McGrath, Ramisetty-Mikler, & Field, 2005) revealed that the incidence of MF violence was more likely to occur among Hispanics (AOR = 3.4, CI = 1.2–9.5) but not Blacks compared with Whites, even after controlling for sociodemographics, alcohol factors, childhood violence, and impulsivity. The recurrence of MF violence was more likely among Black couples (AOR = 2.7, CI = 1.2–6.2) but not Hispanic couples compared with Whites. The only significant ethnic differences in FM partner violence were with recurrence among Black couples (AOR = 3.5, CI = 1.3–9.0) compared with White couples.

Although the NCVS calculates incident-based estimates, data from the 1993 to 1999 NCVS revealed similar patterns to those of the NVAWS with regard to race/ethnicity (Rennison & Welchans, 2000). The rate of nonlethal IPV incidents among Black female victims was higher than that of White females (11.1 and 8.2 per 1,000 population, respectively), but victimization rates for Hispanic males and females (7.7 and 1.3, respectively) were not significantly different from those of their non-Hispanic counterparts (8.4 and 1.4, respectively). When controlling for victim gender and household income, however, rate differences between racial/ethnic groups are no longer significant (Rennison & Planty, 2003). It is possible that Hispanics may have been less likely to report IPV because of legal concerns regarding immigration. Nevertheless, findings from other self-report surveys, such as those previously noted, have demonstrated higher incidence rates for victimization among Hispanic women.

Intimate Partner Homicide

National data used for IPH surveillance are derived from the SHR (Fox & Zawitz, 2004). The IPH rate per 100,000 population between 1976 and 2002 fell among Black males and females in each victim–offender relationship category (i.e., spouse/ex-spouse, boyfriend, girlfriend), whereas the rate declined for White current and former wives and husbands and boyfriends but not girlfriends. The rates per 100,000 population in 2002 were highest among Black girlfriends (4.45) and boyfriends (3.70), followed by Black wives/ex-wives (3.48). Lower rates were found among White girlfriends (1.93) and Black husbands/ex-husbands (1.12). Rates for White male and female spouses/ex-spouses and White boyfriends were less than 1 per 100,000.

On the basis of 1981–1998 data (CDC, 2001), the greatest proportion of White victims are spouses (about 60%) and boyfriends/girlfriends (21%–28%); among Black victims, the distribution is more equal (37% and 42%–48%, respectively). Across all races, same-sex partners constitute less than 1% of offenders among female victims but 3% to 11% of offenders among male victims.

Limitations of Survey Data

Survey data based on general population samples are superior to clinical samples in terms of generalizability. Nevertheless, survey data have their own limitations. This is particularly true when one compares findings across studies. There are wide range of IPV estimates, which is likely due to differences in sampling methodology (e.g., telephone vs. face-to-face interviews), the framing of questionnaires or interviews (e.g., whether the events being assessed are considered crimes vs. partner–spouse conflict), and measures of IPV. Overall, however, one does see a trend toward similar rates of violence victimization and perpetration between cohabiting men and women but elevated rates of victimization among women in studies that do not restrict sampling by cohabitation, such as the NVAWS and the NCVS. Although it is possible that these differences reflect different patterns of violence among cohabiting and noncohabiting individuals, at least one study (Tjaden & Thoennes, 2000c) found higher rates of IPV victimization among women compared with men even after restricting the analysis to cohabiting respondents. As previously noted, general population surveys also capture less severe violence and possibly different typologies of violence than agency data, which may explain the gender symmetry found in the majority of these surveys. As illustrated by the ongoing debate surrounding the issue of gender symmetry and how IPV is measured, more research in these areas will be necessary.

Although general population survey data suggest that IPV occurs more frequently among Blacks and Hispanics compared with Whites, the studies reviewed herein demonstrate diverse results. These findings illustrate the difficulty in comparing ethnic studies, particularly when analytic methods differ. In multivariate analyses, for example, the relationship between ethnicity and IPV may fade depending on what factors are controlled for in the analysis. Furthermore, the gender of the perpetrator appears to affect the relationship between ethnicity and IPV. These issues must be carefully examined in an attempt to compare studies or draw conclusions from even a single survey.

CONCLUSION

IPV is clearly an important public health problem that requires the attention of all sectors of public health. Consistent monitoring is critical to the intervention and prevention of partner violence. As we described in this chapter, the surveillance program for IPV is currently fragmented and has important missing links. Although too numerous to report in full, the Building Data Systems workshop (CDC, 2006b) formed several useful recommendations regarding the monitoring of violence against women that are also applicable to IPV overall (a full set of recommendations may be found in the workshop report). For example, a number of factors to consider in determining the utility and reliability of surveillance-based estimates of IPV were suggested. Methodological factors include periodicity (i.e., ongoing or periodic vs. one time), precision (i.e., large sample size or population based), and the means to explore methodological questions. In addition, the capacity to collect prevalence, incidence, chronicity (i.e., number of episodes per victim per year), violence subtypes, and etiologic and comorbidity data as well as data on health care and social service utilization should be considered.

Collaboration across disciplines and agencies is another critical aspect that must be addressed in considering research strategies (CDC, 2006b). The U.S. Department and Health and Human Services and the Department of Justice, for example, should continue to conduct joint research, such as the NVAWS and the planned NISVS. Coordinated efforts at the local, state, and national level are and will continue to be necessary to adequately conduct IPV surveillance in a consistent manner.

Many of the recommendations made by the Building Data Systems workshop are being addressed, but much remains to be accomplished. Public health officials must focus on the fragmentation of the current surveillance efforts and implement a central surveillance center at the national level to coordinate data across systems. Existing systems must also be supported while promoting the development of and supporting new systems that will bridge existing gaps. As part of this support, it is essential to provide training in data collection to personnel involved in developing and maintaining these systems. Finally, periodic evaluation of the main monitoring indicators of IPV (e.g., prevalence, incidence, homicide) in the general population as well as in other sectors must be developed and supported, such as the health and criminal justice systems. Annual reports on current IPV data should be published to help identify areas in the surveillance systems that need improvement. All of these efforts will more adequately inform our public health policies and practices, improve prevention and intervention efforts, and provide guidance to health and social service providers addressing and responding to IPV.

REFERENCES

Bachman, R. (2000). A comparison of annual incidence rates and contextual characteristics of intimate-partner violence against women from the National Crime Victimization Survey (NCVS) and the National Violence Against Women Survey (NVAWS). *Violence Against Women, 6*, 839–867.

Basile, K. C., Arias, I., Desai, S., & Thompson, M. P. (2004). The differential association of intimate partner physical, sexual, psychological, and stalking violence and posttraumatic stress symptoms in a nationally representative sample of women. *Journal of Trauma and Stress, 17*, 413–421.

Basile, K. C., Swahn, M. H., Chen, J., & Saltzman, L. E. (2006). Stalking in the United States: Recent national prevalence estimates. *American Journal of Preventive Medicine, 31*, 172–175.

Biroscak, B. J., Smith, P. K., & Post, L. A. (2006). A practical approach to public health surveillance of violent deaths related to intimate partner relationships. *Public Health Reports, 121*, 393–399.

Biroscak, B. J., Smith, P. K., Roznowski, H., Tucker, J., & Carlson, G. (2006). Intimate partner violence against women: Findings from one state's ED surveillance system. *Journal of Emergency Nursing, 32*, 12–16.

Bonomi, A. E., Thompson, R. S., Anderson, M., Reid, R. J., Carrell, D., Dimer, J. A., & Rivara, F. P. (2006). Intimate partner violence and women's physical, mental, and social functioning. *American Journal of Preventive Medicine, 30*, 458–466.

Caetano, R., Cunradi, C. B., Clark, C. L., & Schafer, J. (2000). Intimate partner violence and drinking patterns among White, Black, and Hispanic couples in the U.S. *Journal of Substance Abuse, 11*, 123–138.

Caetano, R., McGrath, C., Ramisetty-Mikler, S., & Field, C. A. (2005). Drinking, alcohol problems and the five-year recurrence and incidence of male to female and female to male partner violence. *Alcoholism Clinical and Experimental Research, 29*, 98–106.

Campbell, J. C. (2000). Promise and perils of surveillance in addressing violence against women. *Violence Against Women, 6*, 705–727.

Cazenave, N. A., & Straus, M. (1990). Race, class, network embeddedness, and family violence: A search for potent support systems. In M. A. Straus & R. J. Gelles (Eds.), *Physical violence in American families: Risk factors and adaptations to violence in 8,145 families* (pp. 322–337). New Brunswick, NJ: Transaction.

Centers for Disease Control and Prevention. (2000). Building data systems for monitoring and responding to violence against women: Recommendations from a workshop. *Morbidity and Mortality Weekly Report, 49*(RR-11), 1–15.

Centers for Disease Control and Prevention. (2001). CDC surveillance summaries. *Morbidity and Mortality Weekly Report, 50*(SS-3), 1–15.

Centers for Disease Control and Prevention. (2006a). *Intimate partner violence: CDC activities*. Retrieved May 11, 2006, from http://www.cdc.gov/ncipc/factsheets/ipvactivities.htm

Centers for Disease Control and Prevention. (2006b). *National violent death reporting system*. Retrieved June 21, 2006, from http://www.cdc.gov/ncipc/profiles/nvdrs/default.htm

Coker, A. L., Davis, K. E., Arias, I., Desai, S., Sanderson, M., Brandt, H. M., & Smith, P. H. (2002). Physical and mental health effects of intimate partner violence for men and women. *American Journal of Preventive Medicine, 23*, 260–268.

Davis, K. E., Coker, A. L., & Sanderson, M. (2002). Physical and mental health effects of being stalked for men and women. *Violence and Victims, 17*, 429–443.

DeKeseredy, W. S. (2000). Current controversies on defining nonlethal violence against women in intimate heterosexual relationship: Empirical implications. *Violence Against Women, 6*, 32–50.

Federal Bureau of Investigation. (2006). *NIBRS frequently asked questions*. Retrieved June 21, 2006, from http://www.fbi.gov/ucr/faqs.htm

Fox, J. A., & Zawitz, M. W. (2004). *Homicide trends in the United States*. Washington, DC: U.S. Department of Justice.

Gelles, R. J. (2000). Estimating the incidence and prevalence of violence against women. *Violence Against Women, 6*, 784–804.

Glass, N., Dearwater, S., & Campbell, J. (2001). Intimate partner violence screening and intervention: Data from eleven Pennsylvania and California community hospital emergency departments. *Journal of Emergency Nursing, 27*, 141–149.

Gordon, M. (2000). Definitional issues in violence against women: Surveillance and research from a violence research perspective. *Violence Against Women, 6*, 747–783.

Jasinski, J. L. (2004). Physical violence among White, African American, and Hispanic couples: Ethnic differences in initiation, persistence, and cessation. In B. Fisher (Ed.), *Violence against women and family violence: Developments in research, practice, and policy* (Publication No. NCJ 199704). Washington, DC: U.S. Department of Justice.

Kothari, C. L., & Rhodes, K. V. (2006). Missed opportunities: Emergency department visits by police-identified victims of intimate partner violence. *Annals of Emergency Medicine, 47*, 190–199.

Kramer, A., Lorenzon, D., & Mueller, G. (2004). Prevalence of intimate partner violence and health implications for women using emergency departments and primary care clinics. *Women's Health Issues, 14*, 19–29.

Langford, L., Isaac, N., & Kabat, S. (1998). Homicides related to intimate partner violence in Massachusetts: Examining case ascertainment and validity of the SHR. *Homicide Studies, 2*, 353–377.

Logan, T. K., Leukefeld, C., & Walker, B. (2000). Stalking as a variant of intimate violence: Implications from a young adult sample. *Violence and Victims, 15*, 91–111.

Logan, T. K., Shannon, L., Cole, J., & Walker, R. (2006). The impact of differential patterns of physical violence and stalking on mental health and help-seeking among women with protective orders. *Violence Against Women, 12*, 866–886.

Maxfield, M. G. (1989). Circumstances in supplementary homicide reports: Variety and validity. *Criminology, 27*, 671–695.

McFarlane, J., Soeken, K., Reel, S., Parker, B., & Silva, C. (1997). Resource use by abused women following an intervention program: Associated severity of abuse and reports of abuse ending. *Public Health Nursing, 14*, 244–250.

Mechanic, M. B., Uhlmansiek, M. H., Weaver, T. L., & Resick, P. A. (2000). The impact of severe stalking experienced by acutely battered women: An examination of violence, psychological symptoms and strategic responding. *Violence and Victims, 15*, 443–458.

Mechanic, M. B., Weaver, T. L., & Resick, P. A. (2000). Intimate partner violence and stalking behavior: Exploration of patterns and correlates in a sample of acutely battered women. *Violence and Victims, 15*, 55–72.

National Center for Injury Prevention and Control. (2003). *Costs of intimate partner violence against women in the United States*. Atlanta, GA: Centers for Disease Control and Prevention.

National Victim Center & Crime Victims Research and Treatment Center. (1992). *Rape in America: A report to the nation*. Arlington, VA: Author.

Orchowsky, S., & Weiss, J. (2000). Domestic violence and sexual assault data collection systems in the United States. *Violence Against Women, 6*, 904–911.

Pampel, F. C., & Williams, K. R. (2000). Intimacy and homicide: Compensating for missing data in the SHR. *Criminology, 38*, 661–680.

Rand, M. R. (1997). *Violence-related injuries treated in hospital emergency departments*. Washington, DC: U.S. Department of Justice.

Rennison, C. M. (2003). *Intimate partner violence, 1993–2001*. Washington, DC: U.S. Department of Justice.

Rennison, C. M., & Planty, M. (2003). Nonlethal intimate partner violence: Examining race, gender, and income patterns. *Violence and Victims, 18*, 433–443.

Rennison, C. M., & Welchans, S. (2000). *Intimate partner violence*. Washington, DC: U.S. Department of Justice.

Rodriguez, E., Lasch, K. E., Chandra, P., & Lee, J. (2001). Family violence, employment status, welfare benefits, and alcohol drinking in the United States: What is the relation? *Journal of Epidemiology and Community Health, 55*, 172–178.

Rosen, L. N. (2006). Origin and goals of the "Gender Symmetry" workshop. *Violence Against Women, 12*, 997–1002.

Saltzman, L. E., Fanslow, J. L., McMahon, P. M., & Shelley, G. A. (1999). *Intimate partner violence surveillance: Uniform definitions and recommended data elements* (Version 1.0). Atlanta, GA: Centers for Disease Control and Prevention.

Schafer, J., Caetano, R., & Clark, C. L. (1998). Rates of intimate partner violence in the United States. *American Journal of Public Health, 88*, 1702–1704.

Schafer, J., Caetano, R., & Cunradi, C. B. (2004). A path model of risk factors for intimate partner violence among couples in the United States. *Journal of Interpersonal Violence, 19*, 127–142.

Sorenson, S. B., Upchurch, D. M., & Shen, H. (1996). Violence and injury in marital arguments: Risk patterns and gender differences. *American Journal of Public Health, 86*, 35–40.

Straus, M. A. (1979). Measuring intrafamily conflict and violence: The Conflict Tactics (CT) Scales. *Journal of Marriage and the Family, 41*, 75–88.

Straus, M. A. (1990). The Conflict Tactics Scales and its critics: An evaluation and new data on validity and reliability. In M. A. Straus & R. J. Gelles (Eds.), *Physical violence in American families: Risk factors and adaptations to violence in 8,145 families* (pp. 49–72). New Brunswick, NJ: Transaction.

Straus, M. A. (1993). Physical assaults by wives: A major social problem. In R. J. Gelles & D. R. Loeske (Eds.), *Current controversies on family violence* (pp. 67–87). Newbury Park, CA: Sage.

Straus, M. A. (1999). The controversy over domestic violence by women: A methodological, theoretical, and sociology of science analysis. In X. B. Arriaga & S. Oskamp (Eds.), *Violence in intimate relationships* (pp. 210–221). Thousand Oaks, CA: Sage.

Straus, M. A., & Gelles, R. J. (1990). How violent are American families? Estimates from the National Family Violence Resurvey and other studies. In M. A. Straus & R. J. Gelles (Eds.), *Physical violence in American families: Risk factors and adaptations to violence in 8,145 families* (pp. 95–112). New Brunswick, NJ: Transaction.

Straus, M. A., Hamby, S. L., Boney-McCoy, S., & Sugarman, D. B. (1996). The Revised Conflict Tactics Scales (CTS2): Development and preliminary psychometric data. *Journal of Family Issues, 17*, 283–316.

Straus, M. A., & Smith, C. (1990). Violence in Hispanic families in the United States: Incidence rates and structural interpretations. In M. A. Straus & R. J. Gelles (Eds.), *Physical violence in American families: Risk factors and adaptations to violence in 8,145 families* (pp. 341–368). New Brunswick, NJ: Transaction.

Thacker, S. B. (1996). Surveillance. In M. B. Gregg (Ed.), *Field epidemiology* (pp. 26–50). New York: Oxford University Press.

Thompson, M. P., Basile, K. C., Hertz, M. F., & Sitterle, D. (2006). *Measuring intimate partner violence victimization and perpetration: A compendium of assessment tools*. Atlanta, GA: Centers for Disease Control and Prevention.

Thompson, R. S., Bonomi, A. E., Anderson, M., Reid, R. J., Dimer, J. A., Carrell, D., & Rivara, F. P. (2006). Intimate partner violence: Prevalence, types, and chronicity in adult women. *American Journal of Preventive Medicine, 30*, 447–457.

Tjaden, P., & Thoennes, N. (2000a). *Extent, nature, and consequences of intimate partner violence: Findings from the National Violence Against Women Survey*. Washington, DC: U.S. Department of Justice.

Tjaden, P., & Thoennes, N. (2000b). *Full report of the prevalence, incidence, and consequences of violence against women: Findings from the National Violence Against Women Survey.* Washington, DC: U.S. Department of Justice.

Tjaden, P., & Thoennes, N. (2000c). Prevalence and consequences of male-to-female and female-to-male intimate partner violence as measured by the National Violence Against Women Survey. *Violence and Victims, 6,* 142–161.

Tjaden, P., & Thoennes, N. (2000d). The role of stalking in domestic violence crime reports generated by the Colorado Springs Police Department. *Violence and Victims, 15,* 427–441.

Tjaden, P., Thoennes, N., & Allison, C. J. (1999). Comparing violence over the life span in samples of same-sex and opposite-sex cohabitants. *Violence and Victims, 14,* 413–425.

Turmanis, S. A., & Brown, R. I. (2006). The Stalking and Harassment Behavior Scale: Measuring the incidence, nature, and severity of stalking and relational harassment and their psychological effects. *Psychology and Psychotherapy, 79*(Pt. 2), 183–198.

U.S. Department of Justice. (1995). *Violence against women: Estimates from the redesigned survey.* Washington, DC: Author.

Waller, A. E., & Martin, S. L. (2000). Health related surveillance data on violence against women: State and local sources. *Violence Against Women, 6,* 868–903.

Zlotnick, C. (1998). Partner physical victimization in a national sample of American families: Relationship to psychological functioning, psychosocial factors and gender. *Journal of Interpersonal Violence, 13,* 156–166.

Zlotnick, C., Johnson, D. M., & Kohn, R. (2006). Intimate partner violence and long-term psychosocial functioning in a national sample of American women. *Journal of Interpersonal Violence, 21,* 262–275.

3

THEORETICAL APPROACHES TO THE ETIOLOGY OF PARTNER VIOLENCE

ERICA M. WOODIN AND K. DANIEL O'LEARY

The purpose of this chapter is to review the major theoretical accounts regarding the etiology of partner violence. If one were quite stringent in the application of what is deemed a theoretical account of behavior, there would be relatively few theoretical accounts of partner violence reviewed here. Specifically, among other things, a good theory has the following characteristics: It is heuristic, it generates hypotheses that can be empirically verified, it is not right or wrong but of varied utility in predicting behavior, and it synthesizes a large variety of observations (Hergenhahn, 1982). Given the relatively nascent nature of the field of partner violence, we review depictions that might loosely be defined as theoretical accounts of partner violence but that often do not meet the full criteria for a well-developed theory.

One cannot adequately review theoretical accounts of partner violence without having some sense of the developments in this field across the past 3 decades. The area of partner violence grew out of a grassroots endeavor to obtain services for women who were severely abused, many of whom were married to alcoholic husbands. In 1980, Straus, Gelles, and Steinmetz published their book, *Behind Closed Doors: Violence in the American Family*, which provided the first documentation of the extent of the problem of partner violence in the United States. The grassroots efforts were primarily advocacy based and socially oriented, whereas Straus et al.'s book focused on sociological predictors of partner violence. In the 1980s, psychologists began to show how certain individual characteristics and psychopathologies placed individuals at risk of partner violence. The first long-term longitudinal studies of at-risk children were also initiated during this time, with the goal of tracking familial and environmental risk factors for the development of psychopathology and behavior dysregulation in adulthood. In the 1990s, multivariate modeling became more common, allowing investigators to more accurately examine complex theoretical models. In the early years of the 21st century, several new methodologies drawn from the biological sciences, including behavioral genetics and neuropsychology, also emerged as methods for understanding the biological bases of violence. In the near future it can be expected that cutting-edge techniques such as genetic linkage and brain imaging studies will also be used in the quest to more fully understand the etiology of partner violence.

MAJOR THEORETICAL APPROACHES TO THE ETIOLOGY OF PARTNER VIOLENCE

In the sections that follow, we review the tenets and empirical evidence for the theories of partner violence that have emanated from the last 3 decades, with special emphasis on those theories that have stood the test of time and empirical verification. Theories of partner violence span the gamut, from sociocultural explanations for men's violence against women, to interpersonal theories of the development and maintenance of violence within families, and finally to intrapersonal accounts of characteristics that place individuals at increased risk of behaving violently. These theories range considerably in focus, scope, and empirical evaluation. We also discuss more recent endeavors to integrate and expand on these disparate accounts of partner violence.

Sociocultural Theories

Several of the earliest theories of partner violence focus on social and cultural factors to explain why violence against women is tolerated and even condoned by many societies. Factors such as societal gender roles, male privilege and domination, and patriarchal social structures have been employed to explain the development and continuation of violence against women within a larger sociocultural context.

Gender Roles

Social role theory posits that individuals will act in ways consistent with their beliefs about behavior appropriate to their gender identification (e.g., see Eagly, 1987). Thus, individuals who adhere to more traditionally masculine gender identities will be more likely to engage in a wide variety of aggressive behaviors because these behaviors are sanctioned by the cultural norms for masculinity. One common gender role distinction is the difference between instrumental and expressive belief systems. Traditional masculinity emphasizes instrumentality, or the desire to manipulate objects, the environment, or social situations to achieve goals, whereas traditional femininity emphasizes expressiveness, or the desire to monitor emotionality and maintain social connections (Gill, Stockard, Johnson, & Williams, 1987). Although men are more likely to endorse instrumental beliefs than women, both men and women who endorse instrumental reasons for aggression are more likely to engage in violence perpetration than individuals who endorse expressive reasons. This finding holds true for both general aggression (Archer & Haigh, 1997) and partner violence (Archer & Graham-Kevan, 2003).

Both gender-related characteristics and gender-related beliefs appear to play a role in violence perpetration. Jenkins and Aubé (2002), for instance, found that endorsement of a hostile, controlling, and self-absorbed form of masculinity is related to psychological and physical violence perpetration for both men and women. The authors also found that men who support a traditional male role, or norms reflecting the need for status, toughness, and antifemininity, are more likely to be psychologically aggressive. In contrast, women with less traditional attitudes about the male role are more likely to be psychologically and physically aggressive toward their partners.

A meta-analysis of beliefs about gender and violence found that physically violent men were more likely than nonviolent men to hold attitudes accepting of partner violence but not more likely to endorse traditional male and female gender roles in general (Sugarman & Frankel, 1996). It is interesting that *undifferentiation*, or a lack of either masculine or feminine gender schemas, was most likely among violent men. The authors theorized that men lacking any gender schema might perceive partner violence to be proper male behavior. Relatedly, existing measures of male gender schema may actually be tapping characteristics such as self-reliance and assertiveness; hence lower scores may reflect low self-esteem, a factor frequently associated with partner violence. In sum, the findings from this meta-analysis suggest that attitudes specifically condoning partner violence, rather than masculine gender schemas or adherence to traditional gender roles per se, may be more likely to lead to violence perpetration.

Men who are susceptible to masculine gender role stress, or the tendency to become emotionally provoked when threats to masculinity ideology occur, are also more likely to report negative attributions and negative affect and to endorse verbal aggression in response to hypothetical scenarios involving partner behavior. This susceptibility is particularly pronounced when the behavior of the partner is relevant to the masculine gender (e.g., flirting with another man, canceling a date) and threatening to the man's authority (Franchina, Eisler, & Moore, 2001). Similarly, husbands with a history of physical violence are more likely than nonviolent, maritally distressed husbands to attribute negative intentions to wives' behavior in hypothetical vignettes, particularly when the situations involve jealousy or rejection (Holtzworth-Munroe & Hutchinson, 1993). Hence there is some evidence that susceptibility to threats to the masculine identity increases the likelihood of male partner violence.

Power and Control

Feminist theorists posit that male violence is motivated by not only societal gender roles but also a larger system of male privilege and domination. The Duluth model of batterers' treatment (Pence & Paymar, 1993), for instance, describes violence as part of a system of power and control used to dominate women. The Minnesota Power and Control Wheel describes a series of interrelated control tactics: intimidation; emotional abuse; isolation; minimizing, denying, and blaming; using children; male privilege; economic abuse; and coercion and threats. Physical and sexual violence are considered extreme forms of these tactics.

Dutton and Starzomski (1997) tested the Power and Control Wheel directly by comparing a group of men in batterers' treatment programs with a group of nonviolent men from the community. Batterers scored significantly higher than nonbatterers on several behaviors linked to power and control, including intimidation, emotional abuse, minimization–denial–blaming, and economic abuse. The groups did not differ on coercion, isolation, or male privilege, and the nonbatterers actually scored higher on using children to control their partners.

Some evidence indicates that violence may actually be more likely when men perceive themselves to have less power in a relationship. Babcock, Waltz, Jacobson, and Gottman (1993), for instance, found that among violent married men, greater differences in education and decision-making power favoring wives were associated with higher rates of husband violence. Similarly, newlywed men who perceived themselves as having less power were more likely to be in relationships with destructive marital conflict, which in turn predicted their own physical violence (Leonard & Senchak, 1996). Sagrestano, Heavey, and Christensen (1999) also found that men with less perceived power, as well as women with more perceived power, were more likely to be verbally and physically violent. Hence men may use violence and other forms of power and control to restore what they believe to be a power imbalance in their relationships.

Patriarchy

In addition to power differentials within couples, feminist theorists have also focused on power differences between genders at the societal level. The societal status of women is made up of many factors, including economic, educational, political, and legal equity (e.g., see Collins, Chafetz, Blumberg, Coltrane, & Turner, 1993). Feminist theory posits that societies in which men primarily control these resources will produce institutions reflecting male dominance and legitimizing female subordination within the institutions as well as throughout society (Dobash & Dobash, 1979). Violence is regarded as a means by which men ensure the subordination of women, and fear of the threat of violence is a mechanism to maintain women in subordinate roles within society (e.g., see Stanko, 1995).

Aggregate data have been used in several instances to examine differences across states or countries in male dominance and rates of male violence. States with less female equality, for instance, tend to report higher rates of male physical and sexual assaults (Baron & Straus, 1989; Straus, 1994). Industrialized countries with less educational and occupational equality also document higher rates of sexual, but not physical, assaults against women (Yodanis, 2004). Finally, less gender equality and individualism and more sexist attitudes and approval of wife beating across 52 nations are linked with more physical violence against women (Archer, 2006).

Sociocultural theories of partner violence have been criticized for failing to acknowledge several important facets of physical violence (e.g., see Dutton & Nicholls, 2005). For instance, Archer has argued that women in Westernized societies are at least as likely to be violent against their partners as are men (e.g., see Archer, 2006) and that rates of injury are fairly equivalent across genders (e.g., see Archer, 2000). Furthermore, he noted that in nonshelter samples, women are no more likely than men to report using violence in self-defense (e.g., see Follingstad, Wright, Lloyd, & Sebastian, 1991). Archer's arguments appear to be most cogent when applied to dating and community samples; however, clinical samples indeed show greater violence and injury by men (K. D. O'Leary, 2000). Regardless, violence by women in intimate relationships has not been well addressed in studies designed to address elements of patriarchy across states and countries.

In general, feminist theories of male patriarchy are well developed conceptually but have not undergone extensive empirical evaluation, particularly at the societal level. Although an understanding of individual male patriarchy (i.e., dominance by individual men) is informative, a true test of the theory requires an analysis at the level of society as well (e.g., male dominance across cultures), because patriarchy at the societal level is theorized to be the actual determinant of whether individual men are violent within their own relationships (Yodanis, 2004). Furthermore, Dutton (1994) argued that using regional data on gender equality to predict violence by individual men leads to the ecological fallacy or the mistaken belief that associations existing at the level of the group must also exist at the level of the individual. The relatively recent statistical development of multilevel modeling (e.g., see Raudenbush & Bryk, 2002) should eventually facilitate a full examination of the theory of male patriarchy by allowing for the simultaneous inspection of male dominance at both societal and individual levels.

Interpersonal Theories

In contrast to sociocultural theories, interpersonal theories of partner violence emphasize the unique interpersonal influences that may cause certain individuals within a society to be more likely to engage in partner violence. These include theories that focus on developmental processes, such as social learning and attachment, as well as adult relationship functioning and the link between partner violence and relationship discord.

Social Learning

Social learning theory posits that behaviors and beliefs are transmitted from generation to generation through learning that occurs as a result of direct experiences as well as the observation of others (Bandura, 1977). Individuals are more likely to behave in ways that have been reinforced directly or that have been observed to receive reinforcement in other people. Behavioral learning is theorized to occur as a result of operant and classical conditioning, as well as through cognitive mediational processes. For instance, there is evidence that children of physically abusive parents are at increased risk of engaging in aggressive behaviors in general, and also for developing problems with social information processing that may lead to lifelong difficulties in negotiating close social interactions (Dodge, Bates, & Pettit, 1990).

An extension of social learning theory posits that partner violence is caused in part by exposure to violence in the family of origin, including emotional and physical abuse directed toward the child as well as violence between parents (K. D. O'Leary, 1988). Although the modeling aspect of social learning theory has generally received the most attention and empirical support, the cognitive processing elements (i.e., attitudes toward violence, personal efficacy) may also be important components in understanding partner violence from a social learning perspective. For instance, in a large sample of college men, Reitzel-Jaffe and Wolfe (2001) found that violence in the family of origin was directly related to the perpetration of partner violence and was also mediated by negative beliefs about gender roles and attitudes accepting of partner violence. Similarly, Stith and Farley (1993) found that the link between the observation of violence between parents and severe partner violence in a sample of batterers and alcoholics was mediated by approval of marital violence and low sex role egalitarianism.

One difficulty with understanding the link between family-of-origin violence and adult partner violence is that most studies are retrospective in design. Several recent reports from long-term prospective studies, however, are beginning to fill this void. For example, in a 20-year longitudinal study, exposure to violence between parents and harsh punishment strategies emerged as two of the strongest predictors of both male and female partner violence in young adulthood (Ehrensaft et al., 2003). Capaldi and Clark (1998), in contrast, used a longitudinal multivariate model to demonstrate that antisocial behavior mediated the link between unskilled parenting and males' partner violence but that violence between parents did not predict later aggressive behavior. The former sample was a representative sample, whereas the latter was composed of at-risk males, and sample differences may in part explain the differential results. Hence additional longitudinal studies may be needed to more fully understand the link between early social learning experiences and physical violence in adulthood.

Attachment

Attachment theory is a well-elucidated model of early development and relationship formation that describes the need for infants to establish a secure base with one or more caregivers so that they can safely explore their environment while still being able to seek refuge when necessary (Bowlby, 1980). These early experiences are theorized to shape children's perceptions and beliefs about themselves, their environments, and close relationships in general through a mental representation termed *attachment working models*. When early environmental experiences and relationships with caregivers are warm and supportive, individuals develop secure models for close relationships. In contrast, when experiences are unpredictable, neglectful, or abusing, individuals are more likely to form insecure attachment representations and become either preoccupied by or dismissing of close relationships. These models tend to be stable throughout childhood and into adulthood, but they can also change as a result of new experiences, particularly of an interpersonal nature (Bowlby, 1988).

Dutton (1998) theorized that insecurely attached individuals may be controlling or violent to their partners in reaction to perceived rejection or abandonment, because they have difficulty regulating emotions and self-soothing during situations that trigger fears of abandonment (e.g., see Mikulincer, 1998). Men who engage in partner violence are indeed far more likely to have insecure attachment representations (74%) compared with men in nonviolent, maritally distressed relationships (38%; Babcock, Jacobson, Gottman, & Yerington, 2000), and female partners of violent men are more likely to be insecurely attached as well (Kesner & McKenry, 1998). Violent men in distressed relationships also report more anxiety over abandonment, more need for nurturance, a narrower focus on the partner, and higher levels of jealousy, and these men are more likely to be classified as having a preoccupied attachment style, compared with nonviolent, maritally distressed men (Holtzworth-Munroe, Stuart, & Hutchison, 1997).

There also seem to be differences in the function of violence across insecure attachment types. Babcock et al. (2000) found that preoccupied men engage in the most belligerence during disagreements and that withdrawal behaviors by their wives incite their violence. Dismissing men, in contrast, display the most withdrawal and contempt during disagreements, and defensiveness by their wives precipitates their violence. Babcock et al. theorized that preoccupied men may react to fears of abandonment in an expressive manner, whereas dismissing men may use violence instrumentally to exert control over their wives.

The need for control plays a role in violence severity for insecurely attached individuals as well. Men in batterers' treatment who are both insecurely attached and high in need to control their partners report the most partner violence (Mauricio & Gormley, 2001). Furthermore, in a large sample of college freshman, Follingstad, Bradley, Helff, and Laughlin (2002) found that anxious attachment predicted angry temperament, which predicted attempts to control the partner, which then predicted actual frequency and severity of partner violence. Thus, there is mounting evidence that insecure attachment, particularly of a preoccupied, controlling type, may lead to partner violence in the face of perceived abandonment.

Relationship Discord

The relationship discord model of partner violence, although not well developed theoretically, generally posits that physical violence between partners may occur in part as an outgrowth of a distressed relationship. Partner violence is indeed far more likely for couples experiencing dissatisfaction with their relationships. In one study, over 60% of couples entering marital therapy reported physical violence in the year before entering treatment (Ehrensaft & Vivian, 1996). Relationship dissatisfaction is also linked to violence in engaged couples (O'Leary et al., 1989) and married men in the military (Pan, Neidig, & O'Leary, 1994). In fact, Pan et al. (1994) demonstrated that marital dissatisfaction increased the risk of both mild and severe forms of partner violence by over 100%. Finally, in a meta-analysis of predictors of partner violence, Stith, Smith, Penn, Ward, and Tritt (2004) found that marital dissatisfaction was one of the strongest predictors of partner violence for both men and women.

A direct link between marital dissatisfaction and partner violence may be more likely for women than men. K. D. O'Leary, Malone, and Tyree (1994), for instance, found that marital dissatisfaction at 18 months of marriage predicted wives' physical violence at 30 months; however, there was no such link for husbands. Women's violence may also be in part a reaction to verbal and physical forms of violence by the partner. Jacobson et al. (1994) found that husbands with a history of severe violence described escalating to violence in response to both violent and nonviolent wife behaviors (e.g., defensiveness, withdrawal) but that wives reported escalating to violence mainly in response to psychological abuse or physical violence by their husbands. S. G. O'Leary and Smith Slep (2006) examined self-reported reasons for physical violence in a sample recruited from the community and found that wives were more likely than husbands to escalate to physical violence in response to psychological abuse by their partners. Interestingly, men were more likely than women to engage in partner violence in response to their wives' own physical violence.

In summary, there is considerable support for the link between aspects of relationship discord and partner violence. However, in dating and young married couples, marital dissatisfaction and physical violence are not closely linked (e.g., see K. D. O'Leary et al., 1989). There is also some evidence that violence early in marriage actually places couples at increased risk of relationship dissatisfaction and dissolution over time (e.g., see Lawrence & Bradbury, 2001). Finally, the mechanisms by which relationship dissatisfaction and verbal conflict lead to physical violence remain unclear, and it is possible that underlying factors such as individual psychopathology and personality factors may place couples at increased risk of a variety of destructive relationship behaviors, including violence. Even if this is the case, however, relationship discord is a strong proximal predictor of physical violence for couples married for several years (K. D. O'Leary, Smith Slep, & O'Leary, 2007).

Intrapersonal Theories

In contrast to sociocultural and interpersonal influences, the intrapersonal theories seek to explain partner violence as an outgrowth of individuals' biological and psychological functioning. According to this perspective, factors such as genetic predisposition, levels of anger and hostility, alcohol and drug use, and certain personality disorders may place individuals at greater risk for partner violence perpetration.

Genetic Heritability

The quest to explore a biological predisposition to partner violence is just beginning. Nonetheless, there is considerable evidence regarding genetic influences on aggression in general (e.g., see Janssen et al., 2005). Animal models using mice with genetic mutations, for instance, find that disruptions of genes responsible for various brain enzymes lead to extremely aggressive mice (e.g., see Young et al., 2002). In humans, a genetic predisposition to low levels of monoamine oxidase A (MAOA) expression has been linked to a variety of aggressive and impulsive behaviors (Brunner, Nelen, Breakefield, Ropers, & van Oost, 1993).

The genetic model of partner violence posits that children may develop into violent adults not only because they were exposed to aggressive models during childhood but also because they may have genes that predispose them and their family members to aggressive tendencies. The term *gene–environment interaction* (Plomin, DeFries, & Loehlin, 1977) refers to situations in which genes may interact with the environment to explain why some but not all individuals who are raised in aggressive homes go on to become aggressive themselves as adults (Hines & Saudino, 2002).

Hines and Saudino (2004) examined rates of partner violence in monozygotic and dizygotic twins. Shared genes explained similarities between twins on levels of psychological and physical violence, with any additional variance in violent behavior attributable to nonshared environments. This study thus suggests that genes may play a larger role than shared family environment in predicting which individuals will become violent against their partners. In contrast, Caspi et al. (2002) found that genetic and social environments demonstrated an interaction effect in predicting general antisocial behavior, with children low in MAOA genetic expression and high in parental maltreatment the most likely to become antisocial. Caspi et al.'s findings suggest a diathesis–stress interaction, in which predisposing genetic vulnerability interacts with environmental stressors to lead to the development of antisocial behavior in some individuals.

Thus, the very limited information available at this time is conflicted regarding the relative importance of genetic versus familial influences on antisocial behavior in general and partner violence in particular. However, it does appear that a genetic predisposition to behave aggressively may help to explain why partner violence is transmitted from one generation to the next. In addition, factors such as conduct disorder and substance abuse that predispose individuals toward aggression have also been shown to have genetic predictors (e.g., see Dick et al., 2006), hence genes may also predispose individuals to certain risk factors that then lead to a common pathway of aggressive behavior.

Anger and Hostility

Anger and hostility have long been theorized to play a key role in the perpetration of aggressive acts in general and partner violence in particular. The simplistic anger-leads-to-aggression hypothesis, however, has received little empirical support (e.g., see Tavris, 1989). More empirically based multifaceted models of violence posit that a propensity toward anger leads to aggressive behavior by causing changes in affect, cognition, and arousal levels that then make violence more likely (e.g., see Anderson & Bushman, 2002).

Anger and hostility are generally considered to be separate but related constructs. *Anger* refers to a specific episode involving a change in physiological, cognitive, subjective, and behavioral experiences (Eckhardt, Norlander, & Deffenbacher, 2004), whereas *hostility* is generally defined as a cynical, mistrusting, and denigrating outlook toward others (Miller, Smith, Turner, Guijarro, & Hallet, 1996). It is hypothesized that individuals high in hostility will be more likely to experience frequent and intense angry episodes (e.g., see Eckhardt & Deffenbacher, 1995), and there is indeed evidence that hostile individuals display greater physiological arousal during anger-induction tasks (e.g., see Fredrickson et al., 2000).

Men who are violent against their partners report more anger and hostility compared with nonviolent men (e.g., see Boyle & Vivian, 1996), and anger is a prospective predictor of partner violence in early marriage (Leonard & Senchak, 1996). Men with a history of partner violence also verbalize more aggression during anger arousal than do nonviolent men (Eckhardt, Jamison, & Watts, 2002).

A meta-analysis by Norlander and Eckhardt (2005) found that physically violent men are moderately higher in rates of anger and hostility experience and expression compared with nonviolent men, even when nonviolent men are in distressed relationships. Furthermore, men who are more severely violent are higher in anger and hostility than men who are less severely violent. Hence there is some support for the theory that anger and hostility are linked to partner violence; however, there is little evidence as to the specific mechanism by which anger and hostility lead to acts of violence against a partner. Some argue that a focus on the physiological and psychological reactions of anger and hostility obscures the fact that many individuals are aggressive in only specific circumstances, such as on suspicion of an affair (e.g., see Dutton, 1997).

Alcohol and Drug Use

The link between substance use and partner violence is well documented. Roughly one third of individuals in general population samples report drinking alcohol prior to an act of violence against a partner (Caetano, Schafer, & Cunradi, 2001), and over 90% of individuals involved in police-investigated domestic assaults report drinking or using substances on the day of the assault (Brookoff, O'Brien, Cook, Thompson, & Williams, 1997). Rates of current substance abuse and dependence in batterer treatment populations may be as high as two thirds, with heavier substance abuse associated with more dangerous and frequent physical violence (Brown, Werk, Caplan, & Seraganian, 1999). Heavy alcohol consumption or binge drinking is more closely associated with violence perpetration than more moderate levels of drinking (K. D. O'Leary & Schumacher, 2003).

There are two competing theories regarding the link between substance use and violence (Fals-Stewart, Golden, & Schumacher, 2003). The *proximal effects model* suggests that alcohol and drug use exert a direct effect on violence, through mechanisms such as pharmacological influences on cognitive processing (e.g., see Chermack & Taylor, 1995) or decreased responsibility attributions as a result of the intoxication (Critchlow, 1983). An alternative perspective, the *indirect effects model*, posits that substance use does not lead directly to violence but rather is moderated or mediated by various social, cultural, and personality factors (Gelles, 1993).

In support of the indirect effects model, Margolin, John, and Foo (1998) found that alcohol impairment was not directly related to male partner violence in a community sample but rather was moderated by negative life events and marital dissatisfaction. Only in cases of negative life events or marital dissatisfaction was male alcohol impairment related to violence against a partner. Similarly, Heyman, O'Leary, and Jouriles (1995) found that alcohol use interacted with aggressive personality traits to predict partner violence in early marriage. In contrast to these studies, however, a longitudinal daily diary study demonstrated that male partner violence was far more likely on days of alcohol or substance use (Fals-Stewart, 2003), even after controlling for antisocial personality disorder and relationship distress (Fals-Stewart et al., 2003). Also, there is some evidence that men who achieve remission following individual alcoholism treatment demonstrate clinically significant reductions in violence perpetration compared with before treatment (O'Farrell, Fals-Stewart, Murphy, & Murphy, 2003).

Thus, alcohol and substance use may be both directly and indirectly related to the perpetration of partner violence. In addition, the effects may depend on the sample used, because support for the direct effects model came from a substance-abusing sample, whereas support for the indirect effects model came from community samples. In addition, it is possible that the effect obtained may come from the methodology used, because the Fals-Stewart study used a daily diary methodology, whereas the other studies previously noted were based on retrospective reports about drinking and physical violence.

Personality Disorders

Dutton (1999) argued that personality disorders may mediate the link between factors such as observation of violence in the family of origin and acts of partner violence in adulthood. Of particular note are conduct disorder and antisocial personality disorder, which are characterized by the propensity toward general violence and impulsivity. Children with conduct disorder, for instance, tend to develop a pervasive pattern of poor social skills, peer rejection, and aggressive tendencies that place them at increased risk of partner violence as they enter adulthood (Capaldi & Clark, 1998). In addition, children with conduct disorder during childhood are at greater risk of developing antisocial personality disorder (Moffitt, 1993), suggesting that harmful behavior patterns developed during childhood often transmit to adulthood personality disorders. Finally, antisocial individuals may be even more likely to use coercion and intimidation during conflicts with intimate partners than with other acquaintances, given the proximity and intensity of these relationships (Caspi & Elder, 1988).

A history of conduct disorder does appear to increase the risk of partner violence in adulthood (Capaldi & Clark, 1998; Ehrensaft et al., 2003). There is also evidence of assortative mating in young adulthood, such that men and women with antisocial personality characteristics are more likely to select romantic partners who also possess antisocial tendencies (Capaldi & Crosby, 1997). Finally, antisocial characteristics in young adulthood make partner violence more likely for both men and women (Capaldi & Owen, 2001) and place young men in particular at risk of severe partner violence (Magdol et al., 1997).

Borderline personality disorder (BPD) is also theoretically linked to partner violence. Characterized by instability in personal relationships, self-image, and emotional expression, as well as by behavioral impulsivity (American Psychiatric Association, 2000), individuals with BPD tend to be less able to attenuate emotional arousal in the face of perceived interpersonal threat, and they may be likely to respond in impulsive and aggressive ways, particularly when confronted with tension in close relationships (e.g., see Levy, 2005).

Physically violent men have been shown to exhibit higher levels of BPD characteristics than nonviolent men (e.g., see Hamberger & Hastings, 1991), and borderline features are associated with issues such as fears of abandonment, dependency, and jealousy in violent men (Holtzworth-Munroe, Meehan, Herron, Rehman, & Stuart, 2000). Dutton (1994) conceptualized borderline personality organization (BPO) as representing a continuum of core borderline features, including identity diffusion, primitive defenses, and reality testing, which at high levels are diagnosable as BPD. Dutton, Starzomski, and Ryan (1996) found that physically violent men were higher on BPO than nonviolent men and that more severe violence was associated with greater BPO symptomatology. Hence there is some evidence that borderline characteristics may place men in particular at risk of partner violence. Little is yet known, however, about the link between female borderline characteristics and partner violence or about the specific mechanisms by which borderline personality characteristics lead to acts of violence.

Summary of Major Theories of Partner Violence

Theories of the etiology of partner violence span several levels of analysis, ranging from the influence of societal norms and power inequalities, to the interactions between family members in childhood and adulthood, and finally to individual characteristics that increase the likelihood of violence perpetration. These theories are clearly not mutually exclusive and often draw on elements of other models to more fully explain the development of partner violence in a multifaceted way. We now present several formal multisystemic theories that integrate and expand on the diverse theoretical models presented thus far.

MULTISYSTEMIC THEORIES

Multisystemic perspectives attempt to incorporate sociocultural, interpersonal, and intrapersonal factors into cohesive and multifaceted theories.

Models such as the nested ecological theory, the background-situational model, and the life span developmental systems perspective seek to explain both why partner violence exists in particular cultural and interpersonal contexts as well as why certain individuals are more likely to become violent within any given context.

Nested Ecological Theory

Dutton (1985) proposed a model of partner violence based on ecologically influenced theories of family functioning (e.g., see Bronfenbrenner, 1979), arguing that violence is "multiply determined by forces in the individual, the family, the community, the culture, and the species" (p. 404) and that each level of analysis is nested within a broader level (see Figure 3.1). Cultural factors are nested within constraints imposed by characteristics of the species, community factors are nested within cultural limitations, and so on. The first and broadest level of analysis is the *macrosystem*, or the sociocultural background from which gender inequalities and societal norms about violence emerge. The second level of analysis is the *exosystem*, or the connections between families and the cultures in which they live, such as economic opportunities, degree of contact time between genders, and integration into the community. The third level is the *microsystem*, which includes characteristics of families and individuals that may heighten the likelihood of violence. For instance, the degree of intimacy and independence between partners might interact with men's issues of jealousy and control to produce violence at times when men feel threatened or abandoned. The fourth and narrowest level of analysis is *ontogenetic* factors, or the physiological, cognitive, affective, and behavioral experiences of individuals that make violence more or less likely. For instance, men with violent tendencies may be more likely to misinterpret their own physiological reactions and anger, particularly when they perceive themselves to be high in coercive power toward the person causing the arousal (e.g., the partner). See chapter 5 of this volume for more about the nested ecological theory.

Stith et al. (2004) used the nested ecological theory as a framework for a meta-analysis of predictors of primarily male partner violence. At the exosystem, career and life stress were most closely linked with violence, followed by age, education, employment, and income. At the microsystem, a history of emotional–verbal abuse and forced sex by the aggressor were the strongest predictors, low marital satisfaction and a history of physical violence were moderate predictors, and jealousy was a small predictor. The ontogenetic risk factors were generally moderate, and listed in descending order were illicit drug use, attitudes condoning violence, traditional sex role ideology, anger and hostility, alcohol use, and depression. Notably, elements of the microsystem were some of the largest predictors, suggesting that the

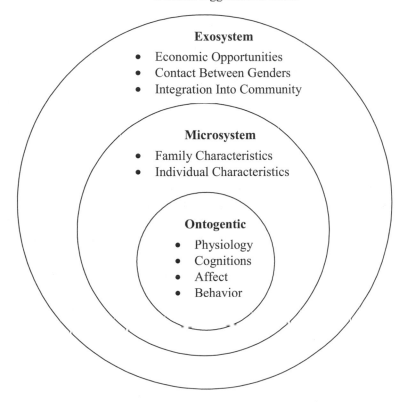

Macrosystem

- Gender Inequalities
- Societal Aggression Norms

Exosystem

- Economic Opportunities
- Contact Between Genders
- Integration Into Community

Microsystem

- Family Characteristics
- Individual Characteristics

Ontogentic

- Physiology
- Cognitions
- Affect
- Behavior

Figure 3.1. Data from Dutton's (1985) nested ecological theory.

immediate environment, particularly a past history of violence, is important for predicting partner violent behavior in men.

Background–Situational Theory

Riggs and O'Leary (1989) proposed a background–situational model of partner violence designed to (a) easily translate into empirically verifiable constructs, (b) explain the high prevalence of female violence in community samples, and (c) extend existing models to adolescent relationships. Background factors, such as cultural and individual characteristics, are posited to explain which individuals will be violent and include factors such as models of violence in intimate relationships; parent violence toward the child; acceptance of violence as a response to conflict, frustration, or threat; psychopathology and neuropathology; arousability and emotionality; aggressive and impulsive personality; and prior use of violence in other settings. Situational factors, such as specific precipitating events, explain which situations are most likely to lead to violence and include relationship conflict, stress, alcohol use, expectation of a positive outcome to the violence, and partner's use of violence. The background–situational model uses predictors other than past partner violence in part because past partner violence is one of the best predictors of future violence. Thus, the predictors within the model reflect factors other than past physical violence to predict physical violence.

Riggs and O'Leary (1996) tested the background–situational model with a large sample of undergraduate students and found that the model explained 60% of the variance in violence perpetration for men and 32% for women. For both men and women, attitudes condoning violence, a history of violent behaviors during childhood, and relationship conflict predicted violent behavior. Family-of-origin violence and general attitudes condoning violence were associated with violence for women but not men. In contrast, Luthra and Gidycz (2006) found that the background–situational model was a much stronger predictor for female college students (83% variance explained) than male college students (30% variance explained). Alcohol use and partner's use of violence predicted violence for both men and women, longer relationship length predicted for men only, and parent–child violence by the father and poor problem-solving abilities predicted violence perpetration for women only. Luthra and Gidycz suggested that differences across studies in prediction by gender may have been due to low base rates of self-reported male violence perpetration in their sample.

The background–situational model has also been replicated in several other populations. In a sample of nearly 3,000 navy recruits (White, Merrill, & Koss, 2001), the model accounted for 67% of the variance in male partner violence and 55% of the variance in female partner violence. Situational factors were much stronger predictors than background factors. Using two samples of high school dating couples, Cano, Avery-Leaf, Cascardi, and O'Leary (1998) found that the model accounted for approximately half of the variance in male (49%–59%) and female (40%–65%) violence. Violence in previous relationships, but not acceptance of violence, was a significant background factor. In terms of situational variables, a partner's use of physical violence and an individual's own level of verbal aggression predicted the use of physical violence, as did a partner's verbal aggression for men. Furthermore, use of dominance and jealousy tactics were predictive of female violence. Thus, the background–situational model accounts for approximately 50% of the variance in partner violence, although the most important predictors for men and women have varied across studies.

Life Span Developmental Systems Perspective

Recently, Capaldi and colleagues (e.g., see Capaldi, Shortt, & Kim, 2005) created a theory of partner violence that focuses more explicitly on developmental antecedents than any previous model. Terming their theory a *life span developmental systems perspective*, Capaldi et al. (2005) argued that existing theories fail to account for the developmental risk factors of violence, as well as the mutuality of violence between genders. This approach integrates biology, contextual factors, and socialization experiences within the family of origin and peer group. Characteristics of both partners are taken into account, both at entry into and over the course of the relationship. Finally, characteristics and changing contexts of the relationship itself are considered.

The full life span developmental systems model posits that the family risk context (e.g., low socioeconomic status, employment problems, parental transitions or divorce) places parents at increased risk of antisocial behavior and depression, as well as unskilled parenting. These parental deficits then set the stage for the development of child conduct problems and depressive symptoms, deviant peer associations, and assortative partnering with other at-risk individuals. Individuals' risk context (e.g., unemployment, arrests) and partners' respective developmental histories place couples at risk of unskilled relationship processes and violence. These unskilled relationship behaviors are theorized to lead eventually to persistent, frequent, and severe forms of violence, as well as to more severe impacts resulting from the violence (Capaldi et al., 2005).

In one of the first longitudinal, multimethod, multi-informant studies of the development of partner violence, at-risk males were followed from childhood to young adulthood and female dating partners were also assessed (e.g., see Capaldi & Clark, 1998; Capaldi & Crosby, 1997). Capaldi and Crosby (1997) found that males with antisocial tendencies were more likely to pair with antisocial females, supporting the assortative mating hypothesis. In a direct test of their model, Capaldi and Clark (1998) found that parents' antisociality predicted unskilled parenting and parental dyadic violence. Unskilled parenting then mediated the link between parents' antisociality and antisociality in the boys in late adolescence. Finally, boys' antisociality predicted their own violence to their partners in early adulthood. The model accounted for 56% of the variance in males' partner violence perpetration. Thus, there is some evidence that a developmental framework is useful for understanding the etiology of partner violence from an intergenerational perspective.

CONCLUSION

The major etiological theories of partner violence discussed in this chapter vary considerably in level of analysis, complexity, and empirical support. Sociocultural theories, which emphasize gender role socialization, male power and control, and patriarchal social institutions, are based on feminist and sociological accounts of why and under what circumstances societies condone violence against women. These theories have received some support from the relatively few studies that have examined their major tenets. Sociocultural theories, however, fail to account for differences in male behavior within a society, as well as the sizable prevalence of nondefensive female violence, and tend to be fairly one dimensional in their account of male violence.

Interpersonal accounts of partner violence attempt to explain why certain families but not others in a society are more likely to transmit partner violence across generations. Social learning from the family of origin, type of attachment, and the degree of distress and conflict within adult relationships are all posited as important familial factors that increase the risk of violence. Interpersonal theories are somewhat less well articulated than are sociocultural accounts of partner violence, even though they often draw from well-developed general theories of development and relationship functioning. Interpersonal theories do, however, successfully explain familial transmission of violence for both men and women and have received considerable empirical support in both cross-sectional and longitudinal studies across a range of populations.

Intrapersonal theories help explain why certain individuals are more likely to be violent, even given the same societal and familial influences. Genetic predisposition, anger and hostility problems, alcohol and drug use, and personality disturbances are theorized to increase the risk of violence. Intrapersonal theories developed partly as an outgrowth of observations made by clinicians treating violent individuals and tend to be the least well developed conceptually. These theories often overlook the context within which many intrapersonal deficits are created and maintained, and they have been criticized for pathologizing behaviors that do not entirely overlap with specific personality or behavioral disturbances. Evidence supporting intrapersonal theories is substantial, although disagreement remains regarding the causal nature of these disorders in partner violence.

Many commonalities also exist across these disparate theories. The assumption that violence is a behavior that is learned through family-of-origin and societal influences pervades many of the models presented herein. Relatedly, many of these models also focus on the mediational role of belief systems and attitudes in understanding how such early experiences translate into violence in adulthood. One marked difference between theories, however, is the extent to which violence is conceptualized as a behavior with possible reinforcing properties. such as the attainment of greater relationship power or social status, or whether violence is considered to represent part of a dysfunctional repertoire of behaviors emanating from biological and environmental vulnerabilities.

Given the importance, empirical support, and inherent limitation of each theoretical perspective, there is now general consensus that multiple viewpoints are needed to account for which societal influences, family environments, and individual characteristics are most likely to lead to partner violence. Multisystemic models, many drawing on advances in multivariate statistical techniques, have begun to evaluate the relative importance of different elements in predicting the onset of partner violence. Multidimensional perspectives will enable an understanding of how distal, intermediate, and proximal factors interact with one another and will also provide a better sense of the relative predictive power of each factor. For example, the meta-analysis by Stith et al. (2004) offers some clues about the relative predictive value of a range of potential factors contributing to the development of partner violence. Furthermore, complex multivariable models of male and female partner violence in large representative community samples from the United States (e.g., see K. D. O'Leary et al., 2007) and Ukraine (e.g., see K. D. O'Leary, Tintle, Bromet, & Gluzman, 2006) demonstrate how family background variables, personality characteristics, and relationship factors interact to predict partner violence. These multivariate models, although not yet fully refined and evaluated, bear great promise to most fully explain the etiology of partner violence. This understanding, in turn, will contribute to the pressing need for theoretically and empirically sound programs to intervene with societies, families, and individuals in the most effective ways possible to reduce the risk of partner violence.

REFERENCES

American Psychiatric Association. (2000). *Diagnostic and statistical manual of mental disorders* (4th ed., text rev.). Washington, DC: Author.

Anderson, C. A., & Bushman, B. J. (2002). Human aggression. *Annual Review of Psychology, 53,* 27–51.

Archer, J. (2000). Sex differences in aggression between heterosexual partners: A meta-analytic review. *Psychological Bulletin, 126,* 651–680.

Archer, J. (2006). Cross-cultural differences in physical aggression between partners: A social-role analysis. *Personality and Social Psychology Review, 10,* 133–153.

Archer, J., & Graham-Kevan, N. (2003). Do beliefs about aggression predict physical aggression to partners? *Aggressive Behavior, 29,* 41–54.

Archer, J., & Haigh, A. M. (1997). Do beliefs about aggressive feelings and actions predict reported levels of aggression? *British Journal of Social Psychology, 36,* 83–105.

Babcock, J. C., Jacobson, N. S., Gottman, J. M., & Yerington, T. P. (2000). Attachment, emotional regulation, and the function of marital violence: Differences between secure, preoccupied, and dismissing violent and nonviolent husbands. *Journal of Family Violence, 15,* 391–409.

Babcock, J. C., Waltz, J., Jacobson, N. S., & Gottman, J. M. (1993). Power and violence: The relation between communication patterns, power discrepancies, and domestic violence. *Journal of Consulting and Clinical Psychology, 61,* 40–50.

Bandura, A. (1977). *Social learning theory*. Oxford, England: Prentice-Hall.

Baron, L., & Straus, M. A. (1989). *Four theories of rape in American society: A state-level analysis*. New Haven, CT: Yale University Press.

Bowlby, J. (1980). *Attachment and loss.* New York: Basic Books.

Bowlby, J. (1988). *A secure base: Parent–child attachment and healthy human development*. New York: Basic Books.

Boyle, D. J., & Vivian, D. (1996). Generalized versus spouse-specific anger/hostility and men's violence against intimates. *Violence and Victims, 11*, 293–317.

Bronfenbrenner, U. (1979). *The ecology of human development: Experiments by nature and design*. Cambridge, MA: Harvard University Press.

Brookoff, D., O'Brien, K., Cook, C. S., Thompson, T. D., & Williams, C. (1997). Characteristics of participants in domestic violence. *Journal of the American Medical Association, 277*, 1369–1373.

Brown, T. G., Werk, A., Caplan, T., & Seraganian, P. (1999). Violent substance abusers in domestic violence treatment. *Violence and Victims, 14*, 179–190.

Brunner, H. G., Nelen, M., Breakefield, X. O., Ropers, H. H., & van Oost, B. A. (1993, October 22). Abnormal behavior associated with a point mutation in the structural gene for monoamine oxidase A. *Science, 262*, 578–580.

Caetano, R., Schafer, J., & Cunradi, C. B. (2001). Alcohol-related intimate partner violence among White, Black, and Hispanic couples in the United States. *Alcohol Research & Health, 25*, 58–65.

Cano, A., Avery-Leaf, S., Cascardi, M., & O'Leary, K. D. (1998). Dating violence in two high school samples: Discriminating variables. *Journal of Primary Prevention, 18*, 431–446.

Capaldi, D. M., & Clark, S. (1998). Prospective family predictors of aggression toward female partners for at-risk young men. *Developmental Psychology, 34*, 1175–1188.

Capaldi, D. M., & Crosby, L. (1997). Observed and reported psychological and physical aggression in young, at-risk couples. *Social Development, 6*, 184–206.

Capaldi, D. M., & Owen, L. D. (2001). Physical aggression in a community sample of at-risk young couples: Gender comparisons for high frequency, injury, and fear. *Journal of Family Psychology, 15*, 425–440.

Capaldi, D. M., Shortt, J. W., & Kim, H. K. (2005). A life span developmental systems perspective on aggression toward a partner. In W. M. Pinsof & J. L. Lebow (Eds.), *Family psychology: The art of the science* (pp. 141–167). New York: Oxford University Press.

Caspi, A., & Elder, G. H., Jr. (1988). Childhood precursors of the life course: Early personality and life disorganization. In E. M. Hetherington, R. M. Lerner, & M. Perlmutter (Eds.), *Child development in life-span perspective* (pp. 115–142). Hillsdale, NJ: Erlbaum.

Caspi, A., McClay, J., Moffitt, T., Mill, J., Martin, J., Craig, I. W., et al. (2002, August 2). Role of genotype in the cycle of violence in maltreated children. *Science, 297*, 851–854.

Chermack, S. T., & Taylor, S. P. (1995). Alcohol and human physical aggression: Pharmacological versus expectancy effects. *Journal of Studies on Alcohol, 56,* 449–456.

Collins, R., Chafetz, J. S., Blumberg, R. L., Coltrane, S., & Turner, J. H. (1993). Toward an integrated theory of gender stratification. *Sociological Perspectives, 36,* 185–216.

Critchlow, B. (1983). Blaming the booze: The attribution of responsibility for drunken behavior. *Personality and Social Psychology Bulletin, 9,* 451–473.

Dick, D. M., Bierut, L., Hinrichs, A., Fox, L., Bucholz, K. K., Kramer, J., et al. (2006). The role of GABRA2 in risk for conduct disorder and alcohol and drug dependence across developmental stages. *Behavior Genetics, 36,* 577–590.

Dobash, R. E., & Dobash, R. (1979). *Violence against wives: A case against the patriarchy.* New York: Free Press.

Dodge, K. A., Bates, J. E., & Pettit, G. S. (1990, December 21). Mechanisms in the cycle of violence. *Science, 250,* 1678–1683.

Dutton, D. G. (1985). An ecologically nested theory of male violence toward intimates. *International Journal of Women's Studies, 8,* 404–413.

Dutton, D. G. (1994). Patriarchy and wife assault: The ecological fallacy. *Violence and Victims, 9,* 167–182.

Dutton, D. G. (1997). A social psychological perspective on impulsivity/intimate violence. In C. D. Webster & M. A. Jackson (Eds.), *Impulsivity: Theory, assessment, and treatment* (pp. 32–41). New York: Guilford Press.

Dutton, D. G. (1998). *The abusive personality: Violence and control in intimate relationships.* New York: Guilford Press.

Dutton, D. G. (1999). Limitations of social learning models in explaining intimate aggression. In X. B. Arriaga & S. Oskamp (Eds.), *Violence in intimate relationships* (pp. 73–87). Thousand Oaks, CA: Sage.

Dutton, D. G., & Nicholls, T. L. (2005). The gender paradigm in domestic violence research and theory: Part 1. The conflict of theory and data. *Aggression and Violent Behavior, 10,* 680–714.

Dutton, D. G., & Starzomski, A. J. (1997). Personality predictors of the Minnesota Power and Control Wheel. *Journal of Interpersonal Violence, 12,* 70–82.

Dutton, D. G., Starzomski, A. J., & Ryan, L. (1996). Antecedents of abusive personality and abusive behavior in wife assaulters. *Journal of Family Violence, 11,* 113–132.

Eagly, A. H. (1987). *Sex differences in social behavior: A social-role interpretation.* Hillsdale, NJ: Erlbaum.

Eckhardt, C. I., & Deffenbacher, J. L. (1995). Diagnosis of anger disorders. In H. Kassinove (Ed.), *Anger disorders: Definition, diagnosis, and treatment* (pp. 27–47). Philadelphia: Taylor & Francis.

Eckhardt, C. I., Jamison, T. R., & Watts, K. (2002). Anger experience and expression among male dating violence perpetrators during anger arousal. *Journal of Interpersonal Violence, 17,* 1102–1114.

Eckhardt, C. I., Norlander, B., & Deffenbacher, J. (2004). The assessment of anger and hostility: A critical review. *Aggression and Violent Behavior, 9*, 17–43.

Ehrensaft, M. K., Cohen, P., Brown, J., Smailes, E., Chen, H., & Johnson, J. G. (2003). Intergenerational transmission of partner violence: A 20-year prospective study. *Journal of Consulting and Clinical Psychology, 71*, 741–753.

Ehrensaft, M. K., & Vivian, D. (1996). Spouses' reasons for not reporting existing marital aggression as a marital problem. *Journal of Family Psychology, 10*, 443–453.

Fals-Stewart, W. (2003). The occurrence of partner physical aggression on days of alcohol consumption: A longitudinal diary study. *Journal of Consulting and Clinical Psychology, 71*, 41–52.

Fals-Stewart, W., Golden, J., & Schumacher, J. A. (2003). Intimate partner violence and substance use: A longitudinal day-to-day examination. *Addictive Behaviors, 28*, 1555–1574.

Follingstad, D. R., Bradley, R. G., Helff, C. M., & Laughlin, J. E. (2002). A model for predicting dating violence: Anxious attachment, angry temperament and need for relationship control. *Violence and Victims, 17*, 35–48.

Follingstad, D. R., Wright, S., Lloyd, S., & Sebastian, J. A. (1991). Sex differences in motivations and effects in dating violence. *Family Relations, 40*, 51–57.

Franchina, J. J., Eisler, R. M., & Moore, T. M. (2001). Masculine gender role stress and intimate abuse: Effects of masculine gender relevance of dating situations and female threat on men's attributions and affective responses. *Psychology of Men & Masculinity, 2*, 34–41.

Fredrickson, B. L., Maynard, K. E., Helms, M. J., Haney, T. L., Siegler, I. C., & Barefoot, J. C. (2000). Hostility predicts magnitude and duration of blood pressure response to anger. *Journal of Behavioral Medicine, 23*, 229–243.

Gelles, R. J. (1993). Alcohol and other drugs are associated with violence: They are not its cause. In R. J. Gelles & D. R. Loseke (Eds.), *Current controversies on family violence* (pp. 182–196). Newbury Park, CA: Sage.

Gill, S., Stockard, J., Johnson, M., & Williams, S. (1987). Measuring gender differences: The expressive dimension and critique of androgyny scales. *Sex Roles, 17*, 375–400.

Hamberger, L. K., & Hastings, J. E. (1991). Personality correlates of men who batter and nonviolent men: Some continuities and discontinuities. *Journal of Family Violence, 6*, 131–147.

Hergenhahn, B. R. (1982). *An introduction to theories of learning.* Englewood Cliffs, NJ: Prentice-Hall.

Heyman, R. E., O'Leary, K. D., & Jouriles, E. N. (1995). Alcohol and aggressive personality styles: Potentiators of serious physical aggression against wives? *Journal of Family Psychology, 9*, 44–57.

Hines, D. A., & Saudino, K. J. (2002). Intergenerational transmission of intimate partner violence: A behavioral genetic perspective. *Trauma, Violence, & Abuse, 3*, 210–225.

Hines, D. A., & Saudino, K. J. (2004). Genetic and environmental influences on intimate partner aggression: A preliminary study. *Violence and Victims, 19*, 701–718.

Holtzworth-Munroe, A., & Hutchinson, G. (1993). Attributing negative intent to wife behavior: The attributions of maritally violent versus nonviolent men. *Journal of Abnormal Psychology, 102*, 206–211.

Holtzworth-Munroe, A., Meehan, J. C., Herron, K., Rehman, U., & Stuart, G. L. (2000). Testing the Holtzworth-Munroe and Stuart (1994) batterer typology. *Journal of Consulting and Clinical Psychology, 68*, 1000–1019.

Holtzworth-Munroe, A., Stuart, G. L., & Hutchinson, G. (1997). Violent versus nonviolent husbands: Differences in attachment patterns, dependency, and jealousy. *Journal of Family Psychology, 11*, 314–331.

Jacobson, N. S., Gottman, J. M., Waltz, J., Rushe, R., Babcock, J., & Holtzworth-Munroe, A. (1994). Affect, verbal content, and psychophysiology in the arguments of couples with a violent husband. *Journal of Consulting and Clinical Psychology, 62*, 982–988.

Janssen, P. A., Nicholls, T. L., Kumar, R. A., Stefanakis, H., Spidel, A. L., & Simpson, E. M. (2005). Of mice and men: Will the intersection of social science and genetics create new approaches for intimate partner violence? *Journal of Interpersonal Violence, 20*, 61–71.

Jenkins, S. S., & Aubé, J. (2002). Gender differences and gender-related constructs in dating aggression. *Personality and Social Psychology Bulletin, 28*, 1106–1118.

Kesner, J. E., & McKenry, P. C. (1998). The role of childhood attachment factors in predicting male violence toward female intimates. *Journal of Family Violence, 13*, 417–432.

Lawrence, E., & Bradbury, T. N. (2001). Physical aggression and marital dysfunction: A longitudinal analysis. *Journal of Family Psychology, 15*, 135–154.

Leonard, K. E., & Senchak, M. (1996). Prospective prediction of husband marital aggression within newlywed couples. *Journal of Abnormal Psychology, 105*, 369–380.

Levy, K. N. (2005). The implications of attachment theory and research for understanding borderline personality disorder. *Development and Psychopathology, 17*, 959–986.

Luthra, R., & Gidycz, C. A. (2006). Dating violence among college men and women: Evaluation of a theoretical model. *Journal of Interpersonal Violence, 21*, 717–731.

Magdol, L., Moffitt, T. E., Caspi, A., Newman, D. L., Fagan, J., & Silva, P. A. (1997). Gender differences in partner violence in a birth cohort of 21-year-olds: Bridging the gap between clinical and epidemiological approaches. *Journal of Consulting and Clinical Psychology, 65*, 68–78.

Margolin, G., John, R. S., & Foo, L. (1998). Interactive and unique risk factors for husbands' emotional and physical abuse of their wives. *Journal of Family Violence, 13*, 315–344.

Mauricio, A. M., & Gormley, B. (2001). Male perpetration of physical violence against female partners. *Journal of Interpersonal Violence, 16,* 1066–1081.

Mikulincer, M. (1998). Adult attachment style and affect regulation: Strategic variations in self-appraisals. *Journal of Personality and Social Psychology, 75,* 420–435.

Miller, T. Q., Smith, T. W., Turner, C. W., Guijarro, M. L., & Hallet, A. J. (1996). Meta-analytic review of research on hostility and physical health. *Psychological Bulletin, 119,* 322–348.

Moffitt, T. E. (1993). Adolescence-limited and life-course-persistent antisocial behavior: A developmental taxonomy. *Psychological Review, 100,* 674–701.

Norlander, B., & Eckhardt, C. (2005). Anger, hostility, and male perpetrators of intimate partner violence: A meta-analytic review. *Clinical Psychology Review, 25,* 119–152.

O'Farrell, T. J., Fals-Stewart, W., Murphy, M., & Murphy, C. M. (2003). Partner violence before and after individually based alcoholism treatment for male alcoholic patients. *Journal of Consulting and Clinical Psychology, 71,* 92–102.

O'Leary, K. D. (1988). Physical aggression between spouses: A social learning theory perspective. In V. B. Van Hasselt, R. L. Morrison, A. S. Bellack, & M. Hersen (Eds.), *Handbook of family violence* (pp. 31–55). New York: Plenum Press.

O'Leary, K. D. (2000). Are women really more aggressive than men in intimate relationships? Comment on Archer. *Psychological Bulletin, 126,* 685–689.

O'Leary, K. D., Barling, J., Arias, I., Rosenbaum, A., Malone, J., & Tyree, A. (1989). Prevalence and stability of physical aggression between spouses: A longitudinal analysis. *Journal of Consulting and Clinical Psychology, 57,* 263–268.

O'Leary, K. D., Malone, J., & Tyree, A. (1994). Physical aggression in early marriage: Prerelationship and relationship effects. *Journal of Consulting and Clinical Psychology, 62,* 594–602.

O'Leary, K. D., & Schumacher, J. A. (2003). The association between alcohol use and intimate partner violence: Linear effect, threshold effect, or both? *Addictive Behaviors, 28,* 1575–1585.

O'Leary, K. D., Smith Slep, A. M., & O'Leary, S. G. (2007). Multivariate models of men's and women's partner aggression. *Journal of Consulting and Clinical Psychology, 75,* 752–764.

O'Leary, K. D., Tintle, N., Bromet, E. J., & Gluzman, S. F. (2006). Descriptive epidemiology of intimate partner aggression in Ukraine. *Social Psychiatry & Psychiatric Epidemiology, 43,* 619–626.

O'Leary, S. G., & Smith Slep, A. M. (2006). Precipitants of partner aggression. *Journal of Family Psychology, 20,* 344–347.

Pan, H. S., Neidig, P. H., & O'Leary, K. D. (1994). Predicting mild and severe husband-to-wife physical aggression. *Journal of Consulting and Clinical Psychology, 62,* 975–981.

Pence, E., & Paymar, M. (1993). *Education groups for men who batter: The Duluth model.* New York: Springer Publishing Company.

Plomin, R., DeFries, J. C., & Loehlin, J. C. (1977). Genotype–environment interaction and correlation in the analysis of human behavior. *Psychological Bulletin, 84,* 309–322.

Raudenbush, S. W., & Bryk, A. S. (2002). *Hierarchical linear models: Applications and data analysis methods* (2nd ed.). Thousand Oaks, CA: Sage.

Reitzel-Jaffe, D., & Wolfe, D. A. (2001). Predictors of relationship abuse among young men. *Journal of Interpersonal Violence, 16,* 99–115.

Riggs, D. S., & O'Leary, K. D. (1989). A theoretical model of courtship aggression. In M. A. Pirog-Good & J. E. Stets (Eds.), *Violence in dating relationships: Emerging social issues* (pp. 53–71). New York: Praeger Publishers.

Riggs, D. S., & O'Leary, K. D. (1996). Aggression between heterosexual dating partners: An examination of a causal model of courtship aggression. *Journal of Interpersonal Violence, 11,* 519–540.

Sagrestano, L. M., Heavey, C. L., & Christensen, A. (1999). Perceived power and physical violence in marital conflict. *Journal of Social Issues, 55,* 65–79.

Stanko, E. A. (1995). Women, crime, and fear. *The Annals of the American Academy of Politics and Social Science, 539,* 46–58.

Stith, S. M., & Farley, S. C. (1993). A predictive model of male spousal violence. *Journal of Family Violence, 8,* 183–201.

Stith, S. M., Smith, D. B., Penn, C. E., Ward, D. B., & Tritt, D. (2004). Intimate partner physical abuse perpetration and victimization risk factors: A meta-analytic review. *Aggression and Violent Behavior, 10,* 65–98.

Straus, M. A. (1994). State-to-state differences in social inequality and social bonds in relation to assaults on wives in the United States. *Journal of Comparative Family Studies, 25,* 7–24.

Straus, M. A., Gelles, R., & Steinmetz, S. K. (1980). *Behind closed doors: Violence in the American family.* Garden City, NY: Anchor Press/Doubleday.

Sugarman, D. B., & Frankel, S. L. (1996). Patriarchal ideology and wife-assault: A meta-analytic review. *Journal of Family Violence, 11,* 13–40.

Tavris, C. (1989). *Anger: The misunderstood emotion* (Rev. ed.). New York: Touchstone Books/Simon & Schuster.

White, J. W., Merrill, L. L., & Koss, M. P. (2001). Predictors of premilitary courtship violence in a navy recruit sample. *Journal of Interpersonal Violence, 16,* 910–927.

Yodanis, C. L. (2004). Gender inequality, violence against women, and fear: A crossnational test of the feminist theory of violence against women. *Journal of Interpersonal Violence, 19,* 655–675.

Young, K. A., Berry, M. L., Mahaffey, C. L., Saionz, J. R., Hawes, N. L., Chang, B., et al. (2002). Fierce: A new mouse deletion of Nr2e1; violent behaviour and ocular abnormalities are background-dependent. *Behavioural Brain Research, 132,* 145–158.

4

RISK FACTORS ASSOCIATED WITH INTIMATE PARTNER VIOLENCE

SANDRA M. STITH AND CATHERINE L. McMONIGLE

In this chapter, we provide an update of the latest research on risk factors for intimate partner violence (IPV; Stith, Smith, Penn, Ward, & Tritt, 2004). Although the science of predicting who will and who will not be violent to their partners is quite inexact, professionals are frequently called on to make informal assessments of future violence. The clinician may want to help the victim understand the level of danger in his or her relationship. The court may ask the clinician for an opinion about how dangerous the offender could be. The use of risk factors in predicting future violence is, of course, important. However, the real value of knowing about risk factors is not to predict who will be violent but to guide prevention efforts. Knowing about risk factors for IPV is necessary for targeted prevention and intervention efforts. For example, we know that relationship conflict is a significant factor for IPV. Therefore, prevention efforts can target reduction of conflict among nonviolent couples. When other risk factors are present, such as stalking or escalating violence, the importance of providing for victim safety to prevent future violence is highlighted. In any case, if the goal is to prevent future violence, it is critical to know which factors increase concern for victim safety and which factors should be targets of intervention, whether in the community, the couple, or the individual.

Because longitudinal research is scarce, we are generally not able to determine that these factors precede violence, only that they tend to co-occur with violence. Therefore, we are careful to describe these factors as markers for violence, not predictors of violence. In addition, it is not always clear whether the risk factors discussed (e.g., fear, strangulation) are simply proxies for a history of more versus less severe IPV because most studies do not control for severity of IPV.

This chapter is divided into three main sections. First, we give special attention to factors that are related to lethal violence. Second, we review risk factors that are shown to be related to IPV but have less evidence that they are related to partner homicide. Because violence risk assessment is a complex process, professionals are most likely to be successful in preventing harm if they make use of evidence-based formal risk instruments. Therefore, third, we discuss tools that could be used to assess the risk of violence. In addition, we offer suggestions for prevention related to each of the risk factors throughout the chapter.

Because most of the risk factor research combines cohabiting couples and married couples, this review pertains to violence in both types of relationships. Literature reviewing risk factors for dating violence is not included in this review. However, previous research has found that risk factors for dating violence are generally parallel to the risk factors for marital violence, and that violent behavior in dating relationships often carries over into marriage (O'Leary et al., 1989; O'Leary, Malone, & Tyree, 1994). Because most of the research addresses male-to-female violence and because women are more likely to be seriously injured in intimate partner relationships, the focus of this review is on male-to-female violence. However, when research addresses female-to-male violence it is included. Violence in same-sex intimate relationships is not included in this review.

RISK FACTORS FOR LETHAL INTIMATE PARTNER VIOLENCE

The effects of IPV are far reaching on both an individual and a societal level. Every year 5.3 million women in the United States are victims of IPV. Almost half of these violent incidents result in injury, and roughly 1,300 result in death (National Center for Injury Prevention and Control, 2003). In the United States, four women are killed every day by their intimate male partners (Stout, 1991). Researchers have found that 30% of female homicides (i.e., *femicides*) are due to intimate partner homicide (Brewer & Paulsen, 1999; Puzone, Saltzman, Kresnow, Thompson, & Mercy, 2000). Conversely, intimate partner homicide accounts for 5% of male homicide victims

(Rennison, 2003). Thus, both men and women are killed by their intimate partners.

Findings from a 12-city femicide study emphasize the need for helping professionals to develop an enhanced familiarity with risk factors that may indicate lethal or severe IPV. Sharps et al. (2001) found that the majority of femicide victims had frequent contact with the health, social, criminal justice, and emergency housing agencies in the year preceding their murder. This study highlights missed opportunities for social services and health care professionals to intervene and prevent further violence and deaths. Additionally, it confirms the urgent need for stronger, more comprehensive prevention efforts. Risk factors for lethal or severe IPV include factors related to (a) victim perception (i.e., victim fear); (b) offender's recent or past history of violent behavior (i.e., evidence of increased frequency or severity of violence, threats to harm or kill self or others, forced or coerced sex, history of choking or strangulating one's partner, and abuse during pregnancy); (c) offender characteristics (i.e., jealousy or stalking behaviors and past criminal behavior); and (d) situational characteristics (i.e., ready access to weapons in the home and victim attempts to leave the relationship).

Factors Related to Victim Perception and Lethal Intimate Partner Violence

The victim's level of fear has been consistently related to male-to-female physical aggression (Cascardi, O'Leary, Lawrence, & Schlee, 1995; Jacobson et al., 1994; H. Johnson, 1995). Women who are victims of partner violence have significantly higher levels of fear than women in discordant but nonabusive relationships (Cascardi et al., 1995; Jacobson et al., 1994). As the severity of abuse increases, so does the victim's fear level (H. Johnson, 1995).

Furthermore, when Weisz, Tolman, and Saunders (2000) entered victims' predictions that severe violence would occur in their relationship within the next year into a regression equation that included factors associated with severe violence in previous research, they found that victims' predictions of future violence was the strongest variable of any studied in predicting the recurrence of violence within the 4 months following the prediction. This analysis did not explore the process of survivors' assessment or how they came to the predictions they made. They may have consciously included other risk factors, such as the level of past violence they had experienced in this relationship. However, the study found that survivors' belief that future violence would occur added significantly to the predictions derived from other known variables. Weisz et al. concluded that these results support the use of "both empirically derived risk variables and survivors' predictions in assessment of danger" (p. 86).

Another study found that a victim's fear that her life was in danger significantly predicted risk of minor and severe injuries due to an assault committed by her intimate partner (Simon et al., 2001). H. Johnson (1995) noted that "in a significant number of cases, [the woman] correctly assesses the potential for life threatening violence by her spouse" (p. 166). It is important to recognize that the victim's perception of risk may not always be accurate. The authors of a recent study (Cattaneo, Bell, Goodman, & Dutton, 2007) used a four-category (i.e., true positive, true negative, false positive, and false negative) version of female victims' accuracy in predicting whether their partner would be physically violent again. They found that, overall, women were more likely to be accurate than to be inaccurate. However, it was more likely that a victim would be a true positive if she had been more frequently stalked by her partner and that it was more likely she would be a false negative if she reported higher levels of substance abuse.

A victim's level of fear should be taken seriously. The victim's fear that she may be seriously injured by her partner should be included as an important risk factor for future severe violence. Women are often socialized to disregard their needs and feelings, which, in terms of IPV, can be dangerous. Dating violence prevention programs should educate participants about the risk factors for IPV. Moreover, in the context of increasing awareness of risk factors, programs should encourage youths to attend to their feelings of fear and emphasize the importance of prioritizing their safety needs. Furthermore, programs should emphasize the accuracy of the connection between participants' feelings of fear and the potential for danger.

Offender's Violent Behavior History and Lethal Intimate Partner Violence

In addition to the victim's level of fear, it is important to consider the offender's previous violent behavior when determining the risk of future lethal violence. In the sections that follow, we examine research related to increased frequency or severity of violence, threats to harm or kill self or others, forced or coerced sex, history of choking or strangulating one's partner, and abuse during pregnancy as risk factors for lethal violence.

Increased Frequency or Severity of Violence

Each abusive relationship has a distinct pattern or cycle of violence. One important pattern involves recent escalation in the frequency or severity of assault. This pattern is associated with imminent risk of violence and with life-threatening assaults (Kropp, 2005).

For example, Campbell et al. (2003) conducted a study involving 220 femicide cases and 343 randomly identified abused women. From each femicide case, two *proxy informants*, or individuals who had knowledge about the victim's relationship with the perpetrator, were identified and interviewed.

When the authors interviewed the abused women who were not murdered, they found that 20% of them experienced an increase in severity of violence before their most recent attack. In contrast, 64% of the femicide victims, according to the proxy informants, experienced an increase in severity of violence before the fatal attack. It is not clear why a pattern of escalating violence occurs in some relationships but not others. However, previous longitudinal analyses have found that those engaged in severe violence were more likely than those engaged in moderate violence to report continued or escalating violence at follow-up (Caetano, Field, Ramisetty-Mikler, & McGrath, 2005). Kropp (2005) proposed that a pattern of escalating violence may reflect an increasing need for more severe levels of violence to maintain control of the partner, desensitization to the use of violence over time, recent stressors, or the onset or recurrence of mental illness. When clinicians see this pattern, they should recognize that risk is elevated.

Threats to Harm or Kill Self or Others

Individuals who threaten to harm or kill themselves or their partners should be taken seriously, and risk management procedures should be put into place to respond to these threats. The U.S. Department of Justice (2000) reported that 32% of partners of victimized women had threatened to kill them, and 18% had threatened them with a weapon. These percentages are similar to the rates reported by male victims. Twenty-seven percent of partners of victimized men had threatened to kill them and 22% had threatened them with a weapon.

Partner threats have been associated with severity of violence and homicide. For example, Moracco, Runyan, and Butts (1998) reviewed 293 partner homicide cases and found that 83.4% of the perpetrators were known to have threatened to kill their partners prior to killing them. Given the empirical link between threats and severity of violence and homicide, it is vital that these threats be taken seriously by clinicians and victims.

Suicide threats and attempts are also significantly more frequent for batterers than for nonbatterers. Suicidality is often indicative of a state of crisis for the offender and is considered a risk factor for spousal violence, including homicide (Kropp, 2005). A link has been demonstrated between dangerousness to self and others (Carcach & Grabosky, 1998; Stack, 1997). A spouse who has threatened to kill a partner is at an increased risk of committing suicide if the spouse follows through with such a threat. Several studies have identified a relationship between intimate partner homicide and offender suicide. For example, Stack (1997) found that homicides in which the victim is a current or ex-spouse increase the odds of the offender committing suicide (8.00 times and 12.68 times, respectively). Carcach and Grabosky (1998) found that nearly 70% of homicide-suicide cases occurred in context of domestic matters (e.g., terminating the relationship, jealousy). Clinicians need to assess thoroughly for threats to harm or kill self or other and respond to such threats appropriately.

Forced or Coerced Sex

A strong relationship exists between the occurrence of physical abuse and forced sex (Painter & Farrington, 1998). Forced sex has also been shown to be related to more severe violence (Gondolf, 1988; Shields & Hanneke, 1983; Weisz et al., 2000) and homicide. Shields and Hanneke's (1983) interviews with 92 wives of violent men found that the more severe the physical abuse, the more likely it was that marital rape had occurred. Campbell's (1989) findings also support a link between forced sex and severity and indicate that abused women who experienced forced sex were significantly more likely to become victims of homicide than battered women who had never been sexually abused by their partners. Thus, forced or coerced sex should be regarded as an important risk factor for severe abuse and homicide and should therefore be included in any assessment of risk of lethal violence.

History of Choking or Strangulating One's Partner

A number of studies have examined the relationship between strangulation and other types of potentially lethal violence or femicide (Campbell et al., 2003; McClane, Strack, & Hawley, 2001; Strack, McClane, & Hawley, 2001). Wilbur et al. (2001) found that strangulation most frequently occurs late in an abusive relationship; thus, women who report that their partner has strangled them are at higher risk of major injury or murder than are battered women who do not report strangulation. Furthermore, in their study of 62 women from shelters, Wilbur et al. found that 87% of the strangled women had also been threatened with death by their abuser, and 70% thought they were going to die while being strangled. Finally, Campbell et al. (2003), in their study comparing risk factors associated with 220 intimate partner femicide victims with risk factors associated with 343 abused control women, found that 56% of female homicide victims had been previously strangled, compared with 10% of victims who had not been murdered.

In an attempt to suggest a protocol for the evaluation and treatment of those who survive strangulation attempts, McClane et al. (2001) emphasized the difficulty in recognizing whether strangulation has occurred. Patients who present to the emergency room reporting that their partner has attempted to strangle them are frequently dismissed because external evidence is often lacking. However, Wilbur et al. (2001) found that nonlethal strangulation can have detrimental medical complications up to 2 weeks after the strangulation incident. Because of the risk of medical complications and the potentially lethal levels of violence that may follow strangulation, it is crucial that clinicians not be among those who dismiss surviving victims of strangulation.

Abuse During Pregnancy

A close look at the research reveals that being pregnant in and of itself is not a risk factor for physical abuse (Campbell, Oliver, & Bullock, 1998; Gelles, 1990; Van Hightower & Gorton, 1998). However, assessing for abuse during pregnancy is extremely important because women abused during pregnancy are at greater risk of being severely abused (Campbell et al., 1998; H. Johnson, 1995; McFarlane, Parker, & Soeken, 1995) and of being killed (Campbell et al., 1998; McFarlane et al., 1995) than are women who are not abused when they are pregnant. For example, H. Johnson (1995) found that violence during pregnancy was 4 times more frequent among women who experienced the most severe forms of violence than among those victimized less severely.

Campbell et al. (1998) compared battered women who were abused during pregnancy with battered women who were not abused during pregnancy and found that those abused during pregnancy were significantly more likely to be at risk of homicide. Similarly, McFarlane et al. (1995) found that women abused during pregnancy reported a higher frequency of 13 out of 14 risk factors for homicide than women abused only before and not during pregnancy. Therefore, women who are abused during pregnancy are more likely to be severely abused and at risk of homicide than are women who are abused but not pregnant, even though being pregnant, in and of itself, may not increase their risk.

In light of these findings, perhaps a closer look at prenatal programs and the information provided by medical personnel to pregnant women is warranted. Although the U.S. Preventive Services Task Force (2004) and the Canadian Task Force on Preventive Health Care (MacMillan & Wathen, 2001) indicated that there is insufficient evidence for or against routine screening for IPV, many experts in the field suggest that this is an important time to screen women for abuse (Sugg, 2006). It is also an important area in which medical personnel can educate women on the seriousness of abuse during pregnancy, the danger it represents for their future and for their unborn child, and the resources available in their community. One potential intervention that has been recommended by the Task Force on Community Preventive Services (2000) is early childhood home visitation for preventing child abuse and neglect. Although there is currently no evidence that early childhood home visitation programs prevent IPV, they have been shown to reduce child maltreatment among at-risk mothers, and those effects are reduced when partner violence is present (Bilukha et al., 2005).

Offender Characteristics and Lethal Intimate Partner Violence

In addition to the offender's previous violent behavior, it is important to consider other offender characteristics when determining the risk of lethal violence. In the sections that follow, we examine research related to jealousy or stalking behaviors and previous criminal behavior unrelated to IPV as risk factors for lethal violence.

Jealousy or Stalking Behaviors

Jealousy is often present in abusive relationships (Weisz et al., 2000) and is related to severity of abuse (Hanson, Cadsky, Harris, & Lalonde, 1997; H. Johnson, 1995; Nielson, Endo, & Ellington, 1992) and homicide (Campbell, 1992). Jealousy has also been shown to be related to escalating violence. Campbell (1992) found that 64% of intimate partner homicide cases involved male jealousy. In addition, interviews with female victims at the time of their court appearance and again 4 months later reveal a significant correlation with batterer accusations of infidelity and the recurrence of severe violence (Weisz et al., 2000).

Stalking presents an additional cause for concern for victims of IPV and is also a risk factor for escalation into life-threatening violence (Kropp, 2005). The most convincing evidence for the risk associated with stalking is from the U.S. Department of Justice (1998) survey of 8,000 women, which found that 81% of physically abused women were also stalked by their abuser and that partners who stalked were 4 times more likely than partners in the general population to abuse their partners. Additionally, Moracco et al. (1998) examined the records of 293 cases of partner homicide and found that stalking occurred prior to the killing in 23.4% of the cases. Thus, jealous and stalking behaviors clearly indicate an elevated risk of abuse and for escalation of abuse.

These findings demonstrate the need for police and law enforcement agencies to take steps to ensure the safety of victims when stalking occurs. These steps may include encouraging victims to request restraining orders and responding to complaints regarding stalking with urgency. Additionally, clinicians should work with stalking victims to develop safety plans to enhance victim safety.

Previous Criminal Behavior Unrelated to Intimate Partner Violence

An offender with a history of violence is at increased risk of partner violence even if the prior violence was not directed at his partner (Kropp, 2005). Both clinicians and researchers have noted that *generally violent* men (i.e., those who are violent both within and outside of the home) often engage in more severe and more frequent partner violence compared with men who are not violent outside the home. For example, on the basis of the reports of 525 battered women, Gondolf (1988) found that the greatest difference among three groups of batterers (i.e., severe, antisocial, and moderate) was the occurrence of arrest for violence outside the home. Whereas only 6% of the moderately abusive men had been violent toward others, 69% of the severe abusers had been violent outside the home.

Furthermore, a link has been demonstrated between the offender's prior criminal record and homicide (Block & Christakos, 1995; Campbell, 1992) and recidivism (Babcock & Steiner, 1999). For example, Campbell (1992) found that almost 70% of partner homicide offenders had a prior arrest record related to violent behavior toward others, and Block and Christakos (1995) found that 40% of the men who killed their partners had been arrested for a violent crime in the past.

In terms of female-perpetrated partner abuse and acts of theft, fraud, vice, and/or physical force, researchers found only a moderate correlation (Moffitt, Krueger, Caspi, & Fagan, 2000). It is clear that more information is needed on female offenders and criminality before conclusions can be made; however, it is evident that prior criminal behavior is an important variable to consider in understanding the risk of male-perpetrated IPV.

This research reveals that many abusers have had contact with the legal system in some form. Intervening to prevent future IPV during offender rehabilitation programs may be an important avenue to consider.

Situational Characteristics and Lethal Intimate Partner Violence

In addition to the offender's behavior and characteristics, certain situational characteristics have been shown to be related to increased risk of lethal IPV. In the sections that follow, we examine research related to ready access to weapons and to victim's attempt to leave the relationship as risk factors for lethal violence.

Ready Access to Weapons

All studies relating to spousal homicide support the notion that access to weapons increases the likelihood of homicide (Kellerman et al., 1993) and that guns are the most common weapons used in these homicides (Moracco et al., 1998). For example, Campbell et al. (2003) found that offender access to a gun and prior threatening with a weapon discriminated femicide victims from other abused women. In contrast to the homicide studies, two studies found that ownership and use of weapons were not risk factors for physical abuse (Hanson et al., 1997; Weisz et al., 2000). Weisz et al. (2000) interviewed abused women at the time they and their partners appeared in court. They found that the use of a weapon before the incident that brought the couple to court was not a significant predictor of severe violence in the 4 months following the interview. However, Gondolf (1988) found that the batterers who were categorized as severe in his cluster analysis were more likely to have used weapons during previous abuse. Therefore, although it is not clear that access to a weapon is generally related to IPV, because access to a weapon has been shown to be related to spousal homicide, it makes sense to be highly cautious if offenders have ready access to guns.

Victim Attempts to Leave the Relationship

One of the most dangerous times for victims of IPV is when the victim attempts to leave or threatens to leave the relationship. Both leaving and threatening to leave have been associated with the occurrence of IPV (H. Johnson, 1995; Moracco et al., 1998; Wilson & Daly, 1993, 1994). In a study of 12,000 women, H. Johnson (1995) found that abuse increased in severity after separation for both mildly and severely abused women.

A link also exists between victims' attempts to leave and homicide risk (Campbell, 1992; Moracco et al., 1998; Wilson & Daly, 1993, 1994). Moracco et al. (1998) found that 50% of the women killed by their partners had threatened to leave, attempted to leave, or had recently separated from their partners. These homicides were more than twice as likely to be preceded by other incidents of IPV when compared with homicides that did not occur in the context of separation.

Similarly, Wilson and Daly (1994) found a history of IPV in 80% of the homicide cases involving separated couples, compared with 35% of the homicide cases involving co-residing couples. Although spousal homicide may occur months or even years after separation, the period immediately following the separation appears to be especially risky for wives. Therefore, separated wives are at greater risk of being killed by their estranged spouses than co-residing wives, particularly immediately following separation. Of course, leaving an offender can also become a protective factor. In fact, Fals-Stewart, Lucente, and Birchler (2002) found that the frequency of both male-to-female and female-to-male physical aggression is lower when days of face-to-face contact is lower. One way to help victims safely leave violent homes is to provide shelter housing services. Some qualitative evidence suggests that women and their children who have escaped violent relationships benefit greatly from shelter or transitional housing services (Whitaker, Baker, & Arias, 2006). However, transitional housing and shelter services are often combined with other services, increasing the difficulty in assessing the impact of shelter housing in reducing revictimization. Offering these services to women leaving abusive relationships appears to help protect victims.

FACTORS FREQUENTLY ASSOCIATED WITH LESS LETHAL INTIMATE PARTNER VIOLENCE

In addition to factors that have been highlighted as risk factors for lethal violence, a number of other factors have been shown to be associated with IPV. These factors include those related to offender behavior, attitudes, or characteristics (including previous physical aggression in current or past intimate relationships, emotional or verbal abuse in current or past intimate partner relationship, high levels of anger or hostility, child abuse, use of power and control, violence in family of origin, and attitudes supporting IPV); mental health issues and disorders (including depression, personality disorders, disorder of emotional attachment, excessive use of drugs or alcohol, and high levels of stress, including financial stress or unemployment); and relationship issues (including high levels of relationship conflict or low levels of relationship satisfaction). Each of these factors should be considered when assessing, intervening, or preventing IPV.

Offender Behavior, Attitudes, or Characteristics

Previous research has found that certain behaviors, attitudes or characteristics of offenders are related to IPV recidivism. In the sections that follow, we examine research related to previous physical aggression, emotional or verbal abuse, anger or hostility, child abuse, use of power and control tactics, violence in the family of origin, and attitudes supporting IPV as risk factors for partner violence recidivism.

Previous Physical Aggression in Current or Past Intimate Relationships

Although recent escalation of the frequency and/or severity of aggression is a strong risk factor for lethal violence, a history of any physical aggression in any intimate relationship is established as a risk factor for recidivism (MacEwen & Barling, 1988; Weisz et al., 2000) and for severe forms of abuse (Aldarondo & Sugarman, 1996; Quigley & Leonard, 1996). In fact, recidivism rates for IPV range from 30% to 70% over a period of 2 years (Dutton, 1995a).

Most studies find that men with longer histories of abuse are more likely to continue being violent and to become more violent than are men with shorter histories of violence (Aldarondo & Sugarman, 1996; Quigley & Leonard, 1996; Weisz et al., 2000). In addition, research by Cantos, Neidig, and O'Leary (1994) suggests that women who have a history of being abusive perpetrate more severe forms of violence against their partners than do women without a history of being abusive. Therefore, it is important to assess both partners for history of violence.

Emotional or Verbal Abuse in Current or Past Intimate Partner Relationships

Emotional or verbal abuse is also an important risk factor for IPV. A significant relationship exists between the severity level of physical violence and the presence of emotional or verbal abuse (Jacobson, Gottman, Gortner, Berns, & Shortt, 1996; Margolin, John, & Foo, 1998; Vivian & Malone, 1997).

Although Stets (1990) found that verbal and physical aggression were significantly correlated, he found that over 50% of the cases involving verbal aggression occurred without physical violence. Similarly, Margolin et al.

(1998) found that whereas 89% of severely violent men were emotionally abusive, only 31% of the emotionally abusive men exhibited severe physical violence. Therefore, it appears that verbal aggression often occurs without physical violence, but rarely does physical violence occur without verbal aggression.

Emotional abuse also appears to be related to physical violence recidivism. Jacobson et al. (1996) studied the differences between those batterers who continued to use severe forms of violence and those who did not. They found that verbal aggression was significantly higher at the time of the initial assessment and 2 years after the initial assessment for husbands who continued to engage in severe violence against their spouse than it was for those who ceased being aggressive. Aldarondo and Sugarman (1996) found that men who reported higher levels of emotional abuse were significantly more likely to continue to use violence over the study's 3-year period. Several studies found the same relationship for women (O'Leary et al., 1994; Sagrestano, Heavey, & Christenson, 1999). For example, O'Leary et al. (1994) found that female psychological aggression 18 months after marriage is predictive of female physical aggression 30 months after marriage.

These findings suggest that a history of verbal or psychological aggression is an important risk assessment factor for both male- and female-perpetrated aggression. A common misconception is that IPV occurs only in the form of physical abuse. Prevention efforts must provide education and awareness of the significant role other forms of abuse play in physical violence and the escalation of violence. There is also some evidence that teaching couples to resolve conflicts with less hostility can reduce the likelihood of IPV.

High Levels of Anger or Hostility

Extensive research has demonstrated that a high level of anger or hostility is a risk factor of husband-to-wife abuse (Dutton, 1995b; Maiuro, Cahn, Vitaliano, & Wagner, 1988; Margolin et al., 1998). In addition, studies by Hanson et al. (1997) and Margolin et al. (1998) have found that severely abusive men score significantly higher on anger or hostility measures compared with nonviolent or less severely abusive men. Furthermore, Dye and Eckhardt (2000) found that college students who were violent toward their partner, regardless of gender, reported expressing more anger-related behaviors and exhibited less control over anger expression than nonviolent participants. Therefore, recognizing the level of anger exhibited by a potential IPV offender may assist the clinician and the potential victim to know when to enact safety measures to help prevent future violence. It is also possible that teaching individuals to handle anger in nonaggressive ways may contribute to the prevention of IPV.

Child Abuse

A strong relationship has been demonstrated between child abuse and the occurrence of IPV (Gondolf, 1988; McCloskey, 1996; Ross, 1996). Father-to-child physical abuse is often associated with the occurrence of husband-to-wife physical abuse. For example, Ross (1996) found that with each additional act of husband-to-wife violence, the odds that the husband will physically abuse a child increased by an average of 12%. Ross also concluded that wife-to-husband abuse was related to women also physically abusing their child or children. The severity level of IPV is also related to the co-occurrence of child abuse and IPV (Gondolf, 1988). Gondolf (1988) found that men who had severely abused their partner were significantly more likely to also report abusing a child than were less severely abusive men.

A clear reciprocal relationship exists between child abuse and IPV, which implies that the presence of either may indicate an elevated risk for families. Thus, there is a need to educate abusers and their partners of the destructive correlation between child abuse and IPV. In addition, child protective workers can play important roles in intervening to prevent IPV as well as child abuse.

Use of Power and Control

A relationship has been demonstrated between IPV and various aspects of the offender's controlling behavior toward the partner. Controlling behavior regarding decision making (Babcock, Waltz, Jacobson, & Gottman, 1993), access to relatives and friends (Cascardi et al., 1995; Dutton, 1995b), access to resources (Weisz et al., 2000), power inequality (Quigley & Leonard, 1996), and perceived power (Sagrestano et al., 1999) have been linked to severe abuse and recidivism. For example, Dutton (1995b) found that violent men were significantly more likely to use forms of dominance and isolation (i.e., control access to resources) compared with a nonviolent control group. Similarly, Cascardi et al. (1995) found that not only did the abused women report more use of controlling behaviors by their husbands than did the community control group, but they also reported experiencing more controlling behavior than women in discordant but nonabusive marriages.

Furthermore, H. Johnson (1995) and M. P. Johnson and Leone (2005) found that controlling behaviors were used much more frequently by men who inflicted serious violence on their wives than by those who did not inflict serious violence. Weisz et al. (2000) found that women's reports that their battering partner had used controlling behaviors in the past were related to severe violence 4 months after the initial interview. Therefore, the offender's use of controlling behavior is related to not only physical aggression but also severity and recidivism. Furthermore, Cantos et al. (1994) compared husbands who had been injured with those who had not been injured by a physically aggressive female partner and found that wives who caused injury were significantly more likely to have threatened to withhold money and to take away children than were physically aggressive women who did not injure their partners. On the basis of these data, it appears that both husbands' and wives' use of control may be related to the occurrence of IPV.

Violence prevention programs should help participants be alert to this type of behavior and the potential negative consequences that can emerge from controlling relationships.

Violence in Family of Origin

The use of family-of-origin violence as a risk factor for IPV is generally supported by the research literature (Aldarondo & Sugarman, 1996; Stith et al., 2000; Sugarman & Hotaling, 1989). Through the intergenerational transmission process, children learn how to act both by experiencing how others treat them and by observing how their parents treat each other. In a meta-analysis of 39 studies, Stith et al. (2000) reported a number of interesting findings relating to this issue. First, they found a weak but significant relationship between both experiencing child abuse and witnessing interparental abuse and subsequently perpetrating IPV, and a similar relationship between witnessing or experiencing abuse and subsequently becoming a victim of IPV. However, they found a much stronger relationship between growing up in a violent home and subsequently perpetrating IPV for males and a much stronger relationship between growing up in a violent home and subsequently becoming a victim of IPV for females.

It is important to note that the presence of violence in the family of origin does not ensure the later development of aggression in intimate relationships. In fact, most children from violent homes do not grow up to be violent adults (Kaufman & Zigler, 1987); therefore, family-of-origin violence is only a small part of understanding the perpetration of couple violence.

However, available research underscores the importance of providing victims of child abuse and witnesses of IPV with a corrective experience of a nurturing relationship. The negative effects of this experience may be counteracted in extrafamilial relationships such as a therapeutic relationship or a mentor/teacher and child relationship. Efforts to prevent the transmission of violence and destructive patterns of relating to others require that children learn new more positive and productive ways of relating and coping.

Attitudes Supporting Intimate Partner Violence

The professional literature suggests that "the most serious and persistent offenders minimize the seriousness of past violence, deflect personal responsibility for the violence, or even deny their involvement in past violence altogether" (Kropp, 2005). A relationship has been demonstrated between the offender's attitudes supporting violence and actual abuse (Hanson et al., 1997; Margolin et al., 1998) and severity of abuse (Hanson et al., 1997; Stith & Farley, 1993; Straus & Yodanis, 1996).

A relationship between women's use of violence and their approval of marital violence has also been found (Stets, 1990; Straus & Yodanis, 1996). For example, Stets (1990) found that wives' approval of marital violence was significantly related to their use of mild and severe forms of physical violence. Similarly, Straus and Yodanis (1996) found that wives' approval of marital violence doubled their odds of inflicting violence against their spouse. Thus, it is important for clinicians to understand the attitudes that offenders have about abusive behavior and to recognize that individuals who have attitudes that minimize or approve of violence are at higher risk of partner violence.

Mental Health Issues and Disorders

In general, men who abuse their spouse appear to have more psychological problems compared with nonviolent men (Riggs, Caufield, & Street, 2000). Four psychological syndromes have been identified as factors for men's perpetration of IPV. Specifically, depression, borderline personality disorder, posttraumatic stress disorder, and substance abuse have been consistently related to perpetration of partner violence. In addition, higher levels of partner violence have been found among individuals experiencing other types of personality disorders (e.g., antisocial, narcissistic, or histrionic), those exhibiting signs of severe mental illness (e.g., delusions, hallucinations, mania, dementia), and those experiencing cognitive or intellectual impairments (e.g., brain damage, mental retardation; Kropp, 2005).

Depression

A number of studies have linked depression and IPV (Dinwiddie, 1992; Pan, Neidig, & O'Leary, 1994; Straus & Yodanis, 1996). One of the first studies to examine this relationship was conducted by Maiuro et al. (1988). They studied depression across a sample of 100 violent men in treatment for anger management and 29 nonviolent control participants. Two thirds of the sample scored within the clinical range for depression. Significantly more men in the domestically violent group scored as depressed than men in the control or general assaulters groups.

Depression has also been linked to the severity of abuse (Pan et al., 1994; Straus & Yodanis, 1996; Vivian & Malone, 1997). For example, in a study of 11,870 men from 38 army bases, Pan et al. (1994) found that men who were mildly or severely physically aggressive reported significantly more depressive symptoms than men who were not physically aggressive. Furthermore, the severely aggressive group reported significantly more depressive symptoms than men in the mildly aggressive group. In fact, for every 20% increase in depressive symptomatology, the odds of being mildly aggressive increased by 30%, whereas the odds of being severely aggressive increased by 74%. Furthermore, while sampling 4,401 (2,557 women and 1,844 men) respondents, Straus and Yodanis (1996) found that a wife's depression doubled her odds of perpetrating physical violence against her spouse. In sum, research finds that depression is a highly relevant factor related to physical abuse for both men and women.

Personality Disorders

Another mental disorder strongly linked to perpetration of IPV is borderline personality disorder. In a series of studies (see Dutton, 1998, for a review), Dutton and his colleagues examined personality profiles of violent men. They found that 45% of self-referred and 27.5% of court-referred wife abusers reached the 85th percentile on the Borderline Scale of the Millon Clinical Multiaxial Inventory—III (Millon, Davis, & Millon, 1997) Furthermore, clients scoring high on borderline personality organization (BPO) scales report greater frequency, magnitude, and duration of anger. They also report greater jealousy and more trauma symptoms, disassociation, anxiety, sleep disturbance, and depression. Partners of these men described a constellation of personality features (e.g., BPO, high anger, fearful attachment, chronic trauma symptoms, recollection of paternal rejection) that accounted for reports of abusiveness by their partner.

Kropp (2005) suggested that mental disorder is likely to be a causal factor leading to impulsive or irrational decisions to act violently toward an intimate partner for some violent offenders. Additionally, he proposed that symptoms of mental disorders can interfere with an offender's ability or motivation to comply with treatment and supervision. Thus, not only should clinicians assess for a variety of mental disorders to understand the risk of future violence, but these disorders should also be a focus of treatment for offenders with these disorders.

Disorder of Emotional Attachment

Dutton (2005) is one of the key contributors in examining abusiveness from an attachment perspective. He suggests that chronic childhood frustration of attachment needs may lead to adult proneness to react to any threat of abandonment or rejection with extreme anger (i.e., intimacy anger). Thus, violence may be a form of protest behavior directed at the assaultive man's attachment figure (i.e., partner) and precipitated by perceived threats of separation or abandonment. The fearful attachment pattern may be most strongly associated with intimacy-anger because fearfully attached individuals desire closeness but experience pervasive interpersonal distrust and fear of rejection.

Excessive Use of Drugs or Alcohol

Excessive use of alcohol and other drugs is related to increased severity of violence and increased occurrence of homicide (Hanson et al., 1997; Kyriacou et al., 1999). Across samples of men receiving inpatient treatment for substance abuse, the prevalence of partner violence in the past year ranged from 58% to 84% (Brown, Werk, Caplan, Shields, & Seraganian, 1998). In outpatient samples of men with alcoholism, the prevalence rate of husband-to-wife violence in the year before treatment ranged from 54% to 66% (Stuart et al., 2003). Also, on those days an abuser drinks, he is more likely to be abusive. Fals-Stewart (2003) found that among men entering treatment for IPV or for substance abuse, partner violence was 5 to 10 times more likely on drinking days than on nondrinking days.

Substance use is also associated with more severe forms of violence (Hanson et al., 1997; Pan et al., 1994; Stith & Farley, 1993). Kyriacou et al. (1999) found alcohol and drug abuse to be associated with an increased risk of women sustaining injury as a result of IPV. Furthermore, some studies support a link between substance use and domestic homicide (Campbell, 1992). A relationship between women's alcohol use and their perpetration of violence has also been found (Sommer, Gordon, & Robert, 1992; Stets, 1990).

Given the demonstrated link between substance abuse and risk of IPV, substance abuse programs are presented with an opportunity to incorporate this information into their treatment program, highlighting the role drugs and alcohol play in abusive behavior. Furthermore, during the past 10 years, a variety of studies documenting the effectiveness of behavioral couples therapy (BCT) for substance abuse on reducing IPV have been undertaken (Fals-Stewart, Bircher, & O'Farrell, 1996; Fals-Stewart, Kashdan, O'Farrell, & Bircher, 2002; O'Farrell, Fals-Stewart, Murphy, Stephan, & Murphy, 2004). These studies have consistently demonstrated a decline in IPV among participants along with a decline in substance abuse. This research team is so convinced about the value of conjoint treatment that in one of their most recent publications they recommend that "providers should use partner-based interventions, particularly BCT, for the majority of substance-abusing patients who have engaged in IPV prior to program entry" (Fals-Stewart & Kennedy, in press).

High Levels of Stress, Including Financial Stress or Unemployment

Employment problems and financial stress are commonly cited risk factors for spousal assault. In general, batterers tend to be unemployed more frequently than nonbatterers (H. Johnson, 1995; Kyriacou et al., 1999; Margolin et al., 1998) and also to have been fired (Aldarondo & Kantor, 1997) or fired from more than one job more frequently than nonbatterers (Dinwiddie, 1992). Several explanations have been offered for the relationship between employment problems, financial stress, and IPV (Kropp, 2005). Financial problems or unemployment may be caused by the offender's psychological problems or personality disorders that are associated with violence. Alternatively, work-related frustration and anger may be displaced onto the partner. Thus, ongoing financial problems and unemployment tend to be associated with future violence and recent problems with the imminence of partner violence.

Families become particularly vulnerable to IPV during periods of stress. Therefore, agencies that work with families under stress, such as welfare agencies and counseling services, should be aware of the increased vulnerability to IPV during these times and offer resources to help these families safely manage stress.

Relationship Issues

A correlation between high levels of relationship discord or low levels of relationship satisfaction and IPV has been identified in a variety of studies (Jacobson et al., 1996; Margolin et al., 1998; Pan et al., 1994; Vivian & Malone, 1997). For example, Pan et al.'s (1994) analysis of 11,870 men from 38 army bases found not only that mildly and severely aggressive men scored higher on marital discord than men who were not physically aggressive but also that severely aggressive men scored significantly higher on marital discord than did mildly aggressive men. Furthermore, researchers have found a relationship between recidivism and relationship discord (Aldarondo & Sugarman, 1996; O'Leary et al., 1994). Aldarondo and Sugarman (1996) interviewed 532 people over a 3-year period and found that men who reported higher levels of marital discord were significantly more likely to engage in violence and to continue to use violence over the 3-year study.

Furthermore, marital discord or decreased marital satisfaction appears to be related to female-perpetrated violence (O'Leary et al., 1994; Sagrestano et al., 1999; Straus & Yodanis, 1996). For example, Straus and Yodanis (1996) found that marital conflict tripled the odds of wife-to-husband physical assault. Also, O'Leary et al. (1994) found that marital discord at 18 months after marriage was significantly correlated with wives' physical aggression 30 months after marriage. Therefore, it makes sense to focus prevention efforts on couples experiencing conflict before physical violence occurs in the relationship.

ASSESSING THE RISK OF FUTURE VIOLENCE

Several instruments are currently being used to aid in predicting future violence (see Roehl & Guertin, 1998, for a review). In this chapter, we look at two: the Danger Assessment (DA) and the Spousal Assault Risk Assessment (SARA).

The DA was developed by Campbell (1986) and is used to assist battered women to understand and assess their relationship for lethality risk. The scale contains two sections. The first section asks the battered woman to write on a calendar the days in the past year that she was abused and to rank the severity of the abuse (ranging from 1 = *slap, pushing, no injuries, and/or lasting pain* to 5 = *use of weapon, wounds from weapon*). The second section contains 15 yes–no items that are related to the risk of homicide (e.g., Is there a gun in the house? Have you ever been beaten by him while you were pregnant?). Refer to Campbell (2004) for the actual instrument.

The SARA was developed by Kropp and Hart (1995, 2000). The SARA provides practitioners with "a set of guidelines for the content and process of a thorough risk assessment" (Dutton & Kropp, 2000, p. 175) and, it is important to note, is not a psychological test. Based on an extensive literature review, the SARA contains 20 items to consider while assessing for future risk. As Dutton and Kropp (2000) explained, "Its purpose is not to provide absolute or relative measures of risk using cutoff scores or norms but rather to structure and enhance professional judgments about risk" (p. 175). Items are scored on a 0 to 2 scale (0 = *absent*, 1 = *subthreshold*, 2 = *present*). The SARA also asks clinicians to indicate whether the item is *critical*, defined as, "those [items], given the circumstances of the case at hand, are sufficient on their own to compel the evaluator to conclude that the individual poses an imminent risk of harm" (Dutton & Kropp, 2000, p. 175). The SARA manual can be purchased from the BC Institute of Family Violence (http://www.bcifv.org), located in British Columbia, Canada.

There is some evidence of the reliability and validity of structured professional judgment guidelines such as the SARA (Douglas & Kropp, 2002). For example, studies indicate that interrater reliability is good to excellent for professional judgments concerning the presence of individual risk factors and overall levels of risk (e.g., see Kropp & Hart, 2000). Furthermore, professional judgments of risk have good criterion-related validity: They correlate substantially with scores on actuarial measures (Kropp & Hart, 2000), they discriminate well between known groups of recidivists and nonrecidivists in retrospective research (Kropp & Hart, 2000), and they predict recidivism in prospective research (e.g., see Belfrage, Fransson, & Strand, 2000; Williams & Houghton, 2004).

CONCLUSION

In this chapter, we reviewed risk factors for IPV that have been identified from extensive research. It is clear that the factors associated with IPV are far too complex to be eliminated by any one specific prevention or intervention program, or even one type of program. A much broader range of prevention efforts is required. Knowledge of risk factors is critical to the management of offender risk and enhancement of victim safety. Furthermore, understanding risk factors is vital to the development of programs to prevent IPV or to prevent its escalation. Intervention or prevention programs should address known risk factors and should determine whether the program they are developing or the intervention they are proposing for an offender or victim target these risk factors.

REFERENCES

Aldarondo, E., & Kantor, G. K. (1997). Social predictors of wife assault cessation. In G. K. Kantor & J. L. Jasinski (Eds.), *Out of darkness: Contemporary perspectives on family violence* (pp. 183–193). Thousand Oaks, CA: Sage.

Aldarondo, E., & Sugarman, D. B. (1996). Risk marker analysis of the cessation and persistence of wife assault. *Journal of Consulting and Clinical Psychology, 64,* 1010–1019.

Babcock, J. C., & Steiner, R. (1999). The relationship between treatment, incarceration, and recidivism of battering: A program evaluation of Seattle's coordinated community response to domestic violence. *Journal of Family Psychology, 13,* 46–59.

Babcock, J. C., Waltz, J., Jacobson, N. S., & Gottman, J. M. (1993). Power and violence: The relation between communication patterns, power discrepancies, and domestic violence. *Journal of Consulting and Clinical Psychology, 61,* 40–50.

Belfrage, H., Fransson, G., & Strand, S. (2000). Prediction of violence using the HCR–20: A prospective study in two maximum security correctional institutions. *Journal of Forensic Psychiatry, 11,* 167–175.

Bilukha, O., Hahn, R. A., Crosby, A., Fullilove, M. T., Liberman, A., Moscicki, E., et al. (2005). The effectiveness of early childhood home visitation in preventing violence: A systematic review. *American Journal of Preventive Medicine, 28,* 11–39.

Block, C. R., & Christakos, A. (1995). Intimate partner homicide in Chicago over 29 years. *Crime and Delinquency, 41,* 496–526.

Brewer, V. E., & Paulsen, D. J. (1999). A comparison of U.S. and Canadian findings on uxoricide risk for women with children sired by previous partners. *Homicide Studies, 3,* 317–332.

Brown, T. G., Werk, A., Caplan, T., Shields, N., & Seraganian, P. (1998). The incidence and characteristics of violent men in substance abuse treatment. *Addictive Behaviors, 23,* 573–586.

Caetano, R., Field, C. A., Ramisetty-Mikler, S., & McGrath, C. (2005). The 5-year course of intimate partner violence among White, Black and Hispanic couples in the United States. *Journal of Interpersonal Violence, 20,* 1039–1057.

Campbell, J. C. (1986). Nursing assessment of risk of homicide for battered women. *Advances in Nursing Science, 3,* 67–85.

Campbell, J. C. (1989). Women's responses to sexual abuse in intimate relationships. *Health Care for Women International, 10,* 335–346.

Campbell, J. C. (1992). "If I can't have you, no one can": Power and control in homicide of female partners. In J. Radford & D. E. H. Russell (Eds.), *Femicide: The politics of women killing* (pp. 99–113). New York: Twayne.

Campbell, J. C. (2004). *Danger assessment.* Retrieved December 18, 2006, from http://www.dangerassessment.com/WebApplication1/pages/product.aspx

Campbell, J. C., Oliver, C. E., & Bullock, L. F. C. (1998). The dynamics of battering during pregnancy. In J. C. Campbell (Ed.), *Empowering survivors of abuse: Health care for battered women and their children* (pp. 81–89). Thousand Oaks, CA: Sage.

Campbell, J. C., Webster, D., Koziol-McLain, J., Block, C., Campbell, D., Curry, M. A., et al. (2003). Risk factors for femicide in abusive relationships: Results from a multisite case control study. *American Journal of Public Health, 93,* 1089–1097.

Cantos, A. L., Neidig, P., & O'Leary, D. K. (1994). Injuries of women and men in a treatment program for domestic violence. *Journal of Family Violence, 9,* 113–124.

Carcach, C., & Grabosky, P. N. (1998). *Murder-suicide in Australia.* Canberra, Australia: Australian Institute of Criminology.

Cascardi, M., O'Leary, K. D., Lawrence, E. E., & Schlee, K. A. (1995). Characteristics of women physically abused by their spouses and who seek treatment regarding marital conflict. *Journal of Consulting and Clinical Psychology, 63,* 616–623.

Cattaneo, L., Bell, M. E., Goodman, L. A., & Dutton, M. A. (2007). Intimate partner violence victims' accuracy in assessing their risk of reabuse. *Journal of Family Violence, 22,* 429–440.

Dinwiddie, S. H. (1992). Psychiatric disorders among wife batterers. *Comprehensive Psychiatry, 33,* 411–416.

Douglas, K., & Kropp, P. R. (2002). A prevention-based paradigm for violence risk assessment: Clinical and research applications. *Criminal Justice and Behavior, 2,* 617–658.

Dutton, D. G. (1995a). *The domestic assault of women: Psychological and criminal justice perspectives.* Vancouver, British Columbia, Canada: University of British Columbia Press.

Dutton, D. G. (1995b). Trauma symptoms and PTSD-like profiles in perpetrators of intimate abuse. *Journal of Traumatic Stress, 8,* 299–316.

Dutton, D. G. (1998). *The abusive personality: Violence and control in intimate relationships,* New York: Guilford Press.

Dutton, D. G. (2005, August). *Application of risk assessment to intervention with domestic violence offenders.* Paper presented at the meeting of the Department of Defense Domestic Violence Intervention/Treatment Protocol Development, Alexandria, VA.

Dutton, D. G., & Kropp, P. R. (2000). A review of domestic violence risk instruments. *Trauma, Violence, & Abuse, 1,* 171–181.

Dye, M., & Eckhardt, C. I. (2000). Anger, irrational beliefs, and dysfunctional attitudes in violent dating relationships. *Violence and Victims, 15,* 334–350.

Fals-Stewart, W. (2003). The occurrence of intimate partner violence on days of alcohol consumption: A longitudinal diary study. *Journal of Consulting and Clinical Psychology, 71,* 41–52.

Fals-Stewart, W., Bircher, G. R., & O'Farrell, T. J. (1996). Behavioral couples therapy for male substance-abusing patients: Effects on relationship adjustment and drug-using behavior. *Journal of Consulting and Clinical Psychology, 64,* 959–972.

Fals-Stewart, W., Kashdan, T. B., O'Farrell, T. J., & Bircher, G. R. (2002). Behavioral couples therapy for drug abusing patients: Effects on partner violence. *Journal of Substance Abuse Treatment, 22,* 87–96.

Fals-Stewart, W., & Kennedy, C. (in press). Addressing intimate partner violence in substance abuse treatment: Overview, options, and recommendations. *Journal of Substance Abuse Treatment, 29*, 5–17.

Fals-Stewart, W., Lucente, S. W., & Birchler, G. R. (2002). The relationship between the amount of face-to-face contact and partners' reports of domestic violence frequency. *Assessment, 9*, 123–130.

Gelles, R. J. (1990). Violence and pregnancy: Are pregnant women at greater risk of abuse? In M. A. Straus & R. J. Gelles (Eds.), *Physical violence in American families* (pp. 279–286). New Brunswick, NJ: Transaction.

Gondolf, E. W. (1988). Who are those guys? Toward a behavioral typology of batterers. *Violence and Victims, 3*, 187–203.

Hanson, R. K., Cadsky, O., Harris, A., & Lalonde, C. (1997). Correlates of battering among 997 men: Family history, adjustment, and attitudinal differences. *Violence and Victims, 12*, 191–209.

Jacobson, N. S., Gottman, J. M., Gortner, E., Berns, S., & Shortt, J. W. (1996). Psychological factors in the longitudinal course of battering: When do the couples split up? When does the abuse decrease? *Violence and Victims, 11*, 371–392.

Jacobson, N. S., Gottman, J. M., Waltz, J., Rushe, R., Babcock, J., & Holtzworth-Munroe, A. (1994). Affect, verbal content, and psychophysiology in the arguments of couples with violent husbands. *Journal of Consulting and Clinical Psychology, 62*, 982–988.

Johnson, H. (1995). *Risk factors associated with non-lethal violence against women by marital partners* (Publication No. NCJ 159900). Washington, DC: U.S. Department of Justice.

Johnson, M. P., & Leone, J. M. (2005). The differential effects of intimate terrorism and situational couple violence. *Journal of Family Issues, 26*, 322–349.

Kaufman, J., & Zigler, E. (1987). Do abused children become abusive parents? *American Journal of Orthopsychology, 57*, 186–192.

Kellerman, A. L., Rivara, F. P., Rushforth, N. B., Banton, J. G., Reay, D. T., Francisco, J. T., et al. (1993). Gun ownership as a risk factor for homicide in the home. *The New England Journal of Medicine, 329*, 1084–1091.

Kropp, P. R. (2005, August). *Risk assessment and risk management of domestic violence offenders*. Paper presented at the meeting of the Department of Defense Domestic Violence Intervention/Treatment Protocol, Alexandria, VA.

Kropp, P. R., & Hart, S. D. (2000). The Spousal Assault Risk Assessment (SARA) guide: Reliability and validity in adult male offenders. *Law and Human Behavior, 24*, 101–118.

Kropp, P. R., Hart, S. D., Webster, C. D., & Eaves, D. (1995). *Manual for the Spousal Assault Risk Assessment Guide* (2nd ed.). Vancouver, British Columbia, Canada: British Columbia Institute on Family Violence.

Kyriacou, D. N., Anglin, D., Taliaferro, E., Stone, S., Tubb, T., Linden, J. A., et al. (1999). Risk factors for injury to women from domestic violence. *The New England Journal of Medicine, 341*, 1892–1898.

MacEwen, K. E., & Barling, J. (1988). Multiple stressors, violence in the family of origin, and marital aggression: A longitudinal investigation. *Journal of Family Violence, 3,* 73–87.

MacMillan, H. L., & Wathen, C. N. (with the Canadian Task Force on Preventive Health Care). (2001). Prevention and treatment of violence against women. In *Systematic review and recommendations* (Tech. Rep. No. 01-04). London, Ontario, Canada: Canadian Task Force.

Maiuro, R. D., Cahn, T. S., Vitaliano, P. P., & Wagner, B. C. (1988). Anger, hostility, and depression in domestically violent versus generally assaultive men and nonviolent control subjects. *Journal of Consulting and Clinical Psychology, 56,* 17–23.

Margolin, G., John, R. S., & Foo, L. (1998). Interactive and unique risk factors for husbands' emotional and physical abuse of their wives. *Journal of Family Violence, 13,* 315–345.

McClane, G. E., Strack, G. B., & Hawley, D. (2001). A review of 300 attempted strangulation cases: Part II. Clinical evaluation of the surviving victim. *The Journal of Emergency Medicine, 21,* 311–315.

McCloskey, L. A. (1996). Socioeconomic and coercive power within the family. *Gender & Society, 10,* 449–463.

McFarlane, J., Parker, B., & Soeken, K. (1995). Abuse during pregnancy: Frequency, severity, perpetrator, and risk factors of homicide. *Public Health Nursing, 12,* 284–289.

Millon, T., Davis, R., Millon, C. (1997). *Manual for the Millon Clinical Multiaxial Inventory—III (MCMI–III)* (3rd ed.). Minneapolis, MN: NCS Pearson.

Moffitt, T. E., Krueger, R. F., Caspi, A., & Fagan, J. (2000). Partner abuse and general crime: How are they the same? How are they different? *Criminology, 38,* 199–232.

Moracco, K. E., Runyan, C. W., & Butts, J. (1998). Femicide in North Carolina. *Homicide Studies, 2,* 422–446.

National Center for Injury Prevention and Control. (2003). *Costs of intimate partner violence against women in the United States.* Atlanta, GA: Centers for Disease Control and Prevention.

Nielson, J. M., Endo, R. K., & Ellington, B. L. (1992). Social isolation and wife abuse: A research report. In E. Viano (Ed.), *Intimate violence: Interdisciplinary perspectives* (pp. 49–59). Washington, DC: Hemisphere.

O'Farrell, T. J., Fals-Stewart, W., Murphy, C. M., Stephan, S. H., & Murphy, M. (2004). Partner violence before and after couples-based alcoholism treatment for male alcoholic patients: The role of treatment involvement and abstinence. *Journal of Consulting and Clinical Psychology, 72,* 202–217.

O'Leary, K. D., Barling, J., Arias, I., Rosenbaum, A., Malone, J., & Tyree, A. (1989). Prevalence and stability of physical aggression. *Journal of Consulting and Clinical Psychology, 57,* 263–268.

O'Leary, K. D., Malone, J., & Tyree, A. (1994). Physical aggression in early marriage: Prerelationship and relationship effects. *Journal of Consulting and Clinical Psychology, 62*, 594–602.

Painter, K., & Farrington, D. P. (1998). Marital violence in Great Britain and its relationship to marital and non-marital rape. *International Review of Victimology, 5*, 257–276.

Pan, H. S., Neidig, P. H., & O'Leary, K. D. (1994). Predicting mild and severe husband-to-wife physical aggression. *Journal of Consulting and Clinical Psychology, 62*, 975–981.

Puzone, C. A., Saltzman, L. E., Kresnow, M., Thompson, M. P., & Mercy, J. A. (2000). National trends in intimate partner homicide, United States, 1976–1995. *Violence Against Women, 6*, 409–426.

Quigley, B. M., & Leonard, K. E. (1996). Desistance of husband aggression in the early years of marriage. *Violence and Victims, 11*, 355–370.

Rennison, C. M. (2003). *Intimate partner violence, 1993–2001.* Washington, DC: U.S. Department of Justice.

Riggs, D. S., Caufield, M. B., & Street, A. E. (2000). Risk for domestic violence: Factors associated with perpetration and victimization. *Journal of Clinical Psychology, 56*, 1289–1316.

Roehl, J., & Guertin, K. (1998). *Current use of dangerousness assessments in sentencing domestic violence offenders.* Pacific Grove, CA: State Justice Institute.

Ross, S. M. (1996). Risk of physical abuse to children of spouse abusing parents. *Child Abuse & Neglect, 20*, 589–598.

Sagrestano, L. M., Heavey, C. L., & Christenson, A. (1999). Perceived power and physical violence in marital conflict. *Journal of Social Issues, 55*, 65–79.

Sharps, P. W., Koziol-McLain, J., Campbell, J., McFarlane, J., Sachs, C., & Xu, X. (2001). Health care providers' missed opportunities for preventing femicide. *Preventive Medicine, 33*, 373–380.

Shields, N. M., & Hanneke, C. R. (1983). Battered wives' reactions to marital rape. In D. Finkelhor, R. J. Gelles, G. T. Hotaling, & M. A. Straus (Eds.), *The dark side of families: Current family violence research* (pp. 131–148). Beverly Hills, CA: Sage.

Simon, T. R., Anderson, M., Thompson, M., Crosby, A. E., Shelley, G., & Sacks, J. J. (2001). Attitudinal acceptance of intimate partner violence among U.S. adults. *Violence and Victims, 16*, 115–126.

Sommer, R., Gordon, B. E., & Robert, M. P. (1992). Alcohol consumption, alcohol abuse, personality and female perpetrated spouse abuse. *Personality and Individual Differences, 13*, 1315–1323.

Stack, S. (1997). Homicide followed by suicide: An analysis of Chicago data. *Criminology, 35*, 435–453.

Stets, J. E. (1990). Verbal and physical aggression in marriage. *Journal of Marriage and the Family, 52*, 501–514.

Stith, S. M., & Farley, C. (1993). A predictive model of male spousal violence. *Journal of Family Violence, 8*, 183–201.

Stith, S. M., Rosen, K. H., Middleton, K. A., Busch, A. L., Lundeberg, K., & Carlson, R. F. (2000). The intergenerational transmission of spouse abuse: A meta-analysis. *Journal of Marriage and the Family, 62,* 640–654.

Stith, S. M., Smith, D. B., Penn, C., Ward, D., & Tritt, D. (2004). Intimate partner physical abuse perpetration and victimization risk factors: A meta-analytic review. *Journal of Aggression and Violent Behavior, 10,* 65–98.

Stout, K. D. (1991). Intimate femicide: A national demographic overview. *Journal of Interpersonal Violence, 6,* 476–485.

Strack, G. B., McClane, G. E., & Hawley, D. (2001). A review of 300 attempted strangulation cases: Part I. Criminal legal issues. *The Journal of Emergency Medicine, 21,* 303–309.

Straus, M. A., & Yodanis, C. L. (1996). Corporal punishment in adolescence and physical assaults on spouses in later life: What accounts for the link? *Journal of Marriage and the Family, 58,* 825–841.

Stuart, G. L., Ramsey, S. E., Moore, T. M., Kahler, C. W., Farrell, L., & Recupero, P. R. (2003). Reductions in marital violence following treatment for alcohol dependence. *Journal of Interpersonal Violence, 13,* 1113–1131.

Sugarman, D. B., & Hotaling, G. T. (1989). Violent men in intimate relationships: An analysis of risk markers. *Journal of Applied Social Psychology, 19,* 1034–1048.

Sugg, N. (2006). What do medical providers need to successfully intervene with intimate partner violence? In S. M. Stith (Ed.), *Prevention of intimate partner violence* (pp. 101–120). New York: Haworth Press.

Task Force on Community Preventive Services. (2000). Introducing the guide to community preventive services: Methods, first recommendations, and expert commentary. *American Journal of Preventive Medicine, 18,* 1.

U.S. Department of Justice. (1998). *Stalking and domestic violence: The third annual report to Congress under the Violence Against Women Act.* Washington, DC: Author.

U.S. Department of Justice. (2000). *Intimate partner violence* (Publication No. NCJ 178247). Washington, DC: Author.

U.S. Preventive Services Task Force. (2004). Screening for family and intimate partner violence: Recommendation statement. *Annals of Internal Medicine, 140,* 382–386.

Van Hightower, N. R., & Gorton, J. (1998). Domestic violence among patients at two rural health care clinics: Prevalence and social correlates. *Public Health Nursing, 15,* 335–362.

Vivian, D., & Malone, J. (1997). Relationship factors and depressive symptomatology associated with mild and severe husband-to-wife physical aggression. *Violence and Victims, 12,* 3–18.

Weisz, A. N., Tolman, R. M., & Saunders, D. G. (2000). Assessing the risk of severe domestic violence: The importance of survivors' predictions. *Journal of Interpersonal Violence, 15,* 75–90.

Whitaker, D. J., Baker, C. K., & Arias, I. (2006). Interventions to prevent intimate partner violence. In L. S. Doll, S. E. Bonzo, J. A. Mercy, D. A. Sleet, & E. N. Haas (Eds.), *Handbook on injury and violence prevention* (pp. 203 –221). New York: Springer-Verlag.

Wilbur, L., Higley, M., Hafield, J., Surprenent, Z., Taliaferro, E. H., Smith, D. J., & Paolo, A. (2001). Survey results of women who have been strangled while in an abusive relationship. *The Journal of Emergency Medicine, 21*, 297–302.

Williams, K., & Houghton, A. B. (2004). Assessing the risk of domestic violence reoffending: A validation study. *Law and Human Behavior, 24*, 437–455.

Wilson, M., & Daly, M. (1993). Spousal homicide risk and estrangement. *Violence and Victims, 8*, 3–15.

Wilson, M., & Daly, M. (1994). Spousal homicide. *Juristat Service Bulletin, 14*, 1–15.

5

THE ASSOCIATION BETWEEN PARTNER VIOLENCE AND CHILD MALTREATMENT: A COMMON CONCEPTUAL FRAMEWORK

DEBORAH M. CAPALDI, HYOUN K. KIM, AND KATHERINE C. PEARS

Over the past 3 decades, numerous studies have documented that partner violence and child maltreatment often co-occur within the family (see Appel & Holden, 1998, for a review). Children whose parents engage in aggression not only are exposed to interparental violence but also are more likely to be maltreated physically as well as psychologically. Such exposure to interparental violence and child maltreatment has negative developmental outcomes affecting emotional, cognitive, and behavioral functioning; school adjustment; and peer relationships (Cicchetti & Toth, 2005; Wolfe et al., 2003). However, such family violence has come to be recognized as a major public health issue only relatively recently (American Psychological Association, 1996; Chalk & King, 1998; Tolan, Gorman-Smith, & Henry, 2006). As discussed by Tolan et al. (2006), much of this recognition of the prevalence and consequences of family violence arose from advocacy efforts within separate areas, including partner or domestic violence, child maltreatment, and elder abuse.

It is also the case that theories regarding causes were developed separately. Thus, intimate partner violence (IPV) has generally been viewed as a unique form of violence and has rarely been studied in the context of other forms of violence, limiting our knowledge on its co-occurrence with other forms of violence, particularly child maltreatment (Appel & Holden, 1998). Additionally, as Tolan et al. (2006) argued, the differences between advocacy goals and research goals have detracted from a broader scientific focus that could lead to understanding co-occurrence issues, including possible common etiological factors. Even within each area of family violence, progress toward understanding the aggression and evidence-based interventions has been impeded by heated controversy (Loseke, Gelles, & Cavanaugh, 2005). If progress is to be made in the field, it is time for greater focus on determining the common and interrelated aspects of IPV and child maltreatment. This would be aided by a parallel greater concentration on the rigor of the research conducted, including the adequacy of conceptual models and study designs.

In this chapter, we focus on the co-occurrence of two forms of aggression against intimates—IPV and child maltreatment—and on the role of antisocial behavior in their etiology. First, we review briefly the prevalence of the co-occurrence of IPV and child maltreatment, predominant theoretical approaches to these forms of violence, and studies regarding similarities and differences in risk factors for these two forms of family violence. We focus particularly on IPV in early adulthood, when such aggression is at its highest prevalence (Rennison, 2001) and when the risk of child maltreatment is highest (Smith Slep & O'Leary, 2001). We then present a theoretical approach that is adaptable to the study of abuse and aggression within family relationships, namely the dynamic developmental systems approach, and we summarize some of our work with the Oregon Youth Study (OYS) sample regarding IPV, child maltreatment, and more general violence that pertains to this theoretical approach. We argue that the model provides a comprehensive framework that can assist in taking an integrated approach to studying family violence. Our focus and conceptual models apply to aggression toward partners and children, including physical violence and verbal aggression, rather than to child sexual abuse or neglect. However, because the relevant research often refers to a broader construct of child maltreatment, some of the literature reviewed here refers to all aspects of such maltreatment.

PREVALENCE OF INTIMATE PARTNER VIOLENCE, CHILD MALTREATMENT, AND CO-OCCURRENCE

The issues related to physical aggression in married, cohabiting, and dating couples have received a great deal of attention from scholars, social activists, and the public. Reports based on national surveys indicate that the rate of violence toward a partner in the prior year for U.S. couples ranges from 17% to 39% (Elliott, Huizinga, & Morse, 1985; Plichta, 1996; Schafer, Caetano, & Clark, 1998; Straus & Gelles, 1990). Moffitt and Caspi (1999) compared the findings of three studies with large samples for rates of any physical aggression toward a partner in late adolescence and young adulthood (under age 25): two U.S. studies with data collection in the mid-1980s, namely the National Family Violence Survey (NFVS; Fagan & Browne, 1994) and the National Youth Survey (Elliott et al., 1985), and 1993–1994 findings from their study with a New Zealand sample. Across these studies, perpetration rates ranged from about 36% to 51% for women and 22% to 43% for men. Surveys including a broader age range for couples tend to find lower rates of violence, with the overall rate of 12% in the NFVS (Straus & Gelles, 1990). These rates are for any physical violence in the past year and include moderately severe items (e.g., pushing, shoving). Such physical aggression toward a partner is the highest at young ages (Straus & Gelles, 1986). Although physical aggression toward a partner has been assumed to be a male-only phenomenon (Walker, 1989), recent studies have consistently found that women and men have engaged in some level of physical aggression toward a partner at relatively equal rates (Archer, 2000). Furthermore, there is accumulating evidence that much physical aggression in couples' relationships is mutual (Capaldi, Shortt, & Crosby, 2003; Cascardi, Langhinrichsen, & Vivian, 1992; McDonald, Jouriles, Tart, & Minze, 2006; Stets & Straus, 1990).

Estimated and reported rates of child maltreatment are considerably lower than those of IPV. It is estimated that approximately 12.4 per 1,000 children (1.2%) were the victims of child maltreatment in 2003 (U.S. Department of Health and Human Services [USDHSS], 2004). Of these, the majority involved neglect, and just 19% involved physical abuse. Community surveys find higher prevalence rates, with physical abuse reported for 4.9% of children on the NFVS (Straus, Sugarman, & Giles-Sims, 1997). Several factors may contribute to the disparity in rates of IPV and child maltreatment other than true differences in rates of the behaviors, particularly definitional issues. Measures used to assess child physical abuse do not include some of the less severe items that are typically included in IPV inventories, which tend to have the highest prevalence (e.g., pushing, shoving). From a surveillance perspective, any act of physical hitting is typically considered to be IPV, but this is not the case for child abuse. For example, spanking one time is not counted as child maltreatment. Physical abuse of children, however, is the second most commonly reported form of child maltreatment and accounts for nearly a quarter (22%) of all fatalities from maltreatment (USDHHS, 2008).

According to Appel and Holden's (1998) review of 31 studies, the base rate of co-occurrence of spouse abuse and physical child maltreatment found in representative community samples was about 6%. In clinical samples of either battered women or physically abused children, the percentage of over-lap ranged from 20% to 100%, and when a conservative definition of child maltreatment was used, the median co-occurrence rate was 40%. Smith Slep and O'Leary (2005) found that 92% of couples who reported severe aggression between the partners also reported severe aggression toward a child, suggesting that, at the most extreme end of the family violence continuum, co-occurrence may be more prevalent. Other studies have demonstrated that children in families in which IPV has occurred are between 2 and 4 times more likely to be abused subsequently than children in families without IPV (e.g., see Cox, Kotch, & Everson, 2003; Lee, Kotch, & Cox, 2004; Rumm, Cummings, Kraus, Bell, & Rivara, 2000). Young age of the parents appears to increase the risk of child maltreatment in addition to the occurrence of IPV (Cox et al., 2003; Rumm et al., 2000).

INTIMATE PARTNER VIOLENCE AND CHILD MALTREATMENT AS UNIQUE

IPV is conceptualized according to some of the predominant theories in the field as a unique type of violence and thus a result of largely different factors than child maltreatment. Gender-based theories are associated with the advocacy movement and are the predominant basis for treatment programs, exemplified by batterer treatment programs. Gender theory views IPV as due to the unequal position of men and women in a society and due to men maintaining their dominant position in society and their control over women (Dobash & Dobash, 1979; Walker, 1984; see also chap. 3, this volume).

Another theory that hypothesizes unique aspects of both IPV and child maltreatment is the intergenerational transmission paradigm, which for almost 20 years has predominated in social learning explanations of aggression toward a partner in adults and of physical child maltreatment. Differing social learning processes in the family of origin are usually emphasized in relation to later aggression toward a partner versus child maltreatment. In the former case, aggression between parents is hypothesized to be observed and directly modeled in later relationships with partners (Rosenbaum & O'Leary, 1981; Stets, 1991; Straus, Gelles, & Steinmetz, 1980; see also chap. 3, this volume). Regarding child maltreatment, physical abuse toward the children themselves is hypothesized to be modeled in later relationships with these children's own offspring, thus resulting in transmission to the third generation. Therefore, although the social-learning paradigm is similar, the mechanisms are frequently hypothesized to be relationship specific and thus unique.

There is some evidence for specific transmission effects. As reviewed in Smith Slep and O'Leary (2001), a number of studies have found associations between witnessing interparental aggression and IPV (O'Leary, Malone, & Tyree, 1994). However, most of these studies have used a single adult reporter to assess both forms of aggression rather than longitudinal data. In one of the few longitudinal studies to examine intergenerational transmission of IPV over a 20-year time span, Ehrensaft et al. (2003) did find that witnessing IPV predicted this behavior in offspring. However, the presence of conduct disorder in the offspring was an even stronger predictor.

Regarding specific intergenerational associations for physical child maltreatment, Pears and Capaldi (2001) found that parents who reported having been abused in childhood were significantly more likely to engage in abusive behaviors toward their own children (as reported by those children). Findings indicated that abuse experienced by the parents, as well as consistency of discipline, depression, and posttraumatic stress disorder (PTSD), were predictive of parental abuse of the child. There were significant interactions between parental history of abuse and consistency of discipline, as well as abuse history, depression, and PTSD. Parents who had been abused themselves and exhibited less consistent discipline of their children were more likely to be abusive toward their children; however, parents who scored in the highest one third of the distribution for a combined score of depression and PTSD and had been abused were less likely than other parents who had experienced abuse to be abusive toward their children. Parents who had experienced multiple acts of abuse and multiple injuries, and thus had experienced more severe abuse, were considerably more likely to become abusive than were the other parents. In another prospective study, Dixon, Brown, and Hamilton-Giachritsis (2005) also found specific effects for transmission of child maltreatment. Families with newborns and at least one parent who was physically or sexually abused as a child were compared with families with no such history. Within 13 months after birth, the prevalence of maltreatment referrals was 16 times higher for families in which a parent had been maltreated. Parenting under age 21, history of mental illness and depression, and residing with a violent adult were risk factors, with young parenting being the strongest.

Despite significant associations between violence in the families of origin and procreation, most people who experienced or witnessed violence as children do not go on to commit violence against their partners or children. This has led to calls for examining the mechanisms by which violence in the family of origin is associated with later family violence (Egeland, 1993; Kaufman & Zigler, 1993). Mediators or developmental pathways have been examined for intergenerational models of aggression toward a partner but less examined for intergenerational maltreatment.

SHARED RISK OF INTIMATE PARTNER VIOLENCE AND CHILD MALTREATMENT

Although specific associations have been found across generations, there is some evidence for common contextual risk factors, as well as pathways or mediators. Two reviews have addressed the issue of concordance between risk factors for IPV and risk factors for child maltreatment. Smith Slep and O'Leary (2001) found considerable overlap in both shared contextual risk factors, such as poverty, stress, and aggression in the family of origin, and the characteristics of the adults involved, including impulsivity, aggression, poor problem solving, depression, and substance use. Organized around an ecological model, Tolan et al. (2006) reviewed risk of IPV and child maltreatment related to contextual and situational factors, individual factors, and relationship factors, concluding that the risk factors overlap substantially. They identified living in poverty, including in disadvantaged neighborhoods, and stress as major contextual risk factors for IPV.

Regarding individual risk factors, histories of low impulse control, prior aggression, and violent victimization are cited, along with other psychopathology, including depression and substance use. A history of poor family-of-origin functioning, including poor parenting, is also a risk factor for IPV. Regarding relationship factors, assortative partnering by antisocial behavior (i.e., if one partner in a romantic relationship has higher-than-average levels of antisocial behavior for their sex, the second partner also shows higher levels) has been found in a number of studies (Capaldi & Crosby, 1997; Krueger, Moffitt, Caspi, Bleske, & Silva, 1998; Moffitt & Caspi, 1999), and high conflict and associated problems such as low relationship satisfaction are also risk factors for IPV. Tolan et al. (2006) cited similar risk factors for child maltreatment as for IPV, including contextual factors of poverty, deprived neighborhoods, and stress; individual characteristics, including poor impulse control and a history of antisocial behavior; and relationship factors, including poorer family functioning, parental discord, and violence between parents.

ANTISOCIAL BEHAVIOR AND PSYCHOPATHOLOGY: A COMMON DEVELOPMENTAL PATHWAY

The overlaps in risk factors at the contextual, individual, and relationship levels suggest similarity in etiologies for these two areas of family violence and for antisocial behavior and violence more generally. There is a general consensus that the development of antisocial behavior involves a prolonged process of interplay between the risk characteristics of individuals and their environments (e.g., see Baltes, 1983; Cairns & Cairns, 1995; Elder, 1985). These environments include social environments created by families and peer groups as well as other key community settings (e.g., schools). The social interactions that occur within each environment may affect antisocial behavior across the life span. Figure 5.1 illustrates the interaction of the individual characteristics of the developing child with the social environment (for simplicity, only parent and peer associations are illustrated). These trans-

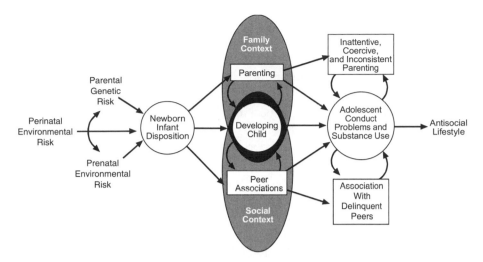

Figure 5.1. Dynamic developmental systems model: Development of antisocial behavior. From *The Handbook of Adolescent Behavioral Problems: Evidence-Based Approaches to Prevention and Treatment* (p. 286), edited by T. P. Gullotta and G. R. Adams, 2005, New York: Springer-Verlag. Copyright 2005 by Springer Science + Business Media. Reprinted with permission.

actions occur within and are affected by larger contextual factors. Bronfenbrenner (1986) conceptualized such settings and processes as a hierarchy of four nested systems involving intrapersonal factors (e.g., temperament), microsystems of face-to-face interactions, behavioral settings (e.g., neighborhood), and, finally, macrocontextual factors involving cultural and community practices. The process of development, including the development of antisocial behavior, may be conceptualized as the functioning of and transactions both across and within biological, psychological, and social systems, with constant feedback and interaction over time; thus, the process may be conceptualized as that of dynamic developmental systems (Capaldi, Shortt, & Kim, 2005).

Findings from the OYS, a 25-year prospective longitudinal study of the development of antisocial and violent behavior, indicated evidence for the intergenerational transmission of aggression toward a partner through unskilled parenting practices and boys' antisocial behavior (Capaldi & Clark, 1998). Similarly, Magdol, Moffitt, Caspi, and Silva (1998) found that, out of a number of contextual and family risk factors, the development of conduct problems and aggressive delinquency was the most consistent predictor of violence toward a partner. Antisocial behavior that develops by adolescence predicts later aggressive behavior toward a romantic partner, not only for young men (e.g., see Capaldi & Clark, 1998; Magdol et al., 1998; Simons & Johnson, 1998) but also for young women (Andrews, Foster, Capaldi, & Hops, 2000; Ehrensaft et al., 2003; Giordano, Millhollin, Cernkovich, Pugh, &

Randolph, 1999; Magdol et al., 1998; Woodward, Fergusson, & Horwood, 2002). This suggests the importance of individual psychopathology as a predictor of aggression for both men and women and some similarity in developmental pathways of aggression toward a partner for men and women, indicating that they both play some active role in physical aggression in couples. Thus, conduct problems seem to be a major developmental pathway leading to violence toward a partner. The fact that childhood maltreatment has been found to be predictive of later conduct problems suggests conduct problems, and possibly associated risk, as the mediator of an association between maltreatment and later aggression toward a partner.

The strength of the association between antisocial behavior and IPV is illustrated by the association with arrest records. There is evidence that the majority of young men who are repeatedly aggressive toward their partners have prior criminal records. Klein (1993) found that close to 80% of men who had civil restraining orders in the state of Massachusetts had prior criminal records in the state, and almost one half had prior arrests for assaults against other men or prior female partners. In the OYS sample, we examined the mean number of non-IPV arrests for three groups of men, namely those with zero, one, or two or more arrests for IPV. The 172 men with no IPV arrest had an average of 4 arrests, whereas the 22 men with 1 such arrest had an average of 8 other arrests, and the 9 men with 2 or more IPV arrests had an average of 13 other arrests. Regarding other adult arrests for violence, the men with no IPV arrests had an average of 0.14 violent arrests, whereas the men with 1 IPV arrest had an average of 0.76, and the men with 2 or more IPV arrests an average of 2.44 other violent arrests in adulthood. Thus, there is strong evidence for the association of antisocial behavior more generally with aggression toward a partner. The effect of antisocial behavior on IPV is increased by the fact that it is a risk factor for both men and women and that higher levels of antisocial behavior in both partners places the couple at greater risk of IPV (Kim & Capaldi, 2004).

Despite the fact that physical abuse of a child is a violent act, less is known about the antisocial behavior of perpetrators of child maltreatment than about that of perpetrators of IPV. According to national child-welfare reports, most child maltreatment is perpetrated by parents, and more mothers than fathers are perpetrators (USDHHS, 2008). In a large-scale review of the literature on the risk factors for child physical abuse, Black, Heyman, and Smith Slep (2001) noted that physically abusive parents (most often mothers) were generally characterized by more impulsivity, a higher tendency to become upset and angry, more negative affect, and more autonomic system reactivity. Additionally, harsh parenting—the use of severe physical punishment that is not necessarily considered abusive—has also been linked in both men and women to having a hostile interpersonal style (Simons, Whitbeck, Conger, & Wu, 1991). Hostility, negative affect, impulsivity, and high reactivity are characteristics of antisocial behavior.

Evidence also suggests that antisocial behavior may be a link in the intergenerational transmission of child maltreatment, specifically, and harsh parenting, more generally. Having experienced maltreatment as a child appears be a risk factor for both antisocial behavior, including violent behavior, and teenage parenthood (Herrenkohl, Herrenkohl, Egolf, & Russo, 1998; Smith, 1996). Given that younger parents are at higher risk of maltreating their children (USDHHS, 2008) as well as being antisocial (Herrenkohl et al., 1998; Thornberry, Smith, & Howard, 1997), this suggests that antisocial behavior might be implicated in the cross-generation transmission of maltreatment. Simons et al. (1991) found that the link between harsh, punitive parenting in one generation and in the next was mediated by hostile personality. Taken together, the evidence suggests a link between antisocial behavior in a parent and his or her physical abuse of children.

THE AGE–VIOLENCE ASSOCIATION

Age of the perpetrators appears to be strongly associated with both violence toward a partner and child maltreatment. Rennison (2001) presented data regarding victimization of women by age from the National Crime Victimization Survey. In 1999, rates for partner violence experienced by women were about 15 to 16 (per 1,000) women ages 16 to 19 and 20 to 24, 9 women ages 25 to 34, 6 women ages 35 to 39, and 3 women ages 50 or older. Thus, the prevalence of partner violence toward women in their teens and early 20s was close to 3 times higher than for those in their late 30s. Evidence for couples' aggression (including female-to-male) more generally indicates relatively high prevalence at younger ages (Smith Slep & O'Leary, 2001; Straus, 1990).

Age also appears to be related to the perpetration of child maltreatment. Data based on national reports of child abuse and neglect demonstrate that for women age shows an inverse association with the likelihood of maltreating a child from age 20 on. For men, this inverse association begins at age 30 (USDHHS, 2008). In their comprehensive review of the risk factors for child physical abuse, Black et al. (2001) found that a number of studies have shown younger parents to be at greater risk of physically abusing their children and that age was the only demographic variable that consistently showed a moderate association with physical abuse.

These findings indicate that developmental factors are related to involvement in both aggression toward a partner and child maltreatment and, thus, indicate the importance of developmental conceptual approaches. Antisocial behaviors generally show improvement with age. For example, the prevalence and frequency of criminal acts peak in late adolescence (Blumstein, Cohen, Roth, & Visher, 1986) and decline quite rapidly thereafter. Aggression toward a partner and child maltreatment may, therefore, show some similar developmental trends to antisocial behavior in general.

A DYNAMIC DEVELOPMENTAL SYSTEMS APPROACH TO UNDERSTANDING INTIMATE PARTNER VIOLENCE AND CHILD MALTREATMENT

Recently, a number of researchers have called for the use of developmental–ecological perspectives that take into account a wide variety of risk and protective contextual, individual, and interpersonal factors and effects of interactions among the factors over time in trying to understand the development of IPV, child maltreatment, and violence more generally (Daro, Edleson, & Pinderhughes, 2004; Knickerbocker, Heyman, Smith Slep, Jouriles, & McDonald, 2007). We have conceptualized behavior in couples as a dynamic developmental system in which behavior in the dyad is inherently interactive and also responsive to developmental characteristics of each of the partners. In addition, behavior is shaped by both broader and more proximal contextual factors. A key characteristic of aggression within couples and aggression toward children is that both involve perpetrators and victims in an ongoing and close family relationship. This makes it likely that the dynamics for each of these types of abuse and aggression will be considerably different from those involved in aggression toward a stranger. Thus, the dynamic developmental systems model, as applied to aggression within an ongoing relationship, involves a conceptual focus on the dyad within the larger contextual setting.

We have built and tested aspects of such an early life span model in a series of studies over the past decade, predominantly using the OYS sample. A summary of the model is depicted in Figure 5.2 and is described in more detail for couples in Capaldi et al. (2005). In taking into account the individual risk characteristics of each partner, as well as risk context and proximal interaction, the model shows continuity with prior conceptualizations, in particular that of Riggs and O'Leary (1989). However, although partner characteristics are considered, the Riggs and O'Leary model focuses less on the dyad and more on the individual's characteristics. A further unique aspect of the dynamic developmental systems model is the emphasis on the importance of development. Thus, the model provides a framework that can aid in understanding developmental risk of violence toward a partner or child, the course of such aggression over time, and bidirectional influences on the behavior and course.

As applied to IPV, the approach emphasizes the importance of considering first the characteristics of both partners as they enter and then move through the relationship, including personality, psychopathology, ongoing social influences (e.g., peer associations), and individual developmental stage. The second emphasis is on the risk context and contextual factors that affect aggression toward a partner, such as whether substances were being used before a fight or the causes of a given fight. The third emphasis is on the nature of the relationship itself, primarily the interaction patterns within the dyad

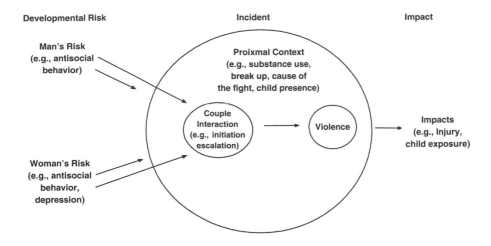

Figure 5.2. Dynamic developmental systems model: Partner violence. From "Typological Approaches to Violence in Couples: A Critique and Alternative Conceptual Approach," by D. M. Capaldi and H. K. Kim, 2007, *Clinical Psychology Review, 27*, p. 259. Copyright 2007 by Elsevier. Reprinted with permission.

as they are initially established and as they change over time, as well as factors affecting the context of the relationship. It is expected that these interactions and violent and abusive behavior will show change over time, and such change is therefore conceptualized as a core element of the model. Although prior risk of each individual is considered in the model, the contribution to negative interactions and aggressive abuse within the relationship may vary from one sided (e.g., one partner may be extremely aggressive, regardless of partner characteristics) to mutual (i.e., each partner contributes to a similar degree to aggression and abuse in the relationship).

The dynamic developmental model can also take into account multiple levels of developmental time in conceptualizing couples' relationships over time. Couples' aggression is related to the age of the partners as well as to the length of the relationship (Capaldi & Crosby, 1997). The developmental stage of the couple's relationship itself, which is related to but not identical with the chronological length of the relationship, may strongly affect the couple's interactions. For example, early stages may be marked by more insecurity and vulnerability to jealousy, and later stages may be marked by more concerns around division of labor and lower levels of satisfaction. For the OYS problem-solving interactions, the most frequently picked topic at Time 1 (ages 17–20 for the young men) was partner's jealousy (chosen by 15% of young men and 14% of young women). At the later ages, partner's jealousy dropped lower in the rankings, whereas issues such as sharing housework were selected more frequently. A unique aspect of the dynamic developmental systems model is that it embraces the changes in context, individual characteristics (e.g., substance use), and the partners themselves (i.e., the introduction of a new partner), and it conceptualizes influences at both the individual and the dyadic interaction levels.

As reflected in Figure 5.2, the findings of our work, along with those of a number of others, have supported the importance of studying behaviors of both partners over time to gain an adequate understanding of the phenomena. For instance, Kim and Capaldi (2004) found that women's antisocial behavior and depressive symptoms accounted for significant additional variance in concurrent levels of the young men's physical and psychological aggression over the men's own psychopathology. Furthermore, women's depressive symptoms also had significant effects over time on the young men's psychological aggression approximately 2 years later. In addition, there was a significant interactive effect of the men's and women's antisocial behavior over time on the young men's psychological aggression.

We have adapted the model to consideration of child maltreatment, as depicted in Figure 5.3. The model shows conceptual parallels to that for IPV and some conceptual similarities to the ecological–transactional model of Cicchetti and Lynch (1993) in the emphasis on transactions across multiple levels of risk factors. Developmental risks that participants bring to the interaction, such as developmental stage, and the proximal contextual factors, such as family stress and parental substance use (Black et al., 2001), combine to result in interactions resulting in aggressive abuse. Similar to the model for IPV, the balance between the developmental risk of the interactants varies from very one sided (e.g., a severely aggressive and violent parent who will be abusive regardless of the child's characteristics) to involving child developmental risks that increase the likelihood of parental abuse toward them, including factors such as mental retardation and physical disabilities (Ammerman, 1990), difficult child temperament, and conduct-problem behaviors (Rohrbeck & Twentyman, 1986). Additionally, age itself is a risk factor for abuse given that older children are at higher risk of physical abuse (although younger children are at risk of maltreatment in general; USDHHS, 2008). The relationship between parent and child always involves differential power, because one is an adult and one a child. Thus, abuse is seen as much more due to parental than child characteristics.

Other unique aspects of child maltreatment are that more than one adult may be involved, at least on the level of being aware that the child is being abused. Smith Slep and O'Leary (2005) found that the most common pattern of physical aggression in the home was that of both parents showing at least some form of physical aggression toward a child. The ways in which the parental or caretaking couple interact and influence each other's parenting behavior is an important aspect of the model, which has not been frequently considered. This is usually considered from the point of view of how more antisocial male partners may have a negative effect on the mother's parenting behaviors. Because men show higher levels of antisocial behavior than do women (Steffensmeier & Allan, 2000), the effect is more likely to be nega-

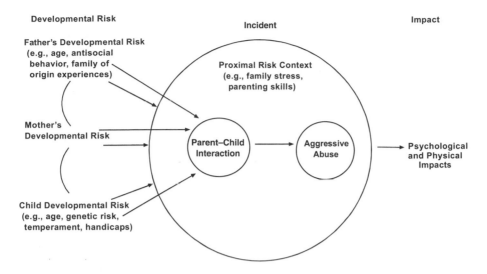

Figure 5.3. Dynamic developmental systems model: Physically and verbally aggressive child maltreatment.

tive from men to women than vice versa. However, female romantic partners can have a negative effect on men's behavior in early adulthood. Capaldi, Kim, and Owen (2008) found for the OYS sample that women's antisocial behavior was predictive of their male partner's persistence in crime and also of adult onset for those men who had not previously been involved in crime, controlling for associated factors such as men's prior criminal history. In another study involving the OYS men's offspring, Capaldi, Pears, Kerr, and Owen (2008) found that women's antisocial behavior and their poor and harsh discipline practices had a deleterious effect on their male partner's discipline practices. This was over and above the parenting the male partner had experienced from his parents as well as his level of antisocial behavior and risk. The dynamics of the parenting dyad and their influences on each other need more consideration in understanding the etiology of both IPV and child maltreatment.

All of the areas in the model represent important targets for investigation as to their role in family violence and its impacts for potentially malleable prevention and intervention points. Programs to reduce prior psychopathology may help prevent aggression toward a partner or child maltreatment. Contextual factors also provide key information. If IPV occurs frequently in the process of divorce or breaking up as was found by Capaldi, Kim, and Owen (2008), treatment could focus around counseling for negotiating such factors as child custody and property division. If the couple is staying together, then counseling on avoiding future violence is indicated, including strategies for nonviolent problem solving, avoiding escalation toward violence, and allowing the partner to take a timeout (Capaldi, Kim, & Owen,

2008). Additionally, for some individuals, drinking or drug use is closely associated with domestic violence and child maltreatment (e.g., see Feingold, Kerr, & Capaldi, 2008; Leonard, Bromet, Parkinson, Day, & Ryan, 1985; Pan, Neidig, & O'Leary, 1994). Therefore, substance use treatment may promote positive change, and there is evidence that interventions reducing alcohol use for male clients with alcoholism are associated with reduced partner violence (O'Farrell, Murphy, Stephan, Fals-Stewart, & Murphy, 2004). In addition, for couples with a child, education as to the negative consequences of violence for the child may provide motivation to the couple to change their behavior.

CONCLUSION

Abusive and aggressive behaviors toward romantic partners and children result in negative physical and psychosocial effects. Such aggressive behaviors toward the individuals with whom one shares close relationships and one's everyday life are a challenge to understand, prevent, and treat. The weight of evidence suggests that engaging in higher levels of antisocial behavior and violence more generally, including violence toward strangers, places an individual at higher risk of perpetrating family aggression and abuse. Furthermore, there is some significant co-occurrence of IPV and child maltreatment and evidence of shared risk factors and etiology. The dynamic developmental systems approach provides a conceptual framework that can encompass the various levels of risk factors, as well as the dyadic interaction of two people within an ongoing relationship. Calls for more integration of the field of family violence (Daro et al., 2004; Smith Slep & O'Leary, 2001; Tolan et al., 2006) are a challenge to the field to move forward in our understanding of family violence by improving conceptual models and identifying shared and unique developmental contributions. Such work will provide the foundation for stronger and more effective evidence-based interventions.

REFERENCES

American Psychological Association. (1996). *Violence and the family: Report of the American Psychological Association Presidential Task Force on Violence and the Family.* Washington, DC: Author.

Ammerman, R. T. (1990). Predisposing child factors. In R. T. Ammerman & M. Hersen (Eds.), *Children at risk: An evaluation of factors contributing to child maltreatment and neglect* (pp. 199–224). New York: Plenum Press.

Andrews, J. A., Foster, S. L., Capaldi, D. M., & Hops, H. (2000). Adolescent and family predictors of physical aggression, communication, and satisfaction in young adult couples: A prospective analysis. *Journal of Consulting and Clinical Psychology, 68,* 195–208.

Appel, A. E., & Holden, G. W. (1998). The co-occurrence of spouse and physical child maltreatment: A review and appraisal. *Journal of Family Psychology, 12,* 578–599.

Archer, J. (2000). Sex differences in aggression between heterosexual partners: A meta-analytic review. *Psychological Bulletin, 126,* 651–680.

Baltes, P. B. (1983). Life-span developmental psychology: Observations on history and theory revisited. In R. M. Lerner (Ed.), *Developmental psychology: Historical and philosophical perspectives* (pp. 79–11). Hillsdale, NJ: Erlbaum.

Black, D. A., Heyman, R. E., & Smith Slep, A. M. (2001). Risk factors for child physical abuse. *Aggression and Violent Behavior, 6,* 121–188.

Blumstein, A., Cohen, J., Roth, J. A., & Visher, C. A. (Eds.). (1986). *Criminal careers and career criminals* (Vol. 1). Washington, DC: National Academies Press.

Bronfenbrenner, U. (1986). Ecology of family as a context for human development: Research perspectives. *Developmental Psychology, 22,* 723–742.

Cairns, R. B., & Cairns, B. D. (1995). Social ecology over time and space. In P. Moen, G. H. Elder Jr., & K. Luscher (Eds.), *Examining lives in context: Perspectives on the ecology of human development* (pp. 397–421). Washington, DC: American Psychological Association.

Capaldi, D. M., & Clark, S. (1998). Prospective family predictors of aggression toward female partners for at-risk young men. *Developmental Psychology, 34,* 1175–1188.

Capaldi, D. M., & Crosby, L. (1997). Observed and reported psychological and physical aggression in young, at-risk couples. *Social Development, 6,* 184–206.

Capaldi, D. M., & Eddy, J. M. (2005). Oppositional defiant disorder and conduce disorder. In T. P. Gullotta & G. R. Adams (Eds.), *The handbook of adolescent behavioral problems: Evidence-based approaches to prevention and treatment* (pp. 283–308). New York: Springer-Verlag.

Capaldi, D. M., & Kim, H. K. (2007). Typological approaches to violence in couples: A critique and alternative conceptual approach. *Clinical Psychology Review, 27,* 253–265.

Capaldi, D. M., Kim, H. K., & Owen, L. D. (2008). Romantic partners' influence on men's likelihood of arrest in early adulthood. *Criminology, 46,* 401–433.

Capaldi, D. M., Pears, K. C., Kerr, D. C. R., & Owen, L. D. (2008). Intergenerational and partner influences on fathers' negative discipline. *Journal of Abnormal Child Psychology, 36,* 347–358.

Capaldi, D. M., Shortt, J. W., & Crosby, L. (2003). Physical and psychological aggression in at-risk young couples: Stability and change in young adulthood. *Merrill-Palmer Quarterly, 49,* 1–27.

Capaldi, D. M., Shortt, J. W., & Kim, H. K. (2005). A life span developmental systems perspective on aggression toward a partner. In W. Pinsof & J. Lebow (Eds.), *Family psychology: The art of the science* (pp. 141–167). New York: Oxford University Press.

Cascardi, M., Langhinrichsen, J., & Vivian, D. (1992). Marital aggression, impact, injury, and health correlates for husbands and wives. *Archives of Internal Medicine, 152*, 1178–1184.

Chalk, R., & King, P. A. (1998). *Violence in families: Assessing prevention and treatment programs.* Washington, DC: National Academies Press.

Cicchetti, D., & Lynch, M. (1993). Toward an ecological/transactional model of community violence and child maltreatment: Consequences for children's development. *Psychiatry, 56*, 96–118.

Cicchetti, D., & Toth, S. L. (2005). Child maltreatment. *Annual Review of Clinical Psychology, 1*, 409–438.

Cox, C. E., Kotch, J. B., & Everson, M. D. (2003). A longitudinal study of modifying influences in the relationship between domestic violence and child maltreatment. *Journal of Family Violence, 18*, 5–17.

Daro, D., Edleson, J. L., & Pinderhughes, H. (2004). Finding common ground in the study of child maltreatment, youth violence, and domestic violence. *Journal of Interpersonal Violence, 19*, 282–298.

Dixon, L., Browne, K., & Hamilton-Giachritsis, C. (2005). Risk factors of parents abused as children: Part I. A mediational analysis of the intergenerational continuity of child maltreatment. *Journal of Child Psychology and Psychiatry, 46*, 47–57.

Dobash, R. E., & Dobash, R. (1979). *Violence against wives: A case against the patriarchy.* New York: Free Press.

Egeland, B. (1993). A history of abuse is a major risk factor for abusing the next generation. In R. J. Gelles & D. R. Loseke (Eds.), *Current controversies on family violence* (pp. 197–208). Newbury Park, CA: Sage.

Ehrensaft, M. K., Cohen, P., Brown, J., Smailes, E., Chen, H., & Johnson, J. (2003). Intergenerational transmission of partner violence: A 20-year prospective study. *Journal of Consulting and Clinical Psychology, 71*, 741–753.

Elder, G. H., Jr. (1985). Perspectives on the life course. In G. H. Elder Jr. (Ed.), *Life course dynamics: Trajectories and transitions* (pp. 23–49). Ithaca, NY: Cornell University Press.

Elliott, D. S., Huizinga, D., & Morse, B. J. (1985). *The dynamics of delinquent behavior: A national survey progress report.* Boulder: University of Colorado.

Fagan, J., & Browne, A. (1994). Violence between spouses and intimates: Physical aggression between women and men in intimate relationships. In A. J. Reiss & J. A. Roth (Eds.), *Understanding and preventing violence: Social influences* (Vol. 3, pp. 115–292). Washington, DC: National Academies Press.

Feingold, A., Kerr, D. C. R., & Capaldi, D. M. (2008). Associations of substance use problems with intimate partner violence for at-risk men in long-term relationships. *Journal of Family Psychology, 22*, 429–438.

Giordano, P. C., Millhollin, T. J., Cernkovich, S. A., Pugh, M. D., & Rudolph, J. L. (1999). Delinquency, identity, and women's involvement in relationship violence. *Criminology, 37*, 17–40.

Herrenkohl, E. C., Herrenkohl, R. C., Egolf, B. P., & Russo, M. J. (1998). The relationship between early maltreatment and teenage parenthood. *Journal of Adolescence, 21,* 291–303.

Kaufman, J., & Zigler, E. (1993). The intergenerational transmission of abuse is overstated. In R. J. Gelles & D. R. Loseke (Eds.), *Current controversies on family violence* (pp. 209–221). Newbury Park, CA: Sage.

Kim, H. K., & Capaldi, D. M. (2004). The association of antisocial behavior and depressive symptoms between partners and risk for aggression in romantic relationships. *Journal of Family Psychology, 18,* 82–96.

Klein, A. (1993). *Spousal/partner assault: A protocol for sentencing and supervision of offenders.* Quincy, MA: Quincy Court.

Knickerbocker, L., Heyman, R. E., Smith Slep, A. M., Jouriles, E. N., & McDonald, R. (2007). Co-occurrence of child and partner maltreatment: Definitions, prevalence, theory, and implications for assessment. *European Psychologist, 12,* 36–44.

Krueger, R. F., Moffitt, T. E., Caspi, A., Bleske, A., & Silva, P. A. (1998). Assortative mating for antisocial behavior: Developmental and methodological implications. *Behavior Genetics, 28,* 173–186.

Lee, L. C., Kotch, J. B., & Cox, C. E. (2004). Child maltreatment in families experiencing domestic violence. *Violence and Victims, 19,* 573–591.

Leonard, K. E., Bromet, E. J., Parkinson, D. K., Day, N. L., & Ryan, C. M. (1985). Patterns of alcohol use and psychically aggressive behavior in men. *Journal of Studies on Alcohol, 46,* 279–282.

Loseke, D. R., Gelles, R. J., & Cavanaugh, M. M. (2005). *Current controversies on family violence.* Thousand Oaks, CA: Sage.

Magdol, L., Moffitt, T. E., Caspi, A., & Silva, P. A. (1998). Hitting without a license: Testing explanations for differences in partner abuse between young adult daters and cohabitors. *Journal of Marriage and the Family, 60,* 41–55.

McDonald, R., Jouriles, E. N., Tart, C. D., & Minze, L. C. (2006, July). *Adjustment in the context of men's severe intimate partner violence: Contributions of other forms of family violence.* Poster presented at the International Family Violence and Child Victimization Research Conference, Portsmouth, NH.

Moffitt, T. E., & Caspi, A. (1999). *Findings about partner violence from the Dunedin Multidisciplinary Health and Development Study* (Publication No. NCJ 170018). Washington, DC: U.S. Department of Justice.

O'Farrell, T. J., Murphy, C. M., Stephan, S. H., Fals-Stewart, W., & Murphy, M. (2004). Partner violence before and after couples-based alcoholism treatment for male alcoholic patients: The role of treatment involvement and abstinence. *Journal of Consulting and Clinical Psychology, 72,* 202–217.

O'Leary, K. D., Malone, J., & Tyree, A. (1994). Physical aggression in early marriage: Prerelationship and relationship effects. *Journal of Consulting and Clinical Psychology, 62,* 594–602.

Pan, H. S., Neidig, P. H., & O'Leary, K. D. (1994). Predicting mild and severe husband-to-wife physical aggression. *Journal of Consulting and Clinical Psychology*, 62, 975–981.

Pears, K. C., & Capaldi, D. M. (2001). Intergenerational transmission of abuse: A two-generation, prospective study of an at-risk sample. *Child Abuse & Neglect*, 25, 1439–1461.

Plichta, S. B. (Ed.). (1996). *Violence and abuse: Implications for women's health*. Baltimore: Johns Hopkins University Press.

Rennison, C. M. (2001). *Intimate partner violence and age of victim, 1993–99* (Publication No. NCJ 19735). Washington, DC: U.S. Department of Justice.

Riggs, D. S., & O'Leary, K. D. (1989). A theoretical model of courtship aggression. In M. A. Pirog-Goood & J. E. Stets (Eds.), *Violence in dating relationships: Emerging social issues* (pp. 53–71). New York: Praeger Publishers.

Rohrbeck, C. A., & Twentyman, C. T. (1986). Multimodal assessment of impulsiveness in abusing, neglecting, and nonmaltreating mothers and their preschool children. *Journal of Consulting and Clinical Psychology*, 54, 231–236.

Rosenbaum, A., & O'Leary, K. D. (1981). Marital violence: Characteristics of abusive couples. *Journal of Consulting and Clinical Psychology*, 49, 63–71.

Rumm, P. D., Cummings, P., Krauss, M. R., Bell, M. A., & Rivara, F. P. (2000). Identified spouse abuse as a risk factor for child maltreatment. *Child Abuse & Neglect*, 24, 1375–1381.

Schafer, J., Caetano, R., & Clark, C. (1998). Rates of intimate partner violence in the United States. *American Journal of Public Health*, 88, 1702–1704.

Simons, R. L., & Johnson, C. (1998). An examination of competing explanations for the intergenerational transmission of domestic violence. In Y. Danieli (Ed.), *International handbook of the Plenum series on stress and coping* (pp. 553–570). New York: Plenum Press.

Simons, R. L., Whitbeck, L. B., Conger, R. D., & Wu, C. (1991). Intergenerational transmission of harsh parenting. *Developmental Psychology*, 27, 159–171.

Smith, C. (1996). The link between childhood maltreatment and teenage pregnancy. *Social Work Research*, 20, 131–141.

Smith Slep, A. M., & O'Leary, S. G. (2001). Examining partner and child maltreatment: Are we ready for a more integrated approach to family violence. *Clinical Child and Family Psychology Review*, 4, 87–107.

Smith Slep, A. M., & O'Leary, S. G. (2005). Parent and partner violence in families with young children: Rates, patterns, and connections. *Journal of Consulting and Clinical Psychology*, 73, 435–444.

Steffensmeier, D., & Allan, E. (2000). Looking for patterns: Gender, age, and crime. In J. Sheley (Ed.), *Criminology: The contemporary handbook* (pp. 85–127). Belmont, CA: Wadsworth.

Stets, J. E. (1991). Psychological aggression in dating relationships: The role of interpersonal control. *Journal of Family Violence*, 6, 97–114.

Stets, J. E., & Straus, M. A. (1990). Gender differences in reporting marital violence and its medical and psychological consequences. In M. A. Straus & R. J. Gelles

(Eds.), *Physical violence in American families: Risk factors and adaptations to violence in 8,145 families* (pp. 151–166). New Brunswick, NJ: Transaction.

Straus, M. A. (1990). Injury and frequency of assault and the "representative sample fallacy" in measuring wife beating and child maltreatment. In M. A. Straus & R. G. Gelles (Eds.), *Physical violence in American families: Risk factors and adaptations to violence in 8,145 families* (pp. 75–91). New Brunswick, NJ: Transaction.

Straus, M. A., & Gelles, R. J. (1986). Societal change and change in family violence from 1975 to 1985 as revealed by two national surveys. *Journal of Marriage and the Family, 48,* 465–478.

Straus, M. A., & Gelles, R. J. (Eds.). (1990). *Physical violence in American families: Risk factors and adaptations to violence in 8,145 families.* New Brunswick, NJ: Transaction.

Straus, M. A., Gelles, R. J., & Steinmetz, S. K. (1980). *Behind closed doors: Violence in the American family.* Garden City, NY: Anchor/Doubleday.

Straus, M. A., Sugarman, D. B., & Giles-Sims, J. (1997). Spanking by parents and subsequent antisocial behavior of children. *Archives of Pediatric and Adolescent Medicine, 151,* 761–767.

Thornberry, T. P., Smith, C. A., & Howard, G. J. (1997). Risk factors for teenage fatherhood. *Journal of Marriage and the Family, 59,* 505–522.

Tolan, P. H., Gorman-Smith, D., & Henry, D. B. (2006). Family violence. *Annual Review of Psychology, 57,* 557–583.

U.S. Department of Health and Human Services. (2004). *Child maltreatment 2002.* Washington, DC: Author.

U.S. Department of Health and Human Services. (2008). *Child maltreatment 2006.* Washington, DC: Author.

Walker, L. E. (1984). *The battered women syndrome.* New York: Springer Publishing Company.

Walker, L. E. (1989). Psychology and violence against women. *American Psychologist, 44,* 695–702.

Wolfe, D. A., Wekerle, C., Scott, K., Straatman, A., Grasley, C., & Reitzel-Jaffee, D. (2003). Dating violence prevention with an at-risk youth: A controlled outcome evaluation. *Journal of Consulting and Clinical Psychology, 71,* 279–291.

Woodward, L. J., Fergusson, D. M., & Horwood, L. J. (2002). Romantic relationships of young people with childhood and adolescent onset antisocial behavior problems. *Journal of Abnormal Child Psychology, 30,* 231–243.

6

HEALTH EFFECTS OF PARTNER VIOLENCE: AIMING TOWARD PREVENTION

JACQUELYN C. CAMPBELL, MARGUERITE L. BATY,
KATHRYN LAUGHON, AND ANNE WOODS

Intimate partner violence (IPV) is a widespread problem in the United States and globally, with increasing evidence of significant effects on the physical and mental health and well-being of women and children. This chapter critically reviews recent research in this area, starting with an overview of prevalence in the health care system, followed by sections on physical health effects (including homicide, attempted homicide, injury, pregnancy-related outcomes, and the emerging area of research on the intersection of IPV and HIV/AIDS), mental health effects, and the other emerging area of research in the integrated biopsychosocial–immunological mechanisms that underlie these health effects, with a final section on implications for prevention and intervention.

In this chapter, we use the 1999 Centers for Disease Control and Prevention (CDC) definition of IPV, which can be summarized as physical and/or sexual assault or threats of assault against a married, cohabitating, or dating current or estranged intimate partner by the other partner, also including emotional abuse and controlling behaviors in a relationship in which there has been physical and/or sexual assault (Saltzman, Fanslow, McMahon, & Shelley, 1999). IPV thus can occur between spouses, girlfriend and boyfriend, former spouses or former boyfriend and girlfriend, or current or former same-sex intimate partners. Although the majority of research examines IPV, we use the term *intimate partner abuse* (IPA) when referring to emotional abuse or controlling behaviors without accompanying physical and/or sexual violence. We have included published research addressing physical and mental health effects of IPV on adolescent and adult victims. There is little research examining physical and mental health effects of IPV on males, so although this research is included, the vast majority of the body of knowledge in this field has been accumulated on studies of females. We have also included Canadian and other international research where identifiable in the usual databases, but there are fewer studies from other countries than from the United States, and some of those studies are published in journals not usually retrieved by electronic searches.

PREVALENCE OF INTIMATE PARTNER VIOLENCE IN HEALTH CARE SETTINGS

Overall prevalence of IPV was covered earlier in this volume (see chap. 2), but specifically, the prevalence of IPV in various health care settings can be seen in Table 6.1. Again, most of this research has been conducted in the United States.

PHYSICAL HEALTH EFFECTS OF INTIMATE PARTNER VIOLENCE

IPV is associated with a wide range of physical health problems. These health problems range from the most severe direct consequence of violence, death through homicide, to injury and chronic illness. Two specific women's health issues—sexually transmitted infections and complications of child-bearing—are also adversely affected by IPV and are also discussed in the sections that follow.

Homicide and Attempted Homicide

IPV has significant negative physical health consequences. The most severe is homicide, with 30% to 40% of murdered women in the United States killed by an intimate partner or former partner (Bachman & Saltzman, 1995; J. C. Campbell et al., 2003; Paulozzi, Saltzman, Thompson, & Holmgreen, 2001), and 67% to 72% of those cases were preceded by domestic violence against the female partner (J. C. Campbell et al., 2003; Morton,

TABLE 6.1
Prevalence of Intimate Partner Violence (IPV)
in Different Health Care Settings

Health care setting	Type and prevalence	Citations
Emergency departments	Trauma directly from IPV: 2%–3% Past-year IPV: 15%–17% Lifetime IPV: 35%	Dearwater et al. (1998); Glass, Dearwater, and Campbell (2001)
Primary care clinics	Past-year IPV: 8%–29% Lifetime IPV: 20%–51%	Bradley, Smith, Long, and O'Dowd (2002); Hegarty and Bush (2002)
Obstetrics (including prenatal and inpatient)	IPV during pregnancy: 6%–21% IPV during postpartum: 13%–21%	J. C. Campbell, Woods, Chouaf, and Parker (2000); J. C. Campbell, Garcia-Moreno, and Sharps (2004); Gazmararian, Lazorick, and Spitz (1996); Harrykisson, Rickert, and Wiemann (2002)
Inpatient mental health	IPV among women with major anxiety and substance abuse disorders: 30% IPV among women with major depression: 40%	Dienemann et al. (2000)

Runyan, Moracco, & Butts, 1998). When male partners are killed by a female spouse or girlfriend or former spouse or girlfriend, between 75% and 85% are preceded by prior IPV against the female partner, with at least 25% of the cases in immediate self-defense (J. C. Campbell, 1992; Hall-Smith, Moracco, & Butts, 1998). Attempted intimate partner homicides against women with severe injury from gunshot and knife wounds are approximately 9 times more common than actual homicides (Glass, Perrin, Campbell, & Soeken, 2007).

Women are at increased risk of IPV-related femicide during the child-bearing year. In a groundbreaking case-control study across 10 cities in the United States, McFarlane, Campbell, Sharps, and Watson (2002) found femicide to be a significant cause of maternal mortality. Among 437 cases of attempted or completed femicide, 5% of victims were murdered while pregnant. The risk of attempted or completed femicide was 3 times higher for women abused during pregnancy (adjusted odds ratio = 3.08, 95% confidence interval [CI] = 2.4–5.5) than for women who were abused but not during pregnancy. Black women were at even greater risk than White women.

Forty-one percent of women who were killed by an intimate partner in the United States used health care agencies for injury, physical problems, or mental health problems in the year prior to their murder (Sharps et al., 2001). Most of those women had not been seen in any other system in the year before their death, suggesting that the health care system could be an important site for the prevention of intimate partner homicide and attempted homicide if abused women were identified and appropriate interventions provided.

Physical Injury

The most obvious of physical health outcomes of IPV is physical injury; nearly half of women who experience IPV report being injured by the abuse, with about 20% seeking medical care for their injuries (Bachman & Saltzman, 1995; U.S. Department of Justice, 2005). Fractures, lacerations, contusions, and tendon or ligament damage to the face, neck, upper torso, breast, or abdomen are the most common (Kyriacou et al., 1999; Varvaro & Lasko, 1993). Short-term sequelae consist of pain and decreased function related to the traumatic injury. Long-term consequences of injury can include neurological problems such as seizures and fainting from possibly undiagnosed traumatic brain syndrome as well as chronic pain (J. C. Campbell, 2002; Coker, Smith, Bethea, King, & McKeown, 2000; McCauley et al., 1995). One of the less well-recognized injuries are those from choking or attempted strangulation, which can result in short-term brain anoxia and resultant long-term neurological symptoms that abused women report significantly more than those not abused (Glass, Laughon, et al., 2007; McClane, Strack, & Hawley, 2001).

Chronic Physical Health Conditions

The effects of IPV may also result in other long-term physical health sequelae. Coker et al.'s (2002) population-based study using the National Violence Against Women Survey in the United States found that women who experienced physical IPV were at 60% increased risk of having a chronic physical health condition, and women reported that the condition interfered with normal activities in the past week. A large case-control study of enrollees in a multisite metropolitan health maintenance organization found that abused women had approximately a 60% higher rate of all physical health problems in the past year compared with never-abused women, even though the abuse could have occurred as long as 8 years prior to the study (J. C. Campbell et al., 2002). Studies measuring the relationship between IPV and health status and health outcomes reported that abused women report a lower level of overall health and significantly more health symptoms than women who were never abused, even when controlling for other risk factors such as age, insurance status, substance use, and witnessing parental violence (J. C. Campbell, 2002; Coker, Smith, et al., 2000; Plichta & Falik, 2001). A dose–response relationship between severity of IPV and degree of physical health problems has also been demonstrated, but even women experiencing low-severity violence report significantly increased symptoms (McCauley, Kern, Kolodner, Derogatis, & Bass, 1998).

Long-term chronic health conditions can present as musculoskeletal problems such as arthritis or chronic back pain; gynecologic symptoms such as sexually transmitted infections (STIs), vaginal bleeding, vaginal infection, chronic pelvic pain, dyspareunia, and urinary tract infections; conditions associated with chronic stress, such as headaches, hypertension, cardiac problems, loss of appetite, abdominal pain, or digestive problems; immune system alterations such as asthma, allergies, rash, diabetes, upper respiratory infections, and even cancer; and central nervous system problems such as seizures probably related to head injury as explained earlier (J. C. Campbell, 2002; Coker, Sanderson, Fadden, & Pirisi, 2000).

Sexually Transmitted Infections

STIs substantially affect the morbidity of women at highest risk of IPV (i.e., poor, minority women of childbearing age), thereby meriting particular discussion. Rates of chlamydia and gonorrhea in the United States are 431 and 126 per 100,0000, respectively, among adult women. Physically and/or sexually abused women are at 2 to 4 times the risk of contracting an STI than their nonabused counterparts, with one population-based study demonstrating women reporting spousal physical abuse in the past year were 3.47 times more likely to have a diagnosis of an STI in the past 5 years than those women who were not physically abused (Plichta & Abraham, 1996). A 2-year longitudinal study found that on enrollment the risk of STIs among physically or sexually abused women was 4.3 times higher than for their nonabused counterparts. After 2 years, the risk remained elevated, at 3.8 times higher (Liebschutz, Feinman, Sullivan, Stein, & Samet, 2000). The increased risk of STIs may have broader health effects, as illustrated by the findings surrounding human papillomavirus (HPV), an STI. HPV is the primary cause of cervical neoplasia (Schiffman & Castle, 2003), and Coker, Sanderson, et al. (2000) found that invasive cervical neoplasia was 4 times more common among sexually abused women.

The intersection between HIV, the most deadly STI, and IPV is increasingly being recognized and definitively documented through persuasive and rigorous, albeit cross-sectional, research (e.g., see Dunkle et al., 2004; Gielen, O'Campo, Faden, & Eke, 1997; Greenwood et al., 2002; Maman et al., 2002; Whetten et al., 2006; Wyatt et al., 2002). In several studies in Africa (Dunkle et al., 2004; Fonck, Els, Kidula, Ndinya-Achola, & Timmerman, 2005; Maman et al., 2002), IPV has been associated with increased positive HIV status as well as increased high-risk sexual behaviors such as not using condoms, having multiple partners, transactional sex for money or drugs, and sex with high-risk partners, although a causal relationship has not been established. Women compose the largest group worldwide contracting HIV; women 15 to 24 years old are 1.6 times as likely to be HIV-positive as their male counterparts (United Nations Population Fund, 2005). In Africa, women are dying of AIDS at rates of more than two to one over men. Eighty percent of new HIV infections among women worldwide occur within marriages or long-term relationships with primary partners, underscoring the roles of IPV and unknown infidelity of male partners in transmission (United Nations Population Fund, 2005).

The research examining the overlap of STIs and IPV provides moderate evidence of a relationship between abuse and increased risk of STIs. In the United States, the samples were drawn from mostly poor minority populations, using convenience sampling (mostly clinic populations), thereby affecting the generalizability of these findings. However, another important note is that these findings relied on self-report and therefore most likely underestimate STI and abuse prevalence for several reasons. Because of perceived stigma and the personal nature of STIs, women may be reluctant to disclose their status to researchers. Additionally, women may not know their status because many STIs can be asymptomatic and therefore infections can go undiagnosed (Institute of Medicine, 1997; Turner et al., 2002). Detection of abuse may have been hindered because many of the studies used vague questions such as "Have you been abused?," which result in lower rates of detection than more specific questions such as "Has your partner slapped, hit, kicked, or shoved you?" One could reasonably imagine that incidence and prevalence of both IPV and STIs in these studies are even higher than reported.

Complications With Pregnancy and Risks for Newborns

During the childbearing period, women are at special risk of IPV with serious sequelae for mother and child. Janssen et al. (2003) found that pregnant women experiencing IPV were at 3.8 times increased risk of antepartum hemorrhage, 3 times increased risk of intrauterine growth restriction, and 8 times increased risk of perinatal death than their nonabused counterparts. Several studies also document a positive association between IPV and abortion, miscarriage, abruptio placenta, low birth weight (LBW), preterm labor, and cesarean section (Gielen, O'Campo, Faden, Kass, & Xue, 1994; Hedin & Janson, 2000; Pallitto, Campbell, & O'Campo, 2006; Renker, 2002). A U.S. population-based dataset shows a small but significant relationship between IPV either prior to or during the pregnancy and LBW, even when adjusting for age, smoking, public assistance, and education (Silverman, Decker, Reed, & Raj, 2005). A meta-analysis of abuse during pregnancy and birth weight found similar relationships between abuse and LBW across studies in the United States and Canada (Murphy, Schei, Myhr, & Du Mont, 2001).

The infant remains at risk even after delivery. McFarlane and Soeken (1999) found that among an ethnically stratified cohort of 121 women who experienced IPV during pregnancy, weight gain from 6 to 12 months was less in infants when abuse of the mother continued after 6 months. Additionally, the risk of child abuse may be particularly severe when abuse occurred during pregnancy, with a significant association of child abuse and IPV shown in several studies (J. C. Campbell & Lewandowski, 1997). This indicates a need for multidisciplinary attention to risk factors for IPV and IPA within pediatric settings.

MENTAL HEALTH EFFECTS OF INTIMATE PARTNER VIOLENCE

Living in a severely abusive relationship also has significant effects on a woman's mental health status. For most abused women, the violence is not a single event but rather a pattern of behavior that repeats over time, for some as often as once a week. Psychological abuse, including emotional abuse and controlling behaviors, usually occurs along with physical violence, with sexual abuse co-occurring also. Between 40% and 45% of physically abused adult women are subjected to physically forced sex, with even more experiencing sexually degrading acts in the relationship (J. C. Campbell & Soeken, 1999). A battered woman lives in realistic fear of further beatings, rape, injury, and possible death.

In both population based and longitudinal community-based studies, multiple mental health problems have been documented in abused women, including depression, posttraumatic stress disorder (PTSD), phobias, anxiety, panic disorders, and substance abuse disorders (Coker et al., 2002; O'Campo et al., 2006; G. L. Roberts, Williams, Lawrence, & Raphael, 1998). A comprehensive meta-analysis by Golding (1999) showed that compared with rates in general populations of women, abused women had significantly greater mean weighted prevalence rates of depression (47.6%; weighted mean odds ratio = 3.8; 95% CI = 3.16–4.57), suicidality (17.9%; weighted mean odds ratio = 3.55; 95%CI = 2.73–4.60), PTSD (63.8%; weighted mean odds ratio = 3.74; 95% CI = 1.02–6.83), alcohol abuse (18.5%; weighted mean odds ratio = 5.56; 95% CI = 3.32–9.31), and drug abuse (8.9%; weighted mean odds ratio = 5.62; 95% CI = 3.55–7.72). The studies drawn for this review were in both community and clinical settings. Two recent primary care studies have supported the strong link between depression and partner abuse for women attending general practitioners (Coid et al., 2003; Hegarty, Gunn, Chondros, & Small, 2004). Recent research suggests that psychological abuse and stalking uniquely contribute to PTSD and depressive symptoms, even after controlling for physical and sexual abuse (Mechanic, Weaver, & Resick, 2008).

Evidence from both population-based and longitudinal community-based studies suggests that whereas depression lessens with decreasing IPV, PTSD appears to be more persistent (Breslau et al., 1998; J. C. Campbell & Soeken, 1999; Kessler, Sonnega, Bromet, Hughes, & Nelson, 1995). For example, among a community sample of 160 abused, postabused, and nonabused women, up to 66% postabused women continued to have PTSD symptoms despite having been out of their abusive relationships an average of 9 years (range = 2–23 years; S. J. Woods, 2000).

Examining depression and PTSD in women who are abused is complicated by the fact that PTSD is a complex disorder that frequently coexists with other mental health disorders. Comorbidity with substance abuse results in more severe sequelae related to health, social functioning, and quality of life (Ballenger et al., 2004; Hirschfeld, 2001). It is unfortunate that many of the empirical studies addressing the mental health effects of abuse, especially less recent investigations, addressed these comorbidities but failed to measure PTSD. One reason for this may be that patients typically do not approach the health care system complaining of PTSD, and primary care providers may not be attuned to a PTSD assessment and diagnosis.

The comorbidity of PTSD and major depression is particularly common among women experiencing IPV (Tolin & Foa, 2006). A small study specifically examining that comorbidity in abused women found that current IPV-related PTSD and depressive symptoms were strongly correlated ($r = -.84$, $p < .001$) and that in 75% of the cases, major depression occurred in the context of PTSD (S. J. Woods et al., 2005). These general associations were supported in a large case-control study of racially balanced, highly educated, middle-class working women, drawn from female HMO enrollees in a metropolitan city in the United States (O'Campo et al., 2006). This study found a far greater prevalence of comorbid depressive and PTSD symptoms among women with a history of IPV (13.1%) than for pure depressive (4.6%) or PTSD (7.1%) symptoms alone.

Substance abuse is also a frequent comorbidity of IPV, with studies reporting abused women to be at increased risk of alcohol, tobacco, recreational drugs, and prescription drug abuse (Coker et al., 2002; McCauley et al., 1998; Silverman, Raj, Mucci, & Hathaway, 2001). Golding's (1999) meta-analysis demonstrated an 18.5% mean prevalence of alcohol abuse or dependence and an 8.9% mean prevalence of drug abuse or dependence among women abused by intimates. A review article also found support for a link between IPV and use of substances in the majority of studies in which both IPV and substance abuse were examined (Logan, Walker, Cole, & Leukefeld, 2002).

BIOPSYCHOSOCIAL–IMMUNOLOGICAL MECHANISMS OF HEALTH EFFECTS IN INTIMATE PARTNER VIOLENCE

IPV and the related mental and physical effects are closely linked to the women's stress levels and stress response from their bodies. The stress-response aspect of these health effects is a fairly new but growing field of research.

Physical Health Conditions and Injuries

Women who experience IPV may live with a combination of ongoing chronic stress and exacerbations of acute stress related to episodes of physical, psychological, and sexual violence. Although the interrelatedness of stress and health has been recognized since ancient times, research establishing causal pathways between IPV and the multitude of physical and mental health effects is sparse. The complex relationships between women's experiences of abuse and poor physical and mental health outcomes point toward multiple causes. Biologically, innate differences in the central and peripheral responses can influence how a person perceives and reacts to stress. Psychologically, stress responses of fear, helplessness, anxiety, depression, PTSD, and other mental health symptoms affect physical health responses. A recent structural equation model analysis found that PTSD symptoms completely mediated the relationship between partner violence and physical health symptoms (R. Campbell, Greeson, Bybee, & Raja, 2008). Social responses to stress, including substance use and abuse, interact with physical and mental health. Each of these factors influences endocrine and immunologic responses to stress, resulting in immune suppression or immune activation. The effects of stress on physical health are mediated by overresponsiveness of the autonomic nervous system or impaired immune system function, and there is strong support for the role of cortisol and catecholamines in this process (Gill & Page, 2006; Rabin, 1999; Rice, 2000). Excessive secretion of these stress hormones in response to a perceived threat stimulate target organs. Organ dysfunction results when this stress response is not effectively modulated.

Certain stress-related illnesses are more commonly reported in physically and sexually abused women. For example, research has demonstrated an association between irritable bowel syndrome and partner abuse. Irritable bowel syndrome is a chronic, painful, functional disorder that is more prevalent in women than in men. Key factors in this gender discrepancy include stress, mental health, and a history of abuse (Payne, 2004). A case-control study of 207 adults (118 with irritable bowel syndrome and/or functional dyspepsia) found significantly greater reports of adult abuse in cases compared with control participants (40% vs. 25%, $p < .05$), and this relationship was mediated by psychosocial factors (Koloski, Talley, & Boyce, 2005), demonstrating the complex interrelationships of abuse, stress, and health.

Headaches are another example of a stress-related symptom consistently found in abused women significantly more often than in women never victimized by IPV (J. C. Campbell, 2002). Increased sympathetic nervous system activity that increases muscle contraction may result in tension headaches and lower back pain. Migraine headaches may also be a result of increased sympathetic response, with increased norepinephrine and serotonin levels causing vasoconstriction, which is responsible for the prodrome of an impending migraine, followed by rapid vasodilation and subsequent pain.

Cardiovascular conditions such as hypertension, chest pain, and palpitations have been strongly linked to sympathetic nervous system reactivity. Stress hormones elevate blood pressure to transport blood to areas where it is needed to engage in the classic fight-or-flight response. In the presence of chronic stress, the increased alpha-adrenergic tone results in increased peripheral vascular resistance and sustained hypertension. The increased risk of hypertension observed in some studies and some populations of abused women (e.g., Black women) may be the result of an interaction among an abuse-triggered chronic stress response and other genetic risk factors for hypertension, often further increased by smoking (Letourneau, Holmes, & Chasedunn-Roark, 1999; Schollenberger et al., 2003).

The increased reported prevalence of allergies, upper respiratory infections, STIs, and urinary tract infections may also be mediated through the complex interactions between the brain and body through direct and/or indirect effects on the central nervous system, immune system, or neuroendocrine-immune pathways. The effects of IPV on immune function may be related to differences in cortisol and cytokine levels, and subsequently on Th cell balance, that occur in relation to the mental health effects of violence, specifically depression and PTSD and comorbid PTSD and depression (A. B. Woods et al., 2005; S. J. Woods et al., 2005). Constantino, Sekula, Rabin, and Stone (2000) demonstrated a significant correlation of depression and *total mitogen response* (i.e., a biological measure of decreased T-cell function) in abused women compared with nonabused women. Unfortunately, there was potential confounding in that investigation because of tobacco use in all the abused women. However, a more recent, better controlled, and larger investigation supported the relationship between compromised immune function measured by leucocytes, lymphocytes, and CD4 cell counts and IPV, mediated by PTSD (S. J. Woods et al., 2005). See Figure 6.1 for the model tested in that study, which helps explain the physical health symptoms and conditions seen in abused women and the interactions of physical and mental health outcomes. Further effects on impaired immune system function in abused women are also likely mediated through the greater prevalence of substance use and abuse, including tobacco, alcohol, and drugs (Gill & Page, 2006; S. J. Woods et al., 2005).

Stress responses may also contribute to the numerous gynecological problems found in battered women. These include autoimmune activation contributing to fibroids, urinary tract infections, and STIs (S. J. Woods et al., 2005).

The chronic pain response seen so often in abused women may well be a combination of the autoimmune system activation and chronic injury. Chronic pain often presents in concert with other symptoms, including fatigue and depression, and this cluster of symptoms is triggered by proinflammatory cytokines (Dantzer, 2004). A well-controlled study of the sickness behavior symptoms of pain–fatigue–depression in a sample of urban

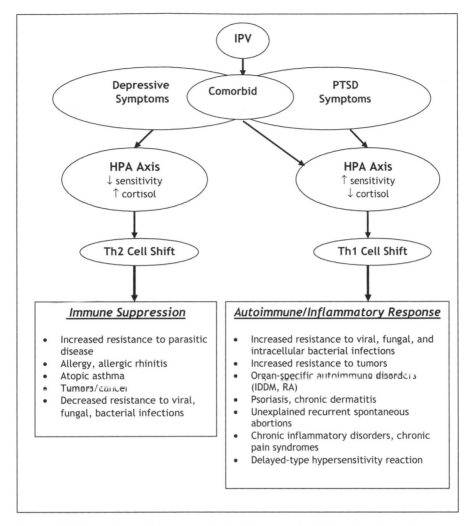

Figure 6.1. Biopsychosocial–immunological framework. IPV = intimate partner violence; PTSD = posttraumatic stress disorder; HPA = hypothalamic–pituitary–adrenocortical axis; Th2 = T helper 2 (Th2) cells; Th1 = T helper 1 (Th1) cells; IDDM = insulin dependent diabetes mellitus; RA = rheumatoid arthritis. From "The Mediation Effect of Posttraumatic Stress Disorder Symptoms on the Relationship of Intimate Partner Violence and IFN-Gamma Levels," by A. B. Woods, G. G. Page, P. O'Campo, L. C. Pugh, D. Ford, and J. C. Campbell, 2005, *American Journal of Community Psychology, 36,* p. 162. Copyright 2005 by Springer Science + Business Media. Reprinted with permission.

primary care patients found that only 10% of nonabused women reported the symptom cluster compared with 45% of women with a history of abuse or current abuse (*p* = .000). In a purposive subsample eliminating women with potential confounders that could medically explain complaints of pain–fatigue–depression, the findings remained and held for all types of abuse—physical, emotional, and sexual. Women with the symptom cluster also had significantly higher mean levels of tumor necrosis factor–alpha (TNF-α; p = .03; A. B. Woods, McKeen, & Page, 2006).

Fibromyalgia, a chronic pain syndrome, is also found more often in abused women. However, the links that have been demonstrated between IPV and fibromyalgia in epidemiological and clinical studies have yet to be explicated physiologically (Alexander et al., 1998; Walker et al., 1997). Studies such as those reviewed earlier are helpful in explaining some of these responses, but much remains to be done in investigating the complex causal pathways by which IPV and IPA affect women's health.

Sexually Transmitted Infections

The causes of increased incidence of STIs among women experiencing IPV or IPA are not known, although a number of plausible mechanisms have been proposed. Forced sex may cause genital injuries that facilitate disease transmission (Liebschutz et al., 2000). In addition, condom use is more difficult to negotiate in violent relationships (Beadnell, Baker, Morrison, & Knox, 2000; Davila & Brackley, 2001; El-Bassel, Gilbert, Rajah, Foleno, & Frye, 2000; Kalichman et al., 1998). A well-controlled study of a nationally representative sample of 973 sexually active dating female adolescents found that, after controlling for sociodemographic factors, number of sexual partners, and history of forced sex, those experiencing current verbal abuse were 56% less likely to use condoms than those not abused (T. A. Roberts, Auinger, & Klein, 2005).

The relationship between high-risk sexual behavior (other than intercourse without condoms) and current or past IPV has also been explored. Behaviors include multiple sexual partners, transactional sex for money or drugs, and sex with high-risk partners (Augenbraun, Wilson, & Allister, 2001; M. Cohen et al., 2000; He, McCoy, Stevens, & Stark, 1998). Although these studies used small convenience samples and cross-sectional designs, significant relationships were found between high-risk sexual behaviors and IPV. Research has also found that men who physically and/or sexually abuse their female partners engaged in more high-risk behaviors than men without such a history (El-Bassel et al., 2001; Neighbors, O'Leary, & Labouvie, 1999; Raj, Silverman, & Amaro, 2004). However, the cross-sectional design of most of the studies precludes drawing conclusions about the causal relationships between violence and disease.

Complications With Pregnancy and Risks for Newborns

How the acute and chronic stress of living with IPV or IPA during pregnancy may affect the pregnancy and neonatal outcomes is not entirely understood. However, increased production of proinflammatory cytokines, especially interleukin (IL)-1β, TNF-α, and interferon (IFN)-γ are important mediators in the cascade of events leading to preterm labor and birth (Farina & Winkelman, 2005; Peltier, 2003). Recent studies have identified significant increased mean levels of the proinflammatory cytokines TNF-α and IFN-γ in women with a history of IPV, although these samples were composed of nonpregnant women (A. B. Woods et al., 2005, 2006). Animal studies have demonstrated structural alterations in the newborn brain, as well as alterations of the hypothalamic pituitary adrenal axis offspring of rodent mothers repeatedly stressed during gestation (Rabin, 1999). More research in this area, incorporating IPV with biological markers of immune function and inflammation, is needed.

Mental Health Effects and Substance Abuse

The mechanism through which IPV leads to mental health problems may seem obvious for conditions such as depression, PTSD, anxiety, phobias, and panic disorders. However, the causal relationship between IPV and substance abuse is less certain. The causes for the increased use of substances in this population of women have not been definitively proven, but some indicators are emerging from studies of women who have experienced a broad range of traumatic experiences. Findings from both longitudinal and cross-sectional studies using causal modeling techniques are beginning to support the notion that trauma precedes substance use rather than the converse (Burnam et al., 1988; Dembo et al., 1987; Grant & Campbell, 1998; Schuck & Widom, 2001). It is likely that major depressive disorder and PTSD mediate the relationship between trauma and substance use. One study directly validated the role of PTSD as a mediator between childhood abuse and adult alcohol use (Epstein, Saunders, Kilpatrick, & Resnick, 1998), and another found depression mediated that relationship between victimization and substance use (Schuck & Widom, 2001). Findings from a longitudinal study of PTSD and drug use show that whereas PTSD increased the risk of drug disorders after exposure to a traumatic event, substance use did not increase the risk of PTSD after a similar event (Chilcoat & Breslau, 1998). A similar study found that having a PTSD diagnosis tripled the odds of a subsequent alcohol-related disorder (Breslau et al., 1998). Kilpatrick, Acierno, Resick, Saunders, and Best's (1997) population-based longitudinal analysis of the relationship between PTSD and substance use found that although existing substance use can lead to increased risk of trauma, and thus increased rates of PTSD, trauma and PTSD preceded the first use of substances. Sullivan and Holt (2008) found that IPV-related PTSD symptoms were significantly associated with substance use. Further research exploring the relationship of substance abuse and PTSD among victims of IPV and IPA is warranted.

More work in this area is needed, but there is strong evidence from large probability samples to support a causal pathway from trauma to PTSD and subsequent substance use in women. The hyperarousal symptoms of PTSD may be dampened by substances, and substance abuse may start out as an effort to self-medicate. The evidence of a relationship between depression and substance abuse is weaker, and the relationships found are possibly explained by the strong degree of comorbidity between PTSD and depression in traumatized women (Kessler et al., 1994; Tolin & Foa, 2006). It is interesting to note that the relationships among trauma, mental health disorders, and substance use are significantly stronger among women than among men (Kessler et al., 1995; MacMillan et al., 2001; Schuck & Widom, 2001; Widom, Weiler, & Cottler, 1999).

IMPLICATIONS FOR PREVENTION AND INTERVENTION

The wide range of health effects associated with IPV serves as a significant impetus for preventing the abuse and for early identification of those at risk of or experiencing either IPV or IPA. To lessen the occurrence and mitigate the negative health effects of IPV and IPA on the well-being of the individuals and families, therapeutic interventions should be instituted on primary and secondary levels. Given the complexity of IPV in relationships, in communities, and in society at large, however, these efforts must be multidimensional.

Primary prevention of IPV and IPA must focus on creating safe environments and establishing behaviors that do not condone IPV or IPA through inaction on community and societal levels. As a health promotion approach, potential benefits of primary prevention include reducing morbidity and mortality, improving quality of life, reducing disparities in IPV and IPA rates by addressing underlying issues, promoting cost-effective use of resources, preventing or decreasing other forms of abuse, and improving health outcomes in known IPV risk areas such as maternal–child health and STIs (L. Cohen, Davis, & Graffunder, 2006).

Given the intergenerational aspect of violent behaviors (Fergusson, Boden, & Horwood, 2006), the long-term mental and physical health effects of witnessing IPV (Bair-Merritt, Blackstone, & Feudtner, 2006), and the association between high-risk behaviors and IPV in adolescents (T. A. Roberts et al., 2005; T. A. Roberts, Klein, & Fisher, 2003; Silverman et al., 2001), prevention of IPV should begin with children. This includes teaching children peaceful conflict resolution skills, respectful communication, and nonbullying behaviors through programs such as the Bullying Prevention Program, endorsed by the Blueprints for Violence Prevention project (Mihalic, Irwin, Elliot, Fagan, & Hansen, 2004). Adolescents can learn healthy relationship skills even before they begin dating, because it has been shown that IPV among adolescents carries with it significant adverse health effects and high-risk behaviors (T. A. Roberts et al., 2005; Silverman et al., 2001). School nurses are well positioned to convey this information through one-on-one interactions or health education classes (Avery-Leaf, Cascardi, O'Leary, & Cano, 1997), but successful programs include schoolwide and community involvement (National Resource Center on Domestic Violence, 2004; Wekerle & Wolfe, 1999; World Health Organization, 2006).

Another approach to primary prevention of IPV is home visitations by community health nurses, which target new mothers, their infants, and the familial setting. In the past, these visitations have primarily taught healthy parenting skills and positive mother–infant interactions, thereby encouraging environments that ensure healthy growth and development of the infant and decreasing the incidence of child maltreatment (Olds et al., 1997; Olds, Henderson, Chamberlin, & Tatelbaum, 1986).

Little research has specifically examined the effect of IPV interventions as part of standardized home visitation protocols, and the results of the major studies that have been done differ. On the one hand, Eckenrode, Ganzel, and Henderson (2000) conducted a study in the 1980s on home visitation interventions that showed a significant decrease in child maltreatment in households with little exposure to IPV. However, treatment effect diminished with the increasing number of IPV incidents reported by the mother, and IPV education and resource referrals were not part of the home visitation protocols. On the other hand, a more recent study by Olds et al. (2004) demonstrated that new mothers visited in their homes by nurses reported less domestic violence in the families, up to 4 years past the birth of their child and 2 years after the visitations were concluded. Therefore, official recommendations for including IPV prevention in home visitation protocols are not possible at this time (Hahn et al., 2003).

Without question, however, these nurses are in unique positions to be able to observe the social and structural environment of their clients, observe familial interactions during the visit, and pick up on subtle indications that IPV or IPA may be present (Evanson, 2006). They must be properly trained on how to identify warning signs and ways to provide support (Evanson, 2006; Tandon, Parillo, Jenkins, & Duggan, 2005), and standard protocols can facilitate the process. Shepard, Elliott, Falk, and Regal (1999) showed that instituting an IPV screening protocol among home-visiting nurses yields higher identification rates, more information sharing, and higher referral. If home-visiting nurses do not include screening for IPV during their sessions and do not intervene to prevent it, an important opportunity for early detection will be passed by and IPV "will probably not be identified until someone has been seriously injured or killed" (Landenburger, Campbell, & Rodriguez, 2004, p. 230).

Primary prevention works to eradicate the problem entirely, but IPV remains prevalent in society. Therefore, most programs to date have focused on secondary or tertiary programs addressing the screening for and the outcomes of IPV. To limit the immediate and long-term health effects of IPV, these interventions are also imperative.

Although the United States Preventive Task Force (2004) found insufficient evidence to recommend universal screening for IPV, other organizations place a priority on this intervention. The Joint Commission on Accreditation of Healthcare Organizations requires accredited hospitals to include methods for identifying, treating, and referring IPV victims in the policies and procedures of their emergency departments and ambulatory settings. Additionally, most of the professional organizations for health care providers endorse screening as a way to identify IPV early on and potentially positively impact health outcomes for their patients. The American Medical Association (1992), the American Academy of Pediatrics (1998), and the American Nurses Association (1991) are among the organizations that have published specific guidelines to encourage and enable their practitioners to incorporate screening and IPV prevention messages into their practices.

Although nurses and other health care providers are well positioned to intercede, lack of proper training of health care providers has been identified as a significant barrier to conducting screenings or even inquiring about IPV and IPA (Waalen, Goodwin, Spitz, Petersen, & Saltzman, 2000). Health care providers who are self-aware of their own perceptions of gender issues and educated on methods to decrease stigma associated with disclosure of IPV and IPA, on effective screening techniques, and on available referral resources can conduct more therapeutic screenings. Such trainings have been evaluated in emergency departments, hospital floors, and primary care settings (Hamberger et al., 2004; Knapp, Dowd, Kennedy, Stallbaumer-Rouyer, & Henderson, 2006; Schoening, Greenwood, McNichols, Heermann, & Agrawal, 2004), after which providers reported raised levels of self-efficacy, comfort, and commitment to include screening as part of their client interactions. By demonstrating respect and interest in the client's well-being as well as providing options, health care providers can give responsive, therapeutic care that meets clients' needs (Chang et al., 2005; Dienemann, Glass, & Hyman, 2005; Zink, Elder, Jacobson, & Klostermann, 2004).

CONCLUSION

Women's health problems associated with IPV have been established by a significant and growing empirical body of research. The problems are certainly serious and widespread, and the associations with IPV may help explain some of the most problematic health disparities between the sexes (e.g., depression) and among racial and ethnic groups (e.g., HIV/AIDS). The economic costs of IPV, which exceed $8.3 billion in direct medical and mental health services as well as lost productivity, place a heavy burden on women, health care providers, and society at large (CDC, 2003; Max, Rice, Finkelstein, Bardwell, & Leadbetter, 2004). This research evidence adds impetus to the policy proposals to use the health care system as a location for prevention efforts and health care professionals as assessors for IPV and IPA and providers of prevention interventions (Chalk & King, 1998; Cohn, Salmon, & Stobo, 2002).

REFERENCES

Alexander, R. W., Bradely, L. A., Alarcon, G. S., Triana-Alexander, M., Aaron, L. A., Alberts, K. R., et al. (1998). Sexual and physical abuse in women with fibromyalgia: Association with outpatient health care utilization and pain medication usage. *Arthritis Care and Research, 11,* 102–115.

American Academy of Pediatrics. (1998). Policy statement: The role of the pediatrician in recognizing and intervening on the behalf of abused women. *Pediatrics, 101,* 1091–1092.

American Medical Association. (1992). *Diagnostic and treatment guidelines on domestic violence.* Chicago: Author.

American Nurses Association. (1991). *Position statement on physical violence against women.* Washington, DC: Author.

Augenbraun, M., Wilson, T. E., & Allister, L. (2001). Domestic violence reported by women attending a sexually transmitted disease clinic. *Sexually Transmitted Diseases, 28,* 143–147.

Avery-Leaf, M. A., Cascardi, M., O'Leary, K. D., & Cano, A. (1997). Efficacy of a dating violence prevention program on attitudes justifying aggression. *Journal of Adolescent Health, 21,* 11–17.

Bachman, R., & Saltzman, L. E. (1995). *Violence against women: Estimates from the redesigned survey* (Publication No. NCJ 154348). Washington, DC: U.S. Department of Justice.

Bair-Merritt, M. H., Blackstone, M., & Feudtner, C. (2006). Physical health outcomes of childhood exposure to intimate partner violence: A systematic review. *Pediatrics, 117,* 278–290.

Ballenger, J. C., Davidson, J. R., Lecrubier, Y., Nutt, D. J., Marshall, R. D., Nemeroff, C. B., et al. (2004). Consensus statement update on posttraumatic stress disorder from the International Consensus Group on Depression and Anxiety. *Journal of Clinical Psychiatry, 65*(Suppl. 1), 55–62.

Beadnell, B., Baker, S. A., Morrison, D. M., & Knox, K. (2000). HIV/STD risk factors for women with violent male partners. *Sex Roles, 42,* 661–689.

Bradley, F., Smith, M., Long, J., & O'Dowd, T. (2002, February 2). Reported frequency of domestic violence: Cross sectional survey of women attending general practice. *BMJ, 324,* 271.

Breslau, N., Kessler, R. C., Chilcoat, H. D., Schultz, L. R., Davis, G. C., & Andreski, P. (1998). Trauma and posttraumatic stress disorder in the community. *Archives of General Psychiatry, 55,* 626–632.

Burnam, M. A., Stein, J. A., Golding, J. M., Siegel, J. M., Sorenson, S. B., Forsythe, A. B., & Telles, C. A. (1988). Sexual assault and mental disorders in a community population. *Journal of Consulting and Clinical Psychology, 56,* 843–850.

Campbell, J. C. (1992). If I can't have you, no one can: Issues of power and control in homicide of female partners. In J. Radford & D. Russell (Eds.), *Femicide: The politics of woman killing* (pp. 99–113). Boston: Twayne.

Campbell, J. C. (2002, April 13). Health consequences of intimate partner violence. *The Lancet, 359*, 1331–1336.

Campbell, J. C., Garcia-Moreno, C., & Sharps, P. W. (2004). Abuse during pregnancy in industrialized and developing countries. *Violence Against Women, 10*, 770–789.

Campbell, J. C., & Lewandowski, L. A. (1997). Mental and physical health effects of intimate partner violence on women and children. *Psychiatric Clinics of North America, 20*, 353–373.

Campbell, J. C., Snow-Jones, A., Dienemann, J., Kub, J., Schollenberger, J., O'Campo, P., & Carlson-Gielen, A. (2002). Intimate partner violence and physical health consequences. *Archives of Internal Medicine, 162*, 1157–1163.

Campbell, J. C., & Soeken, K. (1999). Women's responses to battering over time: An analysis of change. *Journal of Interpersonal Violence, 14*, 21–40.

Campbell, J. C., Webster, D., Koziol-McLain, J., Block, C. R., Campbell, D., Curry, M. A., et al. (2003). Risk factors for femicide in abusive relationships: Results from a multi-site case control study. *American Journal of Public Health, 93*, 1089–1097.

Campbell, J. C., Woods, A. B., Chouaf, K. L., & Parker, B. (2000). Reproductive health consequences of intimate partner violence. *Clinical Nursing Research, 9*, 217–237.

Campbell, R., Greeson, M. R., Bybee, D., & Raja, S. (2008). The co-occurrence of childhood sexual abuse, adult sexual assault, intimate partner violence, and sexual harassment: A meditational model of posttraumatic stress disorder and physical health outcomes. *Journal of Consulting and Clinical Psychology, 76*, 194–207.

Centers for Disease Control and Prevention. (2003). *Costs of intimate partner violence against women in the United States.* Atlanta, GA: Author.

Chalk, R., & King, P. A. (1998). *Violence in families: Assessing prevention and treatment programs.* Washington, DC: National Academies Press.

Chang, J. C., Decker, M. R., Moracco, K. E., Martin, S. L., Petersen, R., & Frasier, P. Y. (2005). Asking about intimate partner violence: Advice from female survivors to health care providers. *Patient Education and Counseling, 59*, 141–147.

Chilcoat, H. D., & Breslau, N. (1998). Posttraumatic stress disorder and drug disorders: Testing causal pathways. *Archives of General Psychiatry, 55*, 913–917.

Cohen, L., Davis, R., & Graffunder, C. (2006). Before it occurs: Primary prevention of intimate partner violence and abuse. In P. Salber & E. Taliaferro (Eds.), *The physician's guide to intimate partner violence and abuse* (pp. 89–100). Volcano, CA: Volcano Press.

Cohen, M., Deamant, C., Barkan, S., Richardson, J., Young, M., Holman, S., et al. (2000). Domestic violence and childhood sexual abuse in HIV-infected women and women at risk for HIV. *American Journal of Public Health, 90*, 560–565.

Cohn, F., Salmon, M. E., & Stobo, J. (2002). *Confronting chronic neglect: The education and training of health care professionals on family violence*. Washington, DC: National Academies Press.

Coid, J., Petruckevitch, A., Chung, W. S., Richardson, J., Moorey, S., & Feder, G. S. (2003). Sexual violence against adult women primary care attenders in east London. *The British Journal of Psychiatry, 183*, 332–339.

Coker, A. L., Davis, K. E., Arias, I., Desai, S., Sanderson, M., & Brandt, H. M. (2002). Physical and mental health effects of intimate partner violence for men and women. *American Journal of Preventive Medicine, 23*, 260–268.

Coker, A. L., Sanderson, M., Fadden, M. K., & Pirisi, L. (2000). Intimate partner violence and cervical neoplasia. *Journal of Women's Health and Gender-Based Medicine, 9*, 1015–1023.

Coker, A. R., Smith, P. H., Bethea, L., King, M. R., & McKeown, R. E. (2000). Physical health consequences of physical and psychological intimate partner violence. *Archives of Family Medicine, 9*, 451–456.

Constantino, R. E., Sekula, L. K., Rabin, B., & Stone, C. (2000). Negative life experiences, depression, and immune function in abused and nonabused women. *Biological Research Nursing, 1*, 190–198.

Dantzer, R. (2004). Cytokine-induced sickness behaviour: A neuroimmune response to activation of innate immunity. *European Journal of Pharmacology, 500*, 399–411.

Davila, Y. R., & Brackley, M. H. (2001). Mexican and Mexican American women in a battered women's shelter: Barriers to condom negotiation for HIV/AIDS prevention. *Issues Mental Health Nursing, 20*, 333–355.

Dearwater, S. R., Coben, J. H., Campbell, J. C., Nah, G., Glass, N., McLoughlin, E., & Bekemeier, B. (1998). Prevalence of intimate partner abuse in women treated at community hospital emergency departments. *The Journal of the American Medical Association, 280*, 433–438.

Dembo, D., Dertke, M., LaVoie, L., Borders, S., Washburn, M., & Schmeidler, J. (1987). Physical abuse, sexual victimization, and illicit drug use: A structural analysis among high risk adolescents. *Journal of Adolescence, 10*, 13–34.

Dienemann, J. A., Boyle, E., Baker, D. G., Resnick, W., Wiederhorn, N., & Campbell, J. C. (2000). Intimate partner abuse among women diagnosed with depression. *Issues in Mental Health Nursing, 21*, 499–513.

Dienemann J. A., Glass, N., & Hyman, R. (2005). Survivor preferences for response to IPV disclosure. *Clinical Nursing Research, 14*, 215–237.

Dunkle, K., Jewkes, R., Brown, R., Gray, G., McIntyre, J., & Harlow, S. (2004, May 1). Gender-based violence, relationship power, and risk of HIV infection in women attending antenatal clinics in South Africa. *The Lancet, 363*, 1415–1421.

Eckenrode, J., Ganzel, B., & Henderson, C. R., Jr. (2000). Preventing child abuse and neglect with a program of nurse home visitation: The limiting effects of domestic violence. *The Journal of the American Medical Association, 284*, 1385–1391.

El-Bassel, N., Fontdevila, J., Gilbert, L., Voisin, D., Richman, B. L., & Pitchell, P. (2001). HIV risks of men in methadone maintenance treatment programs who abuse their intimate partners: A forgotten issue. *Journal of Substance Abuse, 13,* 29–43.

El-Bassel, N., Gilbert, L., Rajah, V., Foleno, A., & Frye, V. (2000). Fear and violence: Raising the HIV stakes. *AIDS Education and Prevention, 12,* 154–170.

Epstein, J. N., Saunders, B. E., Kilpatrick, D. G., Resnick, H. S. (1998). PTSD as a mediator between childhood rape and alcohol use in adult women. *Child Abuse & Neglect, 22,* 223–234.

Evanson, T. A. (2006). Addressing domestic violence through maternal–child health home visiting: What we do and do not know. *Journal of Community Health Nursing, 23,* 95–111.

Farina, L., & Winkelman, C. (2005). A review of the role of proinflammatory cytokines in labor and noninfectious preterm labor. *Biological Research for Nursing, 6,* 230–238.

Fergusson, D. M., Boden, J. M., & Horwood, L. J. (2006). Examining the intergenerational transmission of violence in a New Zealand birth cohort. *Child Abuse & Neglect, 30,* 89–108.

Fonck, K., Els, L., Kidula, N., Ndinya-Achola, J., & Timmerman, M. (2005). Increased risk of HIV in women experiencing physical partner violence in Nairobi, Kenya. *AIDS and Behavior, 9,* 335–339.

Gazmararian, J. A., Lazorick, S., & Spitz, A. M. (1996). Prevalence of violence against pregnant women. *The Journal of the American Medical Association, 275,* 1915–1920.

Gielen, A. C., O'Campo, P., Faden, R. R., & Eke, A. (1997). Women's disclosure of HIV status: Experiences of mistreatment and violence in an urban setting. *Women & Health, 25,* 19–31.

Gielen, A. C., O'Campo, P., Faden, R. R., Kass, N. E., & Xue, X. (1994). Interpersonal conflict and physical violence during the childbearing year. *Social Science & Medicine, 39,* 781–787.

Gill, J., & Page, G. (2006). Psychiatric and physical health ramifications of traumatic events in women. *Issues in Mental Health Nursing, 27,* 711–734.

Glass, N., Dearwater, S., & Campbell, J. (2001). Intimate partner violence screening and intervention: Data from eleven Pennsylvania and California community hospital emergency departments. *Journal of Emergency Nursing, 27,* 141–149.

Glass, N., Laughon, K., Campbell, J., Block, C. R., Hanson, G., Sharps, P. W., & Taliaferro, E. (2007). Non-fatal strangulation is an important risk factor for homicide of women. *The Journal of Emergency Medicine, 35,* 329–335.

Glass, N., Perrin, N., Campbell, J. C., & Soeken, K. (2007). The protective role of tangible support on post-traumatic stress disorder (PTSD) symptoms in urban women survivors of violence. *Research in Nursing and Health, 30,* 558–568.

Golding, J. M. (1999). Intimate partner violence as a risk factor for mental disorders: A meta-analysis. *Journal of Family Violence, 14,* 99–132.

Grant, E. G., & Campbell, J. C. (1998). Abuse, drugs, and crime: Pathways to a vicious cycle. *Journal of Add Nursing, 10,* 15–27.

Greenwood, G. L., Relf, M. V., Huang, B., Pollack, L. M., Canchola, J. A., & Catania, J. A. (2002). Battering victimization among a probability-based sample of men who have sex with men (MSM). *American Journal of Public Health, 92,* 1964–1969.

Hahn, R. A., Bilukha, O. O., Crosby, A., Fullilove, M. T., Liberman, A., Moscicki, E. K., et al. (2003). First reports evaluating the effectiveness of strategies for preventing violence: Early childhood home visitation—Findings from the Task Force on Community Preventive Services. *Morbidity and Mortality Weekly Report, 52*(RR-14), 1–9.

Hall-Smith, P., Moracco, K. E., & Butts, J. (1998). Partner homicide in context. *Homicide Studies, 2,* 400–421.

Hamberger, L. K., Guse, C., Boerger, J., Minsky, D., Pape, D., & Folsom, C. (2004). Evaluation of a health care provider training program to identify and help partner violence victims. *Journal of Family Violence, 19,* 1–11.

Harrykisson, S. D., Rickert, V. I., & Wiemann, C. M. (2002). Prevalence and patterns of intimate partner violence among adolescent mothers during the postpartum period. *Archives of Pediatric Adolescent Medicine, 156,* 325–330.

He, H., McCoy, H. V., Stevens, S. J., & Stark, M. J. (1998). Violence and HIV sexual risk behaviors among female sex partners of male drug users. *Women & Health, 27,* 161–175.

Hedin, L. W., & Janson, P. O. (2000). Domestic violence during pregnancy: The prevalence of physical injuries, substance use, abortions and miscarriages. *Acta Obstetrica Gynecoligica Scandinavia, 79,* 625–630.

Hegarty, K. L., & Bush, R. (2002). Prevalence and associations of partner abuse in women attending general practice: A cross-sectional survey. *Australia New Zealand Journal of Public Health, 26,* 437–442.

Hegarty, K. L., Gunn, J., Chondros, P., & Small, R. (2004, March 13). Association between depression and abuse by partners of women general practice: Descriptive, cross sectional survey. *BMJ, 328,* 621–624.

Hirschfeld, R. M. A. (2001). The comorbidity of major depression and anxiety disorders: Recognition and management in primary care. *Primary Care Companion, Journal of Clinical Psychiatry, 3,* 244–254.

Institute of Medicine. (1997). *The hidden epidemic: Confronting sexually transmitted diseases.* Washington, DC: National Academies Press.

Janssen, P. A., Holt, V. L., Sugg, N. K., Emanuel, I., Critchlow, C. M., & Henderson, A. D. (2003). Intimate partner violence and adverse pregnancy outcomes: A population-based study. *American Journal of Obstetrics & Gynecology, 188,* 1341–1347.

Kalichman, S. C., Williams, E. A., Cherry, C., Belcher, L., & Nachimson, D. (1998). Sexual coercion, domestic violence, and negotiating condom use among low-income African American women. *Journal of Women's Health, 7,* 371–378.

Kessler, R. C., McGonagle, K. A., Zhao, S., Nelson, C. B., Hughes, M., Eshleman, S., et al. (1994). Lifetime and 12-month prevalence of *DSM–III–R* psychiatric disorders in the United States: Results from the National Comorbidity Survey. *Archives of General Psychiatry, 51,* 8–19.

Kessler, R. C., Sonnega, A., Bromet, E., Hughes, M., & Nelson, C. B. (1995). Posttraumatic stress disorder in the National Comorbidity Survey. *Archives of General Psychiatry, 52,* 1048–1060.

Kilpatrick, D. G., Acierno, R., Resick, H. S., Saunders, B. E., & Best, C. L. (1997). A 2-year longitudinal analysis of the relationships between violent assault and substance use in women. *Journal of Consulting and Clinical Psychology, 65,* 834–847.

Knapp, J. F., Dowd, M. D., Kennedy, C. S., Stallbaumer-Rouyer, J., & Henderson, D. P. (2006). Evaluation of a curriculum for intimate partner violence screening in a pediatric emergency department. *Pediatrics, 117,* 110–116.

Koloski, N. A., Talley, N. J., & Boyce, P. M. (2005). A history of abuse in community subjects with irritable bowel syndrome and functional dyspepsia: The role of other psychosocial variables. *International Journal of Gastroenterology, 72,* 86–96.

Kyriacou, D. N., Anglin, D., Taliaferro, E., Stone, S., Tubb, T., Linden, J. A., et al. (1999). Risk factors for injury to women from domestic violence. *The New England Journal of Medicine, 341,* 1892–1898.

Landenburger, K., Campbell, D. W., & Rodriguez, R. (2004). Nursing care of families using violence. In J. Humphreys & J. Campbell (Eds.), *Family violence and nursing practice* (pp. 220–251). Philadelphia: Lippincott Williams & Wilkins.

Letourneau, E. J., Holmes, M., & Chasedunn-Roark, J. (1999). Gynecologic health consequences to victims of interpersonal violence. *Women's Health Issues, 9,* 115–120.

Liebschutz, J. M., Feinman, G., Sullivan, L., Stein, M., & Samet, J. (2000). Physical and sexual abuse in women infected with the human immunodeficiency virus: Increased illness and health care utilization. *Archives of Internal Medicine, 160,* 1659–1664.

Logan, T., Walker, R., Cole, J., & Leukefeld, C. (2002). Victimization and substance abuse among women: Contributing factors, interventions, and implications. *Review of General Psychology, 6,* 325–397.

MacMillan, H. L., Fleming, J. E., Streiner, D. L., Lin, E., Boyle, M. H., Jamieson, E., et al. (2001). Childhood abuse and lifetime psychopathology in a community sample. *American Journal of Psychiatry, 158,* 1878–1883.

Maman, S., Mbwambo, J., Campbell, J. C., Hogan, M., Kilonzo, G. P., Weiss, E., Sweat, M. D. (2002). HIV-1 positive women report more lifetime experiences with violence: Findings from a voluntary HIV-1 counseling and testing clinic in Dar es Salaam, Tanzania. *American Journal of Public Health, 92,* 1331–1337.

Max, W., Rice, D. P., Finkelstein, E., Bardwell, R. A., & Leadbetter, S. (2004). The economic toll of intimate partner violence against women in the United States. *Violence and Victims, 19,* 259–272.

McCauley, J., Kern, D. E., Kolodner, K., Derogatis, L. R., & Bass, E. B. (1998). Relation of low-severity violence to women's health. *Journal of General Internal Medicine, 13,* 687–691.

McCauley, J., Kern, D. E., Kolodner, K., Dill, L., Schroeder, A. F., DeChant, H., et al. (1995). The "battering syndrome": Prevalence and clinical characteristics of domestic violence in primary care internal medicine practices. *Annals of Internal Medicine, 123,* 737–746.

McClane, G. E., Strack, G. B., & Hawley, D. (2001). Violence recognition, management, and prevention: A review of 300 attempted strangulation cases: Part II. Clinical evaluation of the surviving victim. *The Journal of Emergency Medicine, 21,* 311–315.

McFarlane, J., Campbell, J. C., Sharps, P., & Watson, K. (2002). Abuse during pregnancy and femicide: Urgent implications for women's health. *Obstetrics & Gynecology, 100,* 27–36.

McFarlane, J., & Soeken, K. (1999). Weight change of infants age birth to 12 months born to abused women. *Pediatric Nursing, 25,* 19–23.

Mechanic, M. B., Weaver, T. L., & Resick, P. A. (2008). Mental health consequences of intimate partner abuse: A multidimensional assessment of four different forms of abuse. *Violence Against Women, 14,* 634–654.

Mihalic, S., Irwin, K., Elliot, D., Fagan, A., & Hansen, D. (2004). *Blueprints for violence prevention* (Publication No. NCJ 204274). Retrieved January 30, 2008, from http://ojjdp.ncjrs.org/publications/PubAbstract.asp?pubi=11721

Morton, E., Runyan, C. W., Moracco, K. E., & Butts, J. (1998). Partner homicide–suicide involving female homicide victims: A population based study in North Carolina, 1988–1992. *Violence and Victims, 13,* 91–106.

Murphy, C. C., Schei, B., Myhr, T. L., & Du Mont, J. (2001). Abuse: A risk factor for low birth weight? A systematic review and meta-analysis. *Canadian Medical Association Journal, 164,* 1567–1572.

National Resource Center on Domestic Violence. (2004). *Teen dating violence: Overview.* Retrieved January 20, 2008, from http://www.vawnet.org/NRCDVPublications/TAPE/Packets/NRC_TDV.pdf

Neighbors, C. J., O'Leary, A., & Labouvie, E. (1999). Domestically violent and nonviolent male inmates' responses to their partners' requests for condom use: Testing a social-information processing model. *Health Psychology, 18,* 427–431.

O'Campo, P., Kub, J., Woods, A., Garza, M., Jones, S., Gielen, A., et al. (2006). Depression, PTSD, and comorbidity related to intimate partner violence in civilian and military women. *Brief Treatment and Crisis Intervention, 6,* 99–110.

Olds, D. L., Eckenrode, J., Henderson, C. R., Jr., Kitzman, H., Powers, J., Cole, R., et al. (1997). Long-term effects of home visitation on maternal life course and child abuse and neglect: Fifteen-year follow-up of a randomized trial. *The Journal of the American Medical Association, 278,* 637–643.

Olds, D. L., Henderson, C. R., Jr., Chamberlin, R., & Tatelbaum, R. (1986). Preventing child abuse and neglect: A randomized trial of nurse home visitation. *Pediatrics, 78,* 65–78.

Olds, D. L., Robinson, J., Pettitt, L., Luckey, D. W., Holmberg, J., Ng, R. K., et al. (2004). Effects of home visits by paraprofessionals and by nurses: Age 4 follow-up results of a randomized trial. *Pediatrics, 114*, 1560–1568.

Pallitto, C. C., Campbell, J. C., & O'Campo, P. (2006). Is intimate partner violence associated with unintended pregnancy? A review of the literature. *Violence, Trauma, & Abuse, 6*, 217–235.

Paulozzi, L. J., Saltzman, L. E., Thompson, M. P., & Holmgreen, P. (2001). Surveillance for homicide among intimate partners: United States 1981–1998. *Morbidity and Mortality Weekly Report, 50*(SS-3), 1–15.

Payne, S. (2004). Sex, gender, and irritable bowel syndrome: Making the connections. *Gender Medicine, 1*, 18–28.

Peltier, M. R. (2003). Immunology of term and preterm labor. *Reproductive Biology and Endocrinology, 1*, 122–133.

Plichta, S. B., & Abraham, C. (1996). Violence and gynecological health in women < 50 years old. *American Journal of Obstetrics & Gynecology, 174*, 903–907.

Plichta, S. B., & Falik, M. K. (2001). Prevalence of violence and its implications for women's health. *Women's Health Issues, 11*, 244–258.

Rabin, B. S. (1999). *Stress, immune function, and health: The connection.* New York: Wiley.

Raj, A., Silverman, J. G., & Amaro, H. (2004). Abused women report greater male partner risk and gender-based risk for HIV: Findings from a community-based study with Hispanic women. *AIDS Care, 16*, 519–529.

Renker, P. R. (2002). Keep a blank face. I need to tell you what has been happening to me. *The American Journal of Maternal/Child Nursing, 27*, 109–116.

Rice, V. H. (Ed.). (2000). *Handbook of stress, coping, and health: Implications for nursing research, theory, and practice.* Thousand Oaks, CA: Sage.

Roberts, G. L., Williams, G. M., Lawrence, J. M., & Raphael, B. (1998). How does domestic violence affect women's mental health? *Women Health, 28*, 117–129.

Roberts, T. A., Auinger, P., & Klein, J. D. (2005). Intimate partner abuse and the reproductive health of sexually active female adolescents. *Journal of Adolescent Health, 36*, 380–385.

Roberts, T. A., Klein, J. D., & Fisher, S. (2003). Longitudinal effect of intimate partner abuse on high-risk behavior among adolescents. *Archives of Pediatric Adolescent Medicine, 157*, 875–881.

Saltzman, L. E., Fanslow, J. L., McMahon, P. M., & Shelley, G. A. (1999). *Intimate partner violence surveillance: Uniform definitions and recommended data elements* (Version 1.0). Atlanta, GA: Centers for Disease Control and Prevention.

Schiffman, M. H., & Castle, P. (2003). Epidemiologic studies of a necessary causal risk factor: Human papillomavirus infection and cervical neoplasia. *Journal of National Cancer Institute, 95*(6), E2.

Schoening, A. M., Greenwood, J. L., McNichols, J. A., Heermann, J. A., & Agrawal, S. (2004). Effect of an intimate partner violence educational program on the attitudes of nurses. *Journal of Obstetrics, Gynecologic, & Neonatal Nursing, 33*, 572–579.

Schollenberger, J., Campbell, J. C., Sharps, P. W., O'Campo, P., Carlson-Gielen, A., Dienemann, J., & Kub, J. (2003). African American HMO enrollees: Their experiences with partner abuse and its effect on their health and use of medical services. *Violence Against Women, 9*, 599–618.

Schuck, A. M., & Widom, C. S. (2001). Childhood victimization and alcohol symptoms in females: Causal inferences and hypothesized mediators. *Child Abuse & Neglect, 25*, 1069–1092.

Sharps, P. W., Koziol-McLain, J., Campbell, J. C., McFarlane, J., Sachs, C. J., & Xu, X. (2001). Health care provider's missed opportunities for preventing femicide. *Preventive Medicine, 33*, 373–380.

Shepard, M., Elliott, B., Falk, D., & Regal, R. (1999). Public health nurses' responses to domestic violence: A report from the enhanced domestic abuse intervention project. *Public Health Nursing, 16*, 359.

Silverman, J. G., Decker, M. R., Reed, E., & Raj, A. (2005). Intimate partner violence victimization prior to and during pregnancy among women residing in 26 U.S. states: Associations with maternal and neonatal health. *American Journal of Obstetrics & Gynecology, 195*, 140–148.

Silverman, J. G., Raj, A., Mucci, L. A., & Hathaway, J. E. (2001). Dating violence against adolescent girls and associated substance use, unhealthy weight control, sexual risk behavior, pregnancy, and suicidality. *The Journal of the American Medical Association, 286*, 572–579.

Sullivan, T. P., & Holt, L. J. (2008). PTSD symptoms clusters are differentially related to substance use among community women exposed to intimate partner violence. *Journal of Traumatic Stress, 21*, 173–180.

Tandon, S. D., Parillo, K. M., Jenkins, C., & Duggan, A. K. (2005). Formative evaluation of home visitors' role in addressing poor mental health, domestic violence, and substance abuse among low-income pregnant and parenting women. *Maternal and Child Health Journal, 9*, 273–983.

Tolin, D. F., & Foa, E. B. (2006). Sex differences in trauma and posttraumatic stress disorder: A quantitative review of 25 years of research. *Psychological Bulletin, 132*, 959–992.

Turner, C. F., Rogers, S. M., Miller, H. G., Miller, W. C., Gribble, J. N., Chromy, J. R., et al. (2002). Untreated gonococcal and chlamydial infection in a probability sample of adults. *The Journal of the American Medical Association, 287*, 726–733.

United Nations Population Fund. (2005). *State of world population 2005 report.* New York: United Nations.

United States Preventive Services Task Force. (2004). Screening for family and intimate partner violence: Recommendation statement. *Annals of Internal Medicine, 140*, 382–386.

U.S. Department of Justice. (2005). *Family violence statistics: including statistics on strangers and acquaintances.* Retrieved July 7, 2007, from http://www.ojp.usdoj.gov/bjs/pub/pdf/fvs.pdf

Varvaro, F. F., & Lasko, D. L. (1993). Physical abuse as cause of injury in women: Information for orthopaedic nurses. *Orthopaedic Nursing, 12,* 37–41.

Waalen, J., Goodwin, M. M., Spitz, A. M., Petersen, R., & Saltzman, L. E. (2000). Screening for intimate partner violence by health care providers: Barriers and interventions. *American Journal of Preventive Medicine, 19,* 230–237.

Walker, E. A., Keegan, D., Gardner, G., Sullivan, M., Bernstein, D. P., & Katon, W. J. (1997). Psychosocial factors in fibromyalgia compared with rheumatoid arthritis: II. Sexual, physical, and emotional abuse and neglect. *Psychosomatic Medicine, 59,* 572–577.

Wekerle, C., & Wolfe, D. A. (1999). Dating violence in mid-adolescence: Theory, significance, and emerging prevention initiatives. *Clinical Psychology Review, 19,* 435–456.

Whetten, K., Leserman, J., Lowe, K., Stangl, D., Thielman, N., Swartz, M., et al. (2006). Prevalence of childhood sexual abuse and physical trauma in an HIV-positive sample from the deep South. *American Journal of Public Health, 96,* 1028–1030.

Widom, C. S., Weiler, B. L., & Cottler, L. B. (1999). Childhood victimization and drug abuse: A comparison of prospective and retrospective findings. *Journal of Consulting and Clinical Psychology, 67,* 867–880.

Woods, A. B., McKeen, C., & Page, G. G. (2006, October). *Pain–fatigue–depression symptom clusters and TNF-α levels in abused women: A biological explanation of somatization.* Paper presented at the biennial meeting of the National State of the Science in Nursing Research, Washington, DC.

Woods, A. B., Page, G. G., O'Campo, P., Pugh, L. C., Ford, D., & Campbell, J. C. (2005). The mediation effect of posttraumatic stress disorder symptoms on the relationship of intimate partner violence and IFN-gamma levels. *American Journal of Community Psychology, 36,* 159–175.

Woods, S. J. (2000). Prevalence and patterns of posttraumatic stress disorder in abused and postabused women. *Issues Mental Health Nursing, 21,* 309–324.

Woods, S. J., Wineman, M., Page, G. G., Hall, R. J., Alexander, T. S., & Campbell, J. C. (2005). Predicting immune status in women from PTSD and childhood and adult violence. *Advances in Nursing Science, 28,* 306–319.

World Health Organization. (2006). *Recommendations.* Retrieved January 20, 2008, from http://www.who.int/gender/violence/who_multicountry_study/summary_report/chapter6

Wyatt, G. E., Myers, H. F., Williams, J. K., Kitchen, C. R., Loeb, T., Carmona, J. V., et al. (2002). Does a history of trauma contribute to HIV risk for women of color? Implications for prevention and policy. *American Journal of Public Health, 92,* 660–665.

Zink, T., Elder, N., Jacobson, J., & Klostermann, B. (2004). Medical management of intimate partner violence considering the stages of change: Precontemplation and contemplation. *Annals of Family Medicine, 2,* 231–239.

II

PREVENTION AND INTERVENTION

7

PRIMARY PREVENTION OF ADOLESCENT DATING ABUSE PERPETRATION: WHEN TO BEGIN, WHOM TO TARGET, AND HOW TO DO IT

VANGIE A. FOSHEE AND HEATHE LUZ McNAUGHTON REYES

Romantic relationships play an important role in adolescent development. They influence sexuality, intimacy, and identity development; provide social support; influence development of secure attachment; facilitate partner sorting and selection; and influence transformations in family and peer relationships (Bouchey & Furman, 2003; Carver, Joyner, & Udry, 2003; Collins, 2003; Erikson, 1968; Fitch & Adams, 1983; Furman & Shaffer, 2003; Giordano, 2003; Hazan & Shaver, 1987; Koch, 1993; McDaniel, 1969). Through dating, adolescents learn responsibility and cooperation, skills in communicating and interacting with others, and loyalty, trust, and respect. For most adolescents, romantic relationships facilitate healthy development (Furman & Shaffer, 2003); however, for some, the experiences may be detrimental to development. When violence and abuse are part of the romantic relationship, they can interfere with the developmental tasks of adolescents (Bouchey & Furman, 2003; Erikson, 1968; Furman & Flanagan, 1997), dis-

141

tort perceptions of normative behaviors and become inappropriate guides for evaluating future relationships, and have negative psychological and physical consequences (Ackard & Neumark-Sztainer, 2002; Decker, Silverman, & Raj, 2005; Foshee, 1996; Roberts, Auinger, & Klein, 2005; Roberts, Klein, & Fisher, 2003; Silverman, Raj, & Clements, 2004; Silverman, Raj, Mucci, & Hathaway, 2001).

Unfortunately, violence and abuse are prevalent in adolescent romantic relationships. Between 11% and 41% of adolescents report using some form of physical violence against their dating partners (Avery-Leaf, Cascardi, O'Leary, & Cano, 1997; Bennett & Fineran, 1998; Brendgen, Vitaro, Tremblay, & Lavoie, 2001; Cascardi, Avery-Leaf, O'Leary, & Smith Slep, 1999; Chapple, 2003; Foshee, 1996; Gorman-Smith, Tolan, Shiedow, & Henry, 2001; Kinsfogel & Grych, 2004; Malik, Sorenson, & Aneshensel, 1997; O'Keefe, 1997; O'Keeffe, Brockopp, & Chew, 1986; O'Leary & Smith Slep, 2003; Ozer, Tschann, Pasch, & Flores, 2004; Pflieger & Vazsonyi, 2006; Schwartz, O'Leary, & Kendziora, 1997; Simons, Lin, & Gordon, 1998; Watson, Cascardi, Avery-Leaf, & O'Leary, 2001; Wolfe, Scott, Wekerle, & Pittman, 2001). Furthermore, between 4% and 14% of adolescents report using forms of violence against dating partners that are likely to result in serious injury, such as hitting a partner with an object, beating up a partner, and using a knife or gun against a partner (Coker, Smith, McKeown, & King, 2000; Foshee, 1996; Gorman-Smith et al., 2001; J. P. Smith & Williams, 1992). The longitudinal studies that would be required to determine whether dating violence perpetration during adolescence is a predictor of adult domestic violence perpetration have not been conducted. However, it is likely that patterns of abuse set during adolescence continue with adult partners. Thus, intervening to prevent dating violence during adolescence may prevent not only detrimental psychological, physical, and developmental consequences for adolescents but also adult partner violence.

In this chapter, we describe considerations in the primary prevention of adolescent dating abuse perpetration. Described as the cornerstone of good public health (National Research Council, 2001), *primary prevention* has been defined as prevention of a disease or problem before it occurs (Commission on Chronic Illness, 1957). This simple definition, however, introduces many complications. For example, defining when a problem occurs is somewhat subjective. Thus, primary prevention of dating abuse could focus on preventing the first disrespectful dating interaction, behavioral precursors to dating abuse such as bullying and aggression against peers, the first actual act of physical violence against a date, or the negative outcomes from violence such as injury. For the purposes of this chapter, we define *primary prevention* broadly in that we consider appropriate approaches for preventing each of these kinds of outcomes.

The key challenges to primary prevention are knowing when to begin, whom to target, and how to do it (Johnson, 2002). This chapter is organized by those challenges. We describe considerations that go into identifying appropriate ages to target for primary prevention; examine Gordon's (1983, 1987) prevention categories of universal, selective, and indicated and their implications for selecting specific populations to target for prevention; and present findings related to predictors of adolescent dating violence that can be targeted for prevention efforts. We also provide a summary of results from randomized trials of dating violence prevention programs, and we draw from lessons learned over the long and rich history of primary prevention of other adolescent problem behaviors such as substance use, delinquency, and risky sexual behaviors. We conclude with recommendations for future prevention research in the area of adolescent dating abuse.

Throughout the chapter, we review the findings of others and present findings from two of adolescent dating violence studies: the Safe Dates study and the Linkages study. The Safe Dates study was a randomized controlled trial with six waves of data testing the effects of a school-based intervention on the prevention of adolescent dating abuse in a rural North Carolina county (Foshee, Bauman, et al., 2005; Foshee et al., 1998, 2000, 2004). The Linkages study involved collecting seven waves of data on adolescent problem behaviors and contexts of influence with a cohort of 5,220 adolescents who were initially in Grades 6, 7, and 8 from three counties in North Carolina.

WHEN TO BEGIN

In the sections that follow, we describe considerations when timing prevention efforts around the time of dating and when timing prevention efforts prior to dating.

Rationale for Beginning Around the Time of Dating

In *Principles of Effective Prevention Programs*, Nation et al. (2003) emphasized the importance of appropriately timing primary prevention so that interventions are enacted at an age when the topic is relevant but before the problem sets in. Identifying that window for primary prevention of dating violence is particularly challenging because the ages at which dating-related issues become relevant vary considerably, and for many adolescents dating-related issues become relevant when dating violence begins.

During middle school, which typically encompasses Grades 6, 7, and 8, interests in dating generally emerge. Approximately 47.4% of eighth graders (13–14 years old) completing the 2003 Monitoring the Future survey indicated that they had dated (Child Trends Databank, n.d.). In the National Longitudinal Study of Adolescent Health, 55% of 12-year-olds, 30.0% of 13-year-olds, and 44% of 14-year-olds indicated that they had had a special romantic relationship with someone in the previous 18 months (Carver et al.,

2003). Approximately 65.5% of the eighth graders in the Safe Dates study and 56.0% of the eighth graders in the Linkages study reported having been on a date. Zimmer-Gembeck, Siebenbruner, and Collins (2001) found that 25% of girls reported having first dated when they were younger than 13 years old, and Connolly, Pepler, Craig, and Taradash (2000) found that adolescents on average reported initiating dating activities around age 11. Variations in the prevalence of dating and romantic relationship across studies are in part due to variations in definitions of dating and romantic relationships. Although formal dating, when one individual goes out with another individual, has decreased among teens since the 1990s (Child Trends Databank, n.d.), a substantial number of middle school adolescents report informal dating or going out in mixed-sex groups that include a person of romantic interest to the adolescent (Connolly et al., 2000; Feiring & Furman, 2000). These mixed-sex groupings progress during adolescence to pairing off within the group and then to individuals going on a date with another individual (Connolly et al., 2000; Feiring & Furman, 2000). Teens in 10th grade report interacting more with their dating partners than with their siblings, peers, and parents (Laursen & Williams, 1997).

Although dating interests generally emerge in middle school, because of the tremendous variation in the timing of pubertal and cognitive development during adolescence, the age at which dating is perceived as relevant varies substantially across individuals who are the same age. Schools are common locales for dating violence prevention programs, and in any grade, but particularly in the middle school grades, there is variation in the perceived relevance of the topic, which introduces a challenge for programming. We are currently evaluating a family-based program to prevent adolescent dating violence, targeted at parents of 13- to 15-year-old adolescents. However, recruitment of families into the trial is difficult for families with 13-year-old boys because many parents indicate that their son is not yet interested in issues related to dating and they perceive him as too immature for the program. This has not been an issue in recruiting families of 13-year-old girls or families of 14- to 15-year-old girls or boys.

Although topics such as dating violence become relevant for many adolescents during middle school, some evidence suggests that dating violence is already occurring then. A few adolescent dating violence studies have included middle school age adolescents (Bennett & Fineran, 1998; Carlson, 1990; Foshee, 1996), but none have reported prevalence estimates separately for these adolescents. However, we have been able to separate out prevalence estimates for middle school age adolescents in the Linkages and Safe Dates studies. In the Linkages study, 7% of sixth graders, 11.12% of seventh graders, and 11.32% of the eighth graders indicated that they had hit someone they were dating during the previous 3 months. In the Safe Dates data from eighth graders, 34% reported being a perpetrator of psychological dating abuse, 11.86% reported being a perpetrator of moderate levels of physical dating violence, 4.34% reported being a perpetrator of severe forms of physical dating violence, and 2.33% reported being a perpetrator of sexual dating violence.

In addition to point estimates of dating abuse prevalence, trajectories of dating abuse development across adolescence can inform the selection of appropriate ages to begin primary prevention efforts. Using Safe Dates data, random coefficient models of the trajectories from ages 13 to 19 for each type of dating abuse perpetration were computed and tested for linear and quadratic slopes (Foshee et al., in press). The typical pattern of development for psychological abuse was linear and positive, indicating that among adolescents 13 to 19 years old, the use of psychological dating abuse increased over time. The typical pattern of development for moderate physical, severe physical, and sexual dating abuse perpetration was quadratic and negative, indicating that the mean trajectory of each of these increased to a certain peak age and then declined. The peak age for moderate physical dating abuse was 17.1 years (standard error [SE] = 0.81; confidence interval [CI] = 15.50–18.69); the peak age for severe physical dating abuse was 16.3 years (SE = 0.52; CI = 15.26–17.28); and the peak age for sexual dating abuse was 16.3 years (SE = 0.57; CI = 15.22–17.46).

These prevalence and trajectory findings suggest that an appropriate time to begin primary prevention of dating violence is around age 13 or in the eighth grade. This is an age when dating-related topics are relevant for most adolescents and yet most have not experienced dating abuse. Also, early adolescents enjoy relatively plastic or modifiable relationships, and this plasticity decreases the further they advance in the developmental process (Sherrod, Busch-Rossnagel, & Fisher, 2003). Thus, interventions during earlier periods of development may have proportionally greater effects than interventions at later periods (O'Connor, 2003).

Primary Prevention Programs to Address Aggression Before the Time of Dating

Some authors have suggested that strategies for preventing dating violence should begin earlier than adolescence (Cascardi & Avery-Leaf, 2000; Connolly et al., 2000; Wolfe & Jaffe, 1999). Cascardi and Avery-Leaf (2000), for example, suggested that the primary prevention of dating violence among adolescents should begin with efforts targeted at younger children to prevent possible behavioral precursors to dating violence, such as bullying and sexual harassment. Unfortunately, few studies have examined the links between bullying or sexual harassment during childhood or early adolescence and later dating violence. An exception is the study by Connolly et al. (2000), who proposed that a bully's use of aggression to assert dominance and power would generalize to romantic relationships. In their sample of adolescents in Grades 5 through 8, bullies started dating earlier than nonbullies; participated in more types of dating activities; spent more time outside of school with other-sex friends; were more likely to have a current boyfriend or girlfriend; perceived their relationship with their boyfriend or girlfriend as less intimate, affectionate, and durable; were more likely to engage in undesirable activities to keep a boyfriend or girlfriend; and perceived dating relationships as less equitable in relative power. Also, bullies were more likely than nonbullies to be perpetrators and victims of social and physical dating aggression, although the sample for these analyses was very small. On the basis of these findings, Connolly et al. suggested instituting bullying prevention programs as early as elementary grades, when bullying behaviors are just emerging, as a way of preventing dating abuse.

A number of longitudinal studies have found that aggression toward peers by younger boys predicted dating violence (Brendgen et al., 2001; Capaldi & Clark, 1998; Herrenkohl et al., 2004; Lavoie et al., 2002; Simons et al., 1998) and adult spouse or partner abuse (Andrews, Foster, Capaldi, & Hops, 2000; Capaldi, Dishion, Stoolmiller, & Yoerger, 2001; Farrington, 1991; Herrenkohl et al., 2004). Thus, efforts at preventing childhood aggression have been proposed as mechanisms for preventing adolescent dating violence and adult partner violence. Although a number of studies have assessed the effects of aggression prevention programs for school-age children (Thorton, Craft, Dahlberg, Lynch, & Baer, 2000; Tolan & Guerra, 1994; U.S. Department of Health and Human Services, 2001; D. B. Wilson, Gottfredson, & Najaka, 2001; S. J. Wilson, Lipsey, & Derzon, 2003), none have assessed the effectiveness of those programs in preventing dating abuse. However, as the children in those studies become adolescents, assessments may become available of the impact of the general aggression prevention programs on dating abuse prevention.

Given the links noted between being abused as a child and perpetrating partner abuse as an adolescent (Bank & Burraston, 2001; J. P. Smith & Williams, 1992) and an adult (Ehrensaft et al., 2003; Herrenkohl et al., 2004; Magdol, Moffitt, Caspi, & Silva, 1998; D. Smith, 1999), and the protective effects of parental closeness, monitoring, and supervision on partner abuse by adolescents (Brendgen et al., 2001; Capaldi & Clark, 1998; Capaldi & Gorman-Smith, 2003; Chapple, 2003; Lavoie et al., 2002; Pflieger & Vazsonyi, 2006) and adults (Ehrensaft et al., 2003), some authors suggest that adolescent dating abuse prevention should begin during infancy and young childhood with programs to teach parenting skills and home visitation programs for new parents. Again, however, although those programs have been found to be effective in preventing childhood aggression (Dahlberg, 1998; Greene, 1998; Hawkins, Von Cleve, & Catalano, 1991; Kellermann, Fuqua-Whitley, Rivara, & Mercy, 1998; Lally, Mangione, & Honig, 1988; Olds et al., 1999; Reese, Vera, Simon, & Ikeda, 2000; Webster-Stratton & Hammond, 1997), their effectiveness in preventing adolescent dating abuse has not yet been determined.

WHOM TO TARGET

A primary consideration in prevention programming is whom to target for intervention. Gordon's (1983) operational classification of disease prevention is a useful framework for considering whom to target in the primary prevention of dating violence. Gordon proposed three categories of prevention efforts—universal, selective, and indicated—based on the population groups to whom the intervention is targeted and the risk to a person of getting a disease, weighed against the cost, risk, and discomfort of the intervention (Mrazek & Haggerty, 1994). Universal interventions can be advocated for a general population because the benefits of the intervention outweigh the human and economic costs and risks of the intervention for all. Selective interventions are designed for groups whose risk is above average, based primarily on demographic characteristics, and for them the intervention approach used has a more favorable cost–benefit ratio than if the approach were used with a general population. Indicated programs are designed for individuals or groups who are at an even higher risk, and again for them the intervention approach used has a more favorable cost–benefit ratio than if the approach were used with a general population or a selected high-risk sample. Gordon considered all three of these approaches to be prevention approaches in that they are enacted with individuals "who are not, at the time, suffering from any discomfort or disability due to the disease or condition being prevented" (p. 108).

Gordon's (1983) categories suggest that different intervention content and approaches should be used in universal, selective, and indicated dating abuse prevention programs. All of the adolescent dating abuse prevention programs that have been evaluated to date (Avery-Leaf et al., 1997; Feltey, Ainslie, & Geib, 1991; Foshee, Bauman, et al., 2005; Foshee et al., 1998, 2000, 2004; Hilton, Harris, Rice, Krans, & Lavigne, 1998; Jaffe, Sudermann, Reitzel, & Killip, 1992; Jones, 1991; Krajewski, Rybarik, Dosch, & Gilmore, 1996; Lavoie, Vezina, Piche, & Boivin, 1995; Macgowan, 1997; Weisz & Black, 2001) except for one (Wolfe et al., 1996) met Gordon's first criterion for universal programs in that they were implemented in schools for the general population of adolescents, not those with special high-risk characteristics. Whether they met the second criterion for universal programs—that the benefits of the intervention outweigh the costs and risks of the intervention for all—is unknown because little attention has been given to cost–benefit analysis of universal dating violence prevention programs. Thus, little information is available to determine whether the content delivered in these programs is in any way harmful to those at high risk of dating violence or those already involved in abusive relationships. A primary advantage of universal programs is that because large segments of the population are targeted, effects on population-level prevalence are more likely than with selective or indicated programs (Rose, 1992). Another is that delivery of the program is easier because large, already-existing groups are targeted. However, a disadvantage of universal dating abuse prevention programs is that costly resources go into delivering an intervention to many adolescents who would never have used violence against a partner anyway.

Gordon (1983) identified populations for selective interventions primarily on the basis of demographic characteristics that put individuals at risk. Strong associations have been noted between demographic characteristics and various medical conditions and diseases, but findings from studies examining associations between demographic characteristics and adolescent dating violence perpetration are not particularly helpful for identifying high-risk populations for selective dating abuse prevention interventions. Most adolescent dating abuse studies have found that the prevalence of dating abuse perpetration was either nearly the same for boys and girls (Bennett & Fineran, 1998; Capaldi & Crosby, 1997; Johnson-Reid & Bivens, 1999; O'Keeffe et al., 1986; Pflieger & Vazsonyi, 2006; Symons, Groër, Kepler-Youngblood, & Slater, 1994; Wolfe, Wekerle, Reitzel-Jaffe, & Lefebvre, 1998) or greater for girls than boys (Avery-Leaf et al., 1997; Carlson, 1990; Cascardi et al., 1999; Chapple, 2003; Chase, Treboux, O'Leary, & Strassberg, 1998; Foshee, 1996; Hird, 2000; Malik et al., 1997; McCloskey & Lichter, 2003; O'Keefe, 1997; O'Leary & Smith Slep, 2003; Ozer et al., 2004; Plass & Gessner, 1983; Schwartz et al., 1997; Wekerle et al., 2001). These findings suggest that it is appropriate for universal programs aimed at the prevention of dating abuse perpetration to target both boys and girls and that there is not strong evidence for focusing selective interventions on a specific gender. Almost all of the studies that have assessed the association between socioeconomic status (SES) and adolescent dating violence perpetration reported no significant association (Chapple, 2003; Foshee, Linder, MacDougall, & Bangdiwala, 2001; Lavoie et al., 2002; Malik et al., 1997; O'Keefe, 1997; O'Keeffe et al., 1986; Simons et al., 1998), although in several of those studies, there was little variation in SES (Chapple, 2003; Lavoie et al., 2002; Simons et al., 1998). A number of studies have found that after controlling for SES, dating violence perpetration is greatest among Black adolescents, followed by Latino and White adolescents, and finally Asian adolescents (Chapple, 2003; Foshee, Ennett, Bauman, Benefield, & Suchindran, 2005; Malik et al., 1997; O'Keefe, 1997; O'Keeffe et al., 1986; Plass & Gessner, 1983). These findings mirror those from studies of adult intimate partner violence (Field & Caetano, 2004). A number of studies have found that Latino students are at particularly high risk of perpetrating dating violence (Borowsky, Hogan, & Ireland, 1997; Malik et al., 1997; O'Keefe, 1997; O'Keeffe et al., 1986). Significant race differences were found in the Linkages study in the perpetration of psychological and physical dating abuse within the previous 3 months, with more of both types of perpetration by Latino (19.90% and 6.92%, respectively) than Black (18.55% and 2.60%, respectively) or White (15.01% and 27.71%, respectively) adolescents. Thus, more consistent findings have been noted when considering racial/ethnic differences in dating abuse perpetration; however, enough inconsistencies in findings and questions about adequate statistical controls for confounding variables exist to make targeting selective dating abuse prevention on the basis of race/ethnicity tenuous. Furthermore, there have been few dating abuse prevention programs designed for specific racial/ethnic groups.

Indicated programs are targeted at populations at particularly high risk (Gordon, 1983). Many risk factors for dating abuse have been identified, but it would be expensive and difficult to identify adolescents with some of those risk factors. For example, having attitudes that are accepting of dating abuse is a risk factor for dating abuse by boys (Foshee et al., 2001). However, identifying adolescent boys with attitudes that are accepting of dating abuse would involve assessing attitudes about the acceptability of dating abuse in some defined population, identifying a cut point on a scale that would define acceptance of dating abuse, and contacting only those boys whose scores met the cut-point definition and inviting them to be in the intervention, each of which could be logistically difficult, expensive, and ethically questionable. Using psychological abuse against a partner is a precursor to using physical dating violence (O'Leary & Smith Slep, 2003; Ozer et al., 2004), but again, identifying a group of adolescents who are psychologically abusing their dates would be difficult and expensive.

One risk factor that can be easily used to identify groups to target for indicated dating abuse prevention programs is exposure to child abuse and maltreatment. And, in fact, the only dating abuse prevention program that is not a universal program targeted adolescents who had been victims of maltreatment identified through Child Protective Services agencies (Wolfe et al., 2003). Several studies have supported the view that corporal punishment, child abuse, and maltreatment are associated with dating abuse perpetration. Corporal punishment has been found to correlate with (Foshee, Bauman, & Linder, 1999) and predict (Simons et al., 1998) dating abuse perpetration. Also, some researchers have found that child abuse by parents was correlated with dating violence perpetration (Bank & Burraston, 2001; J. P. Smith & Williams, 1992), although others did not find an association (Gray & Foshee, 1997; Malik et al., 1997; O'Keefe, 1997; O'Keeffe et al., 1986). In a longitudinal study limited to boys, harsh parenting practices experienced when the boys were 10 to 12 years old predicted dating violence perpetration by the boys when they were 16 to 17 (Lavoie et al., 2002). Several studies have also found that maltreatment, defined by a composite of a variety of family violence indicators (e.g., exposure to domestic violence, corporal punishment, child abuse, sexual abuse), was positively correlated with dating abuse perpetration (Schwartz et al., 1997; Wekerle et al., 2001; Wolfe et al., 1998, 2001; Wolfe, Wekerle, Scott, Straatman, & Grasley, 2004). However, although evidence shows that children who have been maltreated are at greater risk of using violence against their dating partners, many adolescents who have never been maltreated also use violence against their dating partners, and those adolescents would be overlooked in an indicated program targeted at maltreated children. Therefore, the potential impact of such programs on population-level prevalence is minimal (Rose, 1992). However, an advantage of indicated programs is that by targeting more homogeneous groups, program materials can be tailored so that they are more meaningful to participants (Thorton et al., 2000).

HOW TO DO IT

In the sections that follow, we discuss how to do adolescent dating abuse prevention programming by describing predictors of dating abuse that can be targeted for change in programs, identifying evidenced-based dating abuse prevention programs, and describing how lessons learned from efforts at preventing other adolescent health risk behaviors (e.g., substance use, aggression against peers) can inform the development of dating abuse prevention programs.

Targeting Precursors for Change

Primary prevention approaches target for change factors that cause a particular problem behavior or disease in order to break the chain of causation (Gordon, 1987; Seidman, 1987). These causes then become the mediating variables, or the process through which the intervention is expected to lead to changes in outcomes. However, identifying the causes of adolescent dating violence perpetration is a challenge. Although the soundest evidence for causation comes from experiments, it is impractical and indeed unethical to conduct experiments that manipulate factors to induce dating violence. Thus, to identify factors to target for change, researchers and practitioners are forced to depend on findings from survey research. Unfortunately, most studies on adolescent dating violence have used cross-sectional survey designs that cannot distinguish causes from consequences. Longitudinal survey designs provide better evidence for causation, as long as the analyses control for the temporality of relationships. However, there have been relatively few longitudinal studies of adolescent dating abuse perpetration (Arriaga & Foshee, 2004; Bank & Burraston, 2001; Brendgen et al., 2001; Capaldi & Clark, 1998; Capaldi et al., 2001; Foshee, Ennett, et al., 2005; Foshee et al., 2001; Gorman-Smith et al., 2001; Lavoie et al., 2002; Ozer et al., 2004; Simons et al., 1998; Wolfe et al., 2004), and most of those studies have been with boys only (Brendgen et al., 2001; Capaldi & Clark, 1998; Capaldi et al., 2001; Gorman-Smith et al., 2001; Lavoie et al., 2002; Simons et al., 1998), despite the strong evidence that girls also perpetrate dating violence.

Although one can identify risk factors to target for change from these longitudinal studies, one needs to be aware of the limitations of those studies. For example, the causes of behavior are complex, often involving interactions of multiple biological, intrapersonal, interpersonal, social, and environmental factors (Johnson, 2002; Seidman, 1987), and this level of complexity is not captured well in survey research. This is especially true for adolescent dating violence survey research that has focused primarily on examination of interpersonal and intrapersonal risk factors, with little attention to risk factors at higher levels of the ecological model or interactions between factors at multiple levels. Despite these limitations, however, the closest one can come to identifying causes of dating violence that can be targeted for change is to rely on findings from these longitudinal studies.

Longitudinal Predictors of Dating Abuse Perpetration

Factors that have been found to predict perpetration of dating abuse by boys include trauma symptoms (Wolfe et al., 2004); late childhood and early adolescent antisocial behavior, delinquency, and substance abuse (Capaldi & Clark, 1998; Lavoie et al., 2002; Simons et al., 1998); attitudes that are accepting of dating abuse (Foshee et al., 2001); having a friend involved as a victim or perpetrator of dating abuse (Arriaga & Foshee, 2004); exposure to harsh parenting practices (Lavoie et al., 2002; Simons et al., 1998); exposure to inconsistent discipline (Bank & Burraston, 2001; Simons et al., 1998); and a lack of parental supervision (Brendgen et al., 2001; Capaldi & Clark, 1998; Foshee et al., 2001; Lavoie et al., 2002), monitoring (Simons et al., 1998), and warmth (Simons et al., 1998). Brendgen et al. (2001) found that reactive aggression in early adolescence predicted later dating abuse perpetration by boys, but maternal warmth buffered those effects (Brendgen et al., 2001). In Foshee, Ennett, et al. (2005), the associations between exposure to various types of family violence and initiation of dating violence varied by subgroups based on race, SES, and family structure. For example, corporal punishment was significantly associated with dating violence initiation among Black adolescents whose mothers had low levels of education but not among Black adolescents whose mothers had higher levels of education or among White adolescents with parents at any education level. Being hit with the intention of harm was significantly associated with dating violence initiation among Black adolescents living in two-parent households but not among Black adolescents living in single-parent households or among White adolescents in any family structure. And witnessing parental violence was significantly associated with dating violence initiation among Black adolescents living in single-parent households but not among Black adolescents living in two-parent households or among White adolescents living in any family structure. These associations were found for both boys and girls.

The only factors found to predict dating abuse perpetration by girls are trauma symptoms (especially anger; Wolfe et al., 2004), alcohol use (Foshee et al., 2001), and having a friend involved, whether as a victim or a perpetrator, in dating abuse (Arriaga & Foshee, 2004; Foshee et al., 2001). As previously noted, among some subgroups of Black girls, exposure to family violence predicted dating abuse perpetration (Foshee, Ennett, et al., 2005).

These findings suggest three foci for prevention interventions for both boys and girls. The first focus is changing the family context by promoting improved parenting skills related to discipline, supervision, and monitoring; encouraging parental warmth toward the child or adolescent; and decreasing child and adolescent exposure to harsh parenting practices and domestic violence. Trauma symptoms were also predictors for both boys and girls, but interventions focused on changing the family context would likely decrease trauma symptoms as well. The second focus for prevention of dating abuse perpetration is to prevent behavioral precursors to dating violence, such as antisocial behaviors, aggression, delinquency, and alcohol and substance use. The third area for intervention is the peer group context. Having a friend involved in dating abuse, whether as a victim or a perpetrator, predicted dating abuse perpetration for both boys and girls, and because the study designs were longitudinal and appropriately controlled for the temporality of relationships, it can be concluded that adolescents became perpetrators of dating abuse after rather than before their friend's involvement in dating abuse.

Evaluations of Adolescent Dating Abuse Prevention Programs

The directions for programs suggested by the findings from these longitudinal studies differ from the adolescent dating abuse prevention programs that have actually been implemented and evaluated. To date, 12 adolescent dating abuse prevention programs have been evaluated and the results reported in peer-reviewed journals or books (Avery-Leaf et al., 1997; Feltey et al., 1991; Foshee, Bauman, et al., 2005; Foshee et al., 1998, 2000, 2004; Hilton et al., 1998; Jaffe et al., 1992; Jaycox et al., 2006; Jones, 1991; Krajewski et al., 1996; Lavoie et al., 1995; Macgowan, 1997; Weisz & Black, 2001; Wolfe et al., 2003). All of the programs were developed before the first longitudinal studies of adolescent dating abuse were published in 1998, and thus program content was developed based primarily on correlates found in cross-sectional studies, often adult domestic violence studies or studies of dating abuse among college students. All of the programs evaluated except for one, the Youth Relationships Project (Wolfe et al., 1996), were school-based programs, and the most common risk factors targeted for change were knowledge and attitudes about dating abuse. None of these programs focused on changing the family or peer context or decreasing behavioral precursors to dating abuse.

Many of the evaluations of adolescent dating abuse prevention programs have been hampered by several factors: (a) use of poor designs that did not control for common threats to internal validity; (b) measurement of knowledge, attitudes, and intentions, not actual dating abuse behaviors;

(c) lack of consistency between program goals and the constructs measured; (d) short follow-up periods; (e) use of measures with poor psychometric properties; (f) substantial attrition; and (g) limited generalizability. Theoretically or empirically based mediators of program effects, based on program goals, were rarely specified and examined. Several reviews describe in detail the limitations of evaluations of adolescent dating abuse prevention programs (Cascardi & Avery-Leaf, 2000; Foshee & Matthew, 2007; Hickman, Jaycox, & Aronoff, 2004; O'Leary, Woodin, & Timmons Fritz, 2005; Wekerle & Wolfe, 1999), and therefore we will not go into detail on limitations here. Instead we describe results from the three randomized trials that measured dating abuse behaviors: Jaycox et al.'s (2006) evaluation of their program, Ending Violence: A Curriculum for Educating Teens on Domestic Violence and The Law; Wolfe et al.'s (2003) evaluation of their Youth Relation Project; and the evaluation of the Safe Dates program (Foshee, Bauman, et al., 2005; Foshee et al., 1998, 2000, 2004).

Jaycox et al.'s (2006) Ending Violence curriculum was a three-session school-based curriculum taught by attorneys that focused on legal aspects of dating violence and was designed to alter knowledge and norms about dating abuse, promote favorable attitudes toward seeking help for dating violence, and decrease the prevalence of dating violence perpetration and victimization. For the evaluation, 40 educational tracts from 10 schools that were over 80% Latino were randomly allocated to treatment or control condition. There were significant treatment effects, in the expected directions, on knowledge of the laws related to dating violence, acceptance of female-to-male violence, and likelihood of help-seeking for dating violence, but there were no differences between treatment and control groups in acceptance of male-to-female violence, abusive/fearful dating experiences, or dating violence perpetration or victimization. All program effects had dissipated at the 6-month follow-up except for knowledge of laws and perceived helpfulness of speaking with a lawyer about dating abuse.

The Youth Relationships Project (Wolfe et al., 1996) consists of 18 two-hour-long sessions, led by a man and a woman cofacilitator, conducted with small coeducational groups of adolescents who had been identified as being maltreated. The program has three components: (a) education and awareness of abuse and power dynamics in close relationships, (b) skills development, and (c) social action. The content of these three components was designed to increase knowledge about dating abuse, alter attitudes toward dating abuse, increase understanding of power dynamics in relationships, improve various communication and problem-solving skills, increase awareness of gender stereotypes that contribute to dating abuse, increase perceptions of the negative consequences of dating violence, and increase help-seeking skills. In their evaluation, 158 adolescents, 14 to 16 years old, with a history of maltreatment were randomly allocated to a treatment ($n = 96$) and control ($n = 62$) condition. Data were collected at baseline and then again

4 months later, after an intervention or control period, and then again bi-monthly for a total of seven waves of data. Adolescents in the treatment condition showed significant reductions over time in physical dating abuse perpetration, emotional dating abuse victimization, and victimization from threatening behaviors, but no reductions in emotional abuse perpetration, threatening behaviors toward dates, or physical dating abuse victimization. The program was more effective for boys than for girls in reducing victimization from physical abuse (Wolfe et al., 2003).

Although the Youth Relationships Project was designed to alter many mediating variables, effects of the program on only three proposed mediating variables were examined. The treatment was associated with reductions in trauma symptoms over time but had no effects on hostility or communication and problem-solving skills. An empirical test to determine whether the mediators explained associations between treatment condition and outcomes was not conducted. Again, the findings have limited generalizability because the evaluation was conducted with only maltreated youths and the 158 adolescents in the analyses represented only about 50% of those eligible.

The Safe Dates study includes a 45-minute-long theater production, a 10-session curriculum, and a poster contest (Foshee & Langwick, 2004). Safe Dates was designed to prevent the onset of and promote the cessation of both dating abuse perpetration and victimization. Activities to prevent the onset of abuse were designed to change norms related to dating abuse such as acceptance of dating abuse, perceived sanctions for using dating abuse, and gender stereotyping, as well as to improve conflict management skills such as responses to anger and communication skills. Activities to promote cessation of dating abuse targeted change in those same constructs, along with cognitive factors found to influence decisions to take preventive action, such as beliefs in the need for help and awareness of community resources for help.

Safe Dates was evaluated with a randomized trial, including five follow-up assessments, up to 4 years postintervention. Positive program effects were noted in all four evaluation papers that have been published (Foshee, Bauman, et al., 2005; Foshee et al., 1998, 2000, 2004). Here we summarize the findings from the most recent and comprehensive paper that included assessments up through the fourth follow-up, which was 3 years postintervention (Foshee, Bauman, et al., 2005). Adolescents who were exposed to Safe Dates in the eighth or ninth grade reported less psychological, moderate physical, and sexual dating violence perpetration and less moderate physical dating violence victimization than those who were not, at all four follow-up periods. Additionally, there was a marginal program effect ($p = .07$) on sexual dating violence victimization at all four follow-up periods. Also, adolescents exposed to Safe Dates and who reported at baseline no or average prior involvement in severe physical perpetration reported less severe physical perpetration at all four follow-up periods than the control group. Safe Dates had both primary and secondary prevention effects on all six of these outcomes in that the very first initiation of these behaviors were prevented (primary prevention) and for those who were already involved in dating abuse, these behaviors were reduced or eliminated (secondary prevention). Also, the program was equally effective for boys and girls and for Whites and non-Whites. Safe Dates did not, however, prevent or reduce psychological dating abuse victimization or severe physical dating abuse victimization at any of the four follow-up periods. It also did not reduce severe physical dating abuse perpetration among adolescents who were already using severe forms of dating abuse at baseline. Mediation was tested empirically, and it was found that program effects were mediated primarily by changes in dating violence norms, gender role norms, and awareness of community services. The program did not affect conflict management skills or belief in the need for help. However, the Safe Dates findings also have limited generalizability in that the study was conducted in a primarily rural county in North Carolina. Many significant program effects on both dating violence behaviors and mediating variables continued at the fifth assessment, which was 4 years after intervention exposure (Foshee et al., 2004).

Together these evaluations demonstrate that attitudes and norms related to dating abuse can be changed through intervention, and the Safe Dates evaluation shows that changes in dating abuse norms and attitudes result in changes in actual dating abuse behaviors. Neither of the programs that intended to influence conflict management or problem-solving skills influenced those skills, yet those programs still had positive effects on dating abuse behaviors.

Lessons Learned From Prevention Research on Other Adolescent Problem Behaviors

Although much has been learned from the short history of adolescent dating abuse research, the amount of prevention research on adolescent dating abuse remains limited. However, lessons can be learned from the long and rich history of prevention science related to other adolescent problem behaviors, such as substance use, delinquency, and unprotected sex. There have been over 100 randomized trials of adolescent substance use prevention programs alone. We provide a summary of the history of prevention science research on other adolescent problem behaviors as described by Catalano, Hawkins, Berglund, Pollard, and Arthur (2002). Initial programs aimed at preventing these other adolescent problem behaviors were not informed by theory or empirical research. Later, programs were designed to change predictors of behaviors identified from a growing number of longitudinal studies, to break the chain of causation leading to the problem behavior. The primary predictors targeted for change during this phase were closely related predictors of specific behaviors such as attitudes toward the behavior. Over time, concerns arose that prevention programs were too focused on changing individual-level predictors of behaviors and were ignoring social and environmental predictors and the influence of individual and environmental interactions. Thus, in the next phase, prevention programs began targeting predictors of behavior at higher levels of the ecological model, such as the school environment, neighborhood characteristics, and social policies (Catalano et al., 2002). These programs also incorporated components to enhance protective factors rather than focusing exclusively on reduction of risks; many of the programs were guided by theories of resilience. Then in the 1990s a number of organizations that focused on the well-being of adolescents, such as the Carnegie Council on Adolescent Development (1995), the Annie E. Casey Foundation (1995), and the Robert Wood Johnson Foundation (Roth et al., 1997), began promoting a youth development approach to prevention. This approach grew out of concern that programs focusing on the prevention of single problem behaviors are inadequate because they ignore the co-occurrence of problem behaviors and because being problem free does not necessarily indicate that an adolescent is fully prepared (Pittman, 1991). As a result, programs began to focus on the promotion of healthy development rather than prevention of a single problem behavior.

Adolescent dating abuse research started out in a similar way, but it is behind the trajectory of prevention research on other problem behaviors. The first adolescent dating abuse studies used cross-sectional designs and examined mostly individual-level correlates of dating abuse. Those studies informed the development of the dating abuse prevention programs that have been evaluated to date, which focus on changing individual-level factors and are mostly atheoretical. By 1997, over 40 adolescent dating abuse perpetration studies had been published using cross-sectional designs, but none had used longitudinal designs. Now, over 15 longitudinal adolescent dating abuse perpetration studies have been published, and findings from those studies will inform the next generation of prevention programs. However, the studies still have not examined the influence on dating abuse of factors at higher levels of the ecological model other than the family, such as peer networks, school characteristics, neighborhood characteristics, the media, and policies at the school and community level, as well as their interactions with each other and with individual-level factors. Therefore, there still is not an empirical base to guide the development of interventions targeted at macrolevel changes. Although most of the prevention programs evaluated to date incorporated content to promote the development of protective factors such as problem solving, communication, and conflict resolution skills rather than focusing only on reducing risk, few adolescent dating abuse studies have focused on identifying protective factors or have been guided by resilience theories or frameworks. However, identification of factors that protect adolescents at high risk of dating violence, such as those who have been abused as a child, would be a valuable direction for future prevention research because those findings can guide prevention efforts targeted at high-risk adolescents. Finally, no studies have determined whether prevention programs guided by a youth developmental approach can prevent adolescent dating abuse.

Several researchers who have summarized findings across the prevention research on other adolescent problems behaviors have made recommendations for prevention programming. Catalano et al. (2002) recommended that prevention programs address both risk and protective factors for multiple problems across multiple social domains, consider risk and protective factors that are appropriate for specific developmental stages, target the factors most relevant for a specific developmental stage, and ensure that activities are culturally appropriate for the target population. From their summary of 35 review articles on the characteristics of effective prevention programs for substance use, risky sexual behavior, school failure, and juvenile delinquency, Nation et al. (2003) concluded that prevention programs should (a) be comprehensive (i.e., address multiple risk factors at multiple levels of the socioecological framework); (b) incorporate interactive skills-based components; (c) be of sufficient dosage and include a booster intervention to promote lasting effects; (d) be theory driven (by either etiological theory, by focusing on causes of the behavior, or intervention theory, by focusing on the best methods for changing etiological risks); (e) provide adolescents with opportunities to develop strong positive relationships with others, including parents and peers; and (f) be socioculturally relevant. However, there are many practical and economical barriers to implementing such a comprehensive approach. Extensive reviews of the characteristics of effective violence prevention programs have been conducted by the Centers for Disease Control and Prevention (CDC; Thorton et al., 2000) and the Surgeon General (U.S. Department of Health and Human Services, 2001). The CDC report describes the characteristics of effective parent and family-based, home visiting, social-cognitive, and mentoring strategies. The Surgeon General's report lists skills training, behavior modification and reinforcement, behavioral techniques for classroom management, building school capacity, continuous progress programs, cooperative learning, and positive youth development programs as effective strategies for the prevention of aggression and violence. Although these reviews can be used to guide the development of dating violence prevention programs, it is not known whether these characteristics or approaches will increase the effectiveness of dating abuse prevention programs.

RECOMMENDATIONS FOR FUTURE ADOLESCENT DATING ABUSE PREVENTION SCIENCE

As noted previously, two of the three adolescent dating abuse prevention programs that have been evaluated for effectiveness in preventing dating abuse behaviors with a randomized trial have been found effective—the Safe Dates program and the Youth Relationships Project. Although there has been some dissemination of those programs, it is not widespread. Future studies need to examine factors that influence the adoption and dissemination of effective adolescent dating abuse prevention programs. This research not only will help with dissemination of the programs found effective but also could shed light on how future dating abuse prevention programs should be structured to facilitate their adoption and dissemination.

The programs found effective need to be evaluated in other settings to determine whether positive program effects can be replicated and to facilitate dissemination. For example, Safe Dates was evaluated in a rural North Carolina county, yet it is being used with inner-city Black adolescents, adolescents on Native American reservations, Hispanic adolescents, and French-speaking adolescents in Switzerland. Whether the program is as effective or not with those groups has not been determined. Cultural adaptation of the programs found to be effective and evaluations of those modified programs would also be useful, as would creation and evaluation of new culturally sensitive dating abuse prevention programs.

Future evaluations should use rigorous methods, including randomized designs, so that evaluation findings have more value for guiding practice. Future evaluations also need to clearly identify mediating variables that the program is intended to change, assure that program content matches those mediators, measure mediators, and test for mediation empirically. Through the mediation analyses conducted in the Safe Dates study (Foshee, Bauman, et al., 2005), the process through which the program did and did not influence dating violence is clear and provides guidance for the development of new interventions and for future modifications of Safe Dates.

Only a few adolescent dating violence studies have examined typical patterns of the development of dating abuse across adolescence by testing behavioral trajectories and examined how risk factors for those behaviors vary by adolescent developmental stage (Foshee, Bauman, et al., 2005; Foshee et al., 2008; Foshee & Matthew, 2007; Wolfe et al., 2003). However, findings from those kinds of developmental studies can guide the creation of developmentally appropriate dating abuse prevention programs.

As noted earlier, all but one adolescent dating abuse prevention program have been school based. However, staff at domestic violence and sexual assault organizations, the primary entities providing dating violence and sexual assault programming across the country, often report difficulties in gaining access to schools to offer dating abuse prevention programming; schools are reluctant to take time away from academic activities and may fear parental objections to sensitive content. When schools do allow organizations to offer school-based dating violence and/or date rape prevention activities, staff are often limited to one or two 45-minute sessions, which is insufficient to affect these complex behaviors. Also, when domestic violence and sexual assault organizations deliver dating abuse programs in schools, the focus is typically on victim services rather than prevention. These observations suggest a need for developing effective primary prevention programs that can be administered independent of schools.

As noted earlier, one promising model of dating violence prevention delivery is family-based programs. These have particular promise because (a) families have a significant impact on many of the risk factors for adolescent dating violence; (b) families have a persistent influence on adolescents, suggesting that programs that focus on family change may have long-term effectiveness; (c) the family is still the primary context in which adolescents acquire much of their information and their sense of values, despite the importance of peers during adolescence (Lefkowitz, Romo, Corona, Au, & Sigman, 2000); and (d) family-based programs have been found effective in preventing and reducing other forms of youth violence (Alexander et al., 1998; Borduin et al., 1995; Hawkins et al., 1991; Olds et al., 1999; Webster-Stratton & Hammond, 1997). We are currently in the process of conducting a national randomized trial, funded by the CDC, testing the effectiveness of a family-based adolescent dating abuse prevention program targeted at the families of 13- to 15-year-old adolescents, and findings from that study will become available soon.

Prevention programs that promote change in factors at higher levels of the ecological level than the individual level have been effective for other adolescent problem behaviors (Abbott et al., 1998; Flay, 2000, 2002; Flay & Allred, 2001; Hawkins et al., 1992). For example, the Surgeon General Report on Violence (U.S. Department of Health and Human Services, 2001) concluded that school-based interventions that target change in the social context are more effective than those that attempt to change only individual attitudes, skills, and risk behaviors. Future studies need to examine the influence on adolescent dating abuse of factors at these higher ecological levels so that those findings can guide the development of prevention interventions at these upper levels. For example, findings from the longitudinal studies suggest that the peer context may influence abusive dating behaviors and thus be a point of intervention for primary prevention. However, the surface has barely been scratched in the exploration of how the peer context facilitates or prevents dating abuse, and such studies are crucial for informing interventions targeting changes in the peer context.

Finally, whether bullying, sexual harassment, and youth aggression prevention programs generalize to the prevention of adolescent dating abuse needs to be determined. Several of the large trials assessing the effectiveness of early childhood and youth development programs will have the opportunity to measure dating abuse as the respondents in their studies become adolescents. Thus, we hope that in the future researchers will learn whether those programs are effective in preventing adolescent dating abuse.

REFERENCES

Abbott, R. D., O'Donnell, J., Hawkins, J. D., Hill, K. G., Kosterman, R., & Catalano, R. F. (1998). Changing teaching practices to promote achievement and bonding to school. *American Journal of Orthopsychiatry, 68,* 542–552.

Ackard, D. M., & Neumark-Sztainer, D. (2002). Date violence and date rape among adolescents: Associations with disordered eating behaviors and psychological health. *Child Abuse & Neglect, 26,* 455–473.

Alexander, J., Pugh, C., Parsons, B., Barton, C., Gordon, D., Grotpeter, J., et al. (1998). *Blueprints for violence prevention: Functional family therapy.* Boulder: University of Colorado Press.

Andrews, J. A., Foster, S. L., Capaldi, D., & Hops, H. (2000). Adolescent and family predictors of physical aggression, communication, and satisfaction in young adult couples: A prospective analysis. *Journal of Consulting and Clinical Psychology, 68,* 195–208.

Annie E. Casey Foundation. (1995). *The path of most resistance: Reflections on lessons learned from new futures.* Baltimore, MD: Author.

Arriaga, X. B., & Foshee, V. A. (2004). Adolescent dating violence: Do adolescents follow their friends' or their parents' footsteps? *Journal of Interpersonal Violence, 19,* 162–184.

Avery-Leaf, S., Cascardi, M., O'Leary, K. D., & Cano, A. (1997). Efficacy of a dating violence prevention program on attitudes justifying aggression. *Journal of Adolescent Health, 21,* 11–17.

Bank, L., & Burraston, B. (2001). Abusive home environments as predictors of poor adjustment during adolescence and early childhood. *Journal of Community Psychology, 29,* 195–217.

Bennett, L., & Fineran, S. (1998). Sexual and severe physical violence among high school students: Power beliefs, gender, and relationship. *American Journal of Orthopsychology, 68,* 645–652.

Borduin, C. M., Mann, B. J., Cone, L. T., Henggeler, S. W., Fucci, B. R., Blaske, D. M., & Williams, R. A. (1995). Multisystemic treatment of serious juvenile offenders: Long-term prevention of criminality and violence. *Journal of Consulting and Clinical Psychology, 63,* 569–578.

Borowsky, I. W., Hogan, M., & Ireland, M. (1997). Adolescent sexual aggression: Risk and protective factors. *Pediatrics, 100*(6), E7. doi: 10.1542/peds.100.6.e7

Bouchey, H., & Furman, W. (2003). Dating and romantic relationships in adolescence. In G. R. Adams & M. Berzonsky (Eds.), *The Blackwell handbook of adolescence* (pp. 313–329). Oxford, England: Blackwell.

Brendgen, M., Vitaro, F., Tremblay, R. E., & Lavoie, F. (2001). Reactive and proactive aggression: Predictions to physical violence in different contexts and moderating effects of parental monitoring and caregiving behavior. *Journal of Abnormal Child Psychology, 29,* 293–304.

Capaldi, D. M., & Clark, S. (1998). Prospective family predictors of aggression toward female partners for young at-risk males. *Developmental Psychology, 34,* 1175–1188.

Capaldi, D. M., & Crosby, L. (1997). Observed and reported psychological and physical aggression in young, at-risk couples. *Social Development, 6*, 184–206.

Capaldi, D. M., Dishion, T. J., Stoolmiller, M., & Yoerger, K. L. (2001). Aggression toward female partners by at-risk young men: The contribution of male adolescent friendships. *Developmental Psychology, 37*, 61–73.

Capaldi, D. M., & Gorman-Smith, D. (2003). The development of aggression in young male/female couples. In P. Florsheim (Ed.), *Adolescent romantic relations and sexual behavior: Theory, research, and practical implications* (pp. 243–274). Mahwah, NJ: Erlbaum.

Carlson, B. E. (1990). Adolescent observers of marital violence. *Journal of Family Violence, 5*, 285–299.

Carnegie Council on Adolescent Development. (1995). *Great transitions: Preparing adolescents for a new century.* New York: Carnegie Corporation of New York.

Carver, K., Joyner, K., & Udry, R. (2003). National estimates of adolescent romantic relationships. In P. Florsheim (Ed.), *Adolescent romantic relations and sexual behavior: Theory, research, and practical implications* (pp. 23–56). Mahwah, NJ: Erlbaum.

Cascardi, M., & Avery-Leaf, S. (2000). *Violence against women: Synthesis of research for secondary school officials* (Publication No. NCJ 201342). Washington, DC: U.S. Department of Justice.

Cascardi, M., Avery-Leaf, S., O'Leary, K. D., & Smith Slep, A. M. (1999). Factor structure and convergent validity of the Conflict Tactics Scale in high school students. *Psychological Assessment, 14*, 546–555.

Catalano, R. F., Hawkins, J. D., Berglund, M. L., Pollard, J. A., & Arthur, M. W. (2002). Prevention science and positive youth development: Competitive or cooperative frameworks? *Journal of Adolescent Health, 31*(Suppl.), 230–239.

Chapple, C. (2003). Examining intergenerational violence: Violent role modeling or weak parental controls? *Violence and Victims, 18*, 143–162.

Chase, K. A., Treboux, D., O'Leary, K. D., & Strassberg, Z. (1998). Specificity of dating aggression and its justification among high-risk adolescents. *Journal of Abnormal Child Psychology, 26*, 467–473.

Child Trends Databank. (n.d.). [Child Trends analysis of the Monitoring the Future study, selected years 1976–2004]. Retrieved June 26, 2006, from http://www.childtrendsdatabank.org/indicators/73Dating.cfm

Coker, A. L., Smith, P. H., McKeown, R. E., & King, M. J. (2000). Frequency and correlates of intimate partner violence by type: Physical, sexual, and psychological battering. *American Journal of Public Health, 90*, 553–559.

Collins, W. (2003). More than myth: The developmental significance of romantic relationships during adolescence. *Journal of Research on Adolescence, 13*, 1–24.

Commission on Chronic Illness. (1957). *Chronic illness in the United States* (Vol. 1). Cambridge, MA: Harvard University Press.

Connolly, J., Pepler, D. J., Craig, W. M., & Taradash, A. (2000). Dating experiences of bullies in early adolescence. *Child Maltreatment, 5*, 299–310.

Dahlberg, L. L. (1998). Youth violence in the United States: Major trends, risk factors, and prevention approaches. *American Journal of Preventive Medicine, 14,* 259–272.

Decker, M., Silverman, J. G., & Raj, A. (2005). Dating violence and sexually transmitted disease/HIV testing and diagnosis among adolescent females. *Pediatrics, 116,* 272–276.

Ehrensaft, M. K., Cohen, P., Brown, J., Smailes, E., Chen, H., & Johnson, J. G. (2003). Intergenerational transmission of partner violence: A 20-year prospective study. *Journal of Consulting and Clinical Psychology, 71,* 741–753.

Erikson, E. H. (1968). *Identity: Youth and crisis.* New York: Norton.

Farrington, D. P. (1991). Childhood aggression and adult violence. In D. Pepler & K. Rubin (Eds.), *The development and treatment of childhood aggression* (pp. 5–29). Hillsdale, NJ: Erlbaum.

Feiring, C., & Furman, W. (2000). When love is just a four-letter word: Victimization and romantic relationships in adolescence. *Child Maltreatment, 5,* 293–298.

Feltey, K. M., Ainslie, J. J., & Geib, A. (1991). Sexual coercion attitudes among high school students. *Youth & Society, 23,* 229–250.

Field, C. A., & Caetano, R. (2004). Ethnic differences in intimate partner violence in the U.S. general population. *Trauma, Violence, & Abuse, 5,* 303–317.

Fitch, S. A., & Adams, G. R. (1983). Ego identity and intimacy status: Replication and extension. *Developmental Psychology, 19,* 839–845.

Flay, B. R. (2000). Approaches to substance use prevention utilizing school curriculum plus social environment change. *Addictive Behavior, 25,* 861–885.

Flay, B. R. (2002). Positive youth development requires comprehensive health promotion programs. *American Journal of Health Behavior, 26,* 407–424.

Flay, B. R., & Allred, C. G. (2001). *Evaluations of the Positive Action program: Summary of findings 1978–2001.* Twin Falls, ID: Positive Action.

Foshee, V. A. (1996). Gender differences in adolescent dating abuse prevalence, types, and injuries. *Health Education Research, 11,* 275–286.

Foshee, V. A., Bauman, K. E., Arriaga, X. B., Helms, R. W., Koch, G. G., & Linder, G. F. (1998). An evaluation of Safe Dates, an adolescent dating violence prevention program. *American Journal of Public Health, 88,* 45–50.

Foshee, V. A., Bauman, K. E., Ennett, S. T., Linder, G. F., Benefield, T., & Suchindran, C. (2004). Assessing the long-term effects of the Safe Dates program and a booster in preventing and reducing adolescent dating violence victimization and perpetration. *American Journal of Public Health, 94,* 619–624.

Foshee, V. A., Bauman, K. E., Ennett, S. T., Suchindran, C., Benefield, T., & Linder, G. F. (2005). Assessing the effects of the dating violence prevention program "Safe Dates" using random coefficient regression modeling. *Prevention Science, 6,* 245–258.

Foshee, V. A., Bauman, K. E., Greene, W. F., Koch, G. G., Linder, G. F., & MacDougall, J. E. (2000). The Safe-Dates program: 1-year follow-up results. *American Journal of Public Health, 90,* 1619–1622.

Foshee, V. A., Bauman, K. E., & Linder, G. F. (1999). Family violence and the perpetration of adolescent dating violence: Examining social learning and social control processes. *Journal of Marriage and the Family, 61,* 331–342.

Foshee, V. A., Benefield, T., Suchindran, C., Ennett, S. T., Bauman, K. E., Karriker-Jaffe, K. J., et al. (in press). The development of four types of adolescent dating abuse and selected demographic correlates. *Journal of Research on Adolescence.*

Foshee, V. A., Ennett, S. T., Bauman, K. E., Benefield, T., & Suchindran, C. (2005). The association between family violence and adolescent dating violence onset: Does it vary by race, socioeconomic status, and family structure? *Journal of Early Adolescence, 25,* 317–344.

Foshee, V. A., Karriker-Jaffe, K. J., Reyes, H. L. M., Ennett, S. T., Suchindran, C., Bauman, K. E., & Benefield, T. S. (2008). What accounts for demographic differences in trajectories of adolescent dating violence? An examination of intrapersonal and contextual mediators. *Journal of Adolescent Health, 42,* 596–604.

Foshee, V. A., & Langwick, S. (2004). *Safe Dates: An adolescent dating abuse prevention curriculum* [Program manual]. Center City, MN: Hazelden Publishing and Educational Services.

Foshee, V. A., Linder, F., MacDougall, J. E., & Bangdiwala, S. (2001). Gender differences in the longitudinal predictors of dating violence. *Preventive Medicine, 32,* 128–141.

Foshee, V. A., & Matthew, R. A. (2007). Adolescent dating abuse perpetration: A review of findings, methodological limitations, and suggestions for future research. In D. Flannery, A. Vazonsyi, & I. Waldman (Eds.), *The Cambridge handbook of violent behavior and aggression* (pp. 431–449). New York: Cambridge University Press.

Furman, W., & Flanagan, A. (1997). The influence of earlier relationships on marriage: An attachment perspective. In W. K. Halford & H. J. Markman (Eds.), *Clinical handbook of marriage and couples interventions* (pp. 179–202). Chichester, England: Wiley.

Furman, W., & Shaffer, L. (2003). The role of romantic relationships in adolescence. In P. Florsheim (Ed.), *Adolescent romantic relations and sexual behavior: Theory, research and practical implications* (pp. 3–22). Mahwah, NJ: Erlbaum.

Giordano, P. (2003). Relationships in adolescence. *Annual Review of Psychology, 29,* 257–281.

Gordon, R. (1983). An operational classification of disease prevention. *Public Health Reports, 98,* 107–109.

Gordon, R. (1987). An operational classification of disease prevention. In J. A. Steinberg & M. M. Silverman (Eds.), *Preventing mental disorders* (pp. 20–26). Rockville, MD: U.S. Department of Health and Human Services.

Gorman-Smith, D., Tolan, P. H., Shiedow, A. J., & Henry, D. B. (2001). Partner violence and street violence among urban adolescents: Do the same family factors relate? *Journal of Research on Adolescence, 11,* 273–295.

Gray, H. M., & Foshee, V. A. (1997). Adolescent dating violence: Differences between one-sided and mutually violent profiles. *Journal of Interpersonal Violence, 12,* 126–141.

Greene, M. B. (1998). Youth violence in the city: The role of educational interventions. *Health Education and Behavior, 25,* 175–193.

Hawkins, J. D., Catalano, R. F., Morrison, D. M., O'Donnell, J., Abbott, R. D., & Day, L. E. (1992). The Seattle Social Development Project: Effects of the first four years on protective factors and problem behaviors. In J. McCord & R. Tremblay (Eds.), *Preventing antisocial behavior: Interventions from birth through adolescence* (pp. 139–161). New York: Guilford Press.

Hawkins, J. D., Von Cleve, E., & Catalano, R. F., Jr. (1991). Reducing early childhood aggression: Results of a primary prevention program. *Journal of the American Academy of Child & Adolescent Psychiatry, 30,* 208–217.

Hazan, C., & Shaver, P. (1987). Romantic love conceptualized as an attachment process. *Journal of Personality and Social Psychology, 52,* 511–524.

Herrenkohl, T. I., Mason, W. A., Kosterman, R., Lengua, L. J., Hawkins, J. D., & Abbott, R. D. (2004). Pathways from physical childhood abuse to partner violence in young adulthood. *Violence and Victims, 19,* 123–136.

Hickman, L. J., Jaycox, L. H., & Aronoff, J. (2004). Dating violence among adolescents: Prevalence, gender distribution, and prevention program effectiveness. *Trauma Violence Abuse, 5,* 123–142.

Hilton, N. Z., Harris, G. T., Rice, M. E., Krans, T. S., & Lavigne, S. E. (1998). Antiviolence education in high schools: Implementation and evaluation. *Journal of Interpersonal Violence, 13,* 726–742.

Hird, M. J. (2000). An empirical study of adolescent dating aggression in the U.K. *Journal of Adolescence, 23,* 69–78.

Jaffe, P. G., Sudermann, M., Reitzel, D., & Killip, S. M. (1992). An evaluation of a secondary school primary prevention program on violence in relationships. *Violence and Victims, 7,* 129–146.

Jaycox, L. H., McCaffrey, D., Eiseman, B., Arnoff, J., Shelley, G. A., Collins, R. L., & Marshall, G. N. (2006). Impact of a school-based dating violence prevention program among Latino teens: Randomized controlled effectiveness trial. *Journal of Adolescent Health, 39,* 694–704.

Johnson, R. (2002). Pathways to adolescent health: Early intervention. *Journal of Adolescent Health, 31*(Suppl.), 240–250.

Johnson-Reid, M., & Bivens, L. (1999). Foster youth and dating violence. *Journal of Interpersonal Violence, 14,* 1249–1262.

Jones, L. E. (1991). The Minnesota School Curriculum Project: A statewide domestic violence prevention project in secondary schools. In B. Levy (Ed.), *Dating violence: Young women in danger* (pp. 258–266). Seattle, WA: Seal Press.

Kellermann, A. L., Fuqua-Whitley, D. S., Rivara, F. P., & Mercy, J. (1998). Preventing youth violence: What works? *Annual Review of Public Health, 19,* 271–292.

Kinsfogel, K. M., & Grych, J. H. (2004). Interparental conflict and adolescent dating relationships: Integrating cognitive, emotional, and peer influences. *Journal of Family Psychology, 18,* 505–515.

Koch, P. (1993). Promoting healthy sexual development during early adolescence. In R. M. Lerner (Ed.), *Early adolescence: Perspectives on research, policy and intervention* (pp. 293–307). Hillsdale, NJ: Erlbaum.

Krajewski, S. S., Rybarik, M. F., Dosch, M. F., & Gilmore, G. D. (1996). Results of a curriculum intervention with seventh graders regarding violence in relationships. *Journal of Family Violence, 11,* 93–112.

Lally, J. R., Mangione, P. L., & Honig, A. S. (1988). The Syracuse University Family Development Research Program: Long-range impact on an early intervention with low-income children and their families. In D. R. Powell (Ed.), *Annual advances in applied developmental psychology: Parent education as early childhood intervention* (Vol. 3, pp. 79–104). Norwood, NJ: Ablex.

Laursen, B., & Williams, V. (1997). Perceptions of interdependence and closeness in family and peer relationships among adolescents with and without romantic partners. *New Directions for Child and Adolescent Development, 78,* 3–20.

Lavoie, F., Hebert, M., Tremblay, R. E., Vitaro, F., Vezina, L., & McDuff, P. (2002). History of family dysfunction and perpetration of dating violence by adolescent boys: A longitudinal study. *Journal of Adolescent Health, 30,* 375–383.

Lavoie, F., Vezina, L., Piche, C., & Boivin, M. (1995). Evaluation of a prevention program for violence in teen dating relationships. *Journal of Interpersonal Violence, 10,* 516–524.

Lefkowitz, E. S., Romo, L. F., Corona, R., Au, T. K., & Sigman, M. (2000). How Latino American and European American adolescents discuss conflicts, sexuality, and AIDS with their mothers. *Development Psychology, 36,* 315–325.

Macgowan, M. J. (1997). An evaluation of a dating violence prevention program for middle school students. *Violence and Victims, 12,* 223–235.

Magdol, L., Moffitt, T. E., Caspi, A., & Silva, P. A. (1998). Developmental antecedents of partner abuse: A prospective-longitudinal study. *Journal of Abnormal Psychology, 107,* 375–389.

Malik, S., Sorenson, S. B., & Aneshensel, C. S. (1997). Community and dating violence among adolescents: Perpetration and victimization. *Journal of Adolescent Health, 21,* 291–302.

McCloskey, L. A., & Lichter, E. L. (2003). The contribution of marital violence to adolescent aggression across different relationships. *Journal of Interpersonal Violence, 18,* 390–412.

McDaniel, C. O. (1969). Dating roles and reasons for dating. *Journal of Marriage and the Family, 31,* 97–107.

Mrazek, P., & Haggerty, R. J. (Eds.). (1994). *Reducing risks for mental disorders.* Washington, DC: National Academies Press

Nation, M., Crusto, C., Wandersman, A., Kumpfer, K. L., Seybolt, D., Morrissey-Kane, E., & Davino, K. (2003). What works in prevention: Principles of effective prevention programs. *American Psychologist, 59,* 449–456.

National Research Council, Committee on Future Directions for Behavioral and Social Sciences Research. (2001). *New horizons in health: An integrative approach.* Washington, DC: National Academies Press.

O'Connor, T. G. (2003). Early experiences and psychological development: Conceptual questions, empirical illustrations, and implications for intervention. *Developmental Psychopathology, 15,* 671–690.

O'Keefe, M. (1997). Predictors of dating violence among high school students. *Journal of Interpersonal Violence, 12,* 546–568.

O'Keeffe, N. K., Brockopp, K., & Chew, E. (1986). Teen dating violence. *Social Work, 31,* 465–468.

O'Leary, K. D., & Smith Slep, A. M. (2003). A dyadic longitudinal model of adolescent dating aggression. *Journal of Child and Adolescent Psychology, 32,* 314–327.

O'Leary, K. D., Woodin, E. M., & Timmons Fritz, P. A. (2005). Can we prevent the hitting? Recommendations for preventing intimate partner violence between young adults. *Journal of Aggression, Maltreatment & Trauma, 13,* 125–181.

Olds, D. L., Henderson, C. R., Jr., Kitzman, H. J., Eckenrode, J. J., Cole, R. E., & Tatelbaum, R. C. (1999). Prenatal and infancy home visitation by nurses: Recent findings. *The Future of Children, 9,* 44–65.

Ozer, E. J., Tschann, J. M., Pasch, L. A., & Flores, E. (2004). Violence perpetration across peer and partner relationships: Co-occurrence and longitudinal patterns among adolescents. *Journal of Adolescent Health, 34,* 64–71.

Pflieger, J. C., & Vazsonyi, A. T. (2006). Parenting processes and dating violence: The mediating role of self-esteem in low- and high-SES adolescents. *Journal of Adolescence, 29,* 495–512.

Pittman, K. (1991). *Promoting youth development: Strengthening the role of youth serving and community organizations.* Washington, DC: Academy for Educational Development.

Plass, M. S., & Gessner, J. C. (1983). Violence in courtship relations: A southern sample. *Free Inquiry Into Creative Sociology, 11,* 198–202.

Reese, L. E., Vera, E. M., Simon, T. R., & Ikeda, R. M. (2000). The role of families and care givers as risk and protective factors in preventing youth violence. *Clinical Child and Family Psychology Review, 3,* 61–77.

Roberts, T., Auinger, P., & Klein, J. D. (2005). Intimate partner abuse and the reproductive health of sexually active female adolescents. *Journal of Adolescent Health, 36,* 380–385.

Roberts, T., Klein, J. D., & Fisher, S. (2003). Longitudinal effect of intimate partner abuse on high-risk behavior among adolescents. *Archives of Pediatrics & Adolescent Medicine, 157,* 875–881.

Rose, G. (1992). *The strategy of preventive medicine.* Oxford, England: Oxford University Press.

Roth, J., Brooks-Gunn, J., Galen, B., Murray, L., Silverman, P., Liu, H., et al. (1997). *Promoting healthy adolescence: Youth development frameworks and programs.* New York: Columbia University Press.

Schwartz, M., O'Leary, S. G., & Kendziora, K. T. (1997). Dating aggression among high school students. *Violence and Victims, 12,* 295–305.

Seidman, E. (1987). Toward a framework for primary prevention research. In J. A. Steinberg & M. M. Silverman (Eds.), *Preventing mental disorders* (pp. 2–19). Rockville, MD: U.S. Department of Health and Human Services.

Sherrod, L., Busch-Rossnagel, N. A., & Fisher, C. B. (2003). Applying developmental science: Methods, visions, and values. In R. M. Lerner & L. Steinberg (Eds.), *Handbook of adolescent psychology* (pp. 747–780). New York: Wiley.

Silverman, J., Raj, A., & Clements, K. (2004). Dating violence and associated sexual risk and pregnancy among adolescent girls in the United States. *Pediatrics, 114*, 220–225.

Silverman, J., Raj, A., Mucci, L., & Hathaway, J. (2001). Dating violence against adolescent girls and associated substance use, unhealthy weight control, sexual risk behavior, pregnancy, and suicidality. *The Journal of the American Medical Association, 286*, 572–579.

Simons, R. L., Lin, K., & Gordon, L. C. (1998). Socialization in the family of origin and male dating violence: A prospective study. *Journal of Marriage and the Family, 60*, 467–478.

Smith, D. (1999). *Intergenerational transmission of courtship violence: A meta-analysis*. Falls Church: Virginia Polytechnic Institute.

Smith, J. P., & Williams, J. G. (1992). From abusive household to dating violence. *Journal of Family Violence, 7*, 153–165.

Symons, P. Y., Groër, M. W., Kepler-Youngblood, P., & Slater, V. (1994). Prevalence and predictors of adolescent dating violence. *Journal of Child and Adolescent Psychiatric Nursing, 7*, 14–23.

Thorton, T. N., Craft, C. A., Dahlberg, L. L., Lynch, B. S., & Baer, K. (2000). *Best practices of youth violence prevention: A sourcebook for community action*. Atlanta: Centers for Disease Control and Prevention.

Tolan, P. H., & Guerra, N. G. (1994). *What works in reducing adolescent violence: An empirical review of the field*. Boulder: University of Colorado.

U.S. Department of Health and Human Services. (2001). *Youth violence: A report of the Surgeon General*. Rockville, MD: U.S. Department of Health and Human Services, Substance Abuse and Mental Health Services Administration, and National Institutes of Health.

Watson, J. M., Cascardi, M., Avery-Leaf, S., & O'Leary, K. D. (2001). High school students' responses to dating aggression. *Violence and Victims, 16*, 339–348.

Webster-Stratton, C., & Hammond, M. (1997). Treating children with early-onset conduct problems: A comparison of child and parent training interventions. *Journal of Consulting and Clinical Psychology, 65*, 93–109.

Weisz, A. N., & Black, B. M. (2001). Evaluating a sexual assault and dating violence prevention program for urban youth. *Social Work Research, 25*, 89–100.

Wekerle, C., & Wolfe, D. A. (1999). Dating violence in mid-adolescence: Theory, significance, and emerging prevention initiatives. *Clinical Psychology Review, 19*, 435–456.

Wekerle, C., Wolfe, D. A., Hawkins, D. L., Pittman, A., Glickman, A., & Lovald, B. E. (2001). Child maltreatment, posttraumatic stress symptomatology and adolescent dating violence: Considering the value of adolescent perceptions of abuse and a trauma mediational model. *Development and Psychopathology, 13*, 847–871.

Wilson, D. B., Gottfredson, D. J., & Najaka, S. S. (2001). School-based prevention of problem behaviors: A meta-analysis. *Journal of Quantitative Criminology, 17*, 247–272.

Wilson, S. J., Lipsey, M. W., & Derzon, J. H. (2003). The effects of school-based intervention programs on aggressive behavior: A meta-analysis. *Journal of Consulting and Clinical Psychology, 71*, 136–149.

Wolfe, D., & Jaffe, P. (1999). Emerging strategies in the prevention of domestic violence. *The Future of Children, 9*, 133–144.

Wolfe, D., Scott, K., Wekerle, C., & Pittman, A. (2001). Child maltreatment: Risk of adjustment problems and dating violence in adolescence. *Journal of the American Academy of Child & Adolescent Psychiatry, 40*, 282–289.

Wolfe, D., Wekerle, C., Gough, R., Reitzel-Jaffe, D., Grasley, C., Pittman, A., et al. (1996). *The Youth Relationships manual: A group approach with adolescents for the prevention of woman abuse and the promotion of healthy relationships.* Thousand Oaks, CA: Sage.

Wolfe, D., Wekerle, C., Reitzel-Jaffe, D., & Lefebvre, L. (1998). Factors associated with abusive relationships among maltreated and nonmaltreated youth. *Developmental Psychopathology, 10*, 61–85.

Wolfe, D., Wekerle, C., Scott, K., Straatman, A., & Grasley, C. (2004). Predicting abuse in adolescent dating relationships over 1 year: The role of child maltreatment and trauma. *Journal of Abnormal Psychology, 113*, 406–415.

Wolfe, D., Wekerle, C., Scott, K., Straatman, A., Grasley, C., & Reitzel-Jaffe, D. (2003). Dating violence prevention with at-risk youth: A controlled outcome evaluation. *Journal of Consulting and Clinical Psychology, 71*, 279–291.

Zimmer-Gembeck, M. J., Siebenbruner, J., & Collins, W. A. (2001). Diverse aspects of dating: Associations with psychosocial functioning from early to middle adolescence. *Journal of Adolescence, 24*, 313–336.

8

ADVANCING INTERVENTIONS FOR PERPETRATORS OF PHYSICAL PARTNER VIOLENCE: BATTERER INTERVENTION PROGRAMS AND BEYOND

DANIEL J. WHITAKER AND PHYLLIS HOLDITCH NIOLON

In this chapter, we review intervention approaches for intimate partner violence (IPV) that focus on the perpetrators of IPV. We begin with a description of batterer intervention programs (BIPs), which are the most prominent intervention model for perpetrators. We then discuss a range of other intervention approaches that are at various stages of empirical development, and we conclude with an examination of critical issues for future research and policy consideration, such as addressing IPV typologies, intervening with female and culturally diverse perpetrators, and incorporating new strategies into the modern system of BIPs.

This chapter was authored by employees of the United States government as part of official duty and is considered to be in the public domain. Any views expressed herein do not necessarily represent the views of the United States government, and the author's participation in the work is not meant to serve as an official endorsement.

We use the term *IPV perpetrators* to describe those who have committed acts of physical violence toward an intimate partner. Our focus is on physical violence, because most works reviewed here pertain to acts of physical violence, although a comprehensive definition of IPV includes physical violence, sexual violence, threats of physical and/or sexual violence, and emotional– psychological abuse (Saltzman, Fanslow, McMahon, & Shelley, 1999). We explicitly avoid use of the term *batterer* to describe individuals who perpetrate IPV. The terms batterer and battering have recently been used to describe a specific form of IPV that includes ongoing, recurrent violence, fear, intimidation, and control (Johnson, 1995; Smith, Earp, & DeVellis, 1995). It is clear that much of IPV does not fit this description but is low level, conflict based, and/or reciprocally perpetrated. We use the term *batterer intervention program* or BIP to refer specifically to community-based programs that exist as part of a service system based primarily within the criminal justice system (Gondolf, 2002) to treat identified perpetrators of IPV, mostly court-referred, who may or may not be batterers as just described. We use the term *interventions for IPV perpetrators* to discuss a broader range of strategies that may be used in BIPs or may be implemented and tested in a different context.

BATTERER INTERVENTION PROGRAMS

Today's BIPs are primarily psychoeducational groups for IPV perpetrators that can last up to 52 weeks, depending on the program and the state in which it is conducted. BIPs ostensibly work closely with judicial–legal systems to ensure court-ordered perpetrators attend sessions (although, as discussed later, attrition is a large problem) and coordinate with victim services programs to maximize victim safety (e.g., victims may be notified if perpetrators drop out of a BIP). The format and content of most BIPs are regulated, by either states or counties, by the creation of mandatory or voluntary guidelines (termed *standards*) that prescribe the course and content of BIPs (Austin & Dankwort, 1999). These standards have been controversial because they lack empirical data (Gelles, 2002; Maiuro, Hagar, Lin, & Olson, 2002) and may hamper efforts to improve BIPs.

The dominant treatment model for modern BIPs is rooted in a feminist, psychoeducational approach, which focuses on educating men about the potential root causes of their violence (i.e., gender norms and expectations, power, and control) and on holding men accountable for their behavior (Mederos, 2002; Pence & Paymar, 1983). This approach also reeducates men about the patriarchal structure of society, which reinforces a system of privilege in which some men strive for and feel entitled to power and control over relationship partners. It attempts to change behavior by confronting perpetrators about their violence, getting them to recognize the root causes of violence, shifting their belief systems toward a more egalitarian view of relationships, and encouraging them to take responsibility for their abusive behavior through both didactic strategies and participatory group discussion (e.g., see Pence & Paymar, 1983). More recently, cognitive–behavioral approaches (e.g., see Hamberger, 1997) have been incorporated into BIPs and in many cases are combined with feminist psychoeducational approaches. Cognitive–behavioral approaches focus on the proximal thoughts and emotions that might lead one to engage in violent behavior and teach individuals to challenge and modify those thoughts and emotions that lead to violence. Most modern BIPs use a combination of feminist and cognitive–behavioral approaches, making comparisons between the two approaches difficult (Babcock, Green, & Robie, 2004; Eckhardt, Murphy, Black, & Suhr, 2006).

Although most IPV services that are broadly available have had little evaluation (Wathen & MacMillan, 2003; Whitaker, Baker, & Arias, 2007), BIPs are an exception. Since the early 1980s, a number of studies were conducted attempting to examine the impact of BIPs on IPV perpetration among men. To date, more than 20 experimental or quasi-experimental evaluation studies have been published, along with a number of reviews of those evaluations (Babcock et al., 2004; Eckhardt et al., 2006; Feder & Wilson, 2006; Gondolf, 2002, 2004). A scan of the reviews shows that opinions regarding BIP effectiveness vary from optimistic (Gondolf, 2004) to pessimistic (Eckhardt et al., 2006; Feder & Wilson, 2006) to somewhere in between (Babcock et al., 2004). This diversity of opinions seems to stem from disagreements about optimal evaluation methods and the fact that the strongest evidence for BIPs' effectiveness comes from the least rigorous studies.

Two fairly recent meta-analyses of BIPs come to slightly different conclusions based on different study inclusion criteria. Babcock et al. (2004) included 22 experimental and quasi-experimental studies in their meta-analysis of recidivism and found small effects for BIPs (overall $d = .13$), with no differences by treatment type (i.e., feminist vs. cognitive–behavioral). Babcock et al. noted that even this small treatment effect for BIPs could result in large practical effects nationwide. Feder and Wilson's (2006) meta-analysis of BIP evaluations included only the most rigorous studies ($N = 10$). They found a small overall effect based on police reports of recidivism ($d = .26$), which was heavily influenced by one study, and a null effect based on victim reports ($d = -.00$). They raised a number of questions about the studies included in their review that cast doubt on the reliability of the observed effects, including questions about generalizability, measurement, and retention and comparison issues for studies with quasi-experimental designs.

Gondolf (2002, 2004) offered a different perspective and raised a number of methodological issues regarding the evaluation of BIPs. He argued that BIPs are not well suited for evaluation through experimentation because they are simply one portion of an accountability system for batterers and should not be evaluated apart from the system. Gondolf raised important methodological points about experimental field studies of BIPs. For example, he pointed out that experimental designs can change the system in which a BIP operates, thus making the evaluation artificial if men for control groups are drawn from the same system, which they usually are. Another point is that men in the control group often receive other interventions, making it difficult to evaluate BIPs' impact. Gondolf argued that quasi-experimental studies using advanced analytic procedures are better suited to examining BIP effectiveness and that, when this is done, there is fairly clear evidence to support BIPs' effectiveness. In his four-city study, using a variety of analytic techniques, Gondolf (see Gondolf, 2004, for a summary) used propensity score matching to estimate cumulative recidivism rates over 4 years and found the recidivism rate of men who completed a minimum dose of counseling was almost 50% lower than men who dropped out of treatment (36% vs. 55% recidivism rates for treatment completers and dropouts, respectively).

Most view the BIP data as fairly pessimistic overall. One possible reason is that most modern BIPs have not followed the typical path of psychological or public health interventions that begin with small efficacy studies and move toward larger trials and widespread implementation. BIPs were developed and implemented at a time when the need for programs was considered critical, but no empirical evidence existed on effective interventions. Thus, out of necessity, the practice–advocacy community spearheaded the development of the interventions without the benefit of efficacy trials of the treatment model. As other intervention approaches for IPV perpetrators are developed, it is critical that careful efficacy testing be conducted to understand whether interventions can work before widespread implementation occurs.

PSYCHOTHERAPEUTIC APPROACHES

Critics of psychotherapeutic approaches for IPV perpetrators argue that such approaches are inappropriate for IPV perpetrators because providing a clinical diagnosis pathologizes the behavior, thereby providing an excuse for it rather than ensuring that perpetrators take responsibility for their behavior (Adams, 1988). Others have argued that individually based, psychological therapeutic approaches are more suitable to address IPV perpetration than group-based BIPs. The very large etiologic literature suggests that IPV perpetrators have a range of individual problems, such as anger, hostility, emotional regulation, substance abuse, and personality disorders, that may contribute to perpetration and could be amenable to psychological treatment. Various forms of psychological approaches have been applied to the treatment of IPV perpetrators, including psychodynamic or insight-oriented interventions (Cogan & Porcerelli, 2003), attachment-focused interventions (Sonkin & Dutton, 2003; Stosny, 1995), and dialectical behavior therapy (DBT; Waltz, 2003) for IPV perpetrators with borderline personality disorder.

Psychodynamic or insight-oriented treatments are based on the notion that the perpetrators being treated may have experienced significant trauma and displace their anger onto their intimate partners (Cogan & Porcerelli, 2003; Saunders, 1996). Group (or individual) treatments are designed to provide support and empathy for the processing of these traumas to change current relationship behaviors by changing their internalized relationship schemas or templates (sometimes called *core conflictual relationship themes* or *internalized object relations*). Psychodynamic interventions tend to be unstructured, nonconfrontational, and individualized.

Attachment theory has been applied to adult intimate relationships (e.g., see Hazan & Shaver, 1987) and is beginning to be incorporated into psychotherapy approaches for adults (Cassidy & Shaver, 1999). Studies have found insecure attachment styles to be common among male and female IPV perpetrators (e.g., see Babcock, Jacobson, Gottman, & Yerington, 2000; Dutton, Saunders, Starzomki, & Bartholomew, 1994), which makes sense given that many of the traits that define insecure attachments are common among both male and female IPV perpetrators (e.g., jealousy, hostility, fear of abandonment; see Gormley, 2005, for a review). From an attachment perspective, treatment would be guided by the individual's attachment style, which determines his or her behavioral orientation in relationships. The therapist's role would be to provide a secure base to explore current relationships and develop new means to regulate attachment-related emotions and behavior to reduce the use of violence (Sonkin & Dutton, 2003).

A final individual therapeutic approach we discuss is DBT (Linehan, 1993). DBT is a form of cognitive–behavioral therapy that incorporates Zen and dialectical philosophy. DBT was originally developed to treat individuals who were chronically self-harming and suicidal, and it has been used with populations with other problems, including substance abuse and bulimia. In general, DBT is seen as appropriate for individuals with borderline personality disorder or related traits. DBT has shown success in these groups that are typically difficult to treat (e.g., see Koons et al., 2001; Linehan, Armstrong, Suarez, Allmon, & Heard, 1991). It may also be useful for IPV perpetrators because borderline traits are common among IPV perpetrators (e.g., see Hamberger & Hastings, 1991; Holtzworth-Munroe & Stuart, 1994, for review) and because DBT addresses problems of emotion dysregulation and tries to help provide clients with skills in this area. Additionally, DBT was designed to address multiple problems simultaneously, and IPV perpetrators often have concomitant mental health and/or substance use issues (Gondolf, 2004; Holtzworth-Munroe & Stuart, 1994; Leonard, 2005). Further elaboration of DBT for IPV perpetrators can be found elsewhere (Fruzzetti & Levensky, 2000; Waltz, 2003).

Couples Counseling

Intervening with couples to address partner violence has been highly controversial because of concerns about situations in which the abuser imposes high levels of control, coercion, and intimidation. In such situations, a victim could not be expected to participate in couples treatment, and in fact, it would be dangerous to try to do so.

Several points have converged to suggest that couples treatment for partner violence can be a viable option under certain circumstances. First, there is a growing recognition that there is heterogeneity in the types of partner violence and that much of partner violence may arise from arguments and verbal conflict (e.g., see Cascardi & Vivian, 1995; Johnson, 1995; S. G. O'Leary & Smith Slep, 2006) rather than being a systematic effort by one partner to exert control over the other. Second, it has become widely recognized that physical partner violence is often perpetrated by both partners in the same relationship, referred to as mutual, reciprocal, or bidirectional violence. Although reciprocal violence could result from severe abuse by one partner and self-defensive responses by the other, data suggest that this is not always, or even often, the case. For example, studies have shown that in reciprocally violent relationships both partners tend to initiate violence (Gray & Foshee, 1997; Straus & Gelles, 1995); partners with antisocial tendencies partner together (Kim & Capaldi, 2004; Moffitt, Caspi, Rutter, & Silva, 2001); the communication patterns of violent couples differ from those of nonviolent couples (Burman, John, & Margolin, 1992); and partner variables are important predictors of physical IPV perpetration (Capaldi & Kim, 2007). Finally, in certain circumstances, couples counseling may be preferred by the couple and/or by the primary victim, because the dissolution of the relationship is not always the desired goal of those seeking intervention for an abusive relationship; many individuals who seek couples counseling engage in violence but do not see it as the main problem in the relationship (Ehrensaft & Vivian, 1996; K. D. O'Leary, Vivian, & Malone, 1992). Among Latinos and other ethnic groups, relationship dissolution may be inconsistent with cultural norms, and encouraging it may alienate individuals or couples from seeking help (Perilla & Perez, 2002).

Couples counseling for the cessation of violence is different from standard couples counseling, which aims to decrease relationship problems and increase relationship satisfaction (Heyman & Schlee, 2003; K. D. O'Leary, Heyman, & Neidig, 1999). The goal of couples counseling for IPV cessation is to decrease and stop violence within a relationship. It is based on a systems perspective that assumes that each person's behavior is both a response to their partner's behavior and a stimulus for the partner's subsequent response, and it assumes that much of violence occurs in the context of conflict that escalates into physical violence. Each partner is taught behavioral skills for defusing conflict before it reaches physical aggression. Like many interventions, this approach is useful for only certain types of IPV and would not be appropriate for couples in which violence is used against one partner as a chronic and systematic method of control and dominance, a point that has been made by authors who have recommended couples counseling (Bograd & Mederos, 1999; Heyman & Schlee, 2003; K. D. O'Leary, 2002; Stith, Rosen, McCollum, & Thomsen, 2004).

A few empirical studies have examined couples counseling for IPV cessation, but the results are not clear. Most have used behavioral or cognitive–behavioral treatment methods. Other types of couples treatment (e.g., emotion-focused therapy) have not been evaluated for IPV cessation (see Stith, Rosen, & McCollum, 2003). The studies have used different populations, different study entry criteria, and different comparison groups, thus making comparisons across studies difficult. The largest and perhaps most rigorous study was Dunford's (2000) study of navy personnel. In that study, over 800 couples who had been referred for IPV by the husband were randomly assigned to one of four groups: couples treatment, group treatment for the offenders (similar to a traditional BIP described earlier), rigorous monitoring, or a no-intervention control group. The results showed no differences between any of the four groups at 1-year follow up, but men in all four groups greatly reduced their IPV, with overall recidivism rates at 17% for injuring a partner and 4% for re-arrest. It is important to note that attendance by wives among men assigned to the couples treatment group was relatively low, at about 40% overall, which may have affected the impact of this treatment. Dunford's study has also been criticized for use of a population (naval personnel) with very limited generalizability.

Other studies examining couples counseling have compared group couples counseling with individual couples counseling (Stith et al., 2004) or have compared couples counseling with gender-specific groups (Brannen & Rubin, 1996; K. D. O'Leary et al., 1999). All of these studies have been small, and only Stith et al. (2004) included a no-treatment comparison group. In this study ($N = 51$), Stith et al. found that both group couples counseling and individual couples counseling resulted in lower recidivism rates than a no-treatment control group, with recidivism rates at 6 months of 67% for the no-treatment control group, and 43% and 25% for individual couples counseling and group couples counseling, respectively. Individual couples counseling and the no-treatment control group were not statistically different, though this may have been due to low power, as individual couples counseling reduced recidivism by over a third compared with no treatment. Two other studies (Brannen & Rubin, 1996; K. D. O'Leary et al., 1999) compared couples counseling with gender-specific group treatments. Both studies found IPV reductions over time but with no differences between treatment conditions (neither study included a no-treatment control group). Also, both studies examined safety issues associated with couples counseling and reported no concern (Brannen & Rubin, 1996, used a court-referred population, whereas

K. D. O'Leary et al., 1999, used volunteer couples). Finally, in a study not directly targeting relationship violence, Markman, Renick, Floyd, Stanley, and Clements (1993) compared couples receiving the Prevention and Relationship Enhancement Program (PREP) with control couples over a period of 4 years. They found that couples receiving PREP reported fewer instances of physical violence than control couples. However, baseline IPV was not measured, so it was unclear whether this effect was due to selection bias, a possible primary prevention effect, or a possible secondary prevention effect.

Substance Abuse Treatment

As with couples counseling, the link between substance abuse and IPV perpetration has also been controversial over concerns that ascribing a causal role to substance use will excuse the perpetrator's behavior (e.g., see Zubretsky & Digirolamo, 1996). However, a large body of research shows a strong and consistent relationship between substance use and IPV perpetration. Many studies have shown that men often report having used alcohol prior to perpetrating IPV (Kantor & Straus, 1987; Leonard & Blane, 1992). Also, episodes of male-to-female partner violence tend to co-occur with episodes of drinking, and IPV is more severe when drinking is involved (Testa, Quigley, & Leonard, 2003). Fals-Stewart (2003) found IPV was 8 to 11 times more common on days of drinking compared with days with no drinking, and 17 to 20 times more likely on days of heavy drinking compared with nondrinking days.

Perhaps the most compelling data regarding the nature of the relation between substance use and IPV perpetration come from studies examining whether IPV perpetration decreases with substance use treatment. Several studies have examined IPV perpetration rates among men seeking treatment for substance abuse. One study followed alcoholic men treated with behavioral marital therapy ($N = 88$) and found that the proportion of couples experiencing any violence over the course of treatment changed from 61% at pretreatment to 23% at 1-year posttreatment and 19% at 2-years posttreatment. Moreover, treated alcoholic men's cessation of IPV perpetration was strongly related to their abstaining from alcohol, and those who stayed remitted from alcohol use had rates of IPV that were no higher than matched nonalcoholic control participants (O'Farrell & Murphy, 1995; O'Farrell, Van Hutton, & Murphy, 1999). A second, larger study replicated these findings; men with alcoholism who were treated with behavioral couples' therapy reduced IPV rates from 60% to 24%, and the gains were greatest among couples in which alcohol remittance was maintained (60% to 12%) as compared with couples in which the alcoholic partner relapsed (60% to 30%; O'Farrell, Murphy, Stephan, Fals-Stewart, & Murphy, 2004).

A similar study examined whether individually based (i.e., noncouples) outpatient treatment for people with alcoholism would affect IPV rates. Among the 301 alcoholic men who participated in the study, the IPV rate decreased from 56% at baseline (vs. 14% for baseline control participants) to 25% a year after treatment (vs. 15% for control participants). Again, the greatest decrease in reported IPV perpetration rates was among participants who remained remitted in alcohol use (14%) versus those who relapsed (32%). Finally, a small trial ($N = 80$) compared behavioral couples treatment with individual treatment for substance-using men (Fals-Stewart, Kashdan, O'Farrell, & Birchler, 2002). That study randomly assigned participants to the two intervention groups (but no control group was used) and found that behavioral couples treatment reduced IPV over a 1-year period (43% to 18%) compared with individual treatment (48% to 43%). It is noteworthy that the treatments in these studies did not focus on partner violence, given the difficulty other treatment approaches (e.g., such as those used in BIPs) that have focused on partner violence have had in changing behavior.

Data from studies of batterer intervention treatments also show support for the link between alcohol or substance use and reductions in the use of IPV. In one study of men treated in a BIP, alcohol abuse was related to recidivism after treatment (Hamberger & Hastings, 1990). In addition, Snow-Jones and Gondolf (2001) found that treatment for alcohol abuse following BIP completion reduced the likelihood of reassault by 30% to 40%. In sum, these studies suggest that one potentially effective strategy for reducing partner violence is to target the reduction of substance use among those who perpetrate IPV.

ISSUES IN IMPROVING INTERVENTIONS FOR PERPETRATORS OF INTIMATE PARTNER VIOLENCE

There is much work to do in the development and testing of interventions for IPV perpetrators, and the etiologic literature in several areas must be taken into account in the development of new strategies. A few of these issues— tailoring of treatment to types of IPV perpetrators, intervening with female perpetrators, and cultural issues in IPV interventions—are discussed in the sections that follow.

Tailoring Interventions for Types of Perpetrators

In the etiologic literature on IPV perpetrators, there is much discussion of the variation in form, function, and motivation for IPV perpetration. Perpetrators have been categorized along various dimensions, including severity of aggression (K. D. O'Leary, 1993), personality types (Hamberger & Hastings, 1986), psychological factors coupled with the generality of violence (Holtzworth-Monroe & Stuart, 1994), and motives for battering (Johnson, 1995; Tweed & Dutton, 1988).

Currently, the two most cited typologies of IPV perpetration are Johnson's (1995) conceptualization of violence on the basis of violence frequency and coercive control and Holtzworth-Munroe's (Holtworth-Munroe & Stuart, 1994) typology of abusive men that is based on the frequency and generality of violence and men's personality characteristics. Johnson (1995) asserted that two types of violence are predominant and that each differs in the root causes. *Intimate terrorism* (sometimes called *patriarchal terrorism*) is characterized by recurring, serious violence that is used for the purpose of controlling the partner. *Situational violence* (originally called *common couple violence*) is characterized by aggression that is conflict based, often mutual, and typically low level. Johnson argued that intimate terrorists are most likely to be found when accessing clinical samples (i.e., either men in BIPs or women accessed through IPV services), whereas situational violence is the type of violence tapped by national surveys and community samples of nonidentified perpetrators or victims. Holtzworth-Munroe's typology (Holzworth-Munroe & Stuart, 1994) is based on an integration of findings from a number of other typological studies and contains three types of male IPV perpetrators: family only, borderline dysphoric, and generally violent (a recent revision includes a fourth group, low-level antisocial; Holtzworth-Munroe, Meehan, Herron, Rehman, & Stuart, 2003). The types are hypothesized to differ with respect to the level of violence, generality of violence, and a personality–psychopathology dimension.

Typological approaches such as these indicate different interventions for different types of perpetrators or violence (Cavanaugh & Gelles, 2005; Johnson, 1995; Johnson & Leone, 2005; Saunders, 2001). For instance, Johnson (1995) argued that situational violence may be addressed with strategies such as couples counseling or anger management, but interventions for intimate terrorism, which he suggested is perpetrated almost exclusively by men, must focus on women's safety and helping them leave the relationship. Johnson also noted the dangers of using the wrong intervention for a particular type. Obviously, couples counseling would be dangerous for victims of intimate terrorism. Less obvious, though, is the danger of intervening incorrectly with perpetrators and victims of situational violence. Interventions that focus on the patterns of power and control may alienate individuals perpetrating situational violence; as a result, they may drop out of treatment or conclude that there is no violence problem in their relationships (Johnson & Leone, 2005). Holtzworth-Munroe et al. (2003) suggested that hypotheses may be generated and tested examining how different types of batterers respond to different treatments. For instance, borderline–dysphoric types may benefit from a more process-oriented treatment or a cognitive–behavioral treatment developed specifically for borderline perpetrators. In contrast, generally violent men who have a high degree of antisociality would likely not benefit from insight-oriented therapy but might respond well to cognitive–behavioral treatments. However, Holtzworth-Munroe et al. cautioned against jumping to the conclusion that particular interventions for batterer subtypes are appropriate before further testing.

No studies have tested tailored interventions directly, but in a post hoc analysis, Saunders (1996) found that perpetrators with higher dependent personality scores responded more favorably to the process-oriented psychodynamic treatment, whereas those with antisocial tendencies responded more favorably to feminist cognitive–behavioral treatment. This finding seems consistent with Holtzworth-Munroe's typology of male batterers, but other findings from the study require explanation (e.g., hypomanic men responded better to the feminist cognitive–behavioral treatment; men who reported higher relationship satisfaction prior to treatment responded better to feminist cognitive–behavioral treatment). Also, the validity of study was weakened by high attrition; analyses included less than two thirds of men who enrolled.

Although typologies hold promise for advancing the understanding of IPV perpetrators and how to intervene with them, some researchers have cautioned against viewing typologies as panacea. Capaldi and Kim (2007) pointed out that there is relatively little empirical work validating typologies, that no intervention studies have been tested on the basis of known typologies, and that typologies tend to exclude relationship or dyadic factors that contribute to IPV perpetration. For example, although some of Johnson's assertions about intimate terrorism and situational violence have been supported (e.g., intimate terrorism resulted in greater physical and psychological consequences than situational violence; Johnson & Leone, 2005), others have not (e.g., a large Canadian study found that both men and women perpetrated intimate terrorism; LaRoche, 2005), and few longitudinal studies have examined the stability of violence type (i.e., whether situational violence can develop into intimate terrorism). Holtzworth-Munroe et al. (2003) examined whether the conceptual and empirical distinctions between types of batterers held over time. Some findings were consistent with the model but others were not, and men classified as different types of IPV perpetrators became less distinct over time. Finally, Capaldi and Kim (2007) argued that typologies based on individuals ignore dyadic or partner factors that are related to perpetration. For instance, longitudinal studies have shown that a partner's perpetration (Feld & Straus, 1989; S. G. O'Leary & Smith Slep, 2003) and antisocial behavior (Kim & Capaldi, 2004) predict an individual's later IPV perpetration. Other studies have shown that patterns of IPV perpetration are not strongly related across relationship partners (Capaldi, Shortt, & Crosby, 2003; Whitaker, Le, & Niolon, 2006). Thus, although typologies hold promise for understanding variations in the form and function of partner violence, they are likely only a piece of the puzzle.

Intervening With Female Perpetrators of Intimate Partner Violence

Women's perpetration of IPV has been a highly controversial topic since Straus and Gelles (1995) first found that men and women reported approximately equal frequencies of physically violent acts perpetrated against their partner. Some argue that women's perpetration of physical IPV is an important issue to attend to and address (Archer, 2000; Capaldi & Kim, 2007; Dutton & Nicholls, 2005; Straus, 2004; Whitaker, Haileyesus, Swahn, & Saltzman, 2007), whereas others argue that women's IPV perpetration is generally not serious for a variety of reasons: It is done in response to men's violence, and women are unlikely to injure their partner and are much less likely kill their partner (see Johnson, 2005; Kimmel, 2002; Loseke & Kurz, 2004; Saunders, 2002). From these latter perspectives, stopping men's IPV perpetration violence is primary and would end the most consequential IPV.

A number of arguments have been made that suggest it is important to address women's perpetration of IPV. First, several studies have documented the occurrence of IPV in lesbian intimate relationships, in which women are necessarily the perpetrators, at rates comparable with those of heterosexual relationships (McClennen, 2005). Second, within heterosexual relationships, findings indicate not only that the frequency of physical IPV perpetration is similar in men and women (Archer, 2000) but also that physical IPV is initiated at about the same frequency by men and women (Gray & Foshee, 1997; Straus & Gelles, 1995) and that it is often perpetrated by both partners within a relationship (Straus & Gelles, 1995; Whitaker, Haileyesus, et al., 2007). IPV that is reciprocal may escalate and lead to more serious violence over time, increasing the risk of IPV victimization to one or both partners (e.g., see Capaldi & Owen, 2001; Feld & Straus, 1989). Also, although male IPV perpetrators are more likely to cause injuries than female IPV perpetrators, the overall differences are small (ds = .08 and .15 for reported injuries and seeking medical treatment, respectively; Archer, 2000), and the health impact on men and on lesbian partners is not negligible. Finally, although most studies of health impacts have documented the serious consequences for female victims, some have shown that male victims experience similar physical and psychological harm (Coker et al., 1998; George, 1999; Pimlott-Kubiak & Cortina, 2003).

Warrantless and mandatory arrest policies have increased the number of women arrested for IPV perpetration who subsequently enter BIPs (Hamberger & Arnold, 1990; Martin, 1997). For example, Henning and Feder (2004) found that among individuals arrested over a 3.5-year period in Shelby County, Tennessee, about 17% were women. Whether women should be arrested is controversial. Some data suggest that women arrested for IPV are primarily acting in self-defense (Hamberger & Potente, 1994; Saunders, 1986). Other researchers have argued that women are simply treated more leniently in the criminal justice system (Brown, 2004; Henning & Renauer, 2005). Given that the evidence regarding BIPs' effectiveness for men (for whom they were designed) shows a small effect at best, it is highly questionable whether the same programs will be effective for women.

Some aspects of modern BIPs may be relevant for women (e.g., power and control motives, cognitive–behavioral strategies), but little is known about female IPV perpetrators, especially those arrested for IPV offenses. Studies of women arrested for IPV perpetration show both similarities and difference to male arrestees. Henning, Jones, and Holdford (2003) found that men and women arrested for IPV perpetration were similar in demographic characteristics and childhood experiences but differed with regard to mental health problems: Women perpetrators were more likely to have taken psychotropic medicine, to have attempted suicide, and to have elevated scores on the Millon Clinical Multiaxial Inventory—III (Millon, Davis, & Millon, 1997), whereas men had a stronger history of alcohol abuse and conduct problems as a child. A different analysis found that women were more likely to have used a weapon and to have seriously injured their victims than men, whereas men were more likely to be seen as a threat to their victim and had more past violence and arrests than women (Henning & Feder, 2004). Other studies have found that women arrested for IPV perpetration had high rates of substance and drug use (Carney & Buttell, 2004; Stuart, Moore, Ramsey, & Kahler, 2003), which has also been shown among men.

No controlled studies have examined intervention effectiveness for reducing IPV perpetration among women. Carney and Buttell (2004) reported on data from 139 women who attended (mostly court-ordered) a treatment program for IPV perpetrators in South Carolina. The program used the same curriculum male perpetrators typically receive, a feminist-informed psychoeducational group with cognitive–behavioral elements that also emphasizes accountability. Only 26 women completed or graduated from the program, and 77 (55%) dropped out (36 were still in the program but had not completed). Women who completed the program showed reductions in spouse-specific aggression, propensity for abusiveness, and passive-aggressiveness, and only 1 woman was re-arrested on IPV charges. It is not possible to draw conclusions about treatment effectiveness on this basis of this uncontrolled study. More work is needed to understand women's IPV perpetration, the characteristics of those who enter and stay in treatment, and what treatment models are most appropriate for female IPV perpetrators.

Cultural Tailoring of Intimate Partner Violence Interventions

In many areas, a large proportion of men entering BIPs are racial/ethnic minorities (Gondolf, 2002). As already noted, most BIPs use a single approach to working with perpetrators, one that focuses on patriarchy, power, control, and responsibility and accountability for individual behavior. BIPs' focus on these constructs stems primarily from a Western, White, Anglo-Saxon Protestant cultural perspective and has generally failed to take into account how social and cultural contexts might affect the meaning and use of violence against a partner (Mederos, 2002). For instance, different cultural norms regarding masculinity, gender roles, family responsibilities, and traditions, marriage, and religion could affect why violence occurs and, more important, the process of behavioral change needed to end the violence.

There is some evidence to suggest that traditional BIPs are less effective for Black men than for White men (Gondolf, 1997; Williams, 1998) and that culturally focused programs would be more effective in reducing dropout and reassault rates in Black men (Gondolf & Williams, 2001). However, other studies suggest that there is no difference in traditional programs' effectiveness for Black and White men (Buttell & Carney, 2005; Butell & Pike, 2003), and Gondolf (2007) found that Black men in a culturally focused BIP were actually more likely to reassault a partner than men in a mixed-race BIP. No studies to our knowledge have examined the differential effectiveness of BIPs for Latinos or perpetrators from other cultural backgrounds.

However, many authors have discussed the need to tailor IPV treatments and BIPs to address issues relevant for minority populations. Most discussions have focused on Blacks (e.g., see Donnelly, Smith, & Williams, 2002; Gondolf & Williams, 2001) and Latinos (Almeida & Hudak, 2002; Perilla & Perez, 2002; Ramirez Hernandez, 2002), though discussions of issues facing other groups can also be found (e.g., see Raj & Silverman, 2002). Common focal points of these programs are that they (a) incorporate a cultural focus into both the curricula and the structure of the program; (b) use a critical consciousness framework, in which perpetrators are encouraged, through dialogue and idea exchange, to reevaluate their assumptions about gender roles and the acceptability of violence and to ensure they are consistent with their values; and (c) underscore the importance of having facilitators or group leaders who are either from the same cultural background as the participants or at least trained in cultural focus and sensitivity (Almeida & Hudak, 2002; Donnelly et al., 2002; Gondolf & Williams, 2001; Perilla & Perez, 2002; Ramirez Hernandez, 2002).

Authors have suggested that programs for Black men must address the historical oppression of Blacks in the United States and explore how this oppression may relate to Black men's lack of power in society and to their use of violence (Donnelly et al., 2002; Gondolf & Williams, 2001). It has also been suggested that gender roles among Black have tended to be more fluid and less structured than in the White middle-class community, and this issue should thus be addressed differently in BIPs (Gondolf & Williams, 2001). A final issue is that of racial identity, with some suggestion that Black individuals with a stronger sense of racial identity may respond differently to a tailored versus a nontailored treatment (Gondolf & Williams, 2001).

As with Blacks, specific issues have been addressed in tailored interventions for Latino IPV perpetrators. Generally, those tailored interventions (a) emphasize an ecological perspective, which is central to Latino culture and stresses the importance of considering individuals (and their behavior) in the context of their societal, cultural, social, familial, and so on, environments; (b) address the cultural concepts of masculinity (or *machismo*) and respect, helping Latino men to distinguish between the positive aspects of *machismo* from the aspects that seem to encourage the oppression of women; and (c) incorporate the cultural emphasis on family into their work with Latino men (Perilla & Perez, 2002; Ramirez Hernandez, 2002). These approaches are different from, if not at odds with, the approaches of traditional programs, which tend to portray masculinity in a unidimensional instead of multidimensional framework, and which do not emphasize the batterer's role in the family and the importance of family cohesion.

Although there are few data that speak to the relative efficacy of culturally tailored versus nontailored approaches, some tailored programs have collected their own outcome data. An uncontrolled outcome evaluation of Caminar Latino, a comprehensive program for Latino immigrant families that includes a BIP (Perilla & Perez, 2002), revealed that (a) 90% of the men who were court-mandated completed the entire program, (b) 97% of program participants had not reentered the court system 6 months after program completion, (c) both men and their partners reported a significant decrease in men's use of physical violence from pre- to posttest, and (d) men reported a significant decrease in their use of verbal and emotional abuse from pre- to posttest (their partners reported a reduction, but it did not reach statistical significance). A preliminary analysis of a BIP for incarcerated Black men (Donnelly et al., 2002) indicated that 81% of the men completed the program successfully, and participants showed change in several constructs that could lead to reduced IPV (e.g., knowledge about IPV, greater internalized locus of control). Although these uncontrolled evaluation findings should not be taken as efficacy data, they are promising and at least indicate that the programs are well received by participants who complete them. Whether this is due to the cultural focus remains an empirical question. Future research should rigorously test these types of programs compared with existing programs and with different target populations.

BATTERER INTERVENTION PROGRAMS REVISITED: CHALLENGES TO WIDESPREAD ADOPTION OF NEW MODELS

We agree with several other authors (Eckhardt et al., 2006; Feder & Wilson, 2006) that there is a clear need for an expanded set of interventions for today's BIPs. We have discussed a variety of models, many of which require further development and empirical validation before being ready for widespread adoption. However, state and local standards regulating BIPs, along with local capacities to implement different treatment models, present added challenges to incorporating new intervention strategies into modern

BIPs. Standards for BIPs were developed to regulate treatment approaches to ensure some minimal treatment standards for court-ordered perpetrators. With hundreds of BIPs throughout the United States serving IPV perpetrators, this seems reasonable. However, standards have been criticized as being used to serve an ideology rather than as a way to ensure that empirically supported interventions are offered (Corvo & Johnson, 2003; Dutton & Corvo, 2006; Eckhardt et al., 2006; Gelles, 2002).

A review of BIP standards conducted by Austin and Dankwort (1999) found that a majority emphasized patriarchy as a cause of violence and accountability as a goal of intervention. Most standards cited group formats as the desired mode of intervention, and a majority mentioned feminist psychoeducational and/or cognitive–behavioral groups as the intervention approach. A majority of standards also prohibited several forms of treatment, including one-on-one interventions (68%) and couples counseling (73%). There is little empirical evidence to support these requirements. Maiuro et al. (2002) examined the research base around common elements of 30 states' standards, including modalities and length of treatment, specification of treatment orientation and content, education and training of interventionists, and development and revision of standards. They found little empirical evidence supporting the common trends in standards for BIP treatment. Moreover, they concluded that the most serious concern about strict state standards is in the "risk of stunting the development of new and alternative interventions" (p. 38). A majority of states also had no process for updating standards in a way that ensured the latest research was represented. Thus, for new, empirically supported intervention models to be used in BIPs, work on treatment standards at the state and local level will also be needed.

A second challenge is the feasibility of implementing a range of new models in community-based programs for IPV perpetrators. Earlier in this chapter, we discussed various types of therapeutic approaches and couples counseling. Even if such models were demonstrated to be the most effective way to intervene with IPV perpetrators, the cost and feasibility of mandating (or even giving as a diversionary option) treatment of perpetrators in individualized therapy delivered by master's- or doctoral-level professionals could be prohibitive. More work needs to be done to establish effectiveness and to package these services in a way that could be easily adopted into current systems addressing IPV.

CONCLUSION

There is much work to do on many fronts to develop, test, and broadly implement intervention strategies that will result in a substantial reduction in the repeated perpetration of physical IPV. There is much to learn about the etiology of IPV perpetration, how to craft intervention and prevention efforts based on that etiology, and how to focus the resources available to maximize IPV reduction and achieve the greatest health impact. Our hope is that with new research and promising findings, the broader IPV community will be open to implementing new strategies that have been shown to be most effective in reducing IPV among perpetrators.

REFERENCES

Adams, D. (1988). Treatment models of men who batter: A profeminist analysis. In K. Yllo & M. Bograd (Eds.), *Feminist perspectives on wife abuse* (pp. 176–199). Newbury Park, CA: Sage.

Almeida, R. V., & Hudak, J. (2002). The cultural context model. In E. Aldarando & F. Mederos (Eds.), *Programs for men who batter: Intervention and prevention strategies in a diverse society* (pp. 10-2–10-26). Kingston, NJ: Civic Research Institute.

Archer, J. (2000). Sex differences in aggression between heterosexual partners: A meta-analytic review. *Psychological Bulletin, 26*, 651–680.

Austin, J. B., & Dankwort, J. (1999). Standards for batterer programs: A review and analysis. *Journal of Interpersonal Violence, 14*, 152–68.

Babcock, J. C., Green, C. E., & Robie, C. (2004). Does batterers' treatment work? A meta-analytic review of domestic violence treatment. *Clinical Psychology Review, 23*, 1023–1053.

Babcock, J. C., Jacobson, N. S., Gottman, J. M., & Yerington, T. Y. (2000). Attachment, emotional regulation, and the function of marital violence: Differences between secure, preoccupied, and dismissing violent and nonviolent husbands. *Journal of Family Violence, 15*, 391–409.

Bograd, M., & Mederos, F. (1999). Battering and couples therapy: Universal screening and selection of treatment modality. *Journal of Marital & Family Therapy, 3*, 291–312.

Brannen, S. J., & Rubin, A. (1996). Comparing the effectiveness of gender-specific and couples groups in a court-mandated spouse abuse treatment program. *Research on Social Work Practice, 6*, 405–424.

Brown, G. A. (2004). Gender as a factor in the response of the law-enforcement system to violence against partners. *Sexuality & Culture, 8*, 3–139.

Burman, B., John, R. S., & Margolin, G. (1992). Observed patterns of conflict in violent, nonviolent, and nondistressed couples. *Behavioral Assessment, 14*, 15–37.

Buttell, F. P., & Carney, M. M. (2005). Do batterer intervention programs serve African American and Caucasian batterers equally well? An investigation of a 26-week program. *Research on Social Work Practice, 15*, 19–28.

Buttell, F. P., & Pike, C. K. (2003). Investigating the differential effectiveness of a batterer treatment program on outcomes for African American and Caucasian batterers. *Research on Social Work Practice, 13*, 675–692.

Capaldi, D. M., & Kim, H. K. (2007). Typological approaches to violence in couples: A critique and alternative conceptual approach. *Clinical Psychology Review, 27,* 253–265.

Capaldi, D. M., & Owen, L. D. (2001). Physical aggression in a community sample of at-risk young couples: Gender comparisons for high frequency, injury, and fear. *Journal of Family Psychology, 15,* 425–440.

Capaldi, D. M., Shortt, J. W., & Crosby, L. (2003). Physical and psychological aggression in at-risk young couples: Stability and change in young adulthood. *Merrill-Palmer Quarterly, 49,* 1–27.

Carney, M. M., & Buttell, F. P. (2004). A multidimensional evaluation of a treatment program for female batterers: A pilot study. *Research on Social Work Practice, 14,* 249–258.

Cascardi, M., & Vivian, D. (1995). Context for specific episodes of marital aggression. *Journal of Family Violence, 10,* 265–293.

Cassidy, J., & Shaver, P. R. (Eds.). (1999). *Handbook of attachment: Theory, research, and clinical applications.* New York: Guilford Press.

Cavanaugh, M. M., & Gelles, R. J. (2005). The utility of male domestic violence offender typologies. *Journal of Interpersonal Violence, 20,* 155–166.

Cogan R., & Porcerelli, J. H. (2003). Psychoanalytic psychotherapy with people in abusive relationships: Treatment outcome. *Journal of Aggression, Maltreatment & Trauma, 7,* 29–46.

Coker, A., Davis, K., Arias, I., Desai, S., Sanderson, M., Brandt, H., & Smith, P. H. (1998). Physical and mental health effects of intimate partner violence for men and women. *American Journal of Preventive Medicine, 23,* 260–268.

Corvo, K., & Johnson, P. J. (2003). Vilification of the "batterer": How blame shapes domestic violence policy and interventions. *Aggression and Violent Behavior, 8,* 259–281.

Donnelly, D. A., Smith, L. G., & Williams, O. J. (2002). The batterer education program for incarcerated African-American men, 1997–2000. In E. Aldarando & F. Mederos (Eds.), *Programs for men who batter: Intervention and prevention strategies in a diverse society* (pp. 13-2–13-16). Kingston, NJ: Civic Research Institute.

Dunford, F. W. (2000). The San Diego Navy Experiment: An assessment of interventions for men who assault their wives. *Journal of Consulting and Clinical Psychology, 68,* 468–476.

Dutton, D. G., & Corvo, K. (2006). Transforming a flawed policy: A call to revive psychology and science in domestic violence research and practice. *Aggression and Violent Behavior, 11,* 457–483.

Dutton, D. G., & Nicholls, T. (2005). The gender paradigm in domestic violence research and theory: The conflict of theory and data. *Aggression and Violent Behavior, 10,* 680–714.

Dutton, D. G., Saunders, K., Starzomski, A. J., & Bartholomew, K. (1994). Intimacy-anger and insecure attachment as precursors of abuse in intimate relationships. *Journal of Applied Social Psychology, 24,* 1367–1386.

Eckhardt, C. I., Murphy, C., Black, D., & Suhr, L. (2006). Intervention programs for perpetrators of intimate partner violence: Conclusions from a clinical research perspective. *Public Health Reports, 121*, 369–381.

Ehrensaft, M. K., & Vivian, D. (1996). Spouses' reasons for not reporting existing physical aggression as a marital problem. *Journal of Family Psychology, 10*, 443–453.

Fals-Stewart, W. (2003). The occurrence of partner physical aggression on days of alcohol consumption: A longitudinal diary study. *Journal of Consulting and Clinical Psychology, 1*, 41–52.

Fals-Stewart, W., Kashdan, T. B., O'Farrell, T. J., & Birchler, G. R. (2002). Behavioral couples therapy for drug-abusing patients: Effects on partner violence. *Journal of Substance Abuse Treatment, 22*, 87–96.

Feder, L., & Wilson, D. B. (2006). A meta-analytic review of court mandated batterer treatment programs: Can courts affect abusers' behavior? *Journal of Experimental Criminology, 1*, 239–262.

Feld, S. L., & Straus, M. (1989). Escalation and desistance from wife assault in marriage. *Criminology, 27*, 141–161.

Fruzzetti, A. E., & Levensky, E. R. (2000). Dialectical behavior therapy for domestic violence: Rationale and procedures. *Cognitive and Behavioral Practice, 7*, 435–447.

Gelles, R. J. (2002). Standards for programs for men who batter? Not yet. *Journal of Aggression, Maltreatment & Trauma, 5*, 11–20.

George, M. J. (1999). Invisible touch. *Aggression and Violent Behavior, 8*, 23–60.

Gondolf, E. W. (1997). Patterns of reassault in batterer programs. *Violence and Victims, 12*, 373–387.

Gondolf, E. W. (2002). *Batterer intervention systems: Issues, outcomes, and recommendations*. Thousand Oaks, CA: Sage.

Gondolf, E. W. (2004). Evaluating batterer counseling programs: A difficult task showing some effects and implications. *Aggression and Violent Behavior, 9*, 605–631.

Gondolf, E. W. (2007). Culturally focused batterer counseling for African American men. *Criminology & Public Policy, 6*, 341–366.

Gondolf, E. W., & Williams, O. J. (2001). Culturally focused batterer counseling for African American men. *Trauma, Violence, & Abuse, 2*, 283–295.

Gormley, B. (2005). An adult attachment theoretical perspective of gender symmetry in intimate partner violence. *Sex Roles, 52*, 785–795.

Gray, H. M., & Foshee, V. (1997). Adolescent dating violence: Difference between one-sided and mutually violent profiles. *Journal of Interpersonal Violence, 12*, 126–141.

Hamberger, L. K. (1997). Cognitive behavioral treatment of men who batter their partners. *Cognitive and Behavioral Practice, 4*, 147–169.

Hamberger, L. K., & Arnold, J. (1990). The impact of mandatory arrest on domestic violence perpetrator counseling services. *Family Violence and Sexual Assault Bulletin, 6*, 11–12.

Hamberger, L. K., & Hastings, J. E. (1986). Personality correlates of men who abuse their partners: A cross validation study. *Journal of Family Violence, 1,* 323–341.

Hamberger, L. K., & Hastings, J. E. (1990). Recidivism following spouse abuse abatement counseling: Treatment program implications. *Violence and Victims, 5,* 157–169.

Hamberger, L. K., & Hastings, J. E. (1991). Personality correlates of men who batter and non-violent men: Some continuities and discontinuities. *Journal of Family Violence, 6,* 131–147.

Hamberger, L. K., & Potente, T. (1994). Counseling heterosexual women arrested for domestic violence: Implications for theory and practice. *Violence and Victims, 9,* 125–137.

Hazan, C., & Shaver, P. (1987). Romantic love conceptualized as an attachment process. *Journal of Personality and Social Psychology, 52,* 511–524

Henning, K., & Feder, L. (2004). A comparison of men and women arrested for domestic violence: Who presents the greater threat? *Journal of Family Violence, 19,* 69–80.

Henning, K., Jones, A., & Holdford, R. (2003). Treatment needs of women arrested for domestic violence: A comparison with male offenders. *Journal of Interpersonal Violence, 18,* 839–856.

Henning, K., & Renauer, B. (2005). Prosecution of women arrested for intimate partner abuse. *Violence and Victims, 20,* 171–189.

Heyman, R. E., & Schlee, K. (2003). Stopping wife abuse via physical aggression couples treatment. *Journal of Aggression, Maltreatment & Trauma, 7,* 135–157.

Holtzworth-Munroe, A., Meehan, J. C., Herron, K., Rehman, U., & Stuart, G. L. (2003). Do subtypes of maritally violent men continue to differ over time? *Journal of Consulting and Clinical Psychology, 71,* 728–740.

Holtzworth-Munroe, A., & Stuart, G. L. (1994). Typologies of male batterers: Three subtypes and the differences among them. *Psychological Bulletin, 116,* 476–497.

Johnson, M. P. (1995). Patriarchal terrorism and common couple violence: Two forms of violence against women. *Journal of Marriage and the Family, 57,* 283–294.

Johnson, M. P. (2005). Domestic violence: It's not about gender—or is it? *Journal of Marriage and the Family, 67,* 1126–1130.

Johnson, M. P., & Leone, J. M. (2005). The differential effects of intimate terrorism and situational couple violence: Findings from the National Violence Against Women Survey. *Journal of Family Issues, 26,* 322–349.

Kantor, G. K., & Straus, M. A. (1987). The "drunken bum" theory of wife beating. *Social Problems, 34,* 213–230.

Kim, H. K., & Capaldi, D. M. (2004). The association of antisocial behavior and depressive symptoms between partners and risk for aggression in romantic relationships. *Journal of Family Psychology, 18,* 82–96.

Kimmel, M. S. (2002). "Gender symmetry" in domestic violence: A substantive and methodological research review. *Violence Against Women, 8,* 1332–1363.

Koons, C. R., Robbins, C. J., Tweed, J. L., Lynch, T. R., Gonzales, A. M., Morse, J. Q., et al. (2001). Efficacy of dialectical behavior therapy in women veterans with borderline personality disorder. *Behavior Therapy, 32,* 371–390.

LaRoche, D. (2005). *Aspects of the context and consequences of domestic violence: Situational couple violence and intimate terrorism in Canada in 1999.* Quebec City, Quebec, Canada: Government of Quebec.

Leonard, K. E. (2005). Alcohol and intimate partner violence: When can we say that heavy drinking is a contributing cause of violence? *Addiction, 100,* 422–425.

Leonard, K. E., & Blane, H. T. (1992). Alcohol and marital aggression in a national sample of young men. *Journal of Interpersonal Violence, 7,* 19–30.

Linehan, M. M. (1993). *Cognitive behavioral therapy of borderline personality disorder.* New York: Guilford Press.

Linehan, M. M., Armstrong, H. E., Suarez, A., Allmon, D., & Heard, H. L. (1991). Cognitive behavioral treatment of chronically parasuicidal borderline patients. *Archives of General Psychiatry, 48,* 1060–1064.

Loscke, D. R., & Kurz, D. (2004). Men's violence toward women in the serious social problem. In D. R. Loseke, R. J. Gelles, & M. M. Cavanaugh (Eds.), *Current controversies on family violence* (pp. 79–95). Thousand Oaks, CA: Sage.

Maiuro, R. D., Hagar, T. S., Lin, H., & Olson, N. (2002). Are current state standards for domestic violence perpetrator treatment adequately informed by research? A question of questions. *Journal of Aggression, Maltreatment & Trauma, 5,* 21–44.

Markman, H. J., Renick, M. J., Floyd, F. J., Stanley, S. M., & Clements, M. (1993). Preventing marital distress through communication and conflict management training: A 4-and 5-year follow-up. *Journal of Consulting and Clinical Psychology, 61,* 70–77.

Martin, M. (1997). Double your trouble: Dual arrest in family violence. *Journal of Family Violence, 12,* 139–157.

McClennen, J. C. (2005). Domestic violence between same-gender partners: Recent findings and future research. *Journal of Interpersonal Violence, 20,* 149–154.

Mederos, F. (2002). Changing our visions of intervention: The evolution of programs for physically abusive men. In E. Aldarando & F. Mederos (Eds.), *Programs for men who batter: Intervention and prevention strategies in a diverse society* (pp. 1-2–1-26). Kingston, NJ: Civic Research Institute.

Millon, T., Davis, R., Millon, C. (1997). *Manual for the Millon Clinical Multiaxial Inventory—III (MCMI–III)* (3rd ed.). Minneapolis, MN: NCS Pearson.

Moffitt, T., Caspi, A., Rutter, M., & Silva, P. A. (2001). *Sex differences in antisocial behavior: Conduct disorder, delinquency and violence in the Dunedin Longitudinal Study.* New York: Cambridge University Press.

O'Farrell T. J., & Murphy, C. M. (1995). Marital violence before and after alcoholism treatment. *Journal of Consulting and Clinical Psychology, 63,* 256–262.

O'Farrell, T. J., Murphy, C. M., Stephan, S. H., Fals-Stewart, W., & Murphy, M. (2004). Partner violence before and after couples-based alcoholism treatment for male alcoholic patients: The role of treatment involvement and abstinence. *Journal of Consulting and Clinical Psychology, 72,* 202–217.

O'Farrell, T. J., Van Hutton, V., & Murphy, C. M. (1999). Domestic violence before and after alcoholism treatment: A two-year longitudinal study. *Journal of Studies on Alcohol, 60,* 317–321.

O'Leary, K. D. (1993). Through a psychological lens: Personality traits, personality disorders, and levels of violence. In R. J. Gelles & D. R. Loseke (Eds.), *Current controversies on family violence* (pp. 7–30). Newbury Park, CA: Sage.

O'Leary K. D. (2002). Conjoint therapy for partners who engage in physically aggressive behavior: Rationale and research. *Journal of Aggression, Maltreatment & Trauma, 5,* 145–164.

O'Leary, K. D., Heyman, R. E., & Neidig, P. H. (1999). Treatment of wife abuse: A comparison of gender-specific and conjoint approaches. *Behavior Therapy, 30,* 475–505.

O'Leary, K. D., Vivian, D., & Malone, J. (1992). Assessment of physical aggression in marriage: The need for multimodal method. *Behavioral Assessment, 14,* 5–14.

O'Leary, S. G., & Smith Slep, A. M. (2006). Precipitants of partner aggression. *Journal of Family Psychology, 20,* 344–347.

Pence, E., & Paymar, M. (1983). *Education groups for men who batter: The Duluth model.* New York: Springer Publishing Company.

Perilla, J. L., & Perez, F. (2002). A program for immigrant Latino men who batter within the context of a comprehensive family intervention. In E. Aldarando & F. Mederos (Eds.), *Programs for men who batter: Intervention and prevention strategies in a diverse society* (pp. 11-1–11-31). Kingston, NJ: Civic Research Institute.

Pimlott-Kubiak, S., & Cortina, L. M. (2003). Gender, victimization, and outcomes: Reconceptualizing risk. *Journal of Consulting and Clinical Psychology, 71,* 528–539.

Raj, A., & Silverman, J. (2002). Violence against immigrant women: The roles of culture, context, and legal immigrant status on intimate partner violence. *Violence Against Women, 8,* 367–398.

Ramirez Hernandez, A. (2002). CECEVIM: Stopping male violence in the Latino home. In E. Aldarando & F. Mederos (Eds.), *Programs for men who batter: Intervention and prevention strategies in a diverse society* (pp. 12-2–12-28). Kingston, NJ: Civic Research Institute.

Saltzman, L. E., Fanslow, J. L., McMahon, P. M., & Shelley, G. A. (1999). *Intimate partner violence surveillance: Uniform definitions and recommended data elements.* Atlanta, GA: Centers for Disease Control and Prevention.

Saunders, D. G. (1986). When battered women use violence: Husband abuse or self-defense? *Violence and Victims, 1,* 47–60.

Saunders, D. G. (1996). Feminist–cognitive–behavioral and process–psychodynamic treatments for men who batter: Interaction of abuser traits and treatment model. *Violence and Victims, 11,* 393–414.

Saunders, D. G. (2001). Developing guidelines for domestic violence offenders: What can we learn from related fields and current research. In R. A. Geffner & A. Rosenbaum (Eds.), *Domestic violence offenders: Current interventions, research, and implications for policies and standards* (pp. 235–248). New York: Haworth Press.

Saunders, D. G. (2002). Are physical assaults by wives and girlfriends a major social problem? A review of the literature. *Violence Against Women, 8*, 1424–1448.

Smith, P. H., Earp, J. L., & DeVellis, R. (1995). Measuring battering: Development of the Women's Experiences With Battering (WEB) Scale. *Women's Health: Research on Gender, Behavior, and Policy, 1*, 273–288.

Snow-Jones, A., & Gondolf, E. W. (2001). Time-varying risk factors for reassault among batterer program participants. *Journal of Family Violence, 16*, 345–359.

Sonkin D. J., & Dutton, D. (2003). Treating assaultive men from an attachment perspective. In D. Dutton & D. J. Sonkin (Eds.), *Intimate violence: Contemporary treatment advances* (pp. 105–133). New York: Haworth Press.

Stith, S. M., Rosen, K. H., & McCollum, E. E. (2003). Developing a manualized couples treatment for domestic violence: Overcoming challenges. *Journal of Marital & Family Therapy, 28*, 21–25.

Stith, S. M., Rosen, K. H., McCollum, E. E., & Thomsen, C. J. (2004). Treating intimate partner violence within intact couple relationships: Outcomes of multi-couple vs. individual couple therapy. *Journal of Marital & Family Therapy, 30*, 305–318

Stosny, S. (1995). *Treating attachment abuse: A compassionate approach.* New York: Springer Publishing Company.

Straus, M. A. (2004). Women's violence toward men is a serious social problem. In D. R. Loseke, R. J. Gelles, & M. M. Cavanaugh (Eds.), *Current controversies on family violence* (pp. 55–77). Thousand Oaks CA: Sage.

Straus, M. A., & Gelles, R. J. (1995). How violent are American families? Estimates from the National Family Violence Resurvey and other studies. In M. A. Straus & R. J. Gelles (Eds.), *Physical violence in American families: Risk factors and adaptations to violence in 8,145 families* (pp. 95–112). New Brunswick, NJ: Transaction.

Stuart, G. L., Moore, T. M., Ramsey, S. E., & Kahler, C. W. (2003). Relationship aggression and substance use among women court-referred to domestic violence intervention programs. *Addictive Behaviors, 28*, 1603–1610.

Testa, M., Quigley, B. M., & Leonard, K. E. (2003). Does alcohol make a difference? Within-participants comparison of incidence of partner violence. *Journal of Interpersonal Violence, 18*, 735–743.

Tweed, R. G., & Dutton, D. (1988). A comparison of impulsive and instrumental subgroups of batterers. *Violence and Victims, 13*, 217–230.

Waltz, J. (2003). Dialectical behavior therapy in the treatment of abusive behavior. *Journal of Aggression, Maltreatment & Trauma, 7*, 75–103.

Wathen, C. N., & MacMillan, H. L. (2003). Interventions for violence against women: Scientific review. *Journal of the American Medical Association, 289*, 589–600.

Whitaker, D. J., Baker, C. K., & Arias, I. (2007). Interventions to prevent intimate partner violence. In L. S. Doll, S. E. Bonzo, J. A. Mercy, D. A. Sleet, & E. N. Haas (Eds.), *Handbook on injury and violence prevention* (pp. 203–221). New York: Springer-Verlag.

Whitaker, D. J., Haileyesus, T., Swahn, M. H., & Saltzman, L. (2007). Differences in frequency of violence and reported injury between relationships with reciprocal and nonreciprocal intimate partner violence. *American Journal of Public Health, 97*, 941–947.

Whitaker, D. J., Le, B., & Niolon, P. H. (2006, March). *Continuity in partner violence perpetration and victimization across relationships*. Paper presented at the meeting of the Society for Research on Adolescence, San Francisco, CA.

Williams, O. J. (1998). Healing and confronting the African American male who batters. In R. Carillo & J. Tello (Eds.), *Family violence and men of color: Healing the wounded male spirit* (pp. 74–94). New York: Springer Publishing Company.

Zubretsky, T. M., & Digirolamo, K. M. (1996). The false connection between adult domestic violence and alcohol. In A. R. Roberts (Ed.), *Helping battered women: New perspectives and remedies* (pp. 223–228). New York: Oxford University Press.

9

EXPANDING OUR VISION: USING A HUMAN RIGHTS FRAMEWORK TO STRENGTHEN OUR SERVICE RESPONSE TO FEMALE VICTIMS OF MALE INTIMATE PARTNER VIOLENCE

NANCY GLASS, CHIQUITA ROLLINS, AND TINA BLOOM

> Human rights are universal—violence against women has made human
> rights abuse universal.
> —*Amnesty International (2004, p. iv)*

Over the past 3 decades, there has been a dramatic transformation in the response to intimate partner violence (IPV) across all sectors of society, including the criminal justice system, social services, health care, and public policy (Campbell & Glass, in press; Klein, Campbell, Soler, & Ghez, 1997). Criminal justice system enhancements include easily accessible protection orders, mandatory arrest and prosecution, training for law enforcement officers and judges, increased penalties for IPV perpetration, and domestic violence courts (Campbell & Glass, in press). Victim services agencies provide hotlines, emergency shelters, advocacy programs, counseling, and housing programs. IPV assessment by health care providers, such as emergency departments and primary care and prenatal settings, has increased, and many health care providers have advocacy and counseling programs for victims of IPV. Child welfare programs are beginning to take IPV into account (with mixed results), sometimes offering services in partnership with domestic violence service providers as an integral component of child safety and custody (Carter & Schechter, 1997; Family Violence Prevention Fund, 2003).

Although services and resources allocated to victims of IPV have increased dramatically in the United States, these services have rarely been developed from a human rights framework (Silverman, Mesh, Cuthbert, Slote, & Bancroft, 2004). Elsewhere, IPV has been viewed as part of a wider human rights agenda (DeFrancisco, LaWare, & Palczewski, 2003; Erwin, 2006; Hawkins & Humes, 2002). It is our belief that integration of a human rights framework in mainstream domestic violence victim services will increase the rights and privileges of IPV victims, especially among marginalized communities, and provide linkages to other social justice efforts.

In this chapter, we provide an overview of the evolution of domestic violence victim services, describing key components and characteristics of those services. We then turn to a discussion of IPV as human rights violations and the principles and application of a human rights framework in general. Finally, we advocate for strengthening the existing response to IPV victims within this framework. Although IPV/domestic violence can occur within a primarily respectful, egalitarian, and nonviolent relationship, it often is part of a pattern of ongoing battering, terrorism, control, or degradation and abasement by one partner against the other (Cavanaugh & Gelles, 2005; Johnson, 1995). Our analysis of the application of a human rights framework focuses on this latter form of IPV/domestic violence and on violence perpetrated by male partners against their female partners.

Our choice of terminology throughout the chapter is deliberate. *Domestic violence* and *IPV* are used interchangeably. We use the term *victim*, rather than *survivor*, to emphasize the immediate, ongoing, and current level of victimization of women by intimate partners. Except where indicated, the term *domestic violence victim services* refers to community-based services or organizations specifically designed to meet the needs of victims of IPV. *Intimate partners* may include current or former dates, boyfriends and ex-boyfriends, girlfriends and ex-girlfriends, husbands and ex-husbands, or cohabiting partners and ex-partners (Saltzman, Fanslow, McMahon, & Shelley, 1999) and pertains to both same-sex and opposite-sex relationships. Unless specifically noted, we discuss services as they occur in the United States.

IPV can occur against women or men and be perpetrated by women or men (Garcia-Moreno et al., 2006; Tjaden & Thoennes, 2000). However, the level of violence and its impact differ between men and women. For example, women assaulted by male partners were 7 to 14 times more likely to be beaten up and more than twice as likely to be injured than were men assaulted by female partners (Tjaden & Thoennes, 2000). Women were more likely than men to report ongoing fear and/or having changed their behaviors to accommodate the violent partner. IPV against women takes place in a context of ongoing discrimination against women, as evidenced by higher rates of poverty and lower wages compared with male counterparts, even with similar education and experience (Crenshaw, 1994; Riger, Raja, & Camacho, 2002). This background of discrimination significantly affects women's ability to leave abusive relationships and bolsters men's ability to abuse without consequence (Riger et al., 2002). We focus on a human rights framework to address violence against women by male partners for three reasons: (a) The contextual factors (i.e., higher levels of extreme violence and injury, fear, forced changes in behaviors, poverty, and discrimination against women) underscore the importance of understanding IPV against women, (b) the vast majority of domestic violence services focus on male violence against female partners, and (c) an analysis of gender-based violence is well developed within the human rights framework.

EVOLUTION OF DOMESTIC VIOLENCE VICTIM SERVICES

> Many of us now take for granted that misogynist violence is a legitimate political issue, but let us remember that a little more than two decades ago, most people considered "domestic violence" to be a private concern and thus not a proper subject of public discourse or political intervention. Only one generation separates us from that era of silence. The first speak-out against rape occurred in the early 1970s, and the first national organization against domestic violence was founded toward the end of that decade. (Davis, 2000, The Advent of "Domestic Violence" section, ¶ 2)

In the early 1970s, women talked about their lives in consciousness-raising (CR) groups as part of the women's liberation movement. IPV was a common occurrence among CR group participants and was part of a multi-faceted and widespread domination of women by men, in the home, workplace, and community (Erwin, 2006). Individual women in CR groups began to provide informal support to victims, such as a place to stay and assistance with daily needs. They found that battered women faced three major obstacles to safety: (a) The violent partner continued the violence even after separation, (b) there were few resources available for housing and income for women to support themselves and their children following separation, and (c) legal recourse (e.g., arrest, restraining order) was not available except in the most violent situations. Thus, safety during separation and help in reestablishing a woman's life were important needs to address (Dobash & Dobash, 1992; Loseke, 1991; Pagelow, 1997; L. S. Walker, 1979).

The recognition of barriers faced by victims led to the growth of the *battered women's movement* and two important areas of response. The first was the establishment of nonprofit organizations that provided crisis intervention (i.e., hotlines and emergency shelters) and assistance with navigating mainstream institutions, such as criminal justice and child welfare. The second area was advocacy for change in laws, protocols, and procedures by institutions, such as law enforcement, child welfare, public assistance, health care, mental health, housing, and employment (Shepard & Pence, 1999).

In the 1980s and 1990s, there were significant shifts in the movement and in the pressures on the movement, which had significant effects (both positive and negative), even as the movement was successful in receiving funding and institutionalizing services. These shifts and pressures included a decrease in involvement of racial and ethnic minority women, a decrease in focus on male domination as the root cause of IPV and on changing social norms, with a concomitant increase in the development of the mainstream, gender-neutral framework for interpretation of IPV (Erwin, 2006). As noted by Pleck (1987),

> The battered women's cause had been considerably tamed by the coalitions and compromises it made in order to receive state and federal funding for services. Broadening the movement diluted its feminism and altered the character of battered women's services and the theoretical basis for it. (p. 199)

Racial and ethnic minority women were prominent in the civil rights and women's liberation movements of the 1960s and 1970s; however, their presence in the battered women's movement by the 1980s had decreased. The more radical social change movement had slowly been reoriented to a more liberal feminist (primarily White middle-class) agenda of gradual change, criminalization of IPV, and institutionalization of services for victims (e.g., increased funding, professionalization, collaboration with social control agencies).

The early battered women's movement analysis of male domination as the root cause of IPV was watered down over time. The founding of nonprofit organizations to address IPV brought the movement under the regulation of the laws and processes that govern these organizations. Government and private foundation funding mandated collaboration with institutions, such as law enforcement, housing, and child welfare. To maintain credibility with funding agencies as collaborative partners, these nonprofits faced pressure to use a gender-neutral framework for IPV. Increasing interest in the broader community, including faith-based and other charitable organizations, led to conflicts between views of family issues as private matters and women's autonomy (DeFrancisco et al., 2003; Pleck, 1987).

At the same time that the movement was undergoing these changes, *third-wave feminism* was emerging as an intellectual force. Third-wave feminism (i.e., 1980s to present) is characterized by an expanded awareness of the intersectionality of multiple oppressions faced by women (e.g., race/ethnicity, socioeconomic status, ability), by the perceived need to address the negative images and opinions about feminism and feminists, and by the differential impact of gender oppression faced by poor and minority women (Crenshaw, 1994; Taylor, 1998; R. Walker, 1995). It is the confluence of third-wave feminism, the development of victim services, the shifts in focus described previously, and an international analysis of violence against women as violations of human rights that make this a particularly important moment to propose the application of a human rights framework for domestic violence victim services.

CATEGORIES OF DOMESTIC VIOLENCE VICTIM SERVICES

Despite the changes in focus and the ongoing conflicts and tensions within the domestic violence victim services arena, it remains an important social change movement that has led to the availability of services for victims and their children in most communities. The services provide the opportunity for many victims to find support and assistance in increasing their safety, meeting their and their children's daily living needs, and recovering from the impact of IPV.

The National Census of Domestic Violence Services estimates that a minimum of 47,864 victims and their children access victim services on a single day (National Network to End Domestic Violence, 2007). Services are categorized by crisis- or hotlines, emergency housing, transitional housing, advocacy and case management, legal representation, criminal justice advocacy, children's programs, group services, and advocacy for system change.

1. *Crisis- or hotlines* are accessible 24 hours, 7 days a week, and provide access to other services, safety planning, peer support, and domestic violence information.
2. *Emergency housing* (i.e., shelters, vouchers, and safe homes) is safe, often confidentially located, providing short-term stays (of 60–90 days), living needs, and services for victims and their children. Services include support, safety planning, and access to other services, such as transportation, public assistance, and housing.
3. *Transitional housing or rent assistance* programs provide longer term housing and services (from 90 days to 2 years) either in a dedicated building or in private market or public housing. Services provided are similar to those listed for emergency housing (Renzetti, Edelson, & Bergen, 2001; Saathoff & Stoffel, 1999).
4. *Advocacy and case management* provide support, referrals, and assistance with legal, health, parenting, employment, housing, financial, and educational concerns. Advocates may accompany victims to civil or criminal court hearings, health services, child dependency meetings, or public housing appointments. These services may take the form of culturally

specific services, specifically for racial and ethnically diverse women, women with disabilities, and immigrant women (Orloff & Little, 1999).

5. *Legal representation and advice* are provided by attorneys to IPV victims in civil or criminal legal matters, relating to protection orders, landlord–tenant disputes, child welfare, custody, visitation, or dissolution of marriage.

6. *Criminal justice advocacy* in collaboration with victim services agencies and the criminal justice system, especially law enforcement (Erez, 2002), takes different forms. Advocates are called by the responding police officers to provide immediate crisis intervention services; officer–advocate teams provide follow-up services; or police reports are sent to victim services programs for follow-up services by advocates alone.

7. *Children's programs* respond to the negative consequences associated with the abusive behaviors of the batterer (Bancroft & Silverman, 2002; Carter & Schechter, 1997; Wolak & Finkelhor, 1998). Services focus on safety planning; mother–child interaction and bonding; and health, trauma, behavioral, and educational issues associated with exposure to IPV or child abuse.

8. *Group services* are provided in residential and nonresidential settings and include support groups for children and adults, parenting training, and job training or life skills sessions. They are intended to empower women through education, support, and development of a social network.

9. *Advocacy for system change* seeks the development of a consistent and coordinated response designed to create safety and support for IPV victims and their children and to hold batterers accountable (Edelson & Bible, 2001; Shepard & Pence, 1999). Domestic violence victim services and advocates have worked to change the response of major institutions (e.g., criminal justice, health care, governments, child welfare), through changing laws and assuring appropriate implementation of laws and policies.

Challenges to the value and effectiveness of existing domestic violence victim services have been made in the past 30 years. Concerns include the notion that the services are "Band-Aids" that help only a limited number of women who seek to leave a violent partner and do not address the root societal causes of male violence against women (Davis, 2000). Other concerns relate to barriers in accessing services for victims, including those who have a disability, have worked as a prostitute, are undocumented, have limited English language skills, have mental health or drug or alcohol abuse problems, or have several children, including male children over age 12 who are often not allowed to join their mothers in battered women's shelters (Burman & Chantler, 2005; Byrne, Resnick, Kilpatrick, Best, & Saunders, 1999; Dutton, Kaltman, Goodman, Weinfurt, & Vankos, 2005; El-Khoury et al., 2004).

PRINCIPLES OF HUMAN RIGHTS

The concept of human rights asserts that every person has certain economic, social, and political rights by virtue of his or her humanity (International Council on Human Rights Policy, 2005). In the United States, one generally hears about human rights and human rights violations by other governments, such as genocide, limitation of freedom of speech and association, trafficking, and torture, and, within the United States, violations of the rights of prisoners or enemy combatants (DeFrancisco et al., 2003; Erwin, 2006; Hawkins & Humes, 2002). However, the Universal Declaration of Human Rights (UDHR) goes well beyond these areas in defining human rights and the requirements of governments to take affirmative action to assure these rights, rather than simply refrain from infringing on them (United Nations, 1948).

The widely cited UDHR (United Nations, 1948) was influential in the development of international human rights law. It declares that human rights apply to all human beings without distinction of gender, but it does not specifically address issues related to women or violence against women. The UDHR consists of 30 articles (i.e., subsections) that cover a wide range of personal, civil, economic, political, social, and cultural rights. All of the articles apply to not only government actions or inactions but also the actions of individuals and institutions, as well as the need for governments to respond to violations of human rights.

The articles most closely related to the topic of this chapter include the following:

1. Everyone has the right to life, liberty, and security of person. (Article 3)
2. No one shall be held in slavery or servitude; slavery and the slave trade shall be prohibited in all their forms. (Article 4)
3. No one shall be subjected to torture or to cruel, inhuman, or degrading treatment or punishment. (Article 5)
4. Everyone has the right to recognition before the law, without discrimination, and has the right to an effective remedy for acts violating the fundamental rights granted. (Articles 6, 7, 8)
5. Everyone has the right to a standard of living adequate for the health and well-being of himself [or herself] and of his [or her]

family, including food, clothing, housing, medical care, and necessary social services. Motherhood and childhood are entitled to special care and assistance. (Article 25)

Other articles of the UDHR relevant to the needs of women victims of intimate violence are the rights of employment with a living wage, education, and full participation in society (United Nations, 1948).

Since 1948, there has been a steady refinement and increased understanding of the implications and expectations of the UDHR and the human rights framework. These refinements are found in a series of conventions, declarations, and other documents that further define expectations concerning specific articles or concepts within the UDHR. The first significant international recognition of women's rights as human rights was found in the 1979 Convention on the Elimination of All Forms of Discrimination Against Women (CEDAW), which addresses the right of women to be free from trafficking and prostitution but does not explicitly address IPV, sexual abuse, incest, or rape (United Nations, 1979). In the context of this chapter, it is important to note that the United States is the sole industrialized nation in the world to have failed to ratify the CEDAW.

In the 1990s, there was further progress in the recognition of women's human rights with the adoption of a definition of gender-based violence by the CEDAW Committee. Gender-based violence is violence directed against a woman *because* she is a woman or that affects women disproportionately, including acts that inflict physical, mental, or sexual harm or suffering; threats of such acts; coercion; and other deprivations of liberty (United Nations, 1992). CEDAW was followed by the Declaration on the Elimination of Violence Against Women (DEVAW; United Nations, 1993), the Vienna Declaration (United Nations World Conference on Human Rights, 1993), and the Beijing Declaration and Platform for Action (United Nations Fourth World Conference on Women, 1995). All three of the more recent declarations define violence against women, including violence within the family, as a human rights issue. The DEVAW defines violence against women as

> any act of gender-based violence that results in, or is likely to result in, physical, sexual or psychological harm or suffering to women, including threats of such acts, coercion or arbitrary deprivation of liberty, whether occurring in public or private life. (United Nations, 1993, Article 1)

The Vienna Declaration states that

> the human rights of women . . . are an inalienable, integral and indivisible part of universal human rights. . . . Gender-based violence and all forms of sexual harassment and exploitation . . . are incompatible with the dignity and worth of the human person, and must be eliminated. (United Nations World Conference on Human Rights, 1993, No. 18)

INTIMATE PARTNER VIOLENCE AS A
HUMAN RIGHTS VIOLATION

A variety of writers, organizations, and documents place IPV within the scope of gender-based violence, violence against women, and human rights violations (Amnesty International, 2004; Hawkins & Humes, 2002; National Center for Human Rights Education, n.d.b; Young, 2003). IPV is clearly a violation of the rights articulated in UDHR Article 3 (i.e., the right to personal security) and, in more severe cases, may also violate Articles 4 (i.e., slavery) and 5 (i.e., torture). In more severe cases, the abusive partner or ex-partner not only inflicts physical violence, sexual violence, and psychological abuse but also coercively controls the woman's environment, including income, housing, access to friends and families, work, food, children, culture, and sexuality. Insufficient institutional response from the criminal justice, public health care, and welfare systems may violate Articles 6, 7, and 8, and denial of basic living needs to victims attempting to leave such an abusive situation may violate Article 25 (Young, 2003).

The CEDAW, DEVAW, Beijing Platform, Vienna Declaration, and other documents represent tremendous accomplishments and demonstrate that progress is being made in terms of recognizing violence against women as a component of human rights violations. Although international human rights campaigns geared toward enhancing women's rights have gained momentum, application in the United States of human rights concepts appears to have evolved more slowly. The human rights framework has been regarded as irrelevant and inappropriate for "advanced" democracies such as the United States (DeFrancisco et al., 2003; Silverman et al., 2004). Full application of the UDHR continues to remain controversial in the United States, as demonstrated by the failure of the U.S. Congress to ratify the CEDAW and the lack of a human rights court or forum. In addition, the United States has focused its Bill of Rights and tradition on civil and political rights (e.g., the right to vote, to free speech and association, and to freedom of religion), and some members of Congress have steadfastly opposed economic rights to housing, health care, and a living wage, seeing such rights as supportive of socialism or communism (DeFrancisco et al., 2003) and seeing the rights of women to divorce and determine their reproductive capacity free from male involvement as "antifamily" (Erwin, 2006). Therefore, in this context, U.S. domestic violence victim service advocates, clinicians, and researchers have had access to few resources on how to develop and implement victim services from a human rights framework.

Human Rights Framework and Implementation

A human rights framework and its associated documents provide several important duties, principles, and standards that domestic violence victim services and advocates could use in developing programs and advocating for social or institutional changes. However, domestic violence victim services cannot be the only system held accountable for designing and providing services to victims within the framework. The other systems responsible for services to victims, such as health care, criminal justice, and child welfare, need to join in partnership in applying a human rights framework.

A human rights framework goes beyond the passage of laws and policies by local, state, and national governments. It also defines the duties of those responsible for development and implementation of laws and policies, the principles by which the human rights framework will be implemented, and the standards to evaluate performance (International Council on Human Rights Policy, 2005). The following sections rely on a paradigm and analysis developed by the International Council on Human Rights Policy (2005) to describe the application of a human rights framework to local governments, leaders, and institutions, such as domestic violence victim services, criminal justice system, health care system, child welfare system, and public assistance.

In many communities, without an explicit statement of such, domestic violence victim services are incorporating the duties and principles of a human rights framework. For example, many programs are based on a philosophy of empowerment for victims, and victims are involved in the planning, development, and evaluation of services as members of advisory boards or boards of directors. All domestic violence service providers are required under U.S. law to practice nondiscrimination, and many have developed excellent programs to address the needs of specific, underserved, and marginalized populations in their communities (Donnelly, Cook, van Ausdale, & Foley, 2005; Fraser, McNutt, Clark, Williams-Muhammed, & Lee, 2002; Wolf, Ly, Hobart, & Kernic, 2003). An explicit statement about the use of a human rights framework provides an opportunity for programs to build on their strengths and to more fully apply the duties and principles implicit in the framework.

Duties

A human rights framework defines duties by governments and institutions at three levels (International Council on Human Rights Policy, 2005). The framework is realistic and stresses that the duties of governments and institutions are not without limits. Application of a human rights framework is not a one-time event but rather a complex, multilevel effort that evolves over several years, involving the coordination and integration of multiple systems within a community. Thus, communities and institutions are expected to plan and progressively implement advances, taking into account available resources and the understanding that human rights are interdependent and cannot be achieved all at once.

That communities do not have sufficient resources to immediately imple-ment all elements of a human rights framework should not provide an excuse to perform poorly. Instead, they should use the maximum of available re-sources to fulfill these duties. The three duties outlined in the framework include the following:

1. *Respect for human rights.* National, state, and local govern-ments and institutions should not directly or indirectly de-prive individuals of their rights or establish an institutional system that gives incentives to others to deprive them of their rights; certain cases of IPV, as previously discussed, should be addressed as violations of human rights.
2. *Protect human rights.* National, state, and local governments and institutions should enforce respect for rights; they should prevent those who would deprive another of rights from do-ing so, including individuals who perpetrate IPV.
3. *Fulfill human rights.* Local governments and institutions should create conditions in which rights can be realized; this includes legislative, budgetary, judicial, and other actions that are re-quired to assure an effective response to IPV victims.

Victim services programs can fulfill these duties either directly, through addressing the human rights of victims in their own programs, or indirectly, through advocating for local and state governments and other institutions to employ the principles and standards of the human rights framework.

Principles

A human rights framework has overarching principles that assist in the development and implementation of services (International Council on Human Rights Policy, 2005).

1. *Participation.* Individuals affected by IPV are entitled to par-ticipate in developing, implementing, and monitoring re-sponses and services related to IPV. They are entitled to en-gage critically with decisions that affect them and their families at individual, programmatic, and political levels.
2. *Nondiscrimination (inclusion).* Nondiscrimination stands at the very heart of human rights. Human rights cannot be sustained in an environment of discrimination, and all members of a community benefit from this principle, not just those most likely to be discriminated against. Nondiscrimination and equitable treatment exist when systems protect the rights and empower people who are underserved (i.e., those who are ex-cluded, unpopular, despised, and politically invisible). Indi-viduals have rights, without regard for differences of gender,

race, ethnicity, religion, sexual orientation, nationality, age, class, ability, and language. Nondiscrimination encourages the development of outreach and services specifically for the underserved and the involvement of victims from these populations in the development of these services. Programs are asked to find ways to include all victims in their services and to change rules that limit the provision of services to victims.

3. *Accountability*. Individuals have the rights to be informed, to free expression, and to participate in political processes. Thus, responses and services must be predictable, consistent, and transparent, and there must be a venue for victims to influence or evaluate how the responses and services are delivered. For example, IPV victims should have good information in their preferred language about protective orders; the process must be understandable to them and consistently applied; and they must also have the opportunity to participate in the political process to change protective order statutes or the court protocols used in these cases. IPV victims are entitled to opportunities to speak truth to power and to attain their own political power.

4. *Indivisibility*. Human rights are indivisible, and the loss of one human right, such as that of economic security, undermines all other human rights. Thus, victim services programs should work, in coalition with other community organizations, to assure all human rights, such as economic or environmental justice, universal health care, and prison reform.

Standards

Four standards for services have been outlined in the International Council on Human Rights Policy (2005, p. 22) framework. Victim services programs can use these standards to evaluate their own services within a human rights framework. The standards include the following:

1. *Availability*. Services "should be available in sufficient quantity to meet the needs of the entire population concerned," in this case IPV victims.

2. *Accessibility*. Responses should be "located and distributed so that all members of the population [of IPV victims] can use them without discrimination." This implies that services should be physically accessible, be low cost or free, be in the preferred language, and provide access to vital information about safety and resources.

3. *Acceptability*. Responses "must be provided in a form and manner that respects the cultural values, norms and practices" of

those IPV victims who use them, and "must be relevant, culturally appropriate, and of good quality."

4. *Adaptability.* Responses should be developed and "adapted to the needs of communities and individual [IPV victims] from different social, economic and cultural settings."

To further assist in the application of the human rights framework, we have created questions based on the International Council on Human Rights Policy's (2005) *Local Government and Human Rights: Doing Good Services.* These questions (see Table 9.1) are intended for evaluation and to identify further steps to more completely apply the framework at each stage: educating, planning implementing, monitoring, and evaluating. They incorporate the principles of participation, nondiscrimination, accountability, indivisibility, and the standards of availability, accessibility, adaptability, and acceptability. In addition to questions specifically about the services or projects developed, there are several overarching questions used for process evaluation based on "Integrating Human Rights Into Your Programs" (National Center for Human Rights Education, n.d.a). In the table, we use the term *underserved* to refer to populations or victims who have the most significant barriers or who have been unable or unwilling to access existing services or for whom there are limited or nonexistent services available.

Application of the Framework: An Example

In this section, we use examples from our work to improve the workplace response to low-income immigrant and U.S.-born IPV victims as a means to illustrate how a human rights framework can be applied. The project we describe focuses on abused Latina women, because this population tends to be invisible and excluded from many efforts developed for the workplace, and because the experiences of Latina women seeking health and social services are often shaped by multiple and complex intersections of class, gender, ethnicity, and acculturation (Anzaldúa, 1987, 1990; Sokoloff & Dupont, 2005). The ultimate goal of the project is to change workplace norms and culture related to survivors of IPV, including Latinas, and to increase culturally and linguistically acceptable and accessible IPV information, support, and linkage to community resources.

The inclusion of human rights concepts, duties, and principles in our project evolved over time and with the input of IPV victims and of members of the Latino communities. We had not developed our conceptualization of the use of a human rights framework prior to beginning the current project, but we had taken some steps, as outlined in the next section, that were in alignment with this framework. In this project, we focused on a population that was often excluded from workplace solutions for domestic violence (i.e., abused Latinas working in low-paying sectors). The voices, needs, and ex-

TABLE 9.1
Evaluation of Intimate Partner Violence (IPV) Services Using a Human Rights Framework

Parameter	Concept	Outcome measures
Principles	Participation	1. Do venues exist for meaningful participation of IPV victims in service planning, implementation, monitoring, or evaluation? 2. Have we built in support (including budgets) for victim participation?
	Nondiscrimination	1. Do we have a full understanding of the diversity in our community and/or who the specific community services are intended for? 2. Are services nondiscriminatory and provided on an equal basis to all, and do they include racial/ethnic and sexual minorities, regardless of ability or other characteristic? 3. Are victims able to participate in services without financial, physical, or language barriers? 4. Are there safeguards in place so that specific groups of IPV victims are not discriminated against in their access to services? 5. Are there mechanisms in place to assess that services are welcoming to diverse populations and take their concerns into account? 6. Do the nature and form of participation of IPV victims evolve with changing needs and populations? 7. Is there flexibility in services to adjust to changing needs and demands and to assure that new forms of discrimination do not arise?
	Accountability	1. Are victims involved in planning, monitoring, and evaluating services or in decision-making roles in the agency?
	Indivisibility	1. Do services address other human rights issues, such as housing, poverty, employment, and education, simultaneously with security and safety? 2. Do we have relationships with other human rights organizations and efforts? 3. Do we educate our clients about all their human rights?
Standards	Adaptability	1. Have we allocated sufficient resources, within our means, to support and sustain services and the process for change over time and to assure availability, accessibility, acceptability, and adaptability? 2. Have we built in a mechanism by which the structures, content, and processes of services can evolve over time according to the changing needs and demands of the IPV victims being served?

Availability	1.	How will this project increase the availability of domestic violence victim services, especially for underserved populations?
Accessibility	1.	How are services accessible to all groups in the community, and do they address the needs of the underserved?
	2.	How are services physically and financially accessible to all IPV victims in the community or to the underserved?
Acceptability	1.	How are the content and philosophy of services geared to the cultural diversity of IPV victims or to a specific underserved population?
Global evaluation of process	1.	Have we educated our staff, board members, partnering agencies, funders, victims, and others involved in the project about a human rights framework and how it applies to IPV?
	2.	Have we identified other human rights efforts, locally and globally, that can be used as models or can extend our understanding of the scope of and connection to other human rights issues and resources available?
	3.	Have we made alliances with local social justice groups working on issues such as poverty, gender, and civil or political rights?

periences of this population were included through extensive interviews and the involvement of *promotoras* (i.e., peer health workers) in the research team. Community-based organizations, unions and labor organizations, and Latino community leaders actively participated in the development of the grant and research tools and implementation of the project. We developed a team structure to encourage discussion, input, and shared decision making.

Although it is beyond the scope of this chapter to discuss how a human rights framework can be applied to all elements of victim services efforts, in the sections that follow we describe how the duties and principles can be applied (using our project as a specific example) to five activities: educating, planning, implementing, monitoring, and evaluating services for victims of IPV.

Education

Education related to a human rights framework, IPV as a violation of those rights, and the responsibilities of governments, institutions, and victim services is critical to the success of applying the framework to provision of services and, ultimately, to the prevention of IPV. The audience for such education includes IPV victims, victim services providers, agency board members, funders, policymakers, employers, and community members. This education may start with an inner circle of advocates, administrators, funders, and victims to deepen their understanding of human rights and the opportunities this framework provides to more effectively address IPV and victims' needs. The effort can then expand to include other agencies and individuals. This expansion can further enhance the understanding of the meaning of human rights and the framework, connect the effort to other human rights issues, and lead to the development of new strategies to assure human rights of IPV victims.

Application of a human rights framework to our ongoing project in terms of education included, or will include, the following steps:

1. Educating the project team (i.e., the principal investigator, research assistant, and consultant working on the project) about the human rights framework as previously described. This education occurred after the project had started and is ongoing.
2. Extending this information to the whole project research and development team, including those individuals and entities listed earlier and others. This will require development of handouts and other reading materials that account for different levels of literacy and in multiple languages, as well as information in visual formats (e.g., photo novellas), so that a person does not have to be able to read to learn about IPV and human rights. It also will require taking time in project

meetings to discuss how each of the human rights concepts applies to our project, challenging us to more fully incorporate this framework in the project.

3. Extending information to professional business organizations and employee assistance programs in the community.

4. Including human rights concepts in materials developed in the project for distribution to employers and/or employees.

These steps will occur in an iterative process, with each round of steps bringing new information and new understanding of human rights and IPV. As we present and discuss this information with the project research and development team, we will deepen our knowledge and understanding of human rights in general and as it applies to our community and to the Latino community in Oregon.

Planning

Planning for implementation of services on the basis of a human rights framework may take place at multiple levels consecutively or concurrently. We can include human rights concepts in the materials developed and distributed to employers and employees in the low-paying sectors. At the same time, we can more fully integrate the principles of a human rights framework into the project research and development team, for example, by including more Latina survivors of IPV on the advisory board for the project. As we develop future projects or apply for other grants, we can incorporate core human rights concepts in the design and information presented, and we can assure that groups of IPV victims who are at risk of discrimination and exclusion from services are represented and included as leaders in a meaningful way.

Application of the framework to future project planning could include the steps that follow. These steps can occur before the project starts, including at the stage of writing for funding for the project, or at any point during project implementation.

1. Recruiting, training, and supporting victims of IPV to fully participate and/or take a leadership role in the project, through membership on the project team not as volunteers but as paid employees. Support will include addressing barriers to their full participation, such as access in multiple languages, transportation, economic needs, and child-care needs.

2. Developing a plan for further education of and discussion with the project team, advisory board, and community partners, to identify strategies that the project could implement that would bring it more in line with a human rights framework.

3. Including victims at all steps of the planning, including selecting topics for future projects and assuring that victims least

likely to be included are included (i.e., monolingual Spanish speakers, indigenous peoples who speak Spanish as a second language, and undocumented workers) through partnerships, health care providers, employers, Head Start programs, and schools.

4. Developing culturally appropriate structures and communication strategies to assure that the IPV survivors have meaningful input in the end products.

Implementation

Implementation over time emphasizes the need for IPV victims to continuously provide information to service providers, local government, and institutions about the complexity of their lives, IPV, their needs, and the most appropriate way to delivery requested services. In turn, these institutions must emphasize communication and involvement with IPV victims and processes that are transparent to victims and partner agencies. Survivors may become activated and empowered by collaborative participation in projects with a human rights focus that validates the gravity of what they have endured (Wellesley Centers for Women, 2003).

Application of the framework to our project implementation will be a natural outgrowth of the collaborative relationships with survivors nurtured during the education and planning stages. In our project, supporting and working with victims to implement services guided by the framework could include the following steps:

1. Continuing transparent consultation with and inclusion of victims and paid staff who are also survivors of IPV on an advisory board, to guide the intervention and ensure that it remains responsive to the women for whom it is intended.
2. Developing a mechanism by which changes to the project can be made over time; that is, with ongoing input from victims, to assure that it is responsive to the changes in their communities or individual situations over time.
3. Providing information gathered in the interviews and the research portion of the project to community organizations that advocate for a broader range of economic or social justice issues faced by Latina or other survivors, assuring that the format of the information is accessible to this community.

Monitoring

Monitoring of the services and implementation from a human rights framework perspective is important to assess progress toward more fully realized human rights for victims of IPV, such as a reduction in IPV and improvement in the effectiveness of services. Monitoring the implementation and the services delivered depends on the continued involvement of IPV victims to provide feedback of their specific needs, areas of service improvement, and staff or community training and awareness.

Steps in our project that incorporate a human rights framework in monitoring include the following:

1. Continuing the involvement and participation of victims of IPV in the project team and providing a mechanism by which changes to the project can be made over time with ongoing input from victims.
2. Continuing to provide information to survivors, the community, and organizations about the effectiveness, successes, and failures of this project.
3. Developing, in consultation with victims, a monitoring tool that includes their concerns, observations, and priorities.

Evaluation

Evaluation used the standards previously listed: availability, accessibility, acceptance, and adaptability. Evaluation may be by governments, institutions, funders, service providers themselves, researchers, or IPV victims and should draw on the objectives and priorities identified in the planning phase. In addition to examining the content and quality of services and the level of training and skills of the providers, evaluation can also specifically determine the degree to which domestic violence victim services empowered and successfully addressed the needs of vulnerable and excluded victims, reduced or eliminated discrimination, and had otherwise respected, protected, or fulfilled the human rights of victims of IPV.

Application of the framework to our project evaluation could include the following steps:

1. Developing and implementing evaluation tools in consultation with victims from the Latino community and those employed in low-wage jobs.
2. Reviewing materials, determining how they are incorporated into the workplace, and identifying improvements and effectiveness from the perspective of the victims–employees.
3. Including representatives from the identified population in evaluation of all activities, including as paid workers.

Outcomes of Services Provided From a Human Rights Framework

In the previous sections, we briefly described the range of services currently available for IPV victims and outlined the arguments for IPV as a violation of human rights and of the states' and institutions' responsibilities to affirmatively protect those rights. We also discussed duties, principles, and standards of a human rights framework and how to apply the framework to victim services, providing examples from our work on services in the workplace for victims of IPV. We believe that developing, implementing, and evaluating domestic violence victim services from a human rights framework can offer several positive outcomes that result in a strengthened effort to intervene in or prevent IPV. In the sections that follow, we discuss some of the positive outcomes.

Empowerment

Women who stand at the core of a human rights framework are empowered, with an understanding of the wide variety of human rights that are due to them, including housing, health care, food, living wage, safety, and security, and with an opportunity to have a meaningful role in the development of services for herself and her community. This, in turn, allows women to identify violations of their rights by the IPV abuser and institutions, as well as to identify and assist in the development of solutions to IPV that go beyond the cessation of violence and assure autonomy and restitution of physical health, financial stability, and social standing.

Legal Remedy to Intimate Partner Violence

A human rights framework provides a potential legal remedy for failure of governments and institutions to effectively respond to IPV, because the state, in all its forms, is required to affirmatively support human rights, not just assure that the state itself does not violate those rights. This provides the opportunity to document human rights violations and argue for more robust funding for victim services, health care, economic development, protection from individual perpetrators of IPV, and institutional responses. The recent effort in Massachusetts to document human rights violations in the child welfare system and find redress for the state actions in family court cases is a good model for domestic violence victim services (Silverman et al., 2004). This effort has led to the formation of a grassroots organization of victims and advocates for family court reform, and a partnership between the Women's Bar Association and advocacy groups (Cuthbert et al., 2003; Wellesley Centers for Women, 2003).

Linkages to Other Social Justice Efforts

A human rights framework recognizes that human rights are indivisible and that the achievement of one right is tied to the achievement of other rights. This understanding provides a stronger, more subtle, and encompassing platform for the social change aspects of domestic violence victim services. Many domestic violence victim services acknowledge the gender-based racial, political, legal, educational, and economic inequities that women face. A human rights framework articulates how these factors exist in a multilevel and interlocking relationship (Crenshaw, 1994). The framework provides an opportunity to communicate the intersectionality of these multiple factors to the larger community and to increase the collaborative efforts between other social justice efforts.

Domestic violence advocates have often seen an array of unintended consequences following their advocacy for changes in law, policies, or practice. For example, criminalization of IPV to provide deterrence of the perpetrator and safety for the victim has at the same time supported the continued disproportionate incarceration and criminalization of people of color and other marginalized populations (Rojas Durazo, 2007). A human rights framework provides the opportunity to reach across these divides and to enter into dialogue with other social justice advocates working to assure the human rights of all individuals, including perpetrators of IPV.

Joining With Global Human Rights Movements

We, in the United States, have much to learn from our colleagues worldwide and their analysis of human rights, gender inequities, and the intersectionality of issues. By learning about and joining the global movements for full human rights for women and others, domestic violence victim services in the United States can draw encouragement, strength, and creative ideas from a vibrant array of efforts around the world to end violence against women and to connect to other human rights efforts, especially economic and social rights.

CONCLUSION

Efforts to address the needs of victims of IPV have had impressive successes in terms of the expansion of services in partnership with diverse institutions in rural, suburban, and urban communities, as well as the development of programs to address the needs of marginalized women. The current system includes a wide variety of services to meet the range of complex needs of victims (e.g., housing, shelter, crisis intervention, social support, culturally specific services, assistance negotiating institutions). There have also been significant changes in the laws and practices so that many institutions are more attuned to the needs of victims. However, these successes have not equally assisted all victims of IPV in every community in the United States. This chapter acknowledged the limitations of the current system and encouraged a focus on strengthening domestic violence victim services by developing, implementing, monitoring, and evaluating services from a human rights framework. This framework has the potential to allow services to better respond to important challenges: empowering victims; creating services for those IPV victims who have faced significant barriers in accessing or using existing services; addressing economic, social, or political disparities for IPV victims; and mitigating the unintended negative consequences of laws, policies, and practices.

REFERENCES

Amnesty International. (2004). *It's in our hands: Stop violence against women*. New York: Author.

Anzaldúa, G. E. (1987). *Borderlands/La Frontera: The new mestiza*. San Francisco: Spinsters Aunt Lute.

Anzaldúa, G. E. (1990). *Making faces, making soul—haciendo caras: Creative and critical perspectives by women of color*. San Francisco: Spinsters Aunt Lute.

Bancroft, L., & Silverman, J. (2002). *The batterer as parent: Addressing the impact of domestic violence on family dynamics*. Thousand Oaks, CA: Sage.

Burman, E., & Chantler, K. (2005). Domestic violence and minoritisation: Legal and policy barriers facing minoritised women leaving violent relationships. *International Journal of Law and Psychiatry, 28*, 59–74.

Byrne, C. A., Resnick, H. S., Kilpatrick, D. G., Best, C. L., & Saunders, B. E. (1999). The socioeconomic impact of interpersonal violence on women. *Journal of Consulting and Clinical Psychology, 67*, 362–366.

Campbell, J. C., & Glass, N. (in press). Safety planning, danger, and lethality assessment. In C. E. Mitchell (Ed.), *Health care response to domestic violence*. Oxford, England: Oxford University Press.

Carter, J. S., & Schechter, S. (1997). *Child abuse and domestic violence: Creating community partnerships for safe families: Suggested components of an effective child welfare response to domestic violence*. San Francisco: Family Violence Prevention Fund.

Cavanaugh, M. M., & Gelles, R. J. (2005). The utility of male domestic violence offender typologies: New directions for research, policy, and practice. *Journal of Interpersonal Violence, 20*, 155–166.

Crenshaw, K. W. (1994). Mapping the margins: Intersectionality, identity politics, and violence against women of color. In M. A. Fineman & R. Mykitiuk (Eds.), *The public nature of private violence* (pp. 93–118). New York: Routledge.

Cuthbert, C. V., Slote, K. Y., Silverman, J. G., Driggers, M. G., Bancroft, L., & Mesh, C. J. (2003). Battered mothers vs. U.S. family courts. *Human Rights Dialogue, 2*(10), 12–13.

Davis, A. Y. (2000). The color of violence against women. *ColorLines*. Retrieved October 8, 2008, from http://www.colorlines.com/article.php?ID=72

DeFrancisco, V., LaWare, M. R., & Palczewski, C. H. (2003). The home side of global feminism: Why hasn't the global found a home in the U.S.? *Women and Language, 26*, 100–110.

Dobash, R. E., & Dobash, R. (1992). *Violence against women and social change*. London: Routledge.

Donnelly, D. A., Cook, K. J., van Ausdale, D., & Foley, L. (2005). White privilege, color blindness, and services to battered women. *Violence Against Women, 11*, 6–37.

Dutton, M. A., Kaltman, S., Goodman, L. A., Weinfurt, K., & Vankos, N. (2005). Patterns of intimate partner violence: Correlates and outcomes. *Violence and Victims, 20*, 483–497.

Edelson, J. L., & Bible, A. L. (2001). Collaborating for women's safety: Partnerships between research and practice. In C. M. Renzetti, J. L. Edelson, & R. L. Bergen (Eds.), *Sourcebook on violence against women* (pp. 73–96). Thousand Oaks, CA: Sage.

El-Khoury, M. Y., Dutton, M. A., Goodman, L. A., Engel, L., Belamaric, R. J., & Murphy, M. (2004). Ethnic differences in battered women's formal help-seeking strategies: A focus on health, mental health, and spirituality. *Cultural Diversity & Ethnic Minority Psychology, 10,* 383–393.

Erez, E. (2002). Domestic violence and the criminal justice system: An overview. *Online Journal of Issues in Nursing 7*(1), Article 3. Retrieved October 8, 2008, from http://www.nursingworld.org/MainMenuCategories/ANAMarketplace/ANAPeriodicals/OJIN/TableofContents/Volume72002/No1Jan2002/DomesticViolenceandCriminalJustice.aspx#Erez

Erwin, P. E. (2006). Exporting U.S. domestic violence reforms: An analysis of human rights frameworks and U.S. "best practices." *Feminist Criminology, 1,* 188–206.

Family Violence Prevention Fund. (2003). *Advocacy matters: Helping mothers and their children involved with the child protection system.* San Francisco: Author.

Fraser, I. M., McNutt, L.-A., Clark, C., Williams-Muhammed, D., & Lee, R. (2002). Social support choices for help with abusive relationships: Perceptions of African American women. *Journal of Family Violence, 17,* 363–375.

Garcia-Moreno, C., Jansen, H. A., Ellsberg, M., Heise, L., Watts, C. H., & W.H.O. Multi-Country Study on Women's Health and Domestic Violence Against Women Study Team. (2006, October 7). Prevalence of intimate partner violence: Findings from the WHO multi-country study on women's health and domestic violence. *The Lancet, 368,* 1260–1269.

Hawkins, D., & Humes, M. (2002). Human rights and domestic violence. *Political Science Quarterly, 117,* 231–258.

International Council on Human Rights Policy. (2005). *Local government and human rights: Doing good service.* Geneva, Switzerland: Author.

Johnson, M. P. (1995). Patriarchal terrorism and common couple violence: Two forms of violence against women. *Journal of Marriage and the Family, 57,* 283–294.

Klein, E., Campbell, J., Soler, E., & Ghez, M. (1997). *Ending domestic violence: Changing public perceptions.* Newbury Park, CA: Sage.

Loseke, D. R. (1991). Changing the boundaries of crime: The battered women's social movement and the definition of wife abuse as criminal activity. *Criminal Justice Review, 16,* 249–262.

National Center for Human Rights Education. (n.d.a). *Integrating human rights into your programs.* Retrieved June 19, 2007, from http://www.nchre.org/factsheets.html

National Center for Human Rights Education. (n.d.b). *Violence against women: A human rights violation.* Retrieved June 19, 2007 from http://www.nchre.org/factsheets.html

National Network to End Domestic Violence. (2007). *Domestic violence counts: A 24-hour census of domestic violence shelters and services across the United States.* Washington, DC: Author.

Orloff, L. E., & Little, R. (1999). *Somewhere to turn: Making domestic violence services accessible to battered immigrant women.* Washington, DC: AYUDA.

Pagelow, M. (1997). Battered women: A historical research review and some common myths. *Journal of Aggression, Maltreatment & Trauma, 1*, 97–116.

Pleck, E. (1987). *Domestic tyranny: The making of American social policy against family violence from colonial times to the present.* New York: Oxford University Press.

Renzetti, C. L., Edelson, J. L., & Bergen, R. L. (Eds.). (2001). *Sourcebook on violence against women.* Thousand Oaks, CA: Sage.

Riger, S., Raja, S., & Camacho, J. (2002). The radiating impact of intimate partner violence. *Journal of Interpersonal Violence, 17*, 184–205.

Rojas Durazo, A. C. (2007). "We were never meant to survive": Fighting violence against women and the fourth world war. In INCITE! Women of Color Against Violence (Ed.), *The revolution will not be funded: Beyond the non-profit industrial complex* (pp. 113–128). Redmond, WA: South End Press.

Saathoff, A. J., & Stoffel, E. A. (1999). Community-based domestic violence services. *The Future of Children, 9*, 97–110.

Saltzman, L. E., Fanslow, J. L., McMahon, P. M., & Shelley, G. A. (1999). *Intimate partner violence surveillance: Uniform definitions and recommended data elements.* Atlanta, GA: Centers for Disease Control and Prevention.

Shepard, M. F., & Pence, E. L. (Eds.). (1999). *Coordinating community response to domestic violence: Lessons from Duluth and beyond.* Thousand Oaks, CA: Sage.

Silverman, J. G., Mesh, C. M., Cuthbert, C. V., Slote, K., & Bancroft, L. (2004). Child custody determinations in cases involving intimate partner violence: A human rights analysis. *American Journal of Public Health, 94*, 951–957.

Sokoloff, N., & Dupont, I. (2005). Domestic violence at the intersections of race, class, and gender. *Violence Against Women, 11*, 38–64.

Taylor, U. Y. (1998). Making waves: The theory and practice of Black feminism. *The Black Scholar, 28*, 18–28.

Tjaden, P., & Thoennes, N. (2000). *Extent, nature, and consequences of physical violence: Findings from the National Violence Against Women Survey.* Washington, DC: National Institute of Justice and Centers for Disease Control and Prevention.

United Nations. (1948). *Universal declaration of human rights* (General Assembly Resolution 217 A [III]). Retrieved October 8, 2008, from http://www.un.org/Overview/rights.html

United Nations. (1979). *Convention on the elimination of all forms of discrimination against women* (General Assembly Resolution 34/180). Geneva, Switzerland: Office of the United Nations High Commissioner for Human Rights.

United Nations. (1992). *CEDAW general recommendations 19* (11th session). New York: Committee on the Elimination of Discrimination Against Women.

United Nations. (1993). *Declaration on the elimination of violence against women* (General Assembly Resolution 48/104). Retrieved October 23, 2008 from http://www.un.org/documents/ga/res/48/a48r104.htm

United Nations Fourth World Conference on Women. (1995). *Beijing declaration and platform for action* (A/CONF. 177/20 and A/CONF. 177/20/Add.1). New York: United Nations.

United Nations World Conference on Human Rights. (1993). *Vienna declaration and programme of action* (A/CONF.157/23). Retrieved October 23, 2008 from http://www.unhchr.ch/huridocda/huridoca.nsf/(Symbol)/A.CONF.157.23.En

Walker, L. S. (1979). *The battered woman*. New York: Harper & Row.

Walker, R. (Ed.). (1995). *To be real: Telling the truth and changing the face of feminism*. New York: Anchor Books.

Wellesley Centers for Women. (2003, Fall/Winter). Battered mothers fight to survive the family court system. *Research and Action Report*. Retrieved October 8, 2008, from http://www.wcwonline.org/o-rr25-1b.html

Wolak, J., & Finkelhor, D. (1998). Children exposed to partner violence. In J. L. Jasinski & L. Williams (Eds.), *Partner violence: A comprehensive review of 20 years of research* (pp. 73–111). Thousand Oaks, CA: Sage.

Wolf, M. E., Ly, U., Hobart, M. A., & Kernic, M. A. (2003). Barriers to seeking police help for intimate partner violence. *Journal of Family Violence*, 18, 121–129.

Young, G. (2003). Private pain/public peace: Women's rights as human rights and Amnesty International's report on violence against women. *Journal of Women in Culture and Society*, 28, 1209–1229.

10

CRIMINAL JUSTICE RESPONSES TO PARTNER VIOLENCE: HISTORY, EVALUATION, AND LESSONS LEARNED

N. ZOE HILTON AND GRANT T. HARRIS

In this chapter, we briefly review the history of partner violence in legislation, policing, prosecution, and more recent alternatives to the traditional court process. We then describe the little that is known about the effectiveness of criminal justice responses to partner violence over the past half century. We draw on lessons learned from interventions for other forms of criminal conduct. We take the position that this field embodies some challenges for psychologists and researchers. First, most criminal justice responses to any problem are founded on an essentially lay understanding of human behavior. The implicit assumption is that people (especially men) will use violence if they think they can get away with it, and that punishment will act as both a general and a specific deterrent. Criminal justice responses, once applied, albeit with good intentions and optimism, are rarely subject to rigorous evaluation. However, scientific study reveals that, partly because they are based on too simple an understanding of violent behavior, many criminal justice interventions are ineffective or even counterproductive

(Andrews & Bonta, 1994). In the following historical and contemporary review of criminal justice responses to partner violence, and to men's violence against female partners in particular, we highlight empirical evaluations of their effects.

HISTORY OF CRIMINAL JUSTICE RESPONSES TO PARTNER VIOLENCE

Much of the historic criminal justice response to partner violence has been in reaction to men's violence against their female partners. Such violence has existed across human history and geography (e.g., see Kruttschnitt, 1993; Levinson, 1989). Indeed, aggression between the sexes has probably always been an aspect of life on this planet (Lalumière, Harris, Quinsey, & Rice, 2005). It has probably been so ubiquitous an aspect of human affairs that it has often not been regarded as a matter of public concern. In the 17th century, however, women of the Puritan Massachusetts Bay Colony acquired the right to be free from "bodily correction" by husbands (Pleck, 1989). The goal was to enhance family stability rather than to promote women's rights. Feminists first took up the issue within the temperance movement, placing emancipation above family preservation and criticizing the roles of church and state in perpetuating violence against women (Hilton, 1989). Conservative reformers were more accepted by the end of the 19th century. They established women's and children's protective services and protested judicial lenience in cases of partner violence against women. Although such violence was a crime in most states, convictions were rare and confined to excessive violence or permanent injury (Logan, Walker, Jordan, & Leukefeld, 2006). After the start of the 20th century, however, systematic legal reforms aimed at violence against women fell temporarily silent (Buzawa & Buzawa, 2003), paralleling the abandonment of reformist approaches to criminal justice (Harris & Rice, 1997).

Legislation

With the rise of women's liberation in the industrialized West in the 1960s, feminists reidentified partner violence as a problem perpetuated by society's treating it as a private matter. Legislation and law enforcement became a focus for change. Governments recognized "wife assault" as a legitimate concern requiring a criminal justice response (e.g., see Hilton, 1989). Canada altered its definition of criminal assault: Where wife beating once had been a separate crime subject to imprisonment only if it caused bodily harm, it now was classified as a form of assault in general. Starting with the Pennsylvania Protection From Abuse Act in 1977, by the end of the 20th century most U.S. statutes came to define *assault* as intentionally applying or attempting to apply force without consent, or threatening to do so (see Buzawa & Buzawa, 2003, for a review). Many changes eliminated requirements that misdemeanor assaults be witnessed by a police officer. Some states created separate offenses for partner violence that permitted constitutionally valid attempts to promote innovative sentences such as court-mandated counseling (Buzawa & Buzawa, 2003). Such reforms might have improved police responses to such domestic-specific situations as harassment, but from a practical perspective, poorly drafted legislation, constitutional challenges, and inadequate judicial resources have limited the impact of these reforms (Buzawa & Buzawa, 2003).

New changes continue, including elimination of marital exemptions for sexual assault, increased punishment for domestic assaulters, and mandated responses by police and courts, all supported by the U.S. Violence Against Women Act of 1994 (Buzawa & Buzawa, 2003; Valente, Hart, Zeya, & Malefyt, 2001). Feminist reformers of 100 or even 50 years ago would have been impressed with the array of legislative and policy responses to partner violence and the goal of ending society's endorsement of such violence. Yet, although the law no longer condones partner violence, the problem remains prevalent. Because little was systematically recorded on the rates of partner violence prior to the late 20th-century reforms, it is difficult to know whether changing criminal justice responses have had any effect. Evaluation questions include whether legislative changes actually change practice; for example, do "mandatory" arrest laws actually result in higher rates of arrest? Also, is prosecution more likely and sentencing tougher, and, if so, have the rate and severity of partner violence reduced as a result?

Policing

The police are responsible for transferring partner violence from the privacy of the family to the forensic domain. Under traditional policing models, partner violence was considered a private family matter, apparently by both police and the public. That is, women reported an estimated 2% of partner assaults to the police (Dobash & Dobash, 1979) and many of these reports were ignored (Buzawa & Buzawa, 2003; Dobash & Dobash, 1979; Jaffe, Hastings, Reitzel, & Austin, 1993). Responding officers pressed charges in few cases of partner assault against women, measurably fewer than in assault involving strangers, despite evidence of injuries requiring medical attention (Jaffe et al., 1993). Police officers were discouraged from arresting perpetrators by organizational cultures that emphasized nonintervention and by lack of support from prosecutors and courts (Buzawa & Buzawa, 2003; Dutton, 1988; Jaffe et al., 1993). Few police officers believed that arrest was effective, and, somewhat disturbingly, police officers were more likely than other groups to see the violence as acceptable (Hilton, 1993). Furthermore, partner violence calls were erroneously believed to be a particularly dangerous situation for officers (Elliott, 1989).

In the late 1970s, a social work approach dominated police response to partner violence; law enforcement and arrest were secondary concerns. The approach was seen as successful in part because court referrals decreased in favor of referral to social welfare and mental health facilities (Bard & Berkowitz, 1969). In the 1980s, mounting pressure from battered women's groups and a changing political climate resulted in proarrest legislation. In Canada, many police services initiated policies of laying charges in all cases with reasonable and probable grounds to believe that an assault had taken place, partly in response to a report by the Canadian Advisory Council on the Status of Women (Hilton, 1989; Jaffe et al., 1993). In the United States, the impetus for a revision of policing came in part from the Attorney General's Task Force on Family Violence in 1984 (Buzawa & Buzawa, 2003). There is evidence that new policies did indeed increase arrests (Jaffe et al., 1993). Although mandatory arrest is not consistently applied (e.g., see Hilton, Harris, & Rice, 2007), there is evidence that partner assault now yields criminal justice responses comparable with that for other violent crimes (Dutton 1988; Elliott, 1989). Furthermore, women report a higher proportion of assaults to the police than in the 1970s (e.g., see Logan et al., 2006), and most who called the police under a proarrest policy say that they would do so again (Apsler, Cummins, & Carl, 2003; Jaffe et al., 1993). Victim surveys since the 1980s have indicated that women were mostly satisfied with police responses and experienced less subsequent violence (Buzawa & Buzawa, 2003).

In the first attempt at a rigorous evaluation of the effect of arrest, Sherman and Berk (1984) reported that arrests significantly reduced violence (reported by victims or in official records), compared with separating the couple or giving advice. In similar studies, the effects of arrest were found to vary depending on the delay between arrest and follow-up, whether data were based on victim survey or official reports and such characteristics as whether offenders were unemployed (Berk, Campbell, Klap, & Western, 1992; Pate & Hamilton, 1992; Sherman et al., 1992). Other studies did not support an effect of arrest (Dunford, Huizinga, & Elliott, 1990; Hirschel & Hutchison, 1996), and when data from all five replications were combined, arrest was only slightly related to reductions in partner violence (Maxwell, Garner, & Fagan, 2001).

The proarrest policy has been widely adopted since the 1980s, and little attention has been paid to evaluating its effects (e.g., see Garner, Fagan, & Maxwell, 1995). Randomly controlled trials, although the gold standard for evaluation (e.g., see Sullivan, 2006), exclude severe cases of violence because it may be unethical to deny the protection of the criminal justice system to severely abused victims. Furthermore, in the evaluation studies previously described, officers actually arrested more perpetrators than the research design called for, deviating from randomly assigned responses in favor of arresting perpetrators supposed to receive an alternative intervention, mostly because of the severity of assaults even among misdemeanor cases. Rigorous evaluation has been difficult because characteristics of the perpetrator influence not only the likelihood of arrest but also the apparent effect of arrest, as well as the likelihood of recidivism, arrest notwithstanding. Evaluating arrest requires statistical methods to control for such characteristics. As our understanding of the effects of arrest is likely to depend on quasi-experimental studies, controlling for possible influencing characteristics of the case becomes even more important.

In our own research, conducted with colleagues at the Ontario Provincial Police in Ontario, Canada, we evaluated arrest concurrently with several perpetrator and incident characteristics, particularly prearrest risk of partner violence recidivism. This research was conducted using our recently developed tool for assessing risk of recidivism among men committing partner assault: the Ontario Domestic Assault Risk Assessment (ODARA; Hilton et al., 2004). The ODARA was initially intended for use by frontline police officers, and it includes 13 items, each of which was known to be a statistically significant predictor of repeated assault on the basis of analysis of several hundred cases in police records (e.g., prior police record of partner and other violence, substance abuse, assault on victim while pregnant). In our study of arrests in 522 cases, police were more likely to arrest men who had relatively high prearrest risk than men with relatively low scores, even though the ODARA was not known to the officers but scored retrospectively by the researchers (Hilton et al., 2007). To a lesser extent, arrest was also more likely for more severe assaults. Most notably, arrested men were more likely to commit a new assault against a female partner in the 5-year follow-up; however, this correlation was entirely attributable to the fact that police arrested men who were already higher risk. That is, when arrest and prearrest risk scores were analyzed together, only prearrest risk predicted recidivism. We also examined how much time the accused men actually were at risk to reoffend, by subtracting the amount of time they spent in custody (as a consequence of being arrested and charged for the assault on their partner or for some subsequent criminal offense). There was an interaction between arrest and prearrest risk score, such that among perpetrators with relatively low scores on the ODARA, arrested men spent significantly more time at risk without reassaulting a partner than did men not arrested, whereas, among perpetrators with higher scores, arrested and not-arrested men spent similar time at risk. Thus, arrest might have delayed the repetition of partner assault among relatively low-risk men. We conclude that there is reason to be optimistic that the current widespread policy of arresting and pressing charges in partner violence cases is at least not harmful overall, and possibly beneficial in certain cases. Whether the benefit is directly the result of being arrested per se or whether it depends on some subsequent criminal justice intervention has yet to be fully examined.

Prosecution

Unlike in policing, legislation limiting prosecutorial discretion is not widespread, partly because of potential backlogs at court (Buzawa & Buzawa, 2003). The same informal screening that historically occurred at the policing stage has been observed in prosecution (Buzawa & Buzawa, 2003; Ford & Regoli, 1993), which might even have been exacerbated by increased arrests. Little is known, however, about prosecution rates, possible changes since the reforms of the latter 20th century, and any effects on recidivism. Dutton (1988) reported that about half of men arrested for partner violence in Canada were convicted and half of those were punished with a sentence or fine. In U.S. studies, prosecution rates have varied from 2% to 35% of arrested perpetrators (Dunford et al., 1990; Hirschel & Hutchison, 1996; Sherman & Berk, 1984; see also Ford & Regoli, 1993, for a review), suggesting no consistent approach to prosecution. It is not clear that prosecution and conviction rates for partner violence against women are different from other crimes (Dutton, 1988; Elliott, 1989), and intervention appears to be influenced by the same factors (e.g., severity of the offense, victim and witness cooperation; Elliott, 1989). A relationship between victim and perpetrator is associated with reduced likelihood of prosecution, presumably because of an actual or perceived reduction in victim and witness cooperation, and could account for any differences in the prosecution of partner violence (Elliott, 1989; see also Byrne, Kilpatrick, Howley, & Beatty, 1999; Logan et al., 2006). It does seem clear that victims and prosecutors have divergent perceptions of their roles and responsibilities (Bennett, Goodman, & Dutton, 1999; Ford & Regoli, 1993; see also Landau, 2000; Logan et al., 2006).

Little is known about the effect of prosecution on partner violence recidivism. Fagan (1989) compared prosecuted and nonprosecuted cases and reported that prosecution was attempted in only 27%. Cases in which injuries were less severe tended to exhibit less recidivism when prosecution was attempted, but there was essentially no effect on high-severity cases. Conviction was obtained in 24% of prosecuted cases, but there were too few cases at this stage to draw reliable conclusions about the effects of conviction and sentencing. This finding is similar to what we observed in our study of arrest; that is, to the extent that a history of severe violence is correlated with risk of recidivism (e.g., see Cattaneo & Goodman, 2005), criminal justice responses have an effect, if at all, on lower risk cases; higher risk cases are more likely to recidivate regardless of intervention. More recent studies comparing prosecuted and nonprosecuted cases also failed to find a specific deterrent effect of prosecution, including one study of over 1,000 cases that were prosecutor-declined, dismissed, sentenced to probation, or sentenced to jail; violence history predicted recidivism regardless of prosecution (Davis, Smith, & Nickles, 1998).

Some attempts to limit prosecutorial discretion have been made, particularly with no-drop prosecution policies. In some cases, prosecutors have been required to follow a victim's desire to prosecute, but in others, victims have been compelled to serve as witnesses, subpoenaed, or held in contempt of court if they did not cooperate (Buzawa & Buzawa, 2003). There are claims that abusers are more likely to continue to be violent and to coerce partners into dropping charges when it is optional and that no-drop policies reduce violence.

In an experimental study of partner violence complaints brought directly to the prosecutor's office by female victims rather than by police, cases were randomly assigned to drop-permitted or no-drop conditions (Ford & Regoli, 1993). In the no-drop condition, 6% of cases were actually dropped because the victim failed to appear for court or refused to testify, compared with 46% in the drop-permitted condition. Data reported by Ford and Regoli show that violence during the prosecution process appeared to differ only according to processing time (i.e., the longer the prosecution process, the greater the reported violence), and mean processing time was shorter for drop-permitted cases. Six months after the prosecution process, victims who had been permitted to drop charges tended to report a lower violence rate, but only if they did not drop. Victims who did drop when permitted experienced more violence than the no-drop cases, leading to the somewhat paradoxical conclusion that permitting victims to drop charges gives them the best chance of reduced violence, as long as they do not actually drop the charges. As in the arrest experiments, the randomly assigned prosecutorial track was not realized in a substantial number of cases (35%; Ford & Regoli, 1993). Within the no-drop condition, prosecutorial tracks (i.e., pretrial diversion vs. probation with treatment) made no consistent difference to subsequent violence. Perhaps most important, this unique study revealed much discretion throughout the criminal justice system, particularly at the level of prosecution. Complexities mean that it has been extraordinarily challenging to evaluate criminal justice responses and to identify anything that makes a difference to the outcome of violence.

Alternatives to Traditional Court

Because individual discretion is seen as inherent in its role, the judiciary has been less subject to attempts to limit discretion than other aspects of the criminal justice system. Judges have expressed reluctance to treat partner violence as a crime and often dismissed cases ignoring legislated requirements (see Buzawa & Buzawa, 2003, for a review). Inconsistency in disposition has disturbed observers, but there is little systematic information about what influences judges' decisions or how they can be modified. More attention has focused on other aspects of the court system, particularly mediation.

In the early 20th century, mediation aimed at reconciliation and later focused on resolution of conflict associated with separation (Ellis, 1993). Court-based and private mediation became widespread by the 1980s. Currently, some mediation programs accept partner violence cases, and they vary as to whether an admission of guilt is required and whether services are individual or include couple sessions (see Buzawa & Buzawa, 2003, for a review).

In the 1980s, the Province of Ontario recognized that mediation might pose risks for partner assault victims, but it left the decision to offer service to the mediator (Hilton, 1991; c.f. Ellis, 1993). In our study of court cases brought to resolve disputes arising from divorce mediation, a third of cases involved partner violence against the female partner, but the court did not recognize the violence as having impaired victims' ability to negotiate equitably (Hilton, 1991). Others have observed the no-win situation for victims in mediation: Either the abuse is not seen as undermining the victim's ability to negotiate or tolerate cohabitation or the victim endured excessive violence without leaving and therefore was viewed as condoning the violence (e.g., see Ellis, 1993). Ellis (1993) compared women and men who participated in five sessions of court-referred mediation voluntarily with clients who were required to attend one session to be eligible for legal aid. It is not surprising that legal aid clients reported greater dissatisfaction with mediation and were more likely to report being the victim of physical or verbal aggression after mediation. Similar to Ford and Regoli's (1993) report on prosecution, Ellis's (1993) study indicated that the effect of mediation appeared to vary with whether participation was voluntary. Overall, the best predictors of postseparation aggression were preseparation incidents of controlling and destructive behavior and the victim's fear.

Alternatives to traditional courts, such as special family or domestic violence courts, are increasing in popularity (see Buzawa & Buzawa, 2003, for a review). Ontario has 30 specialized courts under the authority of the Ontario Ministry of the Attorney General (http://www.attorneygeneral. jus.gov.on.ca/english/about/vw/dvc.asp) for a population of 12 million, the most extensive domestic violence court program in Canada. It aims to facilitate prosecution and increase offender accountability, as well as to provide better victim support than traditional courts. Each domestic violence court has an advisory committee, specialist prosecutors, victim and witness assistance, and linguistic interpreters, plus special training for court staff, police, and probation and parole officers. Police evidence collection is modified to the needs of domestic violence victims, and a special (nonempirical) form is used to assess risk factors. Ontario is also experimenting with special victim protection procedures and actuarial risk assessment prior to bail hearings. Domestic violence courts attempt *early intervention* whereby offenders are referred to a Partner Assault Response (PAR) treatment program as a condition of probation, conditional sentence, or bail. The 16-week PAR community treatment is contracted out to social service agencies that provide standardized modules and maintain contact with victims for safety planning, referral, and support.

Coordinated Criminal Justice and Community Responses

The Ontario approach is a simple example of criminal justice and community agency cooperation in responding to partner violence. Civil courts also have a role primarily through protective or restraining orders (see Buzawa & Buzawa, 2003, for a review; see also Buzawa & Buzawa, 1996). Civil court orders have the advantage of speed and efficiency in contrast to the prosecution process and can try to limit offenders' contacts with victims, initiate treatment, and provide grounds for future police action (e.g., through violation of an order). They also represent victim choice and appear to allow the victim more control over the procedure and outcome than prosecution. Such civil orders are controversial because they permit restrictions on a person who is often not present at the hearing and unable to present opposing arguments. Evaluations suggest that many victims who initiate an application for a restraining order fail to complete the process (Zoellner et al., 2000), and many perpetrators are quite undeterred when orders are obtained (e.g., see Kanuha & Ross, 2004; Klein, 1996; Logan et al., 2006). Police enforcement of protective orders can also be limited, especially when they are unaware of them. That is, this civil response is substantially weakened in the absence of a coordinated system.

Models of coordination do exist, however (e.g., the Duluth Domestic Abuse Intervention Project; Shepard, Falk, & Elliott, 2002). Duluth, Minnesota, was one of the first U.S. jurisdictions to adopt mandatory domestic violence arrest, and nongovernmental agencies assisted in developing and monitoring a comprehensive response. Each criminal justice juncture had formal guidelines to limit discretion, including no-drop prosecution. Courts ordered offenders to treatment, and probation officers placed male perpetrators into risk categories on the basis of the history of abuse. Several other states adopted this model, and others have developed coordinated responses with step-by-step instructions for protocols and evaluation (Boles & Patterson, 1997). An evaluation of the Duluth model reported gradually decreasing partner violence recidivism rates (measured by new investigations, charges, or convictions) that achieved statistical significance after 3 years (Shepard et al., 2002). Evaluation of men's treatment in a coordinated community response indicated that incarcerated men were the most likely to recidivate, whereas treatment completers were the least (Babcock & Steiner, 1999). This result is consistent with more recent findings that, regardless of a coordinated response, greater criminal justice intervention and treatment dropout are associated with risk to reoffend (Hilton et al., 2007; Hilton & Harris, 2005).

In Ontario, Ottawa's Partner Assault Support Team (PAST) comprises police officers, prosecutors, victim and witness assistance staff, probation and parole officers, child protection workers, and city government staff. The team works in partnership with a specialized domestic violence court to improve investigation, prosecution, and victim safety. Their coordinated activity is believed to have created referrals for victim safety planning, increased the pressing of charges, and made police surveillance available in certain cases. The coordinated response model in Ottawa also served as the backdrop for the pilot implementation of actuarial risk assessment using the ODARA. The Ottawa City Police Service, prosecutors, and court-based victim services liaise with each other to obtain ODARA scores for male perpetrators and communicate with women's shelters and related agencies with a shared language for discussing risk (Ontario Ministry of the Attorney General, 2006). Although we know of no empirical evaluation of this particular model, the Attorney General of Ontario recognized PAST with an award of excellence in 2006; furthermore, a recent analysis of judicial decision making in Ontario courts concluded that, more often than not, judges strongly condemned partner violence against women, issued custodial sentences, and frequently considered the intimate context of the violence as an aggravating factor (Crocker, 2005).

Criminal Justice Response to Women Perpetrators and Marginalized Groups

Some historians have noted that, in their campaigns against family violence, 19th-century feminist reformers overlooked women who used violence and others who could not be perceived as virtuous wives and mothers (Hilton, 1989). This was partly because reformers depended on positions of influence they had through other, less radical movements (i.e., suffrage and temperance), and it was not until the 1960s that the new women's movement recognized partner violence against women as a problem with its own priority. The need to present battered women as "weak victims" in order to gain legitimacy continued in family courts in the late 20th century (Hilton, 1991; see also Bograd, 2005; Crocker, 2005). Critical analysis of criminal justice responses to partner violence also abandoned women who used violence, substance abusers, and other "less virtuous" victims and has only recently focused on responses to women of color and women in same-sex relationships (e.g., see Sokoloff & Pratt, 2005).

Although mandatory arrest was strongly supported by some scholars in the 1980s (e.g., see Sherman & Berk, 1984), it met later with equally strong criticism for its potential to disempower women (e.g., see Landau, 2000; Martin, 1997). In particular, police were accused of failing to discriminate between true aggressors and those reacting in self-defense, resulting in inappropriate dual arrests or true victims being arrested alone (e.g., see Buzawa & Buzawa, 2003; Coulter, Kuehnle, Byers, & Alfonso, 1999; Ferraro & Pope, 1993; Martin, 1997; Pollack, Battaglia, & Allspach, 2005). Overall, dual

arrests (compared with arrests of a single perpetrator) were less likely to result in any conviction, especially for men, even though the dual-arrest women
(but not the men) often had been victimized in the past (Martin, 1997).
Martin (1997) also observed that 14% of domestic violence cases disposed by
criminal court were single arrests of women. Some arrested women reported
that they used violence in response to partner-initiated violence that went
unheeded by police (Woman Abuse Council of Toronto, 2005).

Historically, criminal punishment was more likely to be imposed on
"Blacks, immigrants, vagrants, and other groups without political, economic
or social power" (Buzawa & Buzawa, 2003, p. 63), perhaps more as a means of
controlling these disadvantaged groups than to assist their victims. Bachman
and Coker (1995), using data from the U.S. National Crime Victimization
Survey, reported not only that Black women were more likely than White
women to report domestic assault to police but also that their partners (97%
of whom were also Black) were more likely to be arrested. Although minority
ethnic groups are overrepresented in lower socioeconomic strata and more
likely to experience partner violence and recidivism (e.g., see Caetano, Field,
Ramisetty-Mikler, & McGrath, 2005; Field & Caetano, 2004; Frias & Angel, 2005), the predictors of self- and partner-reported partner violence are
similar across ethnic groups (including Blacks, Latinos, Whites, and Native
Americans; Aldarondo, Kantor, & Jasinski, 2002; Field & Caetano, 2004;
Oetzel & Duran, 2004; Ramirez, 2005; West, 1998; see also Brownridge, 2003;
Mahoney, Williams, & West, 2001). Some judicial interventions appear to
be equally used and effective across such ethnic groups (McFarlane et al.,
2004; Mears, Carlson, Holden, & Harris, 2001). In treatment programs, however, ethnic minority men might be inappropriately assigned to culturally
insensitive programs or to culturally appropriate but inexperienced parapro-
fessional services (Bograd, 2005). Members of ethnic minorities and socially
disadvantaged groups appear less likely to complete treatment (Babcock &
Steiner, 1999).

Public surveys reveal general agreement that partner violence against
women is a crime (e.g., see Carlson & Worden, 2005; Choi & Edleson, 1995;
Hilton, 1993), whereas victim interviews reveal more ambivalence about
the criminal justice system (e.g., see Crocker, 2005), especially among ethnic minority women, the poor, and lesbians (e.g., see Bograd, 2005; Ferraro
& Pope, 1993). Overall, female victims of partner violence are less satisfied
with every level of the criminal justice system than are female victims of
other assaults (Byrne et al., 1999), and this might be especially true for women
from marginalized and disadvantaged groups, for whom it has been argued
that alternatives to the criminal justice system should be the mainstay of an
effective response (e.g., see Sokoloff & Pratt, 2005; see also Bent-Goodley,
2005).

Less is known about gay and lesbian victims and perpetrators. Out of
134 dual-arrest cases studied by Martin (1997), 6 were gay or lesbian couples

(see also Mahoney et al., 2001). Similarly, research identifying women with disabilities as at risk of partner violence is emerging (e.g., see Cohen, Forte, DuMont, Hyman, & Romans, 2005; Coker, Smith, & Fadden, 2005), but we know of no research examining the response of the criminal justice system to these women or about the interaction with their particular sociolegal issues.

Summary of Criminal Justice Responses to Partner Violence

The past 30 years have seen many changes to the criminal justice system response to partner violence, from legislative changes to the definition of assault and proarrest policies, to attempts to limit prosecutorial discretion and progressive efforts to integrate criminal justice and victim services. Many of these changes have been controversial, and there is little empirical evaluation to resolve debates about what criminal justice response works best. In contrast, there has been a good deal of research into what works for general offender interventions. Given that the risk factors for partner violence and general violence are similar among men (Hilton et al., 2004; Hilton, Harris, & Rice, 2001), we can learn from the lessons of general offender intervention research.

LESSONS FROM INTERVENTIONS FOR CRIMINAL CONDUCT

Like many public services (e.g., public education, publicly funded health care), criminal justice services are not accustomed to being held to an effectiveness standard: The goal is regarded not as achieving measured outcomes, but rather it is regarded simply as the provision of service. Thus, criminal justice systems are expected to provide a continuity of service comprising police investigation, arrest, bail determination, prosecution at trial, incarceration and other criminal sanctions, rehabilitation, and eventual release to the community. Few criminal justice practitioners (e.g., police officers, prosecutors, correctional officials, parole and probation officers) are equipped to measure the effects of their practices scientifically (Gendreau, 2001). Nevertheless, the criminal justice reforms we have described were made with the ostensible intention of reducing partner violence. We note that there have been successful demonstrations of effective criminal justice interventions (Lipsey & Wilson, 1993; Ross, Fabiano, & Ewles, 1988; Wilson & Lipsey, 2001). For example, several demonstrations of the value of multisystemic therapy (MST) for adolescent offenders reveal that comprehensively implemented, coordinated programs can be rigorously evaluated using randomized controlled trials and demonstrate undeniable reductions in subsequent criminal behavior. MST is based on an understanding of crime that emphasizes the social environment. That is, criminal behavior is made more likely by various aspects of the peer, school, and family context. MST seeks to replace every procriminal aspect of the environment with something incompatible with criminal conduct (Borduin et al., 1995; Borduin, Schaeffer, Ronis, & Scott, 2003; Harris & Rice, 2006).

We are not advocating the application of MST to partner violence. Rather, the example shows that, even when problems are severe, it is possible to make a difference. We argue that successful outcomes rest on the application of effective empirically supported interventions. We also think there are other important lessons to be learned from such notable successes. Most important, criminal justice "service as usual" has little to recommend it (Andrews & Bonta, 1994; Gendreau, Cullen, & Bonta, 1994; McGuire, 2000). No variation in criminal justice sanctions, for example, has been demonstrated to be more effective than another. Instead, best practice in the field of criminal justice responses to violent or other crime is based on what has been called the *psychology of criminal conduct*, the scientific study of the personal characteristics and environmental correlates associated with crime (Andrews & Bonta, 1994).

The study of the psychology of criminal conduct relies in turn on two principal research methodologies: the follow-up study and the meta-analysis. First, follow-up studies permit the identification of predictors of relevant outcomes, recidivism being most important (e.g., see Hilton & Harris, 2005). By measuring various aspects of individual offenders and their circumstances, and independently measuring late criminal recidivism, it is possible to identify those characteristics that best distinguish those who later reoffend from those who do not. Selecting and combining such characteristics for their ability to forecast recidivism results in highly replicable systems for the appraisal of the relative risk of criminal or violent recidivism (Hilton et al., 2004; Hilton & Harris, 2005; Quinsey, Harris, Rice, & Cormier, 2006). From among those personal characteristics (and situational contexts) consistently associated with recidivism (e.g., history of alcohol abuse, antisocial peers), it is possible to select the best candidates for intervention. Follow-up studies of prosecution approaches, sentencing options, treatment programs, and community supervision practices can permit the identification of those interventions that independently affect the likelihood of recidivism. Second, meta-analysis permits the numerical combination of results from disparate studies (especially follow-up studies, in this context) to render an overall estimate of effectiveness. Meta-analysis also permits testing and evaluation of variables that might moderate effectiveness (Landenberger & Lipsey, 2005; Lipsey & Wilson, 1993; Wilson & Lipsey, 2001). Although there remain many important questions about best criminal justice practice, especially for partner violence, several conclusions can be drawn:

1. *Variation in criminal sanction has little effect.* In the absence of human service or rehabilitative programs, longer (or shorter) sentences, get-tough sentencing, and scaring offenders straight

have no effect on criminal recidivism (Andrews & Bonta, 1994; Cullen, Blevins, Trager, & Gendreau, 2005; Ferguson, 2002). To the extent that partner violence is criminal conduct, get-tough sentencing of perpetrators is unlikely to affect the risk faced by subsequent victims, beyond incapacitation. The ineffectiveness of punishment, combined with the salutary effects of human service in other domains, suggests that the best chance of reducing partner violence among nonincapacitated perpetrators lies in improving interventions aimed at the perpetrators' characteristics and relationships (Bonta, Wallace-Capretta, & Rooney, 2000).

2. *Intervention targets are not always obvious.* Offenders often report high levels of nonspecific subjective distress, elevated general stress, and low self-esteem compared with nonoffenders. Follow-up research, however, shows that these complaints are unrelated, or even inversely related, to recidivism, making them ineffective targets for intervention (Bonta, Law, & Hanson, 1998). In contrast, marital conflict and substance abuse are associated with partner violence recidivism (Hilton & Harris, 2005), and it makes sense to attempt to alter these aspects in efforts to reduce reassault. Research also shows, however, that people choose their own environments, and it is possible that apparent effects of conflict and substance abuse are attributable to individual differences in antisociality. For example, it might be that people who engage in substance abuse tend to be different from those who do not and that those differences, rather than substance abuse, are actually a direct cause of partner assault. Similarly, some relationship violence seems to be attributable to men and women with aggressive proclivities selectively partnering with each other (Capaldi & Crosby, 1997; Capaldi, Shortt, & Crosby, 2003). Thus, teaching conflict resolution skills and treating substance abuse would be ineffective if partner violence, conflict, and substance abuse were all the result of a more fundamental cause such as general antisociality (Quinsey et al., 2006). The best way to resolve the causal relationship is to rigorously evaluate an intervention aimed at reducing conflict or substance abuse while controlling for antisociality.

3. *Risk factors are highly general.* Meta-analyses of follow-up studies indicate little specificity in the personal characteristics that predict criminal and violent recidivism. With few exceptions, antisocial personality traits (especially psychopathy), history of criminal activity, antisocial and aggressive childhood conduct, and substance abuse consistently predict recidivism in

all offender populations, including men who commit partner violence (e.g., see Hilton & Harris, 2005). In our own research, indicators of general antisociality were so good at assessing the risk of partner violence recidivism among men that variables specific to intimate relationships did not improve the prediction (Hilton, Harris, Rice, Houghton, & Eke, 2008). Although there are now empirically derived actuarial assessments for partner violence specifically, the available data indicate that empirically derived actuarial tools for violence risk in general would perform almost as well.

4. *Not everything helps.* One of the more discouraging empirical facts is that some interventions delivered with remarkable levels of fidelity, enthusiasm, and intensity have failed. Indeed, some even have been associated with poorer outcomes than doing nothing (or service as usual). Such failure can occur when the intervention is based on a faulty or incomplete understanding of the causes of the problem. Regarding partner violence, one cannot assume that varying the criminal justice response will have salutary results, no matter how well intentioned or vigorous. Indeed, with the exception of social learning and skills-teaching approaches (Landenberger & Lipsey, 2005; Lipsey & Wilson, 1993), the empirical foundation for reducing violent crime in adults remains small and equivocal (see Palmer, Brown, & Barrera, 1992). The literature, however, justifies trying other therapeutic approaches (e.g., pharmacological) that are based on scientifically reasonable hypotheses about the cause of violence and are provided in the context of scientifically informative evaluations (Harris & Rice, 1997; Quinsey et al., 2006).

5. *Formal risk assessment informs intervention.* Follow-up research has shown that intervention effectiveness is related to risk (Andrews & Bonta, 1994; Andrews, Bonta, & Wormith, 2006; Andrews & Dowden, 2006). Logically, when offenders are already at very low risk of recidivism, there is little intervention can do to lower that risk further. Indeed, when low-risk offenders are mixed with those at higher risk, there is a reasonable chance that interventions will increase recidivism by low-risk participants (Andrews & Bonta, 1994; Poulin, Dishion, & Burraston, 2001). With respect to partner violence, using the same interventions with all perpetrators without regard to risk level could produce an overall increase in partner violence, or at best, cancel the beneficial effects achieved with relatively higher risk offenders with detrimental effects on the lowest risk offenders.

6. *Effective criminal justice response is likely to be systemic and coordinated.* To make effective use of the knowledge already acquired in this domain, fragmented, piecemeal efforts are unlikely to yield the best effects. The application of the available knowledge is best conceived of as systemic; deciding what to do in an individual case cannot rest on the appraisal of individual circumstances alone. Some kind of overriding policy has to ensure that the right services, aimed at the right targets, are directed with the right intensity at the right perpetrators (Dowden & Andrews, 2003; Gendreau, Goggin, & Smith, 1999; Hanson & Whitman, 1995; Paparozzi & Gendreau, 2005). Such policy would be informed by the strong available evidence indicating that the intensity of intervention efforts should match the level of risk. That is, resources should not be divided equally among cases but applied according to best practice in the delivery of criminal justice service, which has been eloquently articulated as risk–needs–responsivity (Andrews & Bonta, 1994; Bonta et al., 2000).

THE RISK–NEEDS–RESPONSIVITY PRINCIPLES OF EFFECTIVE CRIMINAL JUSTICE SERVICE

The risk principle states that services and their intensity are delivered according to the risk of recidivism. For partner violence, detention, denial of bail, postconviction sentence, and even indefinite incarceral incapacitation would be applied in accordance with the measurable risk of recidivism. Similarly, the probability and intensity of pre- and postconviction community supervision, support to victims, perpetrator treatment, and child protection services would also depend on risk. The absolute proportion of cases that would receive any particular intervention would depend on value judgments reflecting societal "tolerance" of partner violence as well as the available public resources (e.g., funds, probation caseloads, jail beds, shelter spaces, treatment spaces). Formal measures of the risk of partner violence recidivism are available for frontline assessment by both police officers and victim support personnel (e.g., see Campbell, 2007; Hilton et al., 2004; Williams & Houghton, 2004), and more in-depth assessment by mental health professionals and parole or probation officers (Hilton et al., 2008; Kropp & Hart, 2000). Valid actuarial risk assessments combine information from official records (e.g., police rap sheets, correctional case files) with offense details gleaned during police investigation (e.g., victim and witness statements, officers' observations).

Knowing a perpetrator's risk of recidivism does not necessarily provide information as to what to do about that risk. For partner violence, only a tiny fraction of perpetrators could, no matter what their assessed risk, be subjected to indefinite incapacitation (although that would be pursued when feasible; Buzawa & Buzawa, 2003). *Criminogenic needs* are defined as personal or contextual characteristics empirically associated with criminal behavior (Andrews & Bonta, 1994); among men, hostility and substance abuse are examples of criminogenic needs for both partner violence and violent crime in general (Hilton & Harris, 2005). Thus, effective criminal justice services would target these needs in attempting to reduce recidivism rather than attempting to modify perpetrators' self-esteem or fear of punishment (which are empirically unrelated to the behavior of interest). Bail conditions obliging perpetrators to abstain from drinking would not alone be expected to be effective for higher risk perpetrators; pretrial detention or intensive supervision would be used to maximize compliance. Similarly, treatment aimed at reducing substance abuse would be delivered most intensively to those perpetrators of highest risk (those not incapacitated), along with efforts to prevent attrition.

The general offender treatment research indicates that best practices would emphasize social learning approaches that forgo an insight-oriented, emotionally evocative therapeutic approach in favor of social skills training in which participants learn (through modeling, role-play, coaching, and video feedback) prosocial methods to deal with interpersonal conflict (Andrews & Bonta, 1994; Dowden, Antonowicz, & Andrews, 2001; McGuire, 2000). The interpersonal style of criminal justice officials dealing with partner violence perpetrators would model prosocial statements and confront procriminal attitudes. They would eschew authoritarian approaches in favor of a firm-but-fair interpersonal style (Andrews & Bonta, 1994).

We note that meta-analyses of partner violence treatment specifically have not indicated the superiority of any one approach, especially when examining the few controlled studies (Babcock, Green, & Robie, 2004; Feder & Wilson, 2005). Illusory effects can result from comparing treatment completers with dropouts (e.g., see Feder & Wilson, 2005), who are likely to be of higher pretreatment risk, a problem exacerbated by providing the same treatment for all offenders, in violation of the risk principle.

CONCLUSION

For the past several decades, various steps have been taken to increase and expand the criminal justice system's response to partner violence. With the possible exception of proarrest policies, new intervention approaches have been attempted sporadically and nonsystematically. Evaluations, especially rigorous empirical designs, are notably rare in the criminal justice system but have revealed some promising results for police arrest and for social learning approaches to perpetrator interventions. The systematic implementation of criminal justice interventions can generate useful knowledge in many ways. The most obvious examples pertain to the rigorous empirical evaluation of interventions. Thus, randomly assigning perpetrators (at comparable levels of assessed risk) to one of at least two interventions (including a service-as-usual placebo) permits later measurement of the actual reduction in detected partner violence achieved by each intervention. The same approaches can be used to evaluate the effects and cost-effectiveness of many nontherapeutic interventions. Without such evaluative data, rational policy development approaches the impossible. Evaluative data (combined with ongoing in-program assessment of treatment gains) can serve a vital quality control and improvement function within interventions. In more basic terms, an intervention for partner violence is essentially an instantiation of an explanatory theory about its causes. As such, its scientifically valid evaluation is a test of that theory and, however the results turn out, informs and contributes to understanding of the phenomenon at a basic level (Gottfredson, 1984; Quinsey et al., 2006). In this context, we note that the field awaits power-fully effective interventions, perhaps based on as yet unapplied explanations (e.g., see Smuts, 1996). Criminal justice practitioners and researchers are uniquely poised to contribute to applied knowledge in a way that more basic theoreticians never can.

REFERENCES

Aldarondo, E., Kantor, G. K., & Jasinski, J. L. (2002). A risk marker analysis of wife assault in Latino families. *Violence Against Women, 8,* 429–454.

Andrews, D. A., & Bonta, J. (1994). *The psychology of criminal conduct.* Cincinnati, OH: Anderson.

Andrews, D. A., Bonta, J., & Wormith, J. S. (2006). The recent past and near future of risk and/or need assessment. *Crime & Delinquency, 52,* 7–27.

Andrews, D. A., & Dowden, C. (2006). Risk principle of case classification in correctional treatment. *International Journal of Offender Therapy and Comparative Criminology, 50,* 88–100.

Apsler, R., Cummins, M. R., & Carl, S. (2003). Perceptions of the police by female victims of domestic partner violence. *Violence Against Women, 9,* 1318–1335.

Babcock, J. C., Green, C. E., & Robie, C. (2004). Does batterers' treatment work? A meta-analytic review of domestic violence treatment. *Clinical Psychology Review, 23,* 1023–1053.

Babcock, J. C., & Steiner, R. (1999). The relationship between treatment, incarceration, and recidivism of battering: A program evaluation of Seattle's coordinated community response to domestic violence. *Journal of Family Psychology, 13,* 46–59.

Bachman, R., & Coker, A. L. (1995). Police involvement in domestic violence: The interactive effects of victim injury, offender's history of violence, and race. *Violence and Victims*, *10*, 91–106.

Bard, M., & Berkowitz, B. (1969). A community psychology consultation program in police family crisis interventions: Preliminary impressions. *International Journal of Social Psychiatry*, *15*, 209–215.

Bennett, L., Goodman, L., & Dutton, M. A. (1999). Systemic obstacles to the criminal prosecution of a battering partner. *Journal of Interpersonal Violence*, *14*, 761–772.

Bent-Goodley, T. B. (2005). An African-centered approach to domestic violence. *Families in Society*, *86*, 197–205.

Berk, R. A., Campbell, A., Klap, R., & Western, B. (1992). A Bayesian analysis of the Colorado Springs spouse abuse experiment. *The Journal of Criminal Law and Criminology*, *83*, 170–200.

Bograd, M. (2005). Strengthening domestic violence theories. In N. J. Sokoloff & C. Pratt (Eds.), *Domestic violence at the margins* (pp. 25–38). New Brunswick, NJ: Rutgers University Press.

Boles, A. B., & Patterson, J. C. (1997). *Improving community response to crime victims*. Thousand Oaks, CA: Sage.

Bonta, J., Law, M., & Hanson, K. (1998). The prediction of criminal and violent recidivism among mentally disordered offenders: A meta-analysis. *Psychological Bulletin*, *123*, 123–142.

Bonta, J., Wallace-Capretta, S., & Rooney, J. (2000). A quasi-experimental evaluation of an intensive rehabilitation supervision program. *Criminal Justice and Behavior*, *27*, 312–329.

Borduin, C. M., Mann, B. J., Cone, L. T., Henggeler, S. W., Fucci, B. R., Blaske, D. M., & Williams, R. A. (1995). Multisystemic treatment of serious juvenile offenders: Long-term prevention of criminality and violence. *Journal of Consulting and Clinical Psychology*, *63*, 569–578.

Borduin, C. M., Schaeffer, C. M., Ronis, M., & Scott, T. (2003). Multisystemic treatment of serious behavior in adolescents. In C. A. Essau (Ed.), *Conduct and oppositional defiant disorders: Epidemiology, risk factors, and treatment* (pp. 299–318). Mahwah, NJ: Erlbaum.

Brownridge, D. A. (2003). Male partner violence against aboriginal women in Canada. *Journal of Interpersonal Violence*, *18*, 65–83.

Buzawa, E. S., & Buzawa, C. G. (1996). *Do arrests and restraining orders work?* Thousand Oaks, CA: Sage.

Buzawa, E. S., & Buzawa, C. G. (2003). *Domestic violence: The criminal justice response*. Thousand Oaks, CA: Sage.

Byrne, C. A., Kilpatrick, D. G., Howley, S. S., & Beatty, D. (1999). Female victims of partner versus nonpartner violence. *Criminal Justice and Behavior*, *26*, 275–292.

Caetano, R., Field, C. A., Ramisetty-Mikler, S., & McGrath, C. (2005). The 5-year course of intimate partner violence among White, Black, and Hispanic couples in the United States. *Journal of Interpersonal Violence, 20,* 1039–1057.

Campbell, J. C. (Ed.). (2007). *Assessing dangerousness: Violence by sexual offenders, batterers, and child abusers* (2nd ed.). New York: Springer Publishing Company.

Capaldi, D. M., & Crosby, L. (1997). Observed and reported psychological and physical aggression in young, at-risk couples. *Social Development, 6,* 184–206.

Capaldi, D. M., Shortt, J. W., & Crosby, L. (2003). Physical and psychological aggression in at-risk couples: Stability and change in young adulthood. *Merrill-Palmer Quarterly, 49,* 1–27.

Carlson, B. E., & Worden, A. P. (2005). Attitudes and beliefs about domestic violence: Results of a public opinion survey. *Journal of Interpersonal Violence, 20,* 1197–1218.

Cattaneo, L. B., & Goodman, L. A. (2005). Risk factors for reabuse in intimate partner violence: A cross-disciplinary critical review. *Trauma, Violence, & Abuse, 6,* 141–175.

Choi, A., & Edleson, J. L. (1995). Advocating legal intervention in wife assaults: Results from a national survey of Singapore. *Journal of Interpersonal Violence, 10,* 243–258

Cohen, M. M., Forte, T., DuMont, J., Hyman, I., & Romans, S. (2005). Intimate partner violence among Canadian women with activity limitations. *Journal of Epidemiology and Community Health, 59,* 834–839.

Coker, A. L., Smith, P. H., & Fadden, M. K. (2005). Intimate partner violence and disabilities among women attending family practice clinics. *Journal of Women's Health, 14,* 829–838.

Coulter, M. L., Kuehnle, K., Byers, R., & Alfonso, M. (1999). Police-reporting behavior and victim–police interactions as described by women in a domestic violence shelter. *Journal of Interpersonal Violence, 14,* 1290–1298.

Crocker, D. (2005). Regulating intimacy: Judicial discourse in cases of wife assault 1970 to 2000. *Violence Against Women, 11,* 197–226.

Cullen, F. T., Blevins, K. R., Trager, J. S., & Gendreau, P. (2005). The rise and fall of boot camps: A case in common-sense. *Journal of Offender Rehabilitation, 40,* 53–70.

Davis, R. C., Smith, B. E., & Nickles, L. (1998). The deterrent effect of prosecuting domestic violence misdemeanors. *Crime & Delinquency, 44,* 434–442.

Dobash, R. E., & Dobash, R. (1979). *Violence against wives.* New York: Free Press.

Dowden, C., & Andrews, D. A. (2003). Does family intervention work for delinquents? Results of a meta-analysis. *Canadian Journal of Criminology and Criminal Justice, 45,* 327–342.

Dowden, C., Antonowicz, D., & Andrews, D. A. (2001). The effectiveness of relapse prevention with offenders: A meta-analysis. *Journal of Offender Therapy and Comparative Criminology, 47,* 516–528.

Dunford, F. W., Huizinga, D., & Elliott, D. S. (1990). The role of arrest in domestic assault: The Omaha police experiment. *Criminology, 28,* 183–206.

Dutton, D. G. (1988). *The domestic assault of women.* Boston: Allyn & Bacon.

Elliott, D. S. (1989). Criminal justice procedures in family violence crimes. In L. Ohlin & M. Tonry (Eds.), *Family violence* (pp. 427–480). Chicago: University of Chicago Press.

Ellis, D. (1993). Family courts, marital conflict mediation, and wife assault. In N. Z. Hilton (Ed.), *Legal responses to wife assault* (pp. 165–187). Newbury Park, CA: Sage.

Fagan, J. (1989). Cessation of family violence: Deterrence and dissuasion. In L. Ohlin & M. Tonry (Eds.), *Family violence* (pp. 377–426). Chicago: University of Chicago Press.

Feder, L., & Wilson, D. B. (2005). A meta-analytic review of court-mandated batterer intervention programs: Can courts affect abusers' behavior? *Journal of Experimental Criminology, 1,* 239–262.

Ferguson, J. L. (2002). Putting the "what works" research into practice. *Criminal Justice and Behavior, 29,* 472–492.

Ferraro, K. J., & Pope, L. (1993). Irreconcilable differences. In N. Z. Hilton (Ed.), *Legal responses to wife assault* (pp. 96–126). Newbury Park, CA: Sage.

Field, C. A., & Caetano, R. (2004). Ethnic differences in intimate partner violence in the U.S. general population. *Trauma, Violence, & Abuse, 5,* 303–317.

Ford, D. A., & Regoli, M. J. (1993). The criminal prosecution of wife assaulters: Process, problems, and effects. In N. Z. Hilton (Ed.), *Legal responses to wife assault* (pp. 127–164). Newbury Park, CA: Sage.

Frias, S. M., & Angel, R. J. (2005). The risk of partner violence among low-income Hispanic subgroups. *Journal of Marriage and Family, 67,* 552–564.

Garner, J., Fagan, J., & Maxwell, C. (1995). Published findings from the Spouse Assault Replication Program: A critical review. *Journal of Quantitative Criminology, 11,* 3–28.

Gendreau, P. (2001). We must do a better job of cumulating knowledge. *Canadian Psychology, 43,* 205–210.

Gendreau, P., Cullen, F. T., & Bonta, J. (1994). Intensive rehabilitation supervision: The next generation in community corrections? *Federal Probation, 58,* 72–78.

Gendreau, P., Goggin, C., & Smith, P. (1999). The forgotten issue in effective correctional treatment: Program implementation. *International Journal of Offender Therapy and Comparative Criminology, 43,* 180–187.

Gottfredson, G. D. (1984). A theory-ridden approach to program evaluation: A method for stimulating researcher–implementer collaboration. *American Psychologist, 39,* 1101–1112.

Hanson, R. K., & Whitman, R. (1995). A rural, community action model for the treatment of abusive men. *Canadian Journal of Community Mental Health, 14,* 49–59.

Harris, G. T., & Rice, M. E. (1997). Risk appraisal and the management of violent behavior. *Psychiatric Services, 48,* 1168–1176.

Harris, G. T., & Rice, M. E. (2006). Treatment of psychopathy: A review of empirical findings. In C. Patrick (Ed.), *The handbook of psychopathy* (pp. 555–572). New York: Guilford Press.

Hilton, N. Z. (1989). One in ten: The struggle and disempowerment of the battered women's movement. *Canadian Journal of Family Law, 7,* 313–336.

Hilton, N. Z. (1991). Mediating wife assault: Battered women and the "new family." *Canadian Journal of Family Law, 9,* 29–54.

Hilton, N. Z. (1993). Police intervention and public opinion. In N. Z. Hilton (Ed.), *Legal responses to wife assault* (pp. 37–61). Newbury Park, CA: Sage.

Hilton, N. Z., & Harris, G. T. (2005). Predicting wife assault. *Trauma, Violence, & Abuse, 6,* 3–23.

Hilton, N. Z., Harris, G. T., & Rice, M. E. (2001). Predicting violence by serious wife assaulters. *Journal of Interpersonal Violence, 16,* 408–423.

Hilton, N. Z., Harris, G. T., & Rice, M. E. (2007). The decision to arrest for wife assault and the effect on recidivism. *Criminal Justice and Behavior, 34,* 1334–1344.

Hilton, N. Z., Harris, G. T., Rice, M. E., Houghton, R. E., & Eke, A. W. (2008). An in-depth risk assessment for wife assault recidivism: The Domestic Violence Risk Appraisal Guide. *Law and Human Behavior, 32,* 150–163.

Hilton, N. Z., Harris, G. T., Rice, M. E., Lines, K. J., Lang, C., & Cormier, C. A. (2004). A brief actuarial assessment for the prediction of wife assault recidivism: The Ontario Domestic Assault Risk Assessment. *Psychological Assessment, 16,* 267–275.

Hirschel, J. D., & Hutchison, I. W. (1996). Realities and implications of the Charlotte Spousal Abuse Experiment. In E. S. Buzawa & C. G. Buzawa (Eds.), *Do arrests and restraining orders work?* (pp. 54–82). Thousand Oaks, CA: Sage.

Jaffe, P. G., Hastings, E., Reitzel, D., & Austin, G. W. (1993). The impact of police laying charges. In N. Z. Hilton (Ed.), *Legal responses to wife assault* (pp. 62–95). Newbury Park, CA: Sage.

Kanuha, V. K., & Ross, M. L. (2004). The use of temporary restraining orders (TROs) as a strategy to address intimate partner violence. *Violence and Victims, 19,* 343–356.

Klein, A. R. (1996). Re-abuse in a population of court-restrained male batterers. In E. S. Buzawa & C. G. Buzawa (Eds.), *Do arrests and restraining orders work?* (pp. 192–213). Thousand Oaks, CA: Sage.

Kropp, P. R., & Hart, S. D. (2000). The Spousal Assault Risk Assessment (SARA) guide: Reliability and validity in adult male offenders. *Law and Human Behavior, 24,* 101–118.

Kruttschnitt, C. (1993). Violence by and against women: A comparative and cross-national analysis. *Violence and Victims, 8,* 253–270.

Lalumière, M. L., Harris, G. T., Quinsey, V. L., & Rice, M. E. (2005). *The causes of rape: Understanding individual differences in male propensity for sexual aggression.* Washington, DC: American Psychological Association.

Landau, T. C. (2000). Women's experiences with mandatory charging for wife assault in Ontario, Canada: A case against the prosecution. *International Review of Victimology, 7,* 141–157.

Landenberger, N. A., & Lipsey, M. W. (2005). The positive effects of cognitive–behavioral programs for offenders: A meta-analysis of factors associated with effective treatment. *Journal of Experimental Criminology, 1,* 451–476.

Levinson, D. (1989). *Family violence in cross-cultural perspective.* Newbury Park, CA: Sage.

Lipsey, M. W., & Wilson, D. B. (1993). The efficacy of psychological, educational, and behavioral treatment. *American Psychologist, 48,* 1181–1209.

Logan, T. K., Walker, R., Jordan, C. E., & Leukefeld, C. G. (2006). *Women and victimization: Contributing factors, interventions, and implications.* Washington, DC: American Psychological Association.

Mahoney, P., Williams, L. M., & West, C. M. (2001). Violence against women by intimate relationship partners. In C. M. Renzetti, J. L. Edleson, & R. K. Bergen (Eds.), *Sourcebook on violence against women* (pp. 143–178). Thousand Oaks, CA: Sage.

Martin, M. E. (1997). Double your trouble: Dual arrest in family violence. *Journal of Family Violence, 12,* 139–157.

Maxwell, C. D., Garner, J. H., & Fagan, J. A. (2001). The effects of arrest on intimate partner violence: New evidence from the Spouse Assault Replication Program. *National Institute of Justice Research Briefs,* 1–15.

McFarlane, J., Malecha, A., Gist, J., Watson, K., Batten, E., Hall, I., & Smith, S. (2004). Protection orders and intimate partner violence: An 18-month study of 150 Black, Hispanic, and White women. *American Journal of Public Health, 94,* 613–618.

McGuire, J. (2000). Can the criminal law ever be therapeutic? *Behavioral Sciences & the Law, 18,* 413–426.

Mears, D. P., Carlson, M. J., Holden, G. W., & Harris, S. D. (2001). Reducing domestic violence revictimization. *Journal of Interpersonal Violence, 16,* 1260–1283.

Oetzel, J., & Duran, B. (2004). Intimate partner violence in American Indian and/or Alaska Native communities: A social ecological framework of determinants and interventions. *American Indian and Alaska Native Mental Health Research, 11,* 49–68

Ontario Ministry of the Attorney General. (2006). *10th Annual Prix Excelsior Awards.* Toronto, Ontario, Canada: Author.

Palmer, S. E., Brown, R. A., & Barrera, M. E. (1992). Group treatment program for abusive husbands: Long-term evaluation. *American Journal of Orthopsychiatry, 62,* 276–283.

Paparozzi, M. A., & Gendreau, P. (2005). An intensive supervision program that worked: Service delivery, professional orientation, and organizational supportiveness. *The Prison Journal, 85,* 445–466.

Pate, A. M., & Hamilton, E. E. (1992). Formal and informal deterrents to domestic violence: The Dade County spouse assault experiment. *American Sociological Review, 57,* 691–697.

Pleck, E. (1989). Criminal approaches to family violence, 1640–1980. In L. Ohlin & M. Tonry (Eds.), *Family violence* (pp. 19–58). Chicago: University of Chicago Press.

Pollack, S., Battaglia, M., & Allspach, A. (2005). *Women charged with domestic violence in Toronto: The unintended consequences of mandatory charge policies.* Retrieved June 23, 2006, from http://www.womanabuse.ca/womenchargedfinal.pdf

Poulin, F., Dishion, T. J., & Burraston, B. (2001). 3-year iatrogenic effects associated with aggregating high-risk adolescents in cognitive–behavioral preventive interventions. *Applied Developmental Science, 5,* 214–224.

Protection From Abuse Act, 23 Pa.C.S. § 6110 (1977).

Quinsey, V. L., Harris, G. T., Rice, M. E., & Cormier, C. A. (2006). *Violent offenders: Appraising and managing risk* (2nd ed.). Washington, DC: American Psychological Association.

Ramirez, I. L. (2005). Criminal history and assaults on intimate partners by Mexican American and non-Mexican White college students. *Journal of Interpersonal Violence, 20,* 1628–1647.

Ross, R. R., Fabiano, E. A., & Ewles, C. D. (1988). Reasoning and rehabilitation. *International Journal of Offender Therapy and Comparative Criminology, 32,* 29–35.

Shepard, M. F., Falk, D. R., & Elliott, B. A. (2002). Enhancing coordinated community responses to reduce recidivism in cases of domestic violence. *Journal of Interpersonal Violence, 17,* 551–569.

Sherman, L. W., & Berk, R. A. (1984). The specific deterrent effects of arrest for domestic assault. *American Sociological Review, 49,* 261–272.

Sherman, L. W., Schmidt, J. D., Rogan, D. P., Smith, D. A., Gartin, P. R., Cohn, E. G., et al. (1992). The variable effects of arrest on criminal careers: The Milwaukee domestic violence experiment. *The Journal of Criminal Law and Criminology, 83,* 137–169.

Smuts, B. (1996). Male aggression against women: An evolutionary perspective. In D. M. Buss & N. M. Malamuth (Eds.), *Sex, power, conflict: Evolutionary and feminist perspectives* (pp. 231–268). New York: Oxford University Press.

Sokoloff, N. J., & Pratt, C. (Eds.). (2005). *Domestic violence at the margins.* New Brunswick, NJ: Rutgers University Press.

Sullivan, C. M. (2006). Interventions to address intimate partner violence: The current state of the field. In J. R. Lutzker (Ed.), *Preventing violence: Research and evidence-based intervention strategies* (pp. 195–212). Washington, DC: American Psychological Association.

Valente, R., Hart, B. J., Zeya, S., & Malefyt, M. (2001). The Violence Against Women Act of 1994. In C. M. Renzetti, J. L. Edleson, & R. K. Bergen (Eds.), *Sourcebook on violence against women* (pp. 279–302). Thousand Oaks, CA: Sage.

Violence Against Women Act, 42 U.S.C.A. § 13981 (1994).

West, C. M. (1998). Lifting the "political gag order." In J. L. Jasinksi & L. M. Williams (Eds.), *Partner violence: A comprehensive review of 20 years of research* (pp. 184–209). Thousand Oaks, CA: Sage.

Williams, K. R., & Houghton, A. B. (2004). Assessing the risk of domestic violence reoffending: A validation study. *Law and Human Behavior, 28,* 437–455.

Wilson, D. B., & Lipsey, M. W. (2001). The role of method in treatment effectiveness research: Evidence from meta-analysis. *Psychological Methods, 6,* 413–429.

Zoellner, L. A., Feeny, N. C., Alvarez, J., Watlington, C., O'Neill, M., Zager, R., & Foa, E. B. (2000). Factors associated with completion of the restraining order process in female victims of partner violence. *Journal of Interpersonal Violence, 15,* 1081–1099.

11

GENDER SYMMETRY IN PARTNER VIOLENCE: EVIDENCE AND IMPLICATIONS FOR PREVENTION AND TREATMENT

MURRAY A. STRAUS

Physical aggression against marital partners, although long recognized and deplored, has historically been ignored, except in extreme cases, under the guise of protecting the privacy and integrity of the family (Calvert, 1974). The training manual published by the International Association of Chiefs of Police (1967), for example, advised officers to minimize involvement in what were then called *domestic disturbances*. Some cities in the United States followed an informal *stitch rule* under which arrests were made only if there was a wound that required sutures. As a result of efforts by the women's movement starting in the mid 1970s, there has been a reversal of these traditional approaches. In most jurisdictions in the United States and Canada, police are now required or advised to arrest perpetrators of physical attacks on a partner. Concordant with the arrest policy has been the growth of treatment programs for perpetrators. Many courts now offer participation in such programs as an alternative to incarceration. There are about 2,000 such programs in operation in the United States and over 200 in Canada (National Clearinghouse on Family Violence, 2004).

These are tremendous advances, but there is also evidence questioning the effectiveness of the 30-year-long effort to reduce domestic violence. A central point of this chapter is that the effort has been handicapped by conceptualizing physical assaults on a partner in marital or dating relationships (i.e., partner violence) as almost entirely a phenomenon involving male perpetrators and female victims—that is, as a problem of violence against women—and the corollary assumption that the primary cause of partner violence is the patriarchal nature of society and the family. I begin the chapter with a review of the evidence countering this conceptualization. I then summarize studies that show that existing efforts at prevention and treatment of partner violence have had limited success. Finally, I suggest changes in prevention and treatment efforts that recognize gender symmetry in partner violence and the multiplicity of causes that lead to partner violence.

EVIDENCE OF GENDER SYMMETRY

Gender Symmetry in Prevalence and Motivation

More than 200 studies have found that men and women perpetrate partner violence at approximately equal rates and that the most prevalent pattern is mutual violence (Archer, 2002; Fiebert, 2004). Moreover, when it is not mutual, female-only and male-only partner violence occur with about equal frequency among married couples (K. L. Anderson, 2002; Capaldi & Owen, 2001; Gelles & Straus, 1988; Kessler, Molnar, Feurer, & Appelbaum, 2001; McCarroll, Ursano, Fan, & Newby, 2004; Medeiros & Straus, 2007; Moffitt, Caspi, Rutter, & Silva, 2001; Straus, Gelles, & Steinmetz, 2006; Williams & Frieze, 2005). Among young couples and dating couples, the percentage of female-only partner violence exceeds the percentage of male-only partner violence (Straus & Ramirez, 2007; Whitaker, Haileyesus, Swahn, & Saltzman, 2007). This pattern of gender symmetry is true even for severe partner violence, such as kicking, attacks with objects, and choking. However, the injury rate is much higher when the perpetrator is male (Gelles & Straus, 1988). Police statistics and crime survey statistics seem to contradict the idea of gender symmetry because 80% to 99% of the perpetrators identified in such surveys are men (Straus, 1999). This is not because of higher numbers of physical attacks by men but because of the greater probability of injury from attacks by men and greater fear for safety by women (Straus, 1999). These are characteristics that lead to police intervention. Such cases are mistakenly taken as representative of partner violence, even though at least 95% of partner violence cases are not known to the police (Kaufman Kantor & Straus, 1990; Statistics Canada, 2005).

Although there are numerous studies showing substantial rates of sexual coercion by women (P. B. Anderson & Struckman-Johnson, 1998), men predominate as perpetrators of sexual coercion and are much more likely to use physical force to coerce a partner into sex, and stranger rapes are almost exclusively a male crime (Saunders, 2002; U.S. Department of Justice, 2003). Official crime data also suggest that women are more likely to be stalked by their partners and that men are much more likely than women to be perpetrators of parent–child homicide-suicide, that is, cases in which the perpetrator kills himself and family members (Felson, 2002; Saunders, 2002; Statistics Canada, 2005).

Not only do men and women tend to perpetrate physical partner violence at about equal rates, but they tend to do so for similar reasons. The most commonly reported proximate motivations for use of violence among both men and women are coercion, anger, and punishing misbehavior by their partner (Cascardi & Vivian, 1995; Follingstad, Wright, Lloyd, & Sebastian, 1991; Kernsmith, 2005; Stets & Hammons, 2002). For example, Pearson (1997) reported that 90% of the women she studied assaulted their partner because they were furious, jealous, or frustrated. The motive of self-defense, which has often been put forward as an explanation for high rates of female violence, explains only a small proportion of partner violence perpetrated by women (and men; Carrado, George, Loxam, Jones, & Templar, 1996; Felson & Messner, 1998; Pearson, 1997; Sarantakos, 1998; Sommer, 1996). For example, using a college student population, Follingstad et al. (1991) found that perpetrators reported that their motivation was self-defensive about 18% of the time (17.7% for men, 18.5% for women). As violence becomes more severe, there are greater gender differences in the use of violence in self-defense; however, self-defense is still a motivation for a relatively small proportion of violence. For example, in a sample of couples presenting for marital therapy, Cascardi and Vivian (1995) found that 20% of wives and no husbands attributed their use of severe aggression to self-defense.

Gender Differences in Injury and Deaths

The only consistently supported gender difference in partner violence by men and women is that attacks by men cause more fear and injury, including more deaths. Although this may be the only consistently supported gender difference, it is an extremely important difference because it is one of several reasons for the need to continue to provide more services for female victims of partner violence than for male victims. It is also worthwhile to note that such differences are particularly apparent in studies of less common and more severe forms of violence. In general population surveys, estimated annual rates of violence perpetration are high (e.g., 10%–30%; Straus, 1999; Whitaker et al., 2007), men and women are equally likely to perpetrate violence, and rates of injury are low (e.g., 0.4%–28%; Kaufman Kantor & Straus, 1990; Stets & Straus, 1990). Here, differences in the victimization of men and women are not large (in part because there are low rates of injury). In contrast, police statistics and crime surveys, such as the National Violence Against Women Survey, show much greater gender differences. The prevalence rates are much lower (under 2%; Straus, 1999), but the injury rates are much higher (e.g., 50%; Straus, 1999), and women predominate as victims.

Severe Violence Experienced by Men

Although women outnumber men as victims of physical injury, female perpetration of severe violence is not a rare occurrence. In the United States in 1998, 38% of persons killed by a partner were men (Rennison, 2000), and in Canada in 2003, 23% of partner homicide victims were men (Statistics Canada, 2005). Similarly, large numbers of men are severely assaulted and injured, even though not killed, by their partner. Data from the National Crime Victimization Survey (Rennison, 2000) show that between 1993 and 1998, 47,000 men were injured by their partner, 28,090 of whom received medical treatment.

Why Partner Violence by Women Is Not Recognized or Is Denied

The evidence of symmetry in perpetration of partner violence and symmetry in context and motives has been available for more than 25 years. This raises the question of why that evidence has not been perceived. Some of the many factors are presented elsewhere (Straus, 2007b). In addition, there has been an extensive effort to deny and misrepresent the evidence on gender symmetry because many people from the advocacy tradition believe the data are wrong and because they fear it will undermine support of services for female victims (Straus, 2007a).

CRITIQUE OF PAST EFFORTS FOR PREVENTION

Direct prevention efforts have tended to concentrate on raising public awareness of the frequency, pervasiveness, and severity of partner violence with statements that imply that only men are perpetrators and that chronic severe assaults and injury are typical. These public education efforts have contributed to increased funding for services to women victims of abuse and to improved professional training in the dynamics of domestic violence. They have also contributed to a change in public perception on the acceptability of partner violence. However, such changes have been limited to male-perpetrated violence and have not extended to female-perpetrated partner violence. Two pieces of evidence support this assertion.

First, studies of shifts in public opinion on the acceptability of interpersonal violence show reductions in pubic acceptability of male partner violence but no change in the acceptability of female partner violence. From 1968 to 1994, national samples of men and women responded to the question, "Are there situations that you can imagine in which you would approve of a husband slapping his wife's face/wife slapping her husband's face?" There were substantial declines in public approval of a man slapping his wife but no significant reduction in approval of a wife slapping her husband (Straus, 1995; Straus, Kaufman Kantor, & Moore, 1997). More recent data from the International Dating Violence Study show much greater acceptance of female-perpetrated than male-perpetrated minor violence by women in all but 1 of the 32 nations (Douglas & Straus, 2006; Straus, in press). Such data clearly suggest that public messages about aggression in relationships in general have not extended to female-perpetrated partner violence, even though female perpetration is as common or more common than partner violence perpetrated by men.

Data on decline in rates of actual partner violence show similar gender-related differences. In 1975, Straus, Gelles, and Steinmetz conducted the first nationally representative household survey of partner violence (Straus et al., 2006). The survey was repeated using the same measure of partner violence in 1985 (Gelles & Straus, 1988), and again in 1992 by Kaufman Kantor, Jasinski, and Aldarondo (1994). Results show a substantial decrease in the rate of severe assaults on women by male partners but no change for women (Straus, 1995). Canadian data provide a similar picture. Rates of male perpetration showed a slight decline between 1999 and 2004, whereas rates of female perpetration remained statistically stable (Statistics Canada, 2005). Similarly, the U.S. National Crime Victimization Survey found a 60% reduction in male-perpetrated partner violence between 1993 and 2004, but no decrease in female-perpetrated partner violence between 1993 and 2003 and a slight increase in female-perpetrated partner violence between 2003 and 2004 (Catalano, 2006).

PRINCIPLES FOR IMPROVING PREVENTION

To address shortcomings in current prevention efforts, approaches based on recognition of the evidence of symmetry and the heterogeneity of partner violence are needed. An important starting point for reform is recognition that the most frequently occurring forms of partner violence are minor (usually slapping and pushing) and rarely cause physical injury. These forms of violence are perpetrated equally by men and women, mostly in anger. A small but important percentage of partner violence is severe, likely to cause injury, and is experienced more frequently by women than men. However, because I believe that a focus on primary prevention is extremely important, for the reasons presented in the list that follows, the focus needs to be on the widely prevalent minor violence. To paraphrase Cowen (1978), primary prevention of family violence involves lowering its incidence by counteracting harmful circumstances before they have had a chance to produce violence. It does not seek to prevent a specific person from committing a violent act; instead, primary prevention seeks to reduce the risk for a whole population. The outcome envisioned as a result of primary prevention is that, although some individuals may continue to be violent, their number will be reduced. There are a number of reasons why the focus of primary prevention needs to be on minor forms of physical violence and equally on male and female perpetration.

1. Minor and mutual violence is the most prevalent pattern.
2. Severe partner violence, such as punching, choking, and attacks with objects, is already recognized as unacceptable and therefore does not require an educational effort.
3. Prevention of minor violence may prevent escalation into more severe forms of violence.
4. Witnessing violence by either parent contributes to the next generation of partner violence, and therefore partner violence by mothers needs attention commensurate with their equal prevalence rate.
5. Ending partner violence by women is an essential step in preventing violence against women because female violence evokes retaliation and contributes to legitimizing male partner violence (Straus, 2005).
6. A focus on minor violence that rarely results in injury is consistent with the principle that ending a risk factor with a low effect size, but which is broadly prevalent, makes a larger contribution to public health than ending a risk factor with a large effect size, but which characterizes only a small part of the population (P. Cohen, 1996; Rose, 1985; Rosenthal, 1984).
7. A focus on prevention of minor violence by women as well as men reflects the belief that all violence in relationships (except that perpetrated in self-defense) is wrong regardless of whether it causes injury, fear, or distress in the other person.

My emphasis on primary prevention by focusing on minor violence does not mean secondary prevention of severe violence and physical injury should be ignored. (Secondary prevention is intended to prevent reoccurrence of the target behavior.) However, the target population for secondary prevention and the information to be conveyed are different. For secondary prevention, the target population is those already involved in physically violent relationships, as either victims or perpetrators. For such individuals, preventative initiatives need to focus on increasing awareness of supports and broadening recognition of risk factors for severe partner violence (e.g., death threats, suicidality, availability of weapons). A focus on women is necessary because of the predominance of female victims of the most severe violence, although the fact that men are also victims of severe partner violence requires that their needs also be considered.

Distinguishing between primary and secondary prevention is important from both theoretical and practical perspectives. From a theoretical perspective, it helps to counter the belief that physical violence by women is not important because it less often causes fear or injury. Instead, it allows for the assertion that physical violence is wrong, in and of itself. From a practical perspective, it helps to focus attention on the audience most appropriate for each form of prevention. Justice, health, and social service personnel, for example, are primarily concerned with violence that results in or has a high probability of physical injury. Those seeking to promote healthy relationships, as do the programs by Botvin, Griffin, and Nichols (2006; see also Foshee, 2004) and Wolfe, Wekerle, and Scott (1997), are interested in a much wider range of violence because it is distressing, increases the probability of mental health problems and dysfunctional family relationships, and can escalate into severe partner violence.

Principles for Improving Primary Prevention

Principle 1. Assert that, except in self-defense, physical violence is not acceptable, and explicitly state that this applies to girls and women, as well as to boys and men. Given the frequency of violence by both men and women, a first principle that should guide prevention efforts is the recognition that all forms of partner violence, except those used in immediate self-defense, are unacceptable. Because broad shifts in public opinion on the unacceptability of interpersonal violence has focused almost entirely on violence by men, specific focus on women is necessary. In fact, past messages have been so gender biased that terms such as *domestic violence* are now perceived as applying exclusively to male-perpetrated violence. To change that perception, public education campaigns need to explicitly mention perpetration by girls and women as well as by boys and men. Such messages should assert that physical aggression is not an appropriate way for girls and women to gain the attention of their partner, to emphasize a point, or to express anger or other emotions in their relationships. *Coaching Boys Into Men: Your Role in Ending Violence Against Women* (Family Violence Prevention Fund, 2006), which addresses these points for boys, needs to be paralleled by a similar brochure addressed to girls.

One example of a program that addresses partner violence by women as well as men is Safe Dates (Foshee, 2004; Foshee et al., 2005). Another is Choose Respect (http://www.chooserespect.org). This U.S. national initiative, developed by the Centers for Disease Control and Prevention, is designed to help adolescents form healthy relationships to prevent dating abuse before it starts. Teens who access the Web site are provided with a variety of materials, including educational games and videos, posters, tip cards, and fact sheets. One example of a specific prevention initiative targeting young women is a poster that shows a picture of a teen thinking "He made me mad . . ." and then considering a respectful "so we talked it out after school" versus a nonrespectful and verbally aggressive response such as "so I yelled at him in front of his friends." These posters, along with all other materials on the Web site, emphasize the need for young women as well as young men to avoid physical violence, verbal abuse, and emotional abuse.

Principle 2. Increase promotion of positive messages about relationships as a means to prevent partner violence. A second prevention recommendation is to reduce emphasis on the prevalence and severity of partner violence and increase focus on the benefits of positive relationship skills. This recommendation is based on best practice documents for the prevention of other problem behaviors. For example, the Surgeon General's Report (2001) and the Blueprints Violence Prevention Initiative (Mihalic, Erwin, Fagan, Ballard, & Elliott, 2004) recommend that successful programs for bullying and peer violence are those that (among other things) focus on developing positive peer relationship skills.

Studies of healthy relationships suggest that good partnerships share a number of important features, including mutual trust, emotional intimacy, positive effect, a sense of commitment and loyalty, good communication, and the desire to support one's spouse (Bagarozzi, 1997; Fenell, 1993; K. A. Moore et al., 2004). Inadequate communication skills, for example, have been related to the development of aggression against a partner. In a series of observational studies, Gottman (1994, 1998) discovered that failure to regulate reciprocation of negativity and deescalate conflict is a central feature of aggressive relationships and an important contributor to the deterioration of marriages. Moreover, longitudinal studies have shown that poor parent–child communication relates to later perpetration of partner violence (J. A. Andrews, Foster, Capaldi, & Hops, 2000; Capaldi & Clark, 1998). Thus, teaching conflict management skills is a promising focus for prevention efforts.

Resource materials available through the Choose Respect program provide one example of the type of positive messages recommended to prevent partner violence. Other prevention initiatives targeting adolescents have also begun to rely on more positive messages. Two examples are the Making Waves Web site (http://www.mwaves.org) and the Girls Health Web site sponsored by the U.S. Department of Health and Social Services (http://www.girlshealth.gov/index.htm), both of which include sections on characteristics of healthy relationships. Although these messages have the great merit of focusing on relationship skills for both boys and girls, neither of these Web sites use specific examples of girls hitting boys. They therefore fail to counter the belief that physical violence in relationships is an exclusively male behavior. However, these Web sites are at least an improvement over the Web site sponsored by Liz Claiborne, Inc. (http://www.loveisnotabuse.com), which falsely presents teen dating violence as perpetrated by only men (e.g., see the "Question Why" section of the Web site) and focuses primarily on helping women avoid being victims of abuse rather than developing healthy relationship skills as a method of achieving that. Broad public education campaigns to prevent partner violence in adult dating, cohabiting, and marital relationships should follow the lead of the teen prevention resources that focus on the development of healthy relationships skills and that emphasize the need for women, as well as men, to use these skills to avoid physical aggression.

Principle 3. Carefully consider when to use fear as a motivator for change. Prevention messages directed toward women often seem intended to promote fear, in particular, women's fear of men's violence. Public education partner violence posters typically feature a woman with serious injuries or in a situation that is likely to result in serious injuries, often coupled with messages about the dangers of underestimating risk (e.g., "I never thought he could do this to me," "He promised he would change"). Fear-based messages have limited use in prevention. Research from a variety of areas of prevention shows that when presented with fear-based messages, people respond positively only if preventive actions are readily apparent and easily envisioned. If preventive actions are not readily envisioned, fear-based prevention methods contribute to greater denial of the issue. Accordingly, best practice guidelines for prevention advise that if a fear-based message is to be used, it should be paired with a clear positive message on steps that can be taken to avoid the fear-provoking outcome (Ruiter, Abraham, & Kok, 2001). Partner violence preventive messages directed to women fail in this respect. Rather than present ways to avoid being a victim of partner violence, many woman-abuse awareness campaigns emphasize the vulnerability of all women in any form of heterosexual relationship. Such messages risk leaving women without any clear ideas of how to avoid being abused and could inadvertently increase women's denial of the possibility of being a victim of abuse.

Principle 4. Recognize gender in the development of prevention messages. The previous principles emphasized the need to send similar messages about violence and about healthy relationships to both men and women. Although the ultimate messages around avoiding partner violence should be the same, the nature of such messages needs to be informed by a gendered analysis of relationships. Men and women continue to be socialized differently about relationships. As a result, they have different expectations of relationships, face different relationship pressures, and are angered and frustrated by different factors. The realities of male and female socialization also play a significant role in how violence plays out in a relationship when it occurs. For example, it is likely that stereotypes about male self-sufficiency contribute to men's greater reluctance to report even severe, injury-causing victimization to police (Felson & Pare, 2005) and to women's greater vulnerability to being a victim of sexual abuse (Saunders, 2002). A gender-strategic approach to prevention recognizes such differences and uses them to inform education and skill development (Crooks, Wolfe, & Jaffe, 2006).

Principles for Improving Secondary Prevention

In addition to efforts to reduce or prevent partner violence entirely (i.e., primary prevention), it is necessary to engage in efforts to reduce reoccurrence in relationships in which partner violence is occurring (i.e., secondary prevention). Although estimates vary across studies, severe violence, such as choking, beating up a partner, or threatening a partner with a knife or a gun, as well as violence that causes injury, occurs in a small proportion of relationships (Kaufman Kantor & Straus, 1990; Straus, 1991). Because women are about two thirds of victims who suffer injury or death from these more severe forms of partner violence and most of those who do fear for their lives (Pottie Bunge & Locke, 2000), emergency distress lines, shelters, and advocacy services for abused women remain critically important. Justice officials, advocates, and services providers are in critical need of assessment tools and guidelines to assess severity and characteristics of violence in relationships so that women are not inappropriately punished for using violence in self-defense or in response to a long history of brutal victimization, and so that male victims can be recognized.

Although the majority of resources for victims of severe partner violence should target women, the service and victimization prevention needs of male victims should not be ignored, as is now the case. As reviewed earlier, most partner violence is mutual. Male victims as well as female victims deserve information and resources to help them recognize the possibility of injury and escape from further violence. This should include public information messages that focus on the need for men as well as women to give serious consideration to the meaning and potential result of their partner's use of violence. Resources for helping men escape situations in which their partner is being violent are also needed. Such services are starting to become available; for example, the Domestic Abuse Helpline for Men and Women provides a 24-hour phone line (1-888-7HELPLINE) and other services (http://www.dahmw.org/pub).

Injury prevention programs need to accept the reality that men are about a third of those injured or killed by a partner and that the risk of injury to women is greatest when both are violent (Straus & Gozjolko, 2007; Whitaker et al., 2007). Although I do not recommend fear-based messages to raise awareness of male victimization, the danger to men must be given more than a short mention in prevention programs. Prevention programs should explicitly state that although women are more likely than men to be injured by their partners, large numbers of men are also injured or killed, and the greatest risk of injury to women as well as men occurs when there is mutual violence. More research is also needed into these cases so that men can be more appropriately informed of risk factors and so that frontline practitioners can more readily identify both men and women at greatest risk of being injured or killed by a partner.

Finally, services for male victims of partner violence, such as those offered by the Domestic Abuse Helpline for Men and Women, need to be further developed. It is likely that such resources could be built into services already provided for men. When violent crime is considered in general, men far outnumber women as victims (Felson, 2002). Often, male victims of these sorts of crimes appear in homeless shelters; at the YMCA, Salvation Army, Men's Mission, or John Howard Society; or in the care of other such organizations. Staff and administrators of these organizations, like the staff of similar organizations serving women, need training in issues around partner violence to better recognize both violence victimization and perpetration so that the needs of these men can be more adequately met.

Summary

Prevention messages should emphasize the importance of nonviolence by women as well as men. Such messages are important for reducing interpersonal violence generally and for preventing the negative consequences on relationships. Prevention messages are most likely to be successful if they focus on healthy modes of dealing with anger and frustration and if they avoid relying on fear as a motivating factor. Efforts to prevent injury and death resulting from partner violence should continue to focus on female victims. However, recognition of male victimization and provision of services for male victims are needed, including services that will enable men to escape from a dangerously violent situation, such as have been provided for women.

PRINCIPLES FOR IMPROVING TREATMENT

Treatment programs for perpetrators of partner violence have been developed almost exclusively by women and men who embraced the feminist theory that partner violence is used by men to reinforce a patriarchal social hierarchy. Specifically, men were thought to be violent because cultural norms support male dominance over women and provide no penalty for men's violence against women (Dobash & Dobash, 1979; Straus, 1976; Yllo & Bograd, 1988). It was also generally assumed that the men whose violence was recognized (e.g., by arrest, in treatment) were the tip of the iceberg in that they were a normal result of a patriarchal social organization and were typical of a large proportion of male–female relationships.

With the assumption that men's abuse was a result of a patriarchal society, treatment programs focused primarily on "reeducating" men. Men were challenged to give up their dominance in the family, avoid using their privilege as men in society to control women, and become involved in advocating for gender equity. The assumption is that a man who has been violent has the skills and knowledge to behave in healthier ways, he simply chooses not to in order to maintain his entitlement to power over his partner and over women in general. Explanations of violence that referred to any other aspect of men's history (e.g., childhood abuse), circumstances (e.g., alcohol use), family system (e.g., contributions of both partners to conflict), personality (e.g., depression, personality disorder), or interpersonal skills (e.g., lack of communication and problem-solving skills) were viewed as excusing male violence and distracting from the main problem of men's patriarchal and sexist attitudes. Treatments with individuals or couples (e.g., anger control programs, couple treatment) are specifically excluded from state standards for batterer intervention programs (BIPs) in 43% of U.S. states (Rosenbaum & Price, 2007).

Ineffectiveness of Batterer Intervention Programs

There have now been over 50 empirical studies evaluating the success of batterer treatment. These studies generally find that approximately two thirds of men who complete BIPs avoid physical reassault of their partners (Gondolf, 2002). However, men who do not attend BIPs cease assaulting their partners at similar rates. Experimental studies address this question more accurately by randomly assigning men to receive or not receive treatment and then following their progress over time. These studies almost uniformly report that treated and nontreated men reassault their partners at the same rate. In other words, these studies suggest that BIPs are no more effective than nontreatment at reducing assault (Babcock, Green, & Robie, 2004; D. G. Dutton, 2006, 2007; D. G. Dutton & Nicholls, 2005; Levesque & Gelles, 1998; Sartin, Hansen, & Huss, 2006). It is clear that improvements are needed.

In this section, I add my speculations to those of others (D. G. Dutton, 2006; Stuart, 2005) on ways to improve treatment through better recognition of gender symmetry, heterogeneity of partner violence, and multiple risk factors. I make seven suggestions, in the form of principles, for assessment and treatment development. Many of these suggestions are controversial, largely because of past misapplication (or concern about misapplication) to the small proportion of male offenders who are imminently dangerous. However, I suggest that improvements in rates of treatment success are most likely to occur through recognizing that most partner violence is mutual and only a small percentage is terroristic, injury causing, and unidirectional.

Principle 1. Assess all presentations of partner violence for dangerousness and symmetry. A critical first step in improving treatment of partner violence is to critically assess all presenting cases for both bidirectionality and danger-ousness. With rare exceptions, such as some programs for military personnel, the current default assumption is that violence is unidirectional (i.e., male to female), is intended to dominate and subjugate the partner by provoking fear of violence and actual violence, typically involves injury, and is potentially lethal. However, the empirical evidence reviewed earlier shows that at least half of partner violence is bidirectional and that, even in court-based samples, the majority of men in BIPs do not fit the model of high risk of ongoing injury-producing violence (Gondolf, 2002). In recognition of this large body of evidence, the default assumption needs to be replaced by assessment of the actual situation. Treatment of partner violence should start by empirically assessing dangerousness by means of an instrument such as the Danger As-sessment (Campbell, 1995, 2001), assessing symmetry by means of an instru-ment such as the Conflict Tactics Scales (Straus & Douglas, 2004; Straus, Hamby, Boney-McCoy, & Sugarman, 1996), and assessing risk factors for partner violence by means of an instrument such as the Personal and Rela-tionships Profile (Straus, Hamby, Boney-McCoy, & Sugarman, 2007; Straus & Mouradian, 1999). In addition, given the evidence that traumatic brain injury is present in a substantial proportion of perpetrators of partner vio-lence (R. A. Cohen, Rosenbaum, Kane, Warnken, & Benjamin, 1999) and that questions to identify head trauma are a cost-effective and valid method of detecting brain injury, brief screening for brain damage should be routine (Stern, 2004). Because some partner violence is dangerous, assessors should separate men and women during assessment and be prepared with safety plans for victims or potential victims of physical injury. Assessors also need to be well trained, so that they are able to safely follow up on inconsistencies and minimization in reports from men and women.

Principle 2. Avoid exclusive reliance on feminist theory. A second step for reform is to review the theoretical basis of treatment programs for partner violence offenders (D. G. Dutton, 2006; Stuart, 2005). BIPs were originally designed to change men's sexist attitudes and patriarchal entitlements, with the assumption that this attitude change would translate to lower rates of partner violence. Patriarchy has been shown to play an important role in predicting rates of violence at a societal level (i.e., rates of violence are higher in more sexist societies; Archer, 2006; Straus, 1994), and hostile attitudes toward women are consistent predictors of sexual aggression and rape (L. B. Dutton & Straus, 2005; Vega & Malamuth, 2007). In contrast, evidence linking sexism (i.e., holding traditional attitudes toward women) to partner violence in general is weak (T. M. Moore & Stuart, 2005; Sugarman & Frankel, 1996), and there is no support yet for the assumption that changing sexist attitudes of men arrested for assaulting their partners predicts long-term changes in partner violence (Davis, Taylor, & Maxwell, 2000; Faulkner, Stoltenberg, Cogen, Nolder, & Shooter, 1992; Feder & Dugan, 2002; Petrik, Olson, & Subotnik, 1994; Sugarman & Frankel, 1996). For example, Saunders and Hanusa (1986) found that among 92 men completing a 12-week treatment program, changes in attitudes toward women's roles, jealousy, and threat from female competency were unrelated to changes in men's reports of abuse perpetration or their partners' reports of victimization. More important to predicting partner violence and change are men's attitudes about their specific partners and their role in that relationship (T. M. Moore & Stuart, 2005). Thus, although the promotion of gender equality is an important goal for society and is an important step in primary prevention that is likely to reduce societal rates of partner violence, it does not appear to be a critical target for treatment of individual men already demonstrating partner violence.

Another problem for existing treatment programs is the assumption that the primary problem of men in treatment is their sexist beliefs and behavior. In reality, this may be only a minor aspect of their problems Of men who perpetrate that level of violence, a high proportion have previous arrests for other crime, are alcoholic or have alcoholic tendencies, and have narcissistic or antisocial characteristics, and over half identify growing up in families in which their parents were physically abusive or had drug or alcohol problems. The rates for these problems are much higher than population averages and suggest that these men are dealing with a number of co-occurring social and psychological problems that must be addressed if treatment is to be effective.

Principle 3. Consider replacing educational "intervention" with cognitive–behavioral or other empirically validated treatment. The short-term BIPs offered across most of North America may serve the function of indicating the criminal nature of the behavior, but I suggest that this type of reeducation will not be sufficient to promote change. Rather, a more therapeutic orientation is needed. Adopting a therapeutic orientation would have a number of implications for batterer treatment programs. First, group sizes would need to be reduced from 20 to 25 (common in programs using the Duluth Domestic Abuse Intervention Project model) to the 8 to 12 typically recommended for group therapy. For those batterers assessed to have antisocial traits, group treatment may need to be avoided altogether to prevent iatrogenic effects (Dishion, McCord, & Poulin, 1999). In addition, the relationship between therapist and clients (acknowledged as one of the most important nonspecific factor for promoting change) would need to be emphasized to a much greater extent than it is currently. Finally, there needs to be more attention to investigating and using empirically supported treatment strategies.

There is a growing body of literature in support of a more therapeutic orientation to treatment for men who have engaged in criminal forms of partner violence. Taft, Murphy, Elliott, and Morrel (2001) found that therapeutic and group alliance factors were important predictors of reduced recidivism regardless of other major differences in the style of treatment. Similarly, Scott and King (in press) have shown that use of a more supportive and engaging therapeutic style with highly resistant clients reduces dropout and enhances change in abuse-supporting attitudes. Focusing on psychological targets rather than on reeducation has also been supported. On the basis of a broad review of literature, to date, the only variables that have reliably been associated with reductions in abusive behavior are reductions in anger, alcohol and drug use, and level of psychopathology (e.g., level of depression; Scott, 2004). Considerably more research in this area is needed for the development of theoretically and empirically sounds treatments for this client group.

Principle 4. Conduct additional research on treatment needs of men and women who have engaged in partner violence. The concept of "need" in a criminal context (D. A. Andrews & Bonta, 1998) is an attitude, behavior, trait, or other factor that relates directly to an individual's likelihood of reoffending. Because research on treatment for partner violence has focused primarily on *whether* programs are successful rather than *why* programs might succeed, little is known about what might promote change in partner violence. D. G. Dutton (2006) speculated that successful therapy of men who perpetrate partner violence needs to address attachment needs and trauma symptoms. In particular, he emphasized the importance of anger management, stress tolerance, emotional regulation, and a strong relationship between therapist and client in which relationship issues can play out in a therapeutic context. Other theorists, notably Murphy and Eckhardt (2005), include many of these features and emphasize enhancing client motivation to change, training in relationship skills, and addressing cognitive distortions of abusive partners. Both theories assert that change in clients' emotion regulation, particularly anger, and in their patterns of thinking about and reacting to relationships are key components to promoting change. Men's use of alcohol is another promising treatment target. More controversial are theories suggesting that cessation of male violence is contingent of the female partner also ceasing (Feld & Straus, 1989; Straus, 2005) and theories suggesting that other characteristics of the relationship between men and women, such as dyadic patterns of hostility and withdrawal, are most important to promoting change. All of these theories need further empirical investigation with samples of partners who successfully end their use of abusive behaviors both with and without attending treatment.

Principle 5. Develop better strategies to contain high-risk repeat offenders. Although most men charged with assault against their partner avoid subsequent physical abuse, approximately 25% of men in BIPs do reassault their partners (Gondolf, 2002). These repeat offenders are a critical focus of treatment and monitoring efforts. Longitudinal studies suggest that reassaults are most likely to happen quickly, that repeat offenders tend to engage in multiple reoffenses, and that these men are responsible for the majority of injuries to women (Gondolf, 2002).

To date, researchers have been relatively unsuccessful at reliably identifying those men who are at high risk of reassaulting their partners from data available at the beginning of treatment. However, the behavior of men during and after treatment does show moderate predictive ability. For example, men who drop out of treatment and who are drunk in the months following treatment are more likely to reassault. Women's perception of safety is also a significant predictor or men's assaults (Gondolf, 2004; Weisz, Tolman, & Saunders, 2000). These findings suggest that models of ongoing risk management might be superior to early identification efforts. Risk management models involve periodic assessment of short-term risk, treatment or increased monitoring in response to any immediate risk, and repeated risk reassessment over time (Fein, Vossekuil, & Holden, 1995). For example, on the basis of the finding that men who drop out of treatment are more likely to reassault their partners than men who do not dropout, programs should initiate a system of greater justice monitoring and the provision of additional information and support to potential victims of violence, as well as reasonable sanctions for failing to comply with court-ordered treatment. For those who do not succeed at ending their abusive behavior, more intensive and highly monitored treatments should be an option. Drug courts and associated treatment programs have pioneered work in this area, and batterer treatment systems might profitably consider similar models.

Principle 6. Develop theoretically and empirically supported treatment programs for female offenders. There is a critical need for better understanding women arrested for assault against their partners and for the development of empirically supported treatments for this population. In response to pressure from the justice system (in which, recently, women have been arrested in about a quarter of calls for partner assault), many larger cities now run treatment programs for female offenders. These programs tend to combine materials from traditional batterer treatment and from trauma-based counseling approaches. Unfortunately, neither of these treatment approaches are good models. Batterer programs have been built on feminist assumptions that make little sense when applied to female use of violence (i.e., How should women be reeducated to avoid patriarchal attitudes and behaviors?). Trauma-based models, in contrast, focus on resolving the impact of past victimization. Neither programs address needs of female offenders for strategies to better deal with anger, assert needs, resolve interpersonal conflict, and make better relationship choices (if these are indeed needs for this population, as suggested in general population surveys).

Fortunately, there is a growing body of literature on the treatment needs of female offenders (Dowd, Leisring, & Rosenbaum, 2005), their risk of reoffense (e.g., see Henning & Feder, 2004), and the efficacy of treatment for this population (Carney & Buttell, 2004, 2006). In addition, some comprehensive treatment programs have been developed. One example is the VISTA program in New Jersey (Larance, 2006). VISTA uses an ecological model to understand and contextualize women's use of violence. When self-defense motives are identified, women are referred to a companion program for victims of abuse. Assessment is ongoing throughout women's involvement in the program and aims to promote women's understanding of the range of emotions, events, and contributing factors to their use of aggression. Educational group sessions focus on educating women on the links between shame and anger and on the impact of familial expectations on their development, promoting women's responsibility for their behaviors and for use of force in relationships, and developing women's skills for resolving problems and conflicts without violence.

Principle 7. Consider expanding services in couples therapy and restorative justice. Finally, providers of treatment for partner violence should consider significantly expanding the range of services offered to include violent individuals who are not arrested for partner violence. As previously noted, national surveys in the United States and the International Dating Violence Study have found that mutual violence is the typical pattern. Studies that have investigated this issue have found that both partners are violent in half the cases and the remaining half are about equally divided between male-only and female-only partner violence. This means that women are violent in about three quarters of violence cases. Moreover, violence by the female partner is an important risk factor for reoffending (Feld & Straus, 1989; Gelles & Straus, 1988). These data indicate a need for treatment of both partners in a violent relationship, either couples therapy or separately, even when only one partner is the presenting case. The need to attend to both partners in a relationship is made even more pressing in light of the lack of evidence for the effectiveness of BIPs that treat only one partner.

Currently, the most likely professional resource that violent couples are likely to seek is marital therapy. Cascardi, Langhinrichsen, and Vivian (1992) found that almost three quarters of couple-clients seeking marital therapy reported at least one incident of partner violence in the past year, 86% of which were reciprocal. There are a variety of theoretical perspectives on how to best address violence within the context of couples therapy, and they vary on the extent to which both partners are held responsible for escalation of conflict. One of the more promising models seems to be the physical aggression couples treatment program (Heyman & Schlee, 2003; O'Leary, 2001). Under this model, each partner is held responsible for his or her own behavior, but both are taught to recognize cycles of dysfunctional interaction and to respond with deescalation strategies.

For partners who have been arrested for domestic violence, *restorative justice* (Daly & Stubbs, 2007; Mills, 2003, 2008; Strang & Braithwaite, 2002) is a promising approach that needs further trial and research. Restorative justice is an alternative to the current retributive justice system. In the current system the crime is considered an offense against the state, and the state imposes penalties (i.e., retribution). Restorative justice seeks to rectify the harm by including both the victim and the offender as parties in need of restoration. It addresses the harm to the dignity and physical, psychological, economic, and social status of the victim and seeks to reintegrate the offender into society. For a court to assign a case to restorative justice, both the offender and the victim must be willing, and there has to be a danger assessment before proceeding. A meeting is arranged that includes all the stakeholders: the offender, the victim, a representative of the criminal justice system, and key people in the lives of the offender and victim. The offender must acknowledge his or her wrongdoing, and steps to rectify the harm to the victims are developed and agreed on at the meeting. Subsequent to the meeting, the case is monitored. If there is lack of compliance, the case goes back to the standard system of justice.

Both couples therapy and restorative justice must address the potential dangers of couple work in violent relationships. Although this is a critically important issue, most of what has been written reflects a misapplication of data from more extreme forms of violence to all partner abuse. With appropriate screening, including use of instruments such as the Campbell's Danger Assessment Scale (Campbell, 1995, 2001) and the Conflict Tactics Scales (Straus & Douglas, 2004; Straus et al., 1996), couples in which there has been significant injury, or one member of the couple denies violence, or either member of the couple is fearful can be excluded. The limited research that has been done on couples therapy suggests that this form of treatment is at least as successful as group-based treatment for reducing rates of violence recidivism (O'Leary & Cohen, 2007; Stith, Rosen, & McCollum, 2003).

Summary

As with prevention, treatment efforts need to be differentiated according to the severity of partner violence. Different approaches are needed for dangerous offenders than for couples who are situationally violent (Johnson & Ferraro, 2000). Despite that, there are two general principles that must be applied to enhance the effectiveness of partner violence treatment for all but the most extreme and immanently dangerous level. The first principle is that most partner violence is mutual. The second principle is that education about patriarchy and male privilege, although extremely important as an end in itself, is a relatively minor risk factor for partner violence in Euro-American societies and by itself is not likely to result in much change in those receiving this message.

CONCLUSION

Preventing and treating partner violence will require major changes in current modes of intervention. In this chapter se emphasized interventions addressed to females as well as males, interventions that increase interpersonal relationship skills, and, for the more severe levels of partner violence, therapy to change the personality, cognitive, behavioral, and emotional underpinnings of severely abusive behaviors. Such programs exist (e.g., see O'Leary & Cohen, 2007; Stith et al., 2003; Stith, Rosen, McCollum, & Thomsen, 2004) but are not widely used and, as noted previously, are specifically excluded from state-mandated intervention programs in many U.S. states. These interventions need to be offered in a variety of formats, including programs for parents and children to enhance interpersonal relations skills, couples counseling, individual counseling, and group treatment, and with varying levels of criminal justice monitoring. Many other aspects of the needed changes are covered in this book and in D. G. Dutton (2006) and Hamel and Nicholls (2007). Achieving this type of differentiated treatment requires broader awareness of the characteristics of partner violence, more systematic use of existing assessment methods to assess multiple risk factors for partner violence, and development of new instruments so that appropriate screening and referrals can be made to each of these types of services.

REFERENCES

Anderson, K. L. (2002). Perpetrator or victim? Relationships between intimate partner violence and well-being. *Journal of Marriage and the Family, 64*, 851–863.

Anderson, P. B., & Struckman-Johnson, C. (Eds.). (1998). *Sexually aggressive women: Current perspectives and controversies.* New York: Guilford Press.

Andrews, D. A., & Bonta, J. (1998). *The psychology of criminal conduct* (2nd ed.). Cincinnati, OH: Anderson.

Andrews, J. A., Foster, S. L., Capaldi, D., & Hops, H. (2000). Adolescent and family predictors of physical aggression, communication, and satisfaction in young adult couples: A prospective analysis. *Journal of Consulting and Clinical Psychology, 68*, 195–208.

Archer, J. (2002). Sex differences in physically aggressive acts between heterosexual partners: A meta-analytic review. *Aggression and Violent Behavior, 7*, 313–351.

Archer, J. (2006). Cross-cultural differences in physical aggression between partners: A social structural analysis. *Personality and Social Psychology Review, 10*, 133–153.

Babcock, J. C., Green, C. E., & Robie, C. (2004). Does batterers' treatment work? A meta-analytic review of domestic violence treatment. *Clinical Psychology Review, 23*, 1023–1053.

Bagarozzi, D. A. (1997). Marital Intimacy Needs Questionnaire: Preliminary report. *American Journal of Family Therapy, 25*, 285–290.

Botvin, G. J., Griffin, K. W., & Nichols, T. D. (2006). Preventing youth violence and delinquency through a universal school-based prevention approach. *Prevention Science, 7*, 403–408.

Calvert, R. (1974). Criminal and civil liability in husband–wife assaults. In S. K. Steinmetz & M. A. Straus (Eds.), *Violence in the family* (pp. 88–91). New York: Harper & Row.

Campbell, J. C. (Ed.). (1995). *Assessing dangerousness: Violence by sexual offenders, batterers, and child abusers*. Newbury Park, CA: Sage.

Campbell, J. C. (2001). Safety planning based on lethality assessment for partners of batterers in intervention programs. *Journal of Aggression, Maltreatment & Trauma, 5*, 129–143.

Capaldi, D. M., & Clark, S. (1998). Prospective family predictors of aggression toward female partners for at-risk young men. *Developmental Psychology, 34*, 1175–1188.

Capaldi, D. M., & Owen, L. D. (2001). Physical aggression in a community sample of at-risk young couples: Gender comparisons for high frequency, injury, and fear. *Journal of Family Psychology, 15*, 425–440.

Carney, M. M., & Buttell, F. P. (2004). A multidimensional evaluation of a treatment program for female batterers: A pilot study. *Research on Social Work Practice, 14*, 249–258.

Carney, M. M., & Buttell, F. P. (2006). An evaluation of a court-mandated batterer intervention program: Investigating differential program effect for African American and White women. *Research on Social Work Practice, 16*, 571–581.

Carrado, M., George, M. J., Loxam, E., Jones, L., & Templar, D. (1996). Aggression in British heterosexual relationships: A descriptive analysis. *Aggressive Behavior, 22*, 401–415.

Cascardi, M., Langhinrichsen, J., & Vivian, D. (1992). Marital aggression: Impact, injury, and health correlates for husbands and wives. *Archives of Internal Medicine, 152*, 1178–1184.

Cascardi, M., & Vivian, D. (1995). Context for specific episodes of marital violence: Gender and severity of violence differences. *Journal of Family Violence, 10*, 265–293.

Catalano, S. (2006). *Intimate partner violence in the United States*. Retrieved January 9, 2007, from http://www.ojp.usdoj.gov/bjs/intimate/ipv.htm

Cohen, P. (1996). How can generative theories of the effects of punishment be tested? *Pediatrics, 98*, 834–836.

Cohen, R. A., Rosenbaum, A., Kane, R. L., Warnken, W. J., & Benjamin, S. (1999). Neuropsychological correlates of domestic violence. *Violence and Victims, 14*, 397–412.

Cowen, E. (1978). Demystifying primary prevention. In D. G. Forgays (Ed.), *Primary prevention of psychopathology* (pp. 7–24). Hanover, NH: University of New England Press.

Crooks, C. V., Wolfe, D. A., & Jaffe, P. G. (2006). School-based adolescent dating violence prevention: Enhancing effective practice with a gender strategic approach. In K. Kendall-Tackett & S. Giacomoni (Eds.), *Intimate partner violence* (pp. 16-2–16-5). Kingston, NJ: Civic Research Institute.

Daly, K., & Stubbs, J. (2007). Feminist theory, feminist and anti-racist politics, and restorative justice. In G. Johnstone & D. W. Van Ness (Eds.), *Handbook of restorative justice* (pp. 149–170). Cullompton, Devon, England: Willan.

Davis, R. C., Taylor, B. G., & Maxwell, C. D. (2000). *Does batterer treatment reduce violence? A randomized experiment in Brooklyn.* Washington, DC: U.S. Department of Justice.

Dishion, T. J., Mccord, J., & Poulin, F. (1999). When interventions harm: Peer groups and problem behavior. *American Psychologist, 54,* 755–764.

Dobash, E. R., & Dobash, R. P. (1979). *Violence against wives: A case against the patriarchy.* New York: Free Press.

Douglas, E. M., & Straus, M. A. (2006). Assault and injury of dating partners by university students in 19 countries and its relation to corporal punishment experienced as a child. *European Journal of Criminology, 3,* 293–318.

Dowd, L. S., Leisring, P. A., & Rosenbaum, A. (2005). Partner aggressive women: Characteristics and treatment attrition. *Violence and Victims, 20,* 219–233.

Dutton, D. G. (2006). *Rethinking domestic violence.* Vancouver, British Columbia, Canada: University of British Columbia Press.

Dutton, D. G. (2007). Thinking outside the box: Gender and court-mandated therapy. In J. Hamel & T. L. Nicholls (Eds.), *Family interventions in domestic violence: A handbook of gender-inclusive theory and treatment.* New York: Springer Publishing Company.

Dutton, D. G., & Nicholls, T. L. (2005). The gender paradigm in domestic violence research and theory: Part I. The conflict of theory and data. *Aggression and Violent Behavior, 10,* 680–714.

Dutton, L. B., & Straus, M. A. (2005, September). *The relationship between hostility toward the other sex and sexual coercion.* Paper presented at the 10th International Conference on Family Violence, San Diego, CA.

Family Violence Prevention Fund. (2006). *Coaching boys into men: Your role in ending violence against women* [Electronic version]. Retrieved March 22, 2007, from http://endabuse.org/cbim

Faulkner, K., Stoltenberg, C. D., Cogen, R., Nolder, M., & Shooter, E. (1992). Cognitive–behavioral group treatment for male spouse abusers. *Journal of Family Violence, 7,* 37–55.

Feder, L., & Dugan, L. (2002). A test of the efficacy of court-mandated counseling for domestic violence offenders: The Broward experiment. *Justice Quarterly, 19,* 343–375.

Fein, R., Vossekuil, B., & Holden, G. (1995). *Threat assessment: An approach to prevent targeted violence* (Publication No. NCJ 155000). Washington, DC: U.S. Department of Justice.

Feld, S. L., & Straus, M. A. (1989). Escalation and desistance of wife assault in marriage. *Criminology, 27,* 141–161.

Felson, R. B. (2002). *Violence and gender reexamined.* Washington, DC: American Psychological Association.

Felson, R. B., & Messner, S. F. (1998). Disentangling the effects of gender and intimacy on victim precipitation in homicide. *Criminology, 36,* 405–423.

Felson, R. B., & Pare, P.-P. (2005). The reporting of domestic violence and sexual assault by nonstrangers to the police. *Journal of Marriage and Family, 67,* 597–610.

Fenell, D. L. (1993). Characteristics of long-term marriages. *Journal of Mental Health Counseling, 15,* 446–460.

Fiebert, M. S. (2004). References examining assaults by women on their spouses or male partners: An annotated bibliography. *Sexuality & Culture, 8,* 140–177.

Follingstad, D. R., Wright, S., Lloyd, S., & Sebastian, J. A. (1991). Sex differences in motivations and effects in dating violence. *Family Relations, 40,* 51–57.

Foshee, V. A. (2004). *Safe Dates: An adolescent dating abuse prevention curriculum.* Center City, MN: Halzelden Publishing and Educational Services.

Foshee, V. A., Bauman, K. E., Ennett, S. T., Suchindran, C., Benefield, T., & Linder, G. F. (2005). Assessing the effects of the dating violence prevention program "Safe Dates" using random coefficient regression modeling. *Prevention Science, 6,* 245–258.

Gelles, R., & Straus, M. (1988). *Intimate violence: The causes and consequences of abuse in the American family.* New York: Simon & Schuster.

Gondolf, E. W. (2002). *Batterer intervention systems: Issues, outcomes, and recommendations.* Thousand Oaks, CA: Sage.

Gondolf, E. W. (2004). Evaluating batterer counseling programs: A difficult task showing some effects and implications. *Aggression and Violent Behavior, 9,* 605–631.

Gottman, J. M. (1994). *What predicts divorce?* Hillsdale, NJ: Erlbaum.

Gottman, J. M. (1998). Psychology and the study of marital processes. *Annual Review of Psychology, 49,* 169–197.

Hamel, J., & Nicholls, T. L. (Eds.). (2007). *Family interventions in domestic violence: A handbook of gender-inclusive theory and treatment.* New York: Springer Publishing Company.

Henning, K., & Feder, L. (2004). A comparison of men and women arrested for domestic violence: Who presents the greater threat? *Journal of Family Violence, 19,* 69–80.

Heyman, R. E., & Schlee, K. (2003). Stopping wife abuse via physical aggression couples treatment. *Journal of Aggression, Maltreatment & Trauma, 7,* 135–157.

International Association of Chiefs of Police. (1967). *Training Key 16: Handling domestic disturbance calls.* Gaithersburg, MD: Author.

Johnson, M. P., & Ferraro, K. J. (2000). Research on domestic violence in the 1990's: Making distinctions. *Journal of Marriage and the Family, 62,* 948–963.

Kaufman Kantor, G., Jasinski, J. L., & Aldarondo, E. (1994). Sociocultural status and incidence of marital violence in Hispanic families. *Violence and Victims, 9,* 207–222.

Kaufman Kantor, G., & Straus, M. A. (1990). Response of victims and the police to assaults on wives. In M. A. Straus & R. J. Gelles (Eds.), *Physical violence in*

American families: Risk factors and adaptations to violence in 8,145 families (pp. 473–487). New Brunswick, NJ: Transaction.

Kernsmith, P. (2005). Exerting power or striking back: A gendered comparison of motivations for domestic violence perpetration. *Violence and Victims, 20,* 173–185.

Kessler, R. C., Molnar, B. E., Feurer, I. D., & Appelbaum, M. (2001). Patterns and mental health predictors of domestic violence in the United States: Results from the National Comorbidity Survey. *International Journal of Law and Psychiatry, 24,* 487–508.

Larance, L. Y. (2006). Serving women who use force in their intimate heterosexual relationships: An extended view. *Violence Against Women, 12,* 622–640.

Levesque, D., & Gelles, R. J. (1998, June). *Does treatment deduce violence recidivism in men who batter? Meta-analytic evaluation of treatment outcome research.* Paper presented at the Program Evaluation and Family Violence Research Conference, Durham, NH.

McCarroll, J. E., Ursano, R. J., Fan, Z., & Newby, J. H. (2004). Patterns of mutual and nonmutual spouse abuse in the U.S. Army (1998–2002). *Violence and Victims, 19,* 453–468.

Medeiros, R. A., & Straus, M. A. (2007). Risk factors for physical violence between dating partners: Implications for gender-inclusive prevention and treatment of family violence. In J. Hamel & T. L. Nicholls (Eds.), *Family interventions in domestic violence: A handbook of gender-inclusive theory and treatment* (pp. 59–87). New York: Springer Publishing Company.

Mihalic, S., Erwin, K., Fagan, A., Ballard, D., & Elliott, D. (2004). *Successful program implementation: Lessons from Blueprints.* Washington, DC: U.S. Department of Justice.

Mills, L. G. (2003). *Insult to injury: Rethinking our responses to intimate abuse.* Princeton, NJ: Princeton University Press.

Mills, L. G. (2008). *Violent partners: A breakthrough plan for ending the cycle of abuse.* New York: Basic Books.

Moffitt, T. E., Caspi, A., Rutter, M., & Silva, P. A. (2001). *Sex differences in antisocial behavior.* Cambridge, England: Cambridge University Press.

Moore, K. A., Jekielek, S. M., Bronte-Tinkew, J., Guzman, L., Ryan, S., & Redd, Z. (2004). *What is a "healthy marriage"? Defining the concept* (Research brief). Washington, DC: Child Trends.

Moore, T. M., & Stuart, G. L. (2005). A review of the literature on masculinity and partner violence. *Psychology of Men & Masculinity, 6,* 46–61.

Murphy, C. M., & Eckhardt, C. I. (2005). *Treating the abusive partner: An individualized cognitive–behavioral approach.* New York: Guilford Press.

National Clearinghouse on Family Violence. (2004). *Canada's treatment programs for men who abuse their partners.* Ottawa, Ontario, Canada: Minister of Health Canada.

O'Leary, K. D. (2001). Conjoint therapy for partners who engage in physically aggressive behavior: Rationale and research. *Journal of Aggression, Maltreatment & Trauma, 5*, 145–164.

O'Leary, K. D., & Cohen, S. (2007). Treatment of psychological and physical aggression in a couple context. In J. Hamel & T. L. Nicholls (Eds.), *Family interventions in domestic violence: A handbook of gender-inclusive theory and treatment* (pp. 363–380). New York: Springer Publishing Company.

Pearson, P. (1997). *When she was bad: Women and the myth of innocence*. Toronto, Ontario, Canada: Random House.

Petrik, N. D., Olson, R. E. P., & Subotnik, L. S. (1994). Powerlessness and the need to control: The male abuser's dilemma. *Journal of Interpersonal Violence, 9*, 278–285.

Pottie Bunge, V., & Locke, D. (2000). *Family violence in Canada: A statistical profile 2000* (Document No. 85-224-Xie). Ottawa, Ontario, Canada: Statistics Canada.

Rennison, C. M. (2000). *Criminal victimization 1999: Changes 1998–00 with trends 1993–99*. Washington, DC: U.S. Department of Justice.

Rose, G. (1985). Sick individuals and sick populations. *International Journal of Epidemiology, 14*, 32–38.

Rosenbaum, A., & Price, B. (2007, July). *National survey of perpetrator intervention programs*. Paper presented at the International Family Violence Research Conference, Portsmouth, NH.

Rosenthal, R. (1984). *Meta-analytic procedures for social research*. Newbury Park, CA: Sage.

Ruiter, R. A. C., Abraham, C., & Kok, G. (2001). Scary warnings and rational precautions: A review of the psychology of fear appeals. *Psychology & Health, 16*, 613.

Sarantakos, S. (1998, July). *Husband abuse as self-defense*. Paper presented at the International Congress of Sociology, Montreal, Quebec, Canada.

Sartin, R. M., Hansen, D. J., & Huss, M. T. (2006). Domestic violence treatment response and recidivism: A review and implications for the study of family violence. *Aggression and Violent Behavior, 11*, 425–440.

Saunders, D. G. (2002). Are physical assaults by wives and girlfriends a major social problem? A review of the literature. *Violence Against Women, 8*, 1424–1448.

Saunders, D. G., & Hanusa, D. (1986). Cognitive–behavioral treatment of men who batter: The short-term effects of group therapy. *Journal of Family Violence, 1*, 357–372.

Scott, K. L. (2004). Predictors of change among batterers: Application of theories and review of empirical findings. *Trauma, Violence, & Abuse, 5*, 260–184.

Scott, K. L., & King, C. B. (in press). Resistance, reluctance, and readiness in perpetrators of abuse against women and children. *Trauma, Violence, & Abuse*.

Sommer, R. (1996). *Male and female perpetrated partner abuse: Testing a diathesis-stress model*. Unpublished doctoral dissertation, University of Manitoba, Winnipeg, Manitoba, Canada.

Statistics Canada. (2005). *Family violence in Canada: A statistical profile.* Ottawa, Ontario, Canada: Canadian Centre for Justice Statistics.

Stern, J. M. (2004). Traumatic brain injury: An effect and cause of domestic violence and child abuse. *Current Neurology and Neuroscience Reports, 4,* 179–181.

Stets, J. E., & Hammons, S. A. (2002). Gender, control, and marital commitment. *Journal of Family Issues, 23,* 3–25.

Stets, J. E., & Straus, M. A. (1990). Gender differences in reporting of marital violence and its medical and psychological consequences. In M. A. Straus & R. J. Gelles (Eds.), *Physical violence in American families: Risk factors and adaptations to violence in 8,145 families* (pp. 151–166). New Brunswick, NJ: Transaction.

Stith, S. M., Rosen, K. H., & McCollum, E. E. (2003). Effectiveness of couples treatment for spouse abuse. *Journal of Marital & Family Therapy, 29,* 407–426.

Stith, S. M., Rosen, K. H., McCollum, E. E., & Thomsen, C. J. (2004). Treating intimate partner violence within intact couple relationships: Outcomes of multi-couple versus individual couple therapy. *Journal of Marital & Family Therapy, 30,* 305–318.

Strang, H., & Braithwaite, J. (2002). *Restorative justice and family violence.* New York: Cambridge University Press.

Straus, M. A. (1976). Sexual inequality, cultural norms, and wife-beating. In E. C. Viano (Ed.), *Victims and society* (pp. 543–559). Washington, DC: Visage Press.

Straus, M. A. (1991). Conceptualizaton and measurement of battering: Implications for public policy. In M. Steinman (Ed.), *Woman battering: Policy responses* (pp. 19–47). Cincinnati, OH: Anderson.

Straus, M. A. (1994). State-to-state differences in social-inequality and social bonds in relation to assaults on wives in the United-States. *Journal of Comparative Family Studies, 25,* 7–24.

Straus, M. A. (1995). Trends in cultural norms and rates of partner violence: An update to 1992. In S. M. Stith & M. A. Straus (Eds.), *Understanding partner violence: Prevalence, causes, consequences, and solutions* (Vol. II, pp. 30–33). Minneapolis, MN: National Council on Family Relations.

Straus, M. A. (1999). The controversy over domestic violence by women: A methodological, theoretical, and sociology of science analysis. In X. Arriaga & S. Oskamp (Eds.), *Violence in intimate relationships* (pp. 17–44). Thousand Oaks, CA: Sage.

Straus, M. A. (2005). Women's violence toward men is a serious social problem. In D. R. Loseke, R. J. Gelles, & M. M. Cavanaugh (Eds.), *Current controversies on family violence* (2nd ed., pp. 55–77). Newbury Park, CA: Sage.

Straus, M. A. (2007a). Processes explaining the concealment and distortion of evidence on gender symmetry in partner violence. *European Journal of Criminal Policy and Research, 13,* 227–232.

Straus, M. A. (2007b). *Why, despite overwhelming evidence, partner violence by women has not been perceived and often denied.* Durham: University of New Hampshire Family Research Laboratory.

Straus, M. A. (in press). Dominance and symmetry in partner violence by male and female university students in 32 nations. *Children and Youth Services Review.*

Straus, M. A., & Douglas, E. M. (2004). A short form of the Revised Conflict Tactics Scales, and typologies for seventy and mutuality. *Violence and Victims, 19,* 507–520.

Straus, M. A., Gelles, R. J., & Steinmetz, S. K. (2006). *Behind closed doors: Violence in the American family.* New York: Doubleday/Anchor Books.

Straus, M. A., & Gozjolko, K. L. (2007, June). *Intimate terrorism and injury of dating partners by male and female university students.* Paper presented at the Stockholm Criminology Prize Symposium, Stockholm, Sweden.

Straus, M. A., Hamby, S. L., Boney-McCoy, S., & Sugarman, D. B. (1996). The Revised Conflict Tactics Scales (CTS2): Development and preliminary psychometric data. *Journal of Family Issues, 17,* 283–316.

Straus, M. A., Hamby, S. L., Boney-McCoy, S., & Sugarman, D. B. (2007). *Manual for the Personal and Relationships Profile (PRP)* (Rev. ed.). Durham: University of New Hampshire Family Research Laboratory.

Straus, M. A., Kaufman Kantor, G., & Moore, D. W. (1997). Change in cultural norms approving marital violence: From 1968 to 1994. In G. Kaufman Kantor & J. L. Jasinski (Eds.), *Out of the darkness: Contemporary perspectives on family violence* (pp. 3–16). Thousand Oaks, CA: Sage.

Straus, M. A., & Mouradian, V. E. (1999, November). *Preliminary psychometric data for the Personal and Relationships Profile (PRP): A multi-scale tool for clinical screening and research on partner violence.* Paper presented at the meeting of the American Society of Criminology, Toronto, Ontario, Canada.

Straus, M. A., & Ramirez, I. L. (2007). Gender symmetry in prevalence, severity, and chronicity of physical aggression against dating partners by university students in Mexico and USA. *Aggressive Behavior, 33,* 281–290.

Stuart, R. B. (2005). Treatment for partner abuse: Time for a paradigm shift. *Professional Psychology: Research and Practice, 36,* 254–263.

Sugarman, D. B., & Frankel, S. L. (1996). Patriarchal ideology and wife-assault: A meta-analytic review. *Journal of Family Violence, 11,* 13–40.

Surgeon General's Report. (2001). *Youth violence: A report of the Surgeon General.* Washington, DC: U.S. Department of Health and Human Services.

Taft, C. T., Murphy, C. M., Elliott, J. D., & Morrel, T. M. (2001). Attendance enhancing procedures in group counseling for domestic abusers. *Journal of Counseling Psychology, 48,* 51–60.

U.S. Department of Justice. (2003). *Bureau of Justice statistics: Sourcebook of criminal justice statistics.* Washington, DC: Author.

Vega, V., & Malamuth, N. M. (2007). Predicting sexual aggression: The role of pornography in the context of general and specific risk factors. *Aggressive Behavior, 33,* 104–117.

Weisz, A. N., Tolman, R. M., & Saunders, D. G. (2000). Assessing the risk of severe domestic violence: The importance of survivors' predictions. *Journal of Interpersonal Violence, 15,* 75–90.

Whitaker, D. J., Haileyesus, T., Swahn, M., & Saltzman, L. S. (2007). Differences in frequency of violence and reported injury between relationships with reciprocal and nonreciprocal intimate partner violence. *American Journal of Public Health, 97,* 941–947.

Williams, S. L., & Frieze, I. H. (2005). Patterns of violent relationships, psychological distress, and marital satisfaction in a national sample of men and women. *Sex Roles, 52,* 771–784.

Wolfe, D. A., Wekerle, C., & Scott, K. (1997). *Alternatives to violence: Empowering youth to develop healthy relationships.* London: Sage.

Yllo, K., & Bograd, M. (Eds.). (1988). *Feminist perspectives on wife abuse.* Newbury Park, CA: Sage.

III

CONCLUSION

12

FUTURE DIRECTIONS IN PREVENTING PARTNER VIOLENCE

DANIEL J. WHITAKER AND JOHN R. LUTZKER

In chapter 1 of this volume, we focused on the progress made during the past 30 years in recognizing, understanding, and preventing intimate partner violence (IPV). In this concluding chapter, we note that although much progress has been made, there is still much to do, and some of the fundamental questions about IPV remain unanswered. We summarize some of the pertinent issues raised in the preceding chapters and discuss several of the questions that we believe must receive attention from IPV researchers and practitioners in the coming years for future advances in IPV research and practice. These issues include a range of IPV activities, including tracking national IPV rates and trends, advancing theoretical and etiologic research to explain the occurrence of IPV, developing and testing prevention and intervention strategies for IPV, researching bringing on empirically supported interventions to scale, and disseminating community practices that are in line with the best empirical evidence. The issues discussed here are certainly not the only ones we consider important but are a selective set of points that we believe must be addressed to advance the field.

In these discussions, we take a public health perspective and review issues in (a) the area of surveillance of IPV (i.e., tracking IPV rates);

(b) identifying risk and protective factors, including advancing theoretical and empirical research; (c) developing and testing prevention strategies; and (d) implementing and disseminating empirically supported prevention strategies to be used as standard programming and practice.

SURVEILLANCE: TRACKING INTIMATE PARTNER VIOLENCE RATES AND TRAJECTORIES

A first set of issues pertains to understanding national rates and time trends in IPV perpetration and victimization. As noted in this volume (see chap. 2), the elements needed for a complete surveillance system for IPV are not currently in place. Lipsky and Caetano describe many of the current efforts that contribute to the national surveillance effort in IPV. Those include ongoing surveys on health (e.g., the Youth Risk Behavior Surveillance System [YRBSS] and the Behavioral Risk Factor Surveillance System) and crime (e.g., National Crime Victimization Survey [NCVS]), as well as data collected as part of other ongoing violence (e.g., the National Violent Death Reporting System) and injury surveillance systems (e.g., the Web-Based Injury Statistics Query and Reporting System) and on the behavior of school-age youths (e.g., YRBSS). One clear need is for an ongoing survey specifically focused on IPV that would carefully monitor rates and trends and could capture the nuances of rates and trends. Surveys such as the 1975 and 1985 National Family Violence Survey (NFVS; Straus & Gelles, 1995) and the National Violence Against Women Survey (NVAWS) have provided in-depth information from large samples of individuals on IPV but have not been designed to capture time trends. The NFVS was repeated 10 years apart, and the second iteration of NVAWS, termed the National Intimate Partner and Sexual Violence Survey, is being piloted at the time of this writing. It is clear there is a strong need for ongoing survey surveillance for IPV.

The need for ongoing surveillance assumes an agreed-on definition of IPV. In 1999, the Centers for Disease Control and Prevention (CDC) recommended uniform definitions and surveillance data elements (Saltzman, Fanslow, McMahon, & Shelley, 1999), and many authors, including several in this volume, have adopted those definitions (see chaps. 1 and 6). However, other authors have implicitly or explicitly questioned whether the CDC-recommended definitions are suitable for fully understanding IPV. The CDC definitions (Saltzman et al., 1999) include four types of IPV: (a) physical violence, (b) sexual violence, (c) threats of physical or sexual violence, and (d) psychological–emotional abuse occurring in the presence of another type of IPV. Physical violence, for example, is said to include behaviors such as pushing, shoving, throwing objects, slapping, hitting, punching, kicking, using a weapon, and restraining the partner, along with other types of physically aggressive acts. The CDC guidelines also recommend measuring lifetime prevalence of physical IPV, for example, by dichotomizing physical violence as having occurred or not occurred and past-year IPV by counting the number of acts of physical aggression. Many authors have noted that simply counting the number of acts of IPV is a problematic measure in that it does not assess the severity of the acts, the consequences of the acts, or the meaning and motives of those acts (DeKeseredy, Saunders, Schwartz, & Alvi, 1997; Dobash, Dobash, Wilson, & Daly, 2004). Recognition of the shortcomings of simple counts and dichotomous measures of forms of violence has grown from the debate about rates of perpetration of IPV by men versus women (e.g., see Archer, 2000, and commentaries) but applies to all perpetrators of IPV. Likewise, Follingstad (2007) argued that there is a lack of conceptual clarity regarding the construct of psychological abuse and that much more work is needed to better define and measure the variable, particularly if one wants to categorize individuals as psychologically abused or not as is often the case with surveillance efforts.

In addition to definitional issues, there are reporting and response issues that must be understood. Survey surveillance of IPV has yielded different results depending on the context of the survey. Crime surveys yield much lower prevalence rates and greater sex differences in victimization rates, with women appearing more likely to be victimized than men; family violence surveys that describe IPV as resulting from conflict and other reasons yield higher prevalence rates and victimization rates that appear more equal between men and women. For example, the NVAWS yielded annual prevalence rates of 13 and 9 per 1,000 respondents for women and men, respectively (Tjaden & Thoennes, 1998), whereas the corresponding figures in the 1985 NFVS were 116 women and 124 men (Straus & Gelles, 1995). The NCVS, which asks individuals about their experience as crime victims, yields the lowest prevalence rates (3.8 per 1,000 women and 1.3 per 1,000 men in 2004) and the greatest sex differences in IPV victimization (Catalano, 2007).

Finally, the field must thoughtfully consider the utility of survey surveillance methods in which the primary measures have traditionally been focused on lifetime or past-year experiences with any IPV. Many of the individuals who are classified as perpetrators or victims of IPV using these classification criteria have experienced or perpetrated low levels of violence, and such violence is unlikely to result in injury. Some have argued that this practice of "counting hits" has been unproductive and has led the field to focus on nonserious forms of intimate aggression, including aggressive acts perpetrated by women that may be done in self-defense. From this perspective, simple prevalence rates are uninformative and potentially harmful if they cause a diversion of resources away from more problematic IPV. Others have argued that all IPV is important, even low-level IPV, because it may escalate to more serious violence (Feld & Straus, 1989; Whitaker, Haileyesus, Swahn, & Saltzman, 2007), and that preventing a small but widespread problem such as low-level IPV can actually result in a broader population-level impact than focusing on the more severe cases (see chap. 11, this volume). Our view is that both perspectives have value: Counting hits does not in fact tell enough of what one needs to know, and survey surveillance must assess other aspects of IPV to better understand the extent and nature of IPV; however, low-level IPV should not be written off as unimportant for the very reasons just stated. More etiologic work is needed to inform surveillance efforts.

ETIOLOGY: UNDERSTANDING THE CAUSES AND CONSEQUENCES OF INTIMATE PARTNER VIOLENCE

In chapter 1, we suggested that the research community has greatly advanced its understanding of the etiology of IPV. Although this is true, the chapters in this volume highlighted that there is still much, much more to learn about why people perpetrate IPV and how it affects health. Theoretical models have advanced in their complexity significantly, but the empirical evidence in support of those models has lagged (as is often the case). Straus's (2006) exhortation for "less talk and more data" (p. 1087) expresses this point clearly. For example, the well-developed and popular feminist theories of partner violence point to broad societal level factors as the primary influence of partner violence. However, few studies have actually tested this model directly, in large part because those data are so difficult to collect. Analyses by Levinson (1989), Straus (e.g., see Straus, 2004), and Archer (2006) are excellent examples of the kinds of work needed to test theories describing how broad social factors influence IPV. Perhaps the most complete theories are those of Riggs and O'Leary (1989), whose model has been explicitly tested in a number of studies or used as the basis for analyses in others (Cano, Avery-Leaf, Cascardi, & O'Leary, 1998; Riggs & O'Leary, 1996; Tontodonato & Crew, 1992). However, there are many aspects of the model that warrant further explication and testing, especially to inform prevention efforts. Given the much partner violence emerges during adolescences, how do the factors identified in the model change over time? How can sex differences that have been found be incorporated into this model? How do the factors interact to produce IPV? What broad social level factors are important? To reiterate Straus's exhortation, less talk, more data.

A related need is for more developmental studies to understand the emergence of IPV over time. By definition, IPV or dating violence cannot exist without the presence of an intimate or dating partner, and because such partnerships do not typically begin until adolescence, the precursors to IPV prior to this period have received little attention. However, as discussed in chapter 7 of this volume, results from several longitudinal studies are beginning to provide information about the precursors of IPV. Findings indicate that early problem behaviors such as conduct disorders (Capaldi & Clark, 1998; Ehrensaft et al., 2003; Magdol, Moffitt, Caspi, & Silva, 1998), parenting

factors such as use of harsh punishment and interaction style (Brendgen, Vitaro, Tremblay, & Lavoie, 2001; Capaldi & Clark, 1998; Simons, Lin, & Gordon, 1998), and beliefs about peer behaviors (Arriaga & Foshee, 2004) are predictive of future IPV perpetration. Many questions remain unanswered, however, that are critical to the development of primary prevention strategies. One critical question is whether the influences of IPV perpetration change over time as youths develop. In the study of youth violence (or aggression against peers), different trajectories of violence have been identified (Dahlberg & Simon, 2006), along with different predictors of violence at different points in development (Lipsey & Derzon, 1998).

Understanding the trajectories of IPV will help address another important need, and that is to understand how IPV develops in the context of other forms of violence and risk behaviors. In the broader literature on the development of teen problem behaviors, there is a movement to examine the cluster of risk behaviors that tend to co-occur, including violence, delinquency, substance use, risky sexual behavior, and school failure. Violence toward a partner has not traditionally been studied as part of this cluster, but data suggest that it should be. As previously mentioned, early conduct problems and poor parenting have been identified as risk factors for the onset of dating violence and as precursors to other behavior problems as well. But, there may also be specific factors that distinguish dating violence from other teen risk behaviors. Studies that have looked specifically at the overlap between partner and youth violence have found some distinction between the two forms of violence (Gorman-Smith, Tolan, Sheidow, & Henry, 2001), specifically that there are individuals who are unique perpetrators of each type of violence and in some cases unique predictors of each type of violence. Perhaps the most discussed unique predictor is sex, with the data indicating that most peer violence is perpetrated by males, but partner violence is perpetrated by both males and females at equal rates, especially among younger samples (Archer, 2000).

A final etiologic area of focus that will continue to be a major area of study is that of sex and gender and their relationship to IPV. This has been an extraordinarily controversial topic and one that remains central to many researchers and practitioners. Understanding the role of sex and gender has vast implications for prevention programming, as discussed in chapter 11 of this volume. There are many questions about the roles of sex and gender in IPV, but perhaps none is more central than clarifying the role of sex versus gender in IPV. Although many have failed to distinguish between sex and gender, gender scholars make a clear distinction between biological sex (referred to as *sex*) and the social construction of biological sex (referred to as *gender*) that includes a number of attitudinal, personality, and social role constructs and carries implications for perceptions, expectations, and behaviors (Anderson, 2005). Men and women certainly vary in the extent to which they express gender-related beliefs and behavior, and sex does not always correlate strongly (or even weakly) with gender-related constructs. Disentangling the effects of sex from those of gender-related constructs may help resolve the many contentious issues around sex differences in IPV perpetration. For instance, Jenkins and Aube (2002) found that for both male and female college students, negative masculine characteristics were the best predictors of aggressive acts, but there were differential effects of attitudes about the traditional roles of men and women.

PREVENTION AND INTERVENTION DEVELOPMENT AND TESTING

As noted in several of the chapters in this volume (see chaps. 7, 8, 9, 10, and 11), there is still much work to do regarding prevention of and intervention for IPV. There are few empirically supported interventions for either primary (Avery-Leaf & Cascardi, 2002; Whitaker et al., 2006) or secondary prevention of IPV (Wathen & MacMillan, 2003; Whitaker, Baker, & Arias, 2007). Most of the widely available services for IPV prevention have not been empirically tested or have not fared well in empirical testing (Whitaker, Baker, & Arias, 2007). In the sections that follow, we focus on the need to expand prevention and intervention approaches, although rigorous evaluation of currently available services is also critically needed.

New Approaches and Settings for Primary Prevention

Primary prevention is often at the heart of a public health effort to reduce or eliminate a threat to public health. With regard to IPV, the focus on primary prevention efforts for partner violence has been primarily on school-based programs that seek to change the attitudes, beliefs, and behaviors of middle and/or high school students to prevent dating violence (Whitaker et al., 2006). This is an important approach that has resulted in some successes (Foshee et al., 2005), but other approaches will likely be needed to address the full range of factors that influence partner violence perpetration and can be conducted in a variety of settings (see chap. 7, this volume). Many recent studies have begun to identify the early individual, family, and peer-level precursors of partner violence, which may serve as intervention targets for early prevention efforts. Findings that family factors such as communication, discipline, and witnessing interparental violence are early predictors of subsequent partner violence perpetration (Brendgen et al., 2001; Capaldi & Clark, 1998; Ehrensaft et al., 2003; Simons et al., 1998) suggest that intervening with families early may serve to prevent partner violence. Family-based interventions have been used to prevent a range of teen risk behaviors, including violence and delinquency (Henggeler, 1999), substance use (Kumpfer, Alvarado, & Whiteside, 2003), and risky sexual activity (Forehand, Miller, Armistead, Kotchick, & Long, 2004).

Tailoring Prevention and Intervention Strategies

A related prevention and intervention need is to understand whether and how different prevention approaches are needed for different circumstances. Different strategies may be needed to prevent different types of IPV (e.g., physical, sexual, emotional), for IPV occurring in different contexts (e.g., more situational, conflict-based IPV vs. severe battering or intimate terrorism), and for different types of perpetrators (e.g., see Gottman & Jacobson, 1998; Holtzworth-Munroe & Stuart, 1994). Of the potential ways to tailor prevention and intervention strategies, the one that has received the most attention is tailoring treatment to types of perpetrators. Current treatment programs for IPV perpetrators have been criticized for their one-size-fits-all approach (Dutton & Corvo, 2006; Eckhardt, Murphy, Black, & Suhr, 2006), although some have argued otherwise (Gondolf, 2002). And although some studies have compared different treatment models (e.g., see Dunford, 2000; O'Leary, Heyman, & Neidig, 1999; Saunders, 1996), no studies have tested a tailored treatment approach in which some form of validated, structured assessment guides treatment. In chapter 11 of this volume, it was recommended that all partner violent relationships be assessed for danger and the reciprocity of the violence to understand what treatment approaches might be appropriate and effective. Further assessment of psychological and social factors that might influence partner violence would also be needed. Some typology proponents have made clear recommendations that different types of intervention strategies are needed for different kinds of perpetrators (see chap. 8, this volume).

Most prevention and intervention strategies for IPV have focused on physical IPV, although intervention effects of psychological IPV and sexual IPV are typically measured (stalking less often so). There is much evidence to suggest that the forms of IPV correlate, particularly psychological and physical IPV. For instance, studies have found that psychological abuse among couples is a strong predictor of subsequent physical abuse (Murphy & O'Leary, 1989; Schumacher & Leonard, 2005). It is important to address psychological abuse because of its own negative consequences (Coker, Smith, Bethea, King, & McKeown, 2000), but intervening with individuals or couples who use psychological abuse may also be an effective strategy for selected primary prevention because those individuals and couples are at higher risk of becoming physically aggressive.

Much less is known about prevention and intervention strategies for sexual IPV and stalking of an intimate partner. For sexual IPV, there has been little research describing its particular manifestation. As noted earlier, it is generally not known how perpetrators of sexual IPV differ from perpetrators of physical IPV only, and thus suggesting targeted intervention strategies for those individuals is premature at this point but may be needed in the future. Even less information is available about prevention of and intervention for stalking, another form of IPV. Stalking can co-occur with physical violence and sexual violence (Roberts, 2005; Spitzberg, 2002). Additionally, stalkers may have unique psychological and social profiles that would warrant particular kinds of prevention and intervention efforts. Sheridan, Blaauw, and Davies (2003) suggested that intervention strategies for stalking can target the victim, the perpetrator, or the stalking behavior. The most commonly used interventions are criminal justice interventions that focus on the stalking behavior. Spitzberg's (2002) meta-analysis found that protective orders are violated up to 40% of the time, suggesting that more than criminal justice efforts may be needed. Sheridan et al. (2003) suggested that certain types of stalkers (e.g., psychotic stalkers) may be receptive to certain kinds of treatments (e.g., drug treatment). Prevention and intervention efforts targeting the less well-studied forms of IPV—sexual violence and stalking—are badly needed.

Community-Level Prevention

Finally, there is a need in prevention research for a better understanding of broad-based interventions that target community-level variables. Research is in a nascent stage of documenting the impact of community-level variables on IPV above and beyond the impact of individual-level variables. Interventions that change community-level factors may influence IPV rates more broadly than individually focused interventions that can reach only the individuals enrolled in the program. Community-level interventions are a broad category of interventions that include policy changes, mass media campaigns, and other strategies to community-wide variables rather than only among the subset of individuals who happen to be enrolled in any particular trial or program. Unfortunately, the methodological difficulties of community-level intervention research are substantial. These include difficulties in designing interventions of sufficient intensity to reach a broad population, measuring the implementation of the intervention, measuring dosage or the extent to which individuals are receiving the intervention, and having a measurement plan that can adequately capture community-level change on the relevant outcome variables. Broad, population-level interventions may ultimately be a better way to reach large segments of a population, but whether these are possible, cost-effective, and able to reach the individuals at highest risk remains unknown.

IMPLEMENTATION AND DISSEMINATION

The final step in the public health model is the dissemination of evidenced-based practices for widespread implementation. Unfortunately, there are few evidenced-based practices to recommend to practitioners regarding prevention and interventions for IPV. However, it is important to understand implementation and dissemination issues so that prevention and intervention strategies can be developed with an eye toward broad implementation. Scientists generally pay a great deal of attention to gaining knowledge (i.e., internal validity) and relatively less attention to its successful application and dissemination (i.e., external validity). For example, careful attention may be given to constructing a detailed intervention manual, but relatively little attention is given to describing the specific training procedures and criteria for training so that the intervention can be delivered as intended.

Fixsen, Naoom, Blasé, Friedman, and Wallace (2005) reviewed the literature in several practice areas and provided an overview of several of the key issues to consider in effective implementation. They identified several "core implementation components," including staff selection, training, consultation and coaching, staff evaluation, and program evaluation that are needed to effectively implement an evidence-based practice or program. The usual methods of workshops, didactics, and demonstrations have been shown to result in virtually no implementation, whereas practice with feedback and coaching drastically improve implementation (Joyce & Showers, 2002). It is imperative that prevention and intervention strategies for partner violence consider implementation needs such as training and coaching (along with other aspects that may affect implementation) as they develop intervention strategies.

Another issue relevant to implementation and dissemination is economic evaluation. Organizations interested in implementing prevention and intervention programs may want to know how well a program works, but as important to them often is the question of how much it costs. No matter how effective a program may be, an organization cannot implement a program it cannot afford. Likewise, decision makers may also want to know the economic benefits that may be accrued from the program, whether for themselves (e.g., a school may save time by preventing behavior problems), the participants, or all of society. These issues highlight the importance of collecting cost data at the later stages of effectiveness trials and attempting to quantify the benefits of a prevention strategy for various parties (Corso & Lutzker, 2006).

CONCLUSION

The study of IPV has progressed much over the past 30 years, but there is still considerable work to do. Basic questions regarding rates of IPV, causes of IPV, and effective prevention strategies still need more complete answers. It is clear that there should be greater attention on social–ecological variables and less attention on individual victim–perpetrator variables. In this chapter, we highlighted some, but certainly not all, of the questions that must be addressed to further advance the study and prevention of IPV. As evidenced by the chapters in this volume, there is a strong cadre of dedicated researchers and practitioners working to solve the problem of IPV. Our hope is that the next 30 years can be as productive as the past 30.

REFERENCES

Anderson, K. L. (2005). Theorizing gender in intimate partner violence research. *Sex Roles, 52*, 853–865.

Archer, J. (2000). Sex differences in aggression between heterosexual partners: A meta-analytic review. *Psychological Bulletin, 126*, 651–680.

Archer, J. (2006). Cross-cultural differences in physical aggression between partners: A social-role analysis. *Personality and Social Psychology Review, 10*, 133–153.

Arriaga, X. B., & Foshee, V. A. (2004). Adolescent dating violence: Do adolescents follow in their friends', or their parents', footsteps? *Journal of Interpersonal Violence 19*, 162–184.

Avery-Leaf, S., & Cascardi, M. (2002). Dating violence education: Prevention and early intervention strategies. In P. A. Schewe (Ed.), *Preventing violence in relationships: Interventions across the life span* (pp. 79–105). Washington, DC: American Psychological Association.

Brendgen, M., Vitaro, F., Tremblay, R. E., & Lavoie, F. (2001). Reactive and proactive aggression: Predictions to physical violence in different contexts and moderating effects of parental monitoring and caregiving behavior. *Journal of Abnormal Child Psychology, 29*, 293–304.

Cano, A., Avery-Leaf, S., Cascardi, M., & O'Leary, K. D. (1998). Dating violence in two high school samples: Discriminating variables. *Journal of Primary Prevention, 18*, 431–446.

Capaldi, D. M., & Clark, S. (1998). Prospective family predictors of aggression toward female partners for at-risk young men. *Developmental Psychology, 34*, 1175–1188.

Catalano, S. (2007). *Intimate partner violence in the United States*. Washington, DC: U.S. Department of Justice.

Coker, A. L., Smith, P. H., Bethea, L., King, M. R., & McKeown, R. E. (2000). Physical health consequences of physical and psychological intimate partner violence. *Archives of Family Medicine, 9*, 451–457.

Corso, P. S., & Lutzker, J. R. (2006). The need for economic analysis in research on child maltreatment. *Child Abuse & Neglect, 30*, 727–738.

Dahlberg, L. L., & Simon, T. R. (2006). Predicting and preventing youth violence: Developmental pathways and risk. In J. R. Lutzker (Ed.), *Preventing violence: Research and evidence-based intervention strategies* (pp. 97–124). Washington, DC: American Psychological Association.

DeKeseredy, W. S., Saunders, D. G., Schwartz, M. D., & Alvi, S. (1997). The meanings and motives for women's use of violence in Canadian college dating relationships: Results from a national survey. *Sociological Spectrum, 17,* 199–222.

Dobash, R. P., Dobash, R. E., Wilson, M., & Daly, M. (2004). The myth of sexual symmetry in marital violence. In C. Renzetti & R. Bergen (Eds.), *Violence against women* (pp. 31–52). Boston: Rowman & Littlefield.

Dunford, F. W. (2000). The San Diego Navy experiment: An assessment of interventions for men who assault their wives. *Journal of Consulting and Clinical Psychology, 68,* 468–476.

Dutton, D. G., & Corvo, K. (2006). Transforming a flawed policy: A call to revive psychology and science in domestic violence research and practice. *Aggression and Violent Behavior, 11,* 457–483.

Eckhardt, C. I., Murphy, C., Black, D., & Suhr, L. (2006). Intervention programs for perpetrators of intimate partner violence: Conclusions from a clinical research perspective. *Public Health Reports, 121,* 369–381.

Ehrensaft, M. K., Cohen, P., Brown, J., Smailes, E., Chen, H., & Johnson, J. G. (2003). Intergenerational transmission of partner violence: A 20-year prospective study. *Journal of Consulting and Clinical Psychology, 71,* 741–753.

Feld, S. L., & Straus, M. A. (1989). Escalation and desistance of wife assault in marriage. *Criminology, 27,* 141–161.

Fixsen, D. L., Naoom, S. F., Blasé, K. A., Friedman, R. M., & Wallace, F. (2005). *Implementation research: A synthesis of the literature.* Tampa: University of South Florida.

Follingstad, D. R. (2007). Rethinking current approaches to psychological abuse: Conceptual and methodological issues. *Aggression and Violent Behavior, 12,* 439–458.

Forehand, R., Miller, K. S., Armistead, L., Kotchick, B. A., & Long, N. (2004). The Parents Matter! program: An introduction. *Journal of Child and Family Studies, 13,* 1–3.

Foshee, V. A., Bauman, K. E., Ennett, S. T., Suchindran, C., Benefield, T., & Linder, G. (2005). Assessing the effects of the dating violence prevention program "Safe Dates" using random coefficient regression modeling. *Prevention Science, 6,* 245–258.

Gondolf, E. W. (2002). *Batterer intervention systems: Issues, outcomes, and recommendations.* Thousand Oaks, CA: Sage.

Gorman-Smith, D., Tolan, P. H., Sheidow, A. J., & Henry, D. B. (2001). Partner violence and street violence among urban adolescents: Do the same family factors relate? *Journal of Research on Adolescence, 11,* 273–295.

Gottman, J. M., & Jacobson, N. S. (1998). *When men batter women: New insights into ending abusive relationships.* New York: Simon & Schuster.

Henggeler, S. W. (1999). Multisystemic therapy: An overview of clinical procedures, outcomes, and policy implications. *Child Psychology and Psychiatry Review, 4,* 2–10.

Holtzworth-Munroe, A., & Stuart, G. L. (1994). Typologies of male batterers: Three subtypes and the differences among them. *Psychological Bulletin, 116,* 476–497.

Jenkins, S. S., & Aube, J. (2002). Gender differences and gender-related constructs in dating aggression. *Personality and Social Psychology Bulletin, 28,* 1106–1118.

Joyce, B. R., & Showers, B. (2002). *Student achievement through staff development* (3rd ed.). Alexandria, VA: Association for Supervision and Curriculum.

Kumpfer, K. L., Alvarado, R., & Whiteside, H. O. (2003). Family-based interventions for substance use and misuse prevention. *Substance Use & Misuse, 38,* 1759–1787.

Levinson, D. (1989). *Family violence in cross cultural perspective.* Newbury Park, CA: Sage.

Lipsey, M. W., & Derzon, J. H. (1998). Predictors of violent and serious delinquency in adolescence and early adulthood: A synthesis of longitudinal research. In R. Loeber & D. P. Farrington (Eds.), *Serious and violent juvenile offenders: Risk factors and successful interventions* (pp. 86–105). Thousand Oaks, CA: Sage

Magdol, L., Moffitt, T. E., Caspi, A., & Silva, P. A. (1998). Developmental antecedents of partner abuse: A prospective-longitudinal study. *Journal of Abnormal Psychology, 107,* 375–389.

Murphy, C. M., & O'Leary, K. (1989). Psychological aggression predicts physical aggression in early marriage. *Journal of Consulting and Clinical Psychology, 57,* 579–582.

O'Leary, K., Heyman, R. E., & Neidig, P. H. (1999). Treatment of wife abuse: A comparison of gender-specific and conjoint approaches. *Behavior Therapy, 30,* 475–505.

Riggs, D. S., & O'Leary, K. (1989). A theoretical model of courtship aggression. In M. A. Pirog-Good & J. E. Stets (Eds.), *Violence in dating relationships: Emerging social issues* (pp. 53–71). New York: Praeger Publishers.

Riggs, D. S., & O'Leary, K. (1996). Aggression between heterosexual dating partners: An examination of a causal model of courtship aggression. *Journal of Interpersonal Violence, 11,* 519–540.

Roberts, K. A. (2005). Women's experience of violence during stalking by former romantic partners: Factors predictive of stalking violence. *Violence Against Women, 11,* 89–114.

Saltzman, L. E., Fanslow, J. L., McMahon, P. M., & Shelley, G. A. (1999). *Intimate partner violence surveillance: Uniform definitions and recommended data elements* (Version 1.0). Atlanta, GA: Centers for Disease Control and Prevention.

Saunders, D. G. (1996). Feminist–cognitive–behavioral and process–psychodynamic treatments for men who batter: Interaction of abuser traits and treatment models. *Violence and Victims, 11,* 393–414.

Schumacher, J. A., & Leonard, K. E. (2005). Husbands' and wives' marital adjustment, verbal aggression, and physical aggression as longitudinal predictors of physical aggression in early marriage. *Journal of Consulting and Clinical Psychology, 73,* 28–37.

Sheridan, L. P., Blaauw, E., & Davies, G. M. (2003). Stalking: Knowns and unknowns. *Trauma, Violence, & Abuse, 4*, 148–162.

Simons, R. L., Lin, K. H., & Gordon, L. C. (1998). Socialization in the family of origin and male dating violence: A prospective study. *Journal of Marriage and the Family, 60*, 467–478.

Spitzberg, B. H. (2002). The tactical topography of stalking victimization and management. *Trauma, Violence, & Abuse, 3*, 261–288.

Straus, M. A. (2004). Prevalence of violence against dating partners by male and female university students worldwide. *Violence Against Women, 10*, 790–811.

Straus, M. A. (2006). Future research on gender symmetry in physical assaults on partners. *Violence Against Women, 12*, 1086–1097.

Straus, M. A., & Gelles, R. J. (1995). How violent are American families? Estimates from the National Family Violence Resurvey and other studies. In M. A. Straus & R. J. Gelles (Eds.), *Physical violence in American families: Risk factors and adaptations to violence in 8,145 families* (pp. 95–112). New Brunswick, NJ: Transaction.

Tjaden, P., & Thoennes, N. (1998). *Prevalence, incidence, and consequences of violence against women: Findings from the National Violence Against Women Survey.* Washington, DC: U.S. Department of Justice.

Tontodonato, P., & Crew, B. K. (1992). Dating violence, social learning theory, and gender: A multivariate analysis. *Violence and Victims, 7*, 3–14.

Wathen, C. N., & MacMillan, H. L. (2003). Interventions for violence against women: Scientific review. *Journal of the American Medical Association, 289*, 589–600.

Whitaker, D. J., Baker, C. K., & Arias, I. (2007). Interventions to prevent intimate partner violence. In L. S. Doll, S. E. Bonzo, J. A. Mercy, D. A. Sleet, & E. N. Haas (Eds.), *Handbook of injury and violence prevention* (pp. 203–221). New York: Springer-Verlag.

Whitaker, D. J., Haileyesus, T., Swahn, M., & Saltzman, L. S. (2007). Differences in frequency of violence and reported injury between relationships with reciprocal and nonreciprocal intimate partner violence. *American Journal of Public Health, 97*, 941–947.

Whitaker, D. J., Morrison, S., Lindquist, C., Hawkins, S. R., O'Neil, J. A., Nesius, A. M., et al. (2006). A critical review of interventions for the primary prevention of perpetration of partner violence. *Aggression and Violent Behavior, 11*, 151–166.

INDEX

mental health and substance abuse, 125–126

physical health conditions and injuries, 121–124

sexually transmitted infections, 124

BIPs. *See* Batterer intervention programs

Blueprints Violence Prevention Initiative, 252

Borderline personality disorder (BPD), 53

Brain damage, 257

BRFSS. *See* Behavioral Risk Factor Surveillance Survey

Bullying, 145–146

Bullying Prevention Program, 126

Caminar Latino, 183

Canadian Advisory Council on the Status of Women, 222

Cardiovascular conditions, 122

Carnegie Council on Adolescent Development, 156

Case management, 197–198

CDC. *See* Centers for Disease Control and Prevention

CEDAW. *See* Convention on the Elimination of All Forms of Discrimination Against Women

Centers for Disease Control and Prevention (CDC)

Choose Respect program of, 251–252

intimate partner violence defined by, 113–114, 276–277

national survey surveillance by, 24–28

surveillance terms proposed by, 18–23, 276–277

surveys developed by, 18

Child maltreatment/abuse, 93–106

and age–violence association, 101

co-occurrence of spouse abuse and, 95–96

and dating abuse, 149–150

dynamic developmental systems approach to IPV and, 102–106

and interparental violence, 93

IPV as unique from, 96–97

of newborns, 119

prevalence of, 95

as risk factor for IPV, 78–79

shared risk factors for IPV and, 97–101

Children's programs, 198

Chlamydia, 117

Choking

history of, 72

injuries from, 116

Choose Respect, 251–252

Chronic pain response, 122–124

Chronic physical health conditions, 116–117

Civil court orders, 227

Common couple violence, 178

Community-level prevention

batterer intervention programs, 170–172, 183–184

coordination of criminal justice responses and, 227–228

need for research on, 282

Completed rape, as IPV measure, 22

Condom use, 124

Conduct disorder, 52

Conflict Tactics Scales (CTS), 21–23, 257, 262

Control

and couples counseling, 174, 175

IPV and, 44, 79–80. *See also* Intimate partner abuse

Convention on the Elimination of All Forms of Discrimination Against Women (CEDAW), 200, 201

Core conflictual relationship themes, 173

Corporal punishment, dating abuse and, 149, 151

Couples counseling/therapy, 174–176, 261, 262

Courts, alternatives to, 225–227

Crime surveys, 277

Criminal conduct/behavior

psychology of, 231–234

as risk factor for IPV, 74–75, 100

Criminal justice advocacy, 198

Criminal justice responses to IPV, 219–236

alternatives to traditional courts, 225–227

coordination of community responses and, 227–228

data sources for, 26–27

history of, 220–230

legislation, 220–221

lessons from interventions for criminal conduct, 230–234

policing, 221–223

prosecution, 224–225

risk–needs–responsivity principles for, 234–235

by women perpetrators and marginalized groups, 228–230

ABOUT THE EDITORS

Daniel J. Whitaker, PhD, received his doctorate in psychology from the University of Georgia in 1996. He worked as a scientist at the Centers for Disease Control and Prevention (CDC) from 1997 to 2007. In June 2002, he became a team leader in the CDC's Prevention Development and Evaluation Branch, where he led a team of researchers who conducted prevention research in the areas of child maltreatment and intimate partner violence. He became the director of the National SafeCare Training and Research Center in January 2008 and a professor of public health at Georgia State University in August 2008. Dr. Whitaker has published more than 50 articles and book chapters, including articles in the *American Journal of Public Health, Child Maltreatment,* and *Aggression and Violent Behavior.* He has served as the CDC advisor to the American Medical Association's National Advisory Committee on Violence and Abuse and on the advisory boards for Healthy Families Georgia and the National Family Preservation Network.

John R. Lutzker, PhD, is the director of the Center for Healthy Development in the College of Health and Human Science and a visiting professor of public health in the Institute of Public Health at Georgia State University. Previously, he was executive director of the Marcus Institute, and before that he was appointed as distinguished consultant and chief for the Centers for Disease Control and Prevention's Prevention Development and Evaluation Branch, Division of Violence Prevention, National Center for Injury Prevention and Control. He has published over 125 professional articles and chapters and has presented over 350 professional papers. He is a fellow of the American Psychological Association's (APA's) Divisions 12 (Society of Clinical Psychology), 25 (Behavior Analysis), 33 (Intellectual and Developmental Disabilities), 37 (Society for Child and Family Policy and Practice), and 53 (Society of Clinical Child and Adolescent Psychology) and a clinical fellow of the Behavior Therapy and Research Society. Dr. Lutzker is currently associate editor of the *Journal of Positive Behavior Interventions*, and he is on the editorial boards of the *International Journal of Child Health and Human Development*, the *Journal of Family Violence*, *Child & Family Behavior Therapy*, and *Behavioral Interventions*. He is the author of five other books, including *Reducing Child Maltreatment: A Guidebook for Parent Services* (2002, with Kathryn M. Bigelow), and editor of the *Handbook of Child Abuse Research and Treatment* (1998) and *Preventing Violence: Research and Evidence-Based Intervention Strategies* (2006, APA). He is a recent recipient of the James M. Gaudin Outstanding Research Award from the Georgia Professional Society on the Abuse of Children and the Alumni Distinguished Achievement Award from the University of Kansas.